The Social Skills Toolkit:
How to Read People, Speak with Influence, Become Charismatic, and Make Friends Instantly

The Social Skills Toolkit : Table of Contents

THE SOCIAL SKILLS TOOLKIT: *HOW TO READ PEOPLE, SPEAK WITH INFLUENCE, BECOME CHARISMATIC, AND MAKE FRIENDS INSTANTLY*   1

THE SOCIAL SKILLS TOOLKIT :TABLE OF CONTENTS   3

BOOK 1: MASSIVE CHARISMA: *SMALL TALK, CHARM, LIKABILITY, AND HOW TO SUCCEED WITH PEOPLE*   7

PART 1: CULTIVATING A CHARISMATIC AURA   9

CHAPTER 1: SO, WHAT IS CHARISMA ANYWAY?   11
CHAPTER 2: BUILDING REAL-WORLD CHARISMA   25
CHAPTER 3: PUTTING IT ALL TOGETHER   37

PART 2: CREATING CHARISMATIC INTERACTIONS   46

CHAPTER 4: THE BEDROCK OF GOOD COMMUNICATION   47
CHAPTER 5: ENGAGING FULLY   55
CHAPTER 6: SUBTLY CHARISMATIC   69

SUMMARY GUIDE   91

BOOK 2: THE SCIENCE OF READING PEOPLE: *HOW TO UNDERSTAND WHAT PEOPLE ARE REALLY SAYING AND WHY*   96

SECTION 1   98

CHAPTER 1: WHAT STOPS US FROM ACCURATELY PERCEIVING OTHERS?   98

PERCEPTUAL SELECTIVITY   98
ATTRIBUTION   98
STEREOTYPING   99
THE HALO EFFECT   99
PROJECTION   99
PERCEPTUAL SET   100
IMPLICIT PERSONALITY THEORY   100
EXPECTANCY   101

PERCEPTUAL DEFENSE	101
IMPROVING YOUR PERCEPTUAL ACCURACY	101

CHAPTER 2: THE ART OF PERSPECTIVE TAKING — 104

CHAPTER 3: THE FOUR PERSONALITY TYPES AND "PERCEPTUAL POSITIONS" — 108

PERCEPTUAL POSITIONS	111

SECTION 2 — 116

CHAPTER 4: THE FOUR FUNCTIONS OF BEHAVIOR — 116

HOW TO READ PEOPLE USING THE ABC MODEL	118

CHAPTER 5: LEARNING TO READ EMOTIONS — 122

CULTIVATING "EMOTIONAL GRANULARITY"	123
THE REAL WAY TO READ BODY LANGUAGE	124
WHY YOU CAN'T ALWAYS TRUST FACIAL EXPRESSIONS	127

CHAPTER 6: BASELINING — 130

USING BASELINES TO DETECT DECEPTION	131

CHAPTER 7: WATCH WARDROBE, WALK, AND FOOD — 138

CLOTHING SPEAKS	138
IT'S IN THE WAY YOU WALK	141
OBSERVE A PERSON'S FOOD CHOICES	142

SECTION 3 — 146

CHAPTER 8: NLP AND PEOPLE'S META-PROGRAMMING — 146

KINDS OF META-PROGRAMS	147

CHAPTER 9: KEEP YOUR EARS PRICKED FOR WORD CLUES — 154

CHAPTER 10: THE ART OF ASKING THE RIGHT QUESTIONS — 164

BOOK 3: MAKE FRIENDS EASILY: HOW TO CHARM AND CONNECT IN RECORD TIME — 174

CHAPTER 1: GETTING TO KNOW YOU . . . — 176

THE FRIENDSHIP FORMULA — 177
CREATE YOUR OWN REALITY DISTORTION FIELD — 183
RECIPROCAL CURIOSITY — 187

CHAPTER 2: THE FRIENDSHIP MINDSET — 194

THE ART OF ACTIVE LISTENING — 194
HELP PEOPLE THINK OUT LOUD — 196
QUESTION-ASKING — 200
ACTIVE AND CONSTRUCTIVE RESPONDING — 205

CHAPTER 3: TURNING ON THE CHARM — 212

STORYTELLING IN CONVERSATIONS — 212
USING WITTY BANTER IN BUILDING RAPPORT — 217
PRINCIPLES OF SELF-DISCLOSURE — 221

CHAPTER 4: WHEN EGO GETS IN THE WAY — 228

THE NARCISSISM RATIO — 228
ALBRECHT'S RULE OF THREE FOR CONVERSATIONS — 233
INTERRUPTING—OR COOPERATIVELY OVERLAPPING? — 239

SUMMARY — 244

SUMMARY GUIDE — 246

BOOK 4: HOW TO SPEAK EFFECTIVELY: *INFLUENCE, ENGAGE, & CHARM* — 250

CHAPTER 1: COMMUNICATION FUNDAMENTALS — 252

- The Ladder of Inference — 252
- Framing — 256
- Chunking: Adjusting the Zoom Button — 260
- Think Before You Speak — 264

CHAPTER 2: MASTERING STYLE AND TONE — 270

- Eliminate Crutch Words and Empty Language — 270
- Upspeak and the Mystery of Tone — 273
- How to Use Signposts — 277

CHAPTER 3: PAINTING WITH WORDS — 282

- The Art of Vivid Language: Use Imagery and Rhythm — 282
- How to Be a Masterful Storyteller — 286

CHAPTER 4: COMMUNICATION'S MOST UNDERRATED SKILL — 290

- Asking the Right Questions — 290
- How to Be a Truly Effective Listener — 294
- Don't Be a Conversational Narcissist! — 298

CHAPTER 5: WHEN IT ALL GOES WRONG . . . — 302

- Effective Conflict Resolution — 302
- How to Master High-Stakes Discussions and Stabilize Intense Emotions — 306
- Assertive Communication — 310
- Give and Take: The Art of Feedback — 315

SUMMARY GUIDE — 320

BOOK 1: MASSIVE CHARISMA:
Small Talk, Charm, Likability, and How to Succeed With People

Part 1: Cultivating a Charismatic Aura

Chapter 1: So, what is charisma anyway?

There's something about them. People with charisma are just so... *appealing*. They're charming, they're likable and they somehow make everyone gravitate towards them. Is it magic? Is it just a chemistry thing?

If you've ever wanted to be that person in the room with the most magnetic, captivating aura, then this book is for you. When we're in the presence of charismatic people, it can be hard to say precisely why we're so bewitched. Charisma can start to seem like something that you're just born with... or not.

But thankfully, this kind of allure is *not* some mysterious power that only a few possess. It's 100% a social skill that you can practice, even if you don't quite see yourself that way now. Charisma is really a collection of different behaviors and attitudes that radiate a certain very attractive mindset to others. We'll divide our "charisma crash course" into two main parts in the chapters that follow. First, you'll learn how to develop your own unique brand of charm within yourself. Then, in part 2, you'll learn to carry that aura out into the world and broadcast it to those you interact with.

With charisma, you're more empathetic, more engaging, and a much, much better conversationalist. You're interesting *and* interested. And because you're witty and emotionally intelligent, people like you and trust you. It's hard to imagine an area of life that isn't improved with a little charisma – dating, work, friendships. Even chatting to strangers at a bus stop becomes an opportunity for winning people over with enchanting banter!

Before we dive in, though, let's dispel one misconception: being charismatic is NOT about being loud, extroverted or cocky. In fact, by the end of this book, the hope is that you'll see there are many ways to be charming, whether that's being flashy and larger than life, or quietly confident and a little mysterious.

A practical definition

Conveniently for us, in 2018, researchers at the University of Toronto studied the phenomena of charisma and developed a working definition. After studying over 1000 people, the team concluded that charisma was a mix of two things:

1. Affability
2. Influence

Affability broadly means that people are pleasant to be around and easily approachable. However you define it – warmth, pleasantness, friendliness – this is the quality that makes you think, "hm, I like this person!"

Influence is defined as leadership potential, "presence" and the ability to influence and persuade people. Not only did the team discover that it was actually possible to measure these two traits, but also that people were fairly accurate at rating themselves – i.e. when self-ratings were compared to ratings by others, they were more or less the same. They created the General Charisma Inventory (GCI), which you can basically complete yourself right now:

Read the following statements and give yourself a rating from 1 to 5, with 1 for "strongly disagree" and 5 for "strongly agree." The first three are about influence, while the latter three are about affability.

I am someone who...

- *Has a presence in a room*
- *Has the ability to influence people*
- *Knows how to lead a group*
- *Makes people feel comfortable*
- *Smiles at people often*
- *Can get along with anyone*

To score, simply add up the ratings for each, and take that value and divide it by 6. If you scored over 3.7, you can consider your charisma above average. Scored significantly lower than that? Don't worry! It's not as hard as you might think to work on these 6 criteria and boost your charm. Did you score low in influence, affability or both? Interestingly, how charismatic you are has nothing to do with your personality type or overall intelligence (it may have something to do with whether you're male or female, though – more on that later).

So, let's summarize: charisma is characterized by the ability to charm, persuade and attract others, and it contains two broad traits, *affability* and the power to *influence*. These two broad traits can be broken down into 6 smaller characteristics, such as presence and good rapport with others. Let's take a closer look at the basic dos and don'ts of charisma.

Being more influential

Think of a person you consider influential. What are they like? Maybe you picture someone like Oprah Winfrey, who built a veritable empire for herself, and influenced millions of people worldwide. Or maybe you picture Mahatma Gandhi, whose non-violent resistance created an aura of decisiveness so powerful it influenced nations. Maybe the first person to pop into your mind is an old-school friend who everybody seemed to love. Whoever you think of when you hear "influential," that person is probably one thing: confident.

Influential people believe in themselves and communicate the things they're passionate about, so much so that other people feel passionate and confident about those things, too! Think of the most famous political speeches in history and how their speakers could transmit their energy and enthusiasm to the crowd. It's not ever about arrogance or narcissism, though. Instead, it's about that person's *presence*.

Picture someone walking into a room, head held high, smile on their face, body language open. They greet everyone in the room confidently, and when they speak, their voice is sure, crisp and clear. Immediately, they seem to take up a certain amount of space in the room. Compare this to someone who slinks in shyly, shoulders slumped, expression of apprehension all over their face. Without making eye contact, they greet one person and then shuffle off to a corner somewhere, speaking quietly, if at all. It's obvious: this person simply takes up less room.

However, taking up more "space" is not just about being literally larger than life. People try to cheat with this and wear outrageous, attention-grabbing clothing or speak too loudly – this will catch people's attention for a second, but is unlikely to hold it if there is no genuine confidence and gravity in your presence beyond the costume! We don't automatically think that loud, domineering people are confident or charismatic. This proves that it's about so much more than who is making the most noise, but a kind of relaxed, open poise that communicates a deeper level of confidence.

DO THIS: Before you walk into a room or start a conversation, literally stand tall and stretch your arms high over your head. Take deep breaths. Imagine a light at the center of your chest. This light is who you are, the best of you, and what you have to offer the world. Imagine proudly and courageously shining this light out when you move around the world, with open body language and a smile. Another option is to visualize – imagine, for example, that you're a proud, regal lion or even a king or queen. If you like, remind yourself of your achievements or of a compliment you've been given. Allow *that* to guide your posture and demeanor.

One final way to immediately get into this open, optimistic posture is to imagine that the people you're about to encounter are *already* your friends, and that you will be received warmly. Imagine that you're meeting old, much-loved friends who are dying to see you. Carry that unguarded expectation and optimism into any new interaction.

DON'T DO THIS: If you have a core belief that certain people or situations are threatening, then this attitude will manifest in your expression, your posture and your voice. You will transmit an attitude (no matter how subtle or unconscious) or fearfulness, reluctance or hostility – and that will immediately destroy any chance of charisma. So, whatever you do, *don't* enter into any interaction where you're quietly thinking, "these people hate me." This attitude will make you shrivel, shrink and fold into yourself, immediately taking up less space and losing presence in the room.

In the same vein, try not to inhabit a mindset of force or desperation. This can be subtle, but if you are running a tape in your head that goes *don't let other people see how uncomfortable you are, play it cool, look confident OR ELSE*, then you are actually going to transmit that feeling of fear and not a feeling of confidence (which, remember, is characteristically calm, not frantic).

What about influencing others? Presence is one thing, but to encourage others to think or do certain things, you'll need to have one important thing: energy. You have to not only believe in yourself (confidence, taking up space) but believe in what you're saying. If you can genuinely muster enthusiasm and optimism for your point of view, people will be more attracted to it. If you're non-committal? Others will respond in the same lukewarm way, if they pay attention at all.

DO THIS: Find your real passion, and speak fervently about it. You can't fake enthusiasm. People can tell when they're being manipulated or advertised to – but they love it when others are fired up with their own mission, and are following their own north star. They love that enthusiasm so much they want to follow that north star, too! Whether you're trying to get people to do something or not, speak out about what matters to you (even if you will actually "lose" some people in the process!).

Passionate about animal rights? About good food? A sport? Have you always been zealous about a particular hobby, interest or view? Then say so! At the very least, be bold and confident in stating what you like and want. Don't sit on the fence. Do you have an unusual preference or opinion? Share it proudly, without diluting your true feelings.

DON'T DO THIS: "Uh, I don't know, what do *you* think?" Not very inspiring, right? Banish these words from your vocabulary. Even though you might feel that way inside, don't second guess or self-doubt out loud. Charismatic people are relaxed, confident and sure of themselves. So, if you portray anxiety, uncertainty or doubt in the value of your ideas, you can expect others to do the same.

One thing to be on guard about is regurgitating the passion and enthusiasm of other people… in other words, being inauthentic. Here's a secret: You don't have to conform! If you can genuinely express a unique, truly original perception that has not been heavily influenced by whatever everyone else thinks, you will immediately appear more interesting and distinct. Plus, this communicates confidence *and* intelligence – because not only are you able to think for yourself, but you are strong enough to convey that instead of going along with convention for the sake of it.

Finally, make a point of not complaining, whining or expressing dissatisfaction about yourself. It's the opposite of inspiring passion. Here's another secret: people don't really mind if others are wrong or different, so long as they are confidently, authentically so! If your unusual opinion or experience is presented respectfully and in the spirit of good conversation, it will always be better received than if you merely parroted the same old things people always do.

Finally, what about leadership? If you are confident and can speak clearly about your passions, then you will automatically find yourself in the position of leading others. The good news is that there is really no such thing as a "natural" leader – if you have a compelling and genuine vision, and you communicate that well to others, they will be inspired to follow.

DO THIS: Speak TO people and not AT them. What do they value? What do they want? How do they make sense of the world? Speak to your audience's highest selves. When you talk to them, communicate so that you *center their perspective,* rather than your own. Make your vision so real for them they can taste it.

For example, if you're part of a committee and you're trying to get people to see the wisdom of a new plan you're proposing, you might listen to the way they speak and reflect that back to them, using their words and not your own. You might adjust how you speak to frame the plan to align with their values and principles. "I know that you're a family man, and you're as concerned as I am about child safeguarding."

DON'T DO THIS: Treat people as objects to be moved. Force and manipulation might work in the very short term but ultimately fail. You may have a brilliant idea, but if you force it on others with no respect for them, they won't listen. Avoid appealing to your audience's lowest selves – the part of them that responds from fear or hate or negativity. This will not be felt as influence, but manipulation. "Well, you have kids. Wouldn't you feel really guilty if you let something bad happen to them?"

Being more affable

Many politicians are quite influential… but nobody *likes* them. Influence is only half of charisma – people also need to like you. Many people who struggle with socializing fail to realize the most important part of being likeable: making other people feel good. It's not about getting others to think you're great; rather, it's about making sure they feel comfortable, listened to, and respected. When people feel that they are liked in this way, then, as if by magic, they like *you*.

Being more affable is easy once you get out of your own head. The easiest (almost too easy) way to be more affable is simply to smile. Smile as often as you can. Remember that people cannot see into your inner experience – they can only see what you're broadcasting on your face. So be aware of your facial muscles and what they're communicating. Check in occasionally and consciously remind yourself to loosen your jaw, unclench your forehead muscles and gently lift the corners of your mouth.

DO THIS: You don't have to grin from ear to ear constantly. But *encourage* yourself to smile more, especially if you're someone who considers themselves a little pessimistic or grumpy! How your face moves is a part of your body language. You can practice genuine smiles by thinking of things that make you happy. It's a trick photographers use: they ask their models to imagine someone they love, or remember a hilarious moment. They can't help but smile or laugh. A smile doesn't have to be enormous to have an effect – as long as it's warm and genuine, it will have an effect.

Making other people feel comfortable is a big part of affability. It's easy to imagine why:

Person A: Good looking, intelligent, accomplished, fascinating, and makes you feel at ease

Person B: Good looking, intelligent, accomplished, fascinating, and makes you feel like garbage

Person A has charisma… person B is just intimidating, or even an outright bully!

Putting other people at ease takes emotional intelligence and empathy (which we'll cover at length in a later chapter). A certain degree of emotional and social maturity is required: charismatic people don't see social interactions as a chance to boast or as a battleground in which they demolish their opponents. Rather, they genuinely like other people and enjoy interacting with them. Ask yourself honestly, do you enter conversations with a genuine desire to listen to what other people say? Do you approach other people with curiosity to learn what they could teach you?

The best way to put other people at ease and make them comfortable is to pay attention to them. Listen to what they're saying (not what you *think* they're saying!) and show that you value and respect that perspective, rather than just barging in to share your own. You will win people's trust and admiration if you treat them with care.

DO THIS: Remember details. How do you feel when people don't spell your name right or completely forget what you told them in detail just yesterday? *Unheard*. A dazzling and interesting person who barely acknowledges your existence is not charismatic – they're more like a self-involved diva or celebrity. Instead, make a point of listening with care to what you're told. Remember facts that people tell you, and bring them up casually in later conversations. If you can do this and engage with others as though they're genuinely the most fascinating person on the planet (in that moment, they are!), then you will instantly boost your appeal.

DON'T DO THIS: Interrupt. It's something so easy and so tempting to do, and it so quickly destroys rapport. When you interrupt, you're basically telling the other person, "What I'm saying is more important than what you're saying." Obviously, this will not make them feel comfortable. Wait a few seconds after they finish speaking before you speak. Some of us tend to interrupt others for purely innocent reasons. We might get excited about what we're hearing and, without thinking, jump in to share our thoughts, perhaps even trying to finish the other person's sentence for them. It's an easy habit to fall into, but just as easy to be mindful and bite your tongue.

Beware of more subtle forms of interrupting, too. If you continually change the topic, ignore what's been said, or deliberately steer the conversation to yourself over and over again, the effect is the same. Let go of any conversational agenda and let the other person take charge and steer things for a while.

Finally, charismatic people get along with everybody. This is important – they don't just get along with those they like or those they're similar to, but *everybody*. Two things can help you get on better with people, whoever they are: optimism and non-judgment.

Charismatic people are positive people. They're solution oriented, resilient, and look on the bright side. They live in the moment and are flexible and adaptable. They see the good in themselves (self-confidence) but also the good in others. They see conversations as opportunities for learning and connection, and challenges as invitations to improve – that is, they're curious. If you are constantly negative, you bring an entirely different energy to interactions. You have an aura of difficulty, resistance, opposition, or just plain old dissatisfaction. Who would be attracted to that? The truth is that even when we think we're saying and doing all the right things, our underlying emotional frequency can still be felt by those around us. If you add judgment into this mix, things are even worse.

DO THIS: Express gratitude often and openly. Something magical happens when you demonstrate appreciation, and you'll instantly come across as more positive. It can be a simple question of saying, "wow, here comes some beautiful rain! My garden is going to love all this water," instead of complaining bitterly about the lack of sunshine. Even better if you can express gratitude for the other person, instead of criticism. Rather than dwelling on how weird you find someone, say instead, "That's what I love about you, you're not like anyone else I know!"

DON'T DO THIS: Judge. That includes yourself! Avoid gossiping or complaining about others, but especially avoid talking negatively about yourself. It may seem harmless (some people even believe that a good gossip session brings people together!), but it ultimately makes you look negative and insecure, and it gives others the unconscious feeling that you might apply that same attitude to everyone else, including them. Instead, say something constructive or at the least keep criticisms to yourself. Ask a question or shine the light on the other person. Keep it playful and open-ended.

And there you have it – we have demystified charisma and pinned it down to six very practical, very simple skills you can try today, in your very next conversation:

1. Open up your posture and take up space; assume that people are already your friends
2. Speak up about your passions and drop self-doubting language
3. Address people's higher selves and their values to influence and win them over
4. Use happy memories to encourage yourself to smile more
5. Show people you're paying attention by remembering conversational details, and never interrupt, to put them at ease
6. Express gratitude rather than criticism and judgment, to appear more optimistic

As you can see, none of the above require any magical powers or special talents – with a little effort and practice, they can all be measured, learnt and developed.

Zooming in on personal charisma

Ronald E Riggio is the Henry R. Kravis Professor of Leadership and Organizational Psychology at Claremont McKenna College in California, and he's been studying charisma for decades, particularly when it comes to leadership. For Riggio, personal charisma is basically a complicated mix of social skills that allows people to *deeply affect others on an emotional level*, primarily using communication. It's not just that you possess a group of nifty skills, but that all the skills come together cohesively, making a deep impact on other people emotionally.

Whether on a social or emotional level, charismatic people are

1. expressive
2. sensitive to other people's expression, and
3. able to control both of these masterfully, according to the context and their own needs

Emotional awareness and *social* intelligence are key here, and with enough practice, you can bring both skills together into one big, charming package. It's interesting to note that the things we might associate with charisma (intelligence, being "right," accomplishments, social status, wealth, attractiveness, etc.) are not what it's all about. Let's look at what Riggio calls the six foundational building blocks of charisma. Each is based on how well we send messages (expressiveness), receive them (sensitivity), or control ourselves. Take careful note how each of these six can be developed intentionally.

Emotional expressiveness

You know who isn't charismatic? A robot. Stoic, restrained or emotionless people may be read as cold and unengaged. Remember our definition: charisma is about making an *emotional* impact on people. You don't do that with a list of rational arguments. You do that by expressing emotion yourself. Spontaneously and genuinely express how you feel. When you're animated and energetic, you seem more alive, more intelligent and more engrossing. When you demonstrate that you can be moved, that you have an opinion, and that you're dynamic and changeable, you appear more human and more trustworthy to others.

DO THIS: To be more expressive… use expressions. Allow your face to be animated. As you talk, imagine that all the sound is muted, or that your audience is hard of hearing, and you have to mime a little. Could an audience guess your meaning from your facial expression alone? Communicate with *all* of your body – use hand gestures and postures. If you're telling a funny story, inject a dramatic pause before the punchline, modulate your voice, and use big, broad gestures and facial expressions to add color and interest. Not sure how? Watch standup comedians with the sound off and look at how they use their bodies to express themselves. Sometimes, a whole world of meaning can be communicated by a well-timed eyebrow lift or a single outlandish adjective. If this seems difficult, one easy trick to remember is just to be moved by your own story. If you're saying something funny, laugh and let your face reflect the joy you have in recounting the tale. If you're trying to communicate an astonishing anecdote, literally pause and let your face reflect that amazement – your audience won't be able to help going along with you as they listen.

DON'T DO THIS: Be boring in your speech. Instead, use colorful and inventive language. Don't rush to get to the end (unconfident people do this because they're unconvinced they deserve much "airtime"), and don't downplay what you're saying (for example, "Oh, so I guess you could say it was kind of amazing… but anyway…"). Be a little unexpected and fresh, describe things in unusual ways, or use unique turns of phrase. On a related note, steer clear of swearing – not because it's vulgar, but because it's uncreative! If you must be vulgar, at least find a novel way to do it…

Emotional sensitivity

Being a sophisticated communicator is not just about sending a clear message, but receiving other people's messages, too. You simply cannot connect with people emotionally if you don't even know what emotions they're experiencing. You need to be able to accurately perceive other people's emotions – and respond to what you see. This is the ability to notice when you've lost someone's attention, when they're feeling uncomfortable, or when you're connecting with them. In other words, it's empathy.

In a later chapter, we'll look more closely at exactly how to improve empathy skills, but for the time being, it's enough to know that *empathy is nothing more than a heightened ability to truly perceive another person's reality.* You only need to pay attention. Truth be told, many of us are bad at this not because it's difficult, but because we don't actually take the time to ask ourselves what the other person is feeling. Becoming good at "reading people" takes time and practice.

DO THIS: Want to know what people feel? Ask them! The question alone already communicates a willingness to empathize, and that's worth a lot. It can be very refreshing and attractive when someone says, "Can I just be really honest with you for a second?" Ask where they're at emotionally, and then genuinely listen to the answer you receive, without judgment

DON'T DO THIS: Make assumptions. Yes, empathy helps you read body language, but often, no single gesture or expression means anything; if you're talking to a stranger, it's difficult to find patterns in their behavior since you don't have a "baseline" and there's nothing to compare it to. It's easier to just read the room! Pay close attention to how people respond to you in the moment, before you say or do the next thing. This stops you from getting carried away in a monologue or being insensitive to your listener's emotional wavelength. It also gives you time to correct faulty assumptions.

Emotional control

Genuinely charismatic people are never out of control. They always seem to be aware of and in command of themselves, so they never end up losing their temper or indulging in emotional displays they're later embarrassed about. But, this is difficult. How can we be "emotionally expressive" while also controlling our emotions? Don't those contradict?

The truth is that charm and charisma do contain an element of artifice. While charisma may be spontaneous and genuine, it is never unaware. In other words, charismatic people know how to turn the charm on and off, as needed. They know how to "act" to a certain extent, downplaying certain emotions if necessary. For example, they can smile and relax even when they feel nervous, and stay quiet when they know it's no use arguing. Emotional control allows people to stay ultra-calm even in the face of insults or chaos.

DO THIS: Get into the habit of slowing down to breathe. We can blurt things without thinking when we're flustered or overwhelmed, but literally a second or two of deep breathing can center us and remind us that we're in control of how we handle ourselves. Pause before you respond so you can gather yourself.

DON'T DO THIS: Get defensive. Ever. If you're ever feeling in over your head, use humor. Playfully making fun of the situation or dropping in an unexpected quip can defuse tension. Respond to rudeness, mistakes or sudden setbacks (your own or other's!) with lightness.

Maintain your emotional "frame" and remind yourself that nothing and nobody can *make* you feel or behave in a certain way. Be less emotionally reactive by just brushing things off instead of getting flustered by them.

Social expressiveness

This refers to sociability and being able to engage and express yourself in social situations. It could mean holding your own in a social group, or public speaking with confidence. Social expressiveness is most often associated with extroversion, but it doesn't need to be – even if you're an introvert, it doesn't mean you can't articulate yourself confidently in social situations. This area may feel challenging for people who don't find socializing easy, but the good news is that it improves with consistent practice.

DO THIS: Yes, it's true that everyone says to "be yourself" and act natural, but for this social skill, it may work to do the opposite: act a little. Watch videos of talk show hosts, standup comedians, actors or public personalities you admire for their charisma. Watch what they do and copy them. Granted, you don't want to base your entire identity on this persona, but it can be a great way to kick start your own innate charisma and give you some practice and confidence.

Consider signing up for a public speaking course, or joining an improv class, dance troupe or amateur drama group. Try standup comedy, an open mic night or simply speak up more in groups. You may be petrified at first, but practice really does make perfect. Frame the exercise as simply having a laugh rather than performing perfectly. You'll lower the stakes and teach yourself not to let fear of failure get in the way.

DON'T DO THIS: Be a slob, i.e., careless with how you dress and present yourself. Much of our communication happens before we even open our mouths. Think about what your clothing and accessories are saying about you, and challenge yourself to take a risk and express your individuality a little more. It may sound too obvious, but many amazing conversations have been spurred by people wearing provocative slogan t-shirts!

Social sensitivity

Just as you can become more masterful in what you communicate to others and how, you can also improve your ability to read what others are broadcasting. An impressive person is nice to *look at* from afar, but a charismatic person is nice to *be with*. When you're in their presence, you feel seen and listened to, you feel that they're the most interesting person you've ever met… and also, somehow, that you are more interesting than you remember!

It's the difference between watching a perfectly choreographed dance performance on a stage, versus being up close and personal with a good dancer, who is dancing *with* us, responding spontaneously and sensitively in every moment. This ability to feel and respond to people dynamically is down to social sensitivity. When people lack this ability, it starts to feel like you're both in separate worlds, having two conversations that have nothing to do with each other.

DO THIS: Practice being sensitive to overall surroundings and context. The next time you're in a new social situation, pause and read the situation before speaking or acting. What is the "energy" of the room? If the group shared one broad emotion and intention at this moment, what would it be? More practically, what are the social conventions and cultural assumptions around this gathering?

Watch people. Devote an hour or so to (unobtrusively) observe others passing by, and just notice what's going on with them. Especially try to read their *emotions*, and how those emotions are reflected in their bodies, faces, voices, everything.

It may sound odd, but meditating can also make you a better listener, which can improve your communication and empathy skills, which can make you more charismatic. Often, we rush into conversations with an agenda or assumptions about who the other person is. However, if you're mindful, you can stop and just look at what is actually in front of you. Drop your expectations, judgments and preconceptions and just neutrally observe what is happening. You may find yourself so much more in tune with others!

DON'T DO THIS: Avoid talking about yourself. Even if you're not bragging or boasting, constantly turning the conversation to *your* ideas, *your* experiences, and *your* opinions is boring. Instead, next time you're tempted to say something about yourself, deliberately choose to ask the other person a question. Most people don't actually conceal themselves; there's a world of fascinating information right there, if you only care to ask!

Social control

Finally, the social role-playing skill that charismatic people are especially good at, which non-charismatic people never even consider: social control. This can be difficult to describe, especially to people who think of social interaction in terms of authenticity and honesty. The truth is, however, that all human social interaction is deliberate, purposeful and rule-bound. In other words, we all play roles – even when we're ourselves!

If you have above-average social control, you're able to skilfully switch roles depending on the situation and your goals. You may play up your artistic, carefree side when on a date, but switch to hard-nosed taskmaster at work, where it matters. You may be very aware of how others perceive you, and choose to gently present a particular version of yourself to them, according to what you're trying to achieve.

Now, for some people, this skill can look dishonest or manipulative – and taken too far, it can be! But you only need to see someone who doesn't possess this skill to understand why it's so important. Do you know "blunt" people who insist on speaking their minds regardless of social context or the negative ramifications? Using a little poise, grace and etiquette is actually an intelligent way to control social situations to your advantage. Don't confuse rudeness, roughness or lack of social awareness with authenticity. At the same time, don't assume that "wearing a mask" is always disingenuous.

DO THIS: Learn to love small talk. Many introverts loathe small talk, and prefer deep, meaty topics. But this is no different from going on a first date and taking your clothes off before you've said hello! Small talk is not small – it's an important, necessary part of creating trust and rapport with people, so that you can *build* connections over time. To get good at small talk, just practice more. Chat to waiters, people in supermarket lines or the guy on the help line.

DON'T DO THIS: Don't avoid strangers. Challenge yourself to speak to new people as often as you can. Most of us tend to steer clear of interactions with people we don't know, but they can be a rich source of insight and practice for social skills. Don't worry if you encounter awkwardness – charismatic people are unfazed by this and just keep going!

When you encounter a charismatic person, they can initially appear to be outside of the ordinary somehow, as though they are breaking the social rules or doing something very radical. Truthfully, they *are* playing by the rules; they're just playing very well! People can make the mistake of thinking that charisma and magnetism are fixed personal qualities that belong to people, like attractiveness. But really, charisma is *relational* – it's something that emerges in context, in conversations and dynamic interactions with people. That's why we cannot be more charismatic by simply working on ourselves, for example, by dressing nicer. Charisma only happens when we know how to play the social game – and that means it's not about us but about *other people*.

Let's go back to our definition: a charismatic person is one who is **likeable**, and one who can **influence** others. And according to Riggio, they're people who are good at impacting others on an emotional level, because they know how to express themselves, how to perceive others, and how to control the situation. How do you compare to this description?

In the next chapter, we will look at concrete ways to become more charismatic, but before we do, let's take a personal inventory. In a journal or notebook, try to answer the following questions to pinpoint which areas you most need to work on:

To measure your influence

Do I have presence in a room?

Am I able to persuade, convince and influence others?

Am I comfortable with and able to lead a group?

To measure your likeability

Do people generally feel comfortable around me?

Do I smile genuinely and often?

Do I get along with all kinds of people?

To measure emotional skills

Am I emotionally expressive?

Am I able to read, listen to and empathize with the emotions of others?

Am I good at emotional self-regulation, and can I control my feelings (hiding them if necessary?)

To measure social skills

Am I comfortable expressing myself in public, such as in groups?

Am I in tune with social rules, etiquette and cultural contexts?

Do I know how to play a role, wear a mask and control how others perceive me?

If you answer each of the above honestly, you'll start to see a clear picture of where you are currently, and get an idea of what to focus on and improve. Perhaps you discover that you're an emotionally intelligent person with enormous empathy and sensitivity, but you lack confidence in social rules. Maybe you're good at leading and inspiring others, but miss out because you're not likeable – or vice versa!

However you measure up, though, remember that *anyone* can be charismatic, and by understanding your own unique strengths and weaknesses in this area, you've taken a real step towards becoming the most likeable and magnetic version of yourself!

Summary

- Charming people may seem to possess a mysterious quality nobody else does, but charisma is a knowable set of social and emotional behaviors that anyone can learn.
- Charisma can be defined as a blend of likeability and influence. Charismatics have presence in a room, can impact and persuade others, can lead, but also know how to put people at ease, are warm, smile often, and get along with anyone.
- Practice taking up more space in a room, and examine any core beliefs that may negatively impact your posture and expression. Believe deep down that other people are not a threat and that you have something worthwhile to communicate.
- Speak openly about your passions, and when you address others, speak to their highest selves. Smile often and remember the details of what people tell you.
- Don't interrupt, judge, complain, gossip or express negativity. Instead, express gratitude and optimism.
- Ronald Riggio broke charisma into 3 social and emotional functions: expressiveness, sensitivity to other people's expressiveness, and self-control.

- To be more charismatic, express yourself emotionally with colorful language and dynamic facial expressions. Pay attention to people's nonverbal expression, but don't be afraid to ask directly about how others feel.
- To improve emotional control, slow down, breathe and become present, rather than reacting mindlessly.
- Acting and improv can help you improve social skills, and the ability to consciously wear a social mask. Pay attention to how you're physically presenting yourself and dress with care and deliberation.
- Finally, learn to "people watch" and get into the habit of asking more questions instead of talking about yourself in conversations.

Chapter 2: Building real-world charisma

We've fleshed out a usable definition of charisma and broken it down into its parts. And hopefully, you've been able to zoom in on all those parts of charisma that you're already getting right, and those that need a little more work. This leads us to the obvious next question: how do we get better?

First things first: your charisma won't look like anyone else's charisma. This makes sense – think of any famous charismatic people from history, and they're all different from one another; Marilyn Monroe, Stalin and Steve Jobs were all enigmatic characters, but in very different ways! This is precisely what Olivia Fox Cabane, author of *The Charisma Myth*, found, i.e., that there are different types of charisma.

Just as you can imagine that Marilyn Monroe would make a pretty poor Stalin, and that Steve Jobs would fail hard to charm people in the way that Marilyn Monroe charmed them, you will be most charismatic when you are leaning into YOUR charisma style, rather than trying to ape someone else's.

Cabane listed four general categories, but even within these groups, it's easy to see the endless possible variations. Recall that charisma is made up of two factors: power and affability. Depending on the relative proportions of these two, you get slightly different expressions of charisma.

The focused charismatic

This is a state of high presence (which is a kind of high power) paired with moderate affability (which makes sense because the focus is on the *other* person).

This is someone who places deep, undivided attention on others, and makes them feel like "the most important person in the room." Talk show hosts (it's Oprah Winfrey again!) build their brands on this kind of charisma, as do motivational speakers – and cult leaders!

You'll know this is your preferred charisma style if you're often told you're a good listener. Focus charismatics are people that know that the best way to shine is to show off others to their best. If you often find yourself in the guru role of guiding people to be the best they can be, this may be your strong area. A focus charismatic can ooze charm and class in a totally subtle and often invisible way. Think about a religious leader, a persuasive healer/therapist type, or a gentle but powerful moral character who gets their way by prompting others to agree with them of their own will.

The visionary charismatic

A visionary charismatic is more affable than the focused charismatic, but a little less powerful.

A visionary can paradoxically get more done and be more impactful because they seem a little more like "one of us" and not like lofty personages that nobody could ever imitate. This tends to make them a little more likable too. Whereas the focus charismatic might be the awe-inspiring ideological leader in a company, the visionary is the one who bridges the gap between this awe and more ordinary life. They turn the dream into reality by communicating a vision not yet accomplished.

Recall Riggio's theory about emotional and social expressiveness – we are drawn to those who can move us to see their inspiring vision of the future, especially if they have the enthusiasm and energy to campaign for that vision. Think about Steve Jobs building a following devoted to his vision of the future, or Martin Luther King Junior's rousing speeches. Innovators and creative people can excel at visionary charisma, too, since they need to convince others to buy into a vision that only they can see.

If you've ever managed to get people rallied together on a passion project, and if your visions seem infectious, you might have this type of charisma.

The kind charismatic

This is the combination of high affability but the lowest power of all the charismatic types.

Emotional connection is powerful stuff – think of Buddhist Zen master Thich Nhat Hanh and how profoundly he influences people without any conventional trappings of wealth and power. He does so purely on an emotional and spiritual level, with genuine warmth and compassion.

Fred McFeely Rogers (affectionately Mister Rogers from the children's TV show *Mister Roger's Neighborhood*) was a much-loved media icon who inspired countless people with simple, wholesome messages. He was not just a cheerful and reassuring part of millions of people's childhoods – he became a role model and ideological icon spreading lessons of civility, tolerance, and belief in your own self-worth.

If you're a person who can drastically elevate situations with kindness, mercy, empathy and benevolence, this form of charisma may be your strongest. Note, however, that the relatively low power here does not mean *no* power. No charismatic will do without at least average or a little higher than average power – it's just that the focus is on affability, and their power is filtered through this kindness.

The authoritative charismatic

Finally, a more classic picture of a charismatic leader – like Stalin or Hitler, people with this style of influence use power and status to position themselves as authorities, experts or leaders.

This combination is low affability and high power. You might argue that if affability is low enough, then you are not dealing with a charismatic person at all, but a dominating bully or despot!

Such people seem to naturally command control, and effortlessly lead others. Do you frequently find that other people defer to your judgment or put you in charge of important tasks? Do you find that even those people who don't actually like you very much still tend to respect and follow you regardless? You might be better at exuding this kind of charisma than the other types.

As you can see from the four types, there is usually a trade-off between power and affability – though you would ideally want the highest possible power and the highest possible affability, in reality it's usually the case that as one increases, the other decreases. Note again, though, that charismatic people are never *low* in either power or affability.

Furthermore, this isn't to say that these are the only types. If you think of famous charismatics from history, you'll find many that don't fit the mold – in fact, their uniqueness itself is a source of both power and affability. Some may inspire and lead people because of their bravery and strength (sporting heroes; those who beat the odds after disease or injury), some may captivate and enthrall people with immense beauty, grace or sex appeal (the starlets from Hollywood's Golden Era), others may capture people's admiration through humor, creativity or originality (Robin Williams' comic genius could hit on an emotional level) and others may garner attention because they're moral or even spiritual crusaders (think of how Greta Thunberg commanded a room with her righteous indignation about climate change).

What about you? You may not yet feel confident in your own charismatic abilities, but you're probably beginning to get a sense for the *style* of that potential charisma, according to your own personality, values and experiences.

Think carefully about your interests and passions, your talents (are you a good communicator? Energetic? Determined?), and what people tend to respond to instinctively when you're around. The lesson here is that you shouldn't worry too much if you don't quite see yourself in the conventional descriptions of "charismatic leader" – you can be an engaging, fascinating person with a massive presence in a room, in a way that's all your own!

Fox Cabane's approach

Olivia Fox Cabane's model of charisma is pretty simple. She suggests that there are actually three main components:

POWER

PRESENCE

WARMTH

Power is here defined as the capacity to impact others, while presence is the ability to be fully engaged and attentive to the moment. Finally, warmth is about perceived goodwill or benevolence, or the degree to which people believe you will use your power and presence in their best interest. Again, all three of these are primarily emotional and about how people *feel* – charisma is not rational!

We can recognize these factors as analogous to the influence, presence and affability we discussed in the last chapter. From Cabane's point of view, different charisma styles vary in their relative proportions of these three special ingredients. For example, authoritative charismatics tend to blow everyone out of the water when it comes to power and presence, but tend to be a little weaker on warmth. Kind and focused charismatics excel in emotional warmth but may lack a little in the power department.

Once you have an idea of your current charisma quotient, and a few clues on your personal style, you have two options for improving yourself:

1. You can lean into your unique style and amplify it
2. You can balance out by cultivating those aspects you lack, so you're more rounded

Either way, always keep in mind that charisma is most powerful when it's personal and genuine, so keep checking in with your authentic values, the things that fire you up, and your natural gifts. With that in mind, let's look at some practical exercises to start tapping into your inner charm. Use these the next time you're heading into a meeting, going on a date, spending time with friends or family or speaking in public.

Exercise 1: Make yourself comfortable

We've seen that charismatic people are confident and have presence. They trust in themselves and their message, and they unapologetically take up space in the room. On a very basic level, though, confidence = comfort. It means being at home in your own skin, at ease with others, and comfortable in the world in general. This is why people advise to "walk into a room like you own it." Because when you are comfortable, you can *relax and expand* your awareness outwards to engage emotionally with others. When you're uncomfortable, every fiber of your being will communicate that, and act as a barrier to your power, presence and warmth.

Start simple and think about what you're wearing. It's infinitely better to wear something you're genuinely comfy in rather than a nice outfit that's too scratchy, too tight, too restrictive or too awkward. For Cabane, physical and mental discomfort are the biggest obstacles to building charisma. And physical tension *will* manifest as social and emotional tension. Think also about your general physical wellbeing. Ensure that you're not hungry or thirsty, tired, ill or too hot/cold. If you're going to be outside, plan ahead to make sure you're not distracted by the sun glaring in your eyes, or the wind blowing your hair around, or the wrong footwear.

Before you head out to a social interaction, pause for a moment and check in with yourself, body and mind. Remind yourself that how things *look* is not as important as how they *feel*. A silk tie or a gorgeous evening gown might be conventional symbols of style and good taste, but if they make you feel bad, then that is what you will transmit socially. Make sure that your physical situation supports you and allows you to express yourself freely, with minimal distraction. If something is getting in the way, get rid of it.

Exercise 2: Use ritual and visualization

Being charismatic is a state of mind. And just like an athlete needs to warm up before a big game or race, you need to warm up emotionally and psychologically before you wow everyone with charm. To extend the metaphor, if you jump into a marathon without stretching beforehand, you're going to be creaky and potentially injure yourself. Likewise, if you just jump into a challenging social situation without any thought or planning, you're going to fumble.

Ritual can be the perfect "social warm up." Not only does it allow us to get into the right mindset, but the mere fact of us planning ahead, taking charge and paying deliberate attention to our strategy will make us feel more in control and more confident. Remember that charisma is a social game, and the best players are those that take it seriously!

What kind of ritual is best? That depends on the state of mind you're trying to cultivate.

Imagine an important job interview coming up and wanting to dazzle your interviewers. It's a sales position, so you need to display both authoritative and focused charisma to charm the interviews and show them you know how to do the job. Truthfully, you're feeling nervous and unsure of yourself, so you know that you're going to need to demonstrate immense social and emotional control.

Hours before the interview, you start psyching yourself up. You listen to energizing music you know always puts you in a good mood. You run over a few mantras and affirmations to focus your mind. You plan your outfit and practice a few responses in a mirror. Finally, you spend time in active visualization. This could go a few different ways: you might imagine in detail how you want the interview to go, seeing yourself smiling, confidently taking charge of the room, and mentally rehearsing your posture, tone of voice and overall attitude.

You could also visualize someone you admire and who demonstrates the mindset you're trying to convey. You could picture being that person, as though you're temporarily using their persona as a mask to give you confidence. What would that person say and do in this situation? You could also use more abstract visualization, for example, imagining in vivid detail that all the stress is leaving your body in the form of literal negative words that float away off the surface of your skin, while a warm glow comes up from the ground and fills you up with energy, conviction and confidence. After the visualization, you imagine that this warmth stays with you, and that you carry it into the interview like a powerful talisman or magic spell. Speaking of talismans, maybe you have a lucky charm or special ritual that helps make the occasion feel auspicious – you wear a sentimental accessory, treat yourself, light a candle, say a prayer or plan to do something rewarding afterwards.

Exercise 3: Be present, build presence

Fox Cabane has a slightly different take on the idea of presence. For her, a person builds presence when they themselves are… present. This means being fully anchored in the moment, rather than having your attention elsewhere. The more present you are, the more genuinely you can engage others, respond sensitively to minute changes in the conversational flow, and observe others' emotional states. It's also far easier to be felt as warm if you are present, focused and paying attention to the person in front of you!

That means that one of the biggest ways to sabotage our charisma is to be so distracted by the idea of what we should be doing that we are pulled away from the present. If you guessed that mindfulness practice will help with presence, then you guessed right. Anxiety can kill your charismatic aura because it takes you out of the moment – and the moment is exactly where the people you need to connect with are! Mindfulness is a tool that can help you reduce anxiety and boost awareness whether you practice it alone, in preparation for a social situation, or in that situation as it unfolds.

Again, the way you use mindfulness depends on your aims. Consider the following examples.

A person trying to improve their warmth and affability realizes that judgment gets in the way of them connecting with people. They try a "loving kindness" meditation every morning, where they practice extending compassion and understanding to everyone. Sitting quietly and with focus, they imagine a person they love, and focus on this feeling of acceptance and warmth. Then, they imagine someone they only like, but practice feeling this same warmth for them, too. Next, they imagine someone they are neutral about, and so on, until they reach a person they actively dislike. They work hard to find feelings of kindness for them, and for the fact that they are human beings who deserve compassion and respect regardless.

While such a person may find that this practice generally improves their outlook and makes them more tolerant and accepting people, another might simply commit to finding little "windows" of awareness in every social interaction. Pausing, coming to the present and reminding themselves to be aware of their body and breath in the moment, they become more relaxed and dynamically engaged. Perhaps they notice that their voice or body language is conveying stress, so they consciously choose to loosen up. Perhaps they realize they're hogging the conversation and graciously decide to let the other person take the stage for a while.

One great way of building presence is to *take your time*. Anxiety, lack of presence, and rushing all go hand in hand. If you find yourself feeling tense in a moment, just pause. Breathe. Anchor in the present and in your 5 senses. What can you smell? See? Taste, even? Slow down and just get comfy in the moment. It's usually our stressful ruminations about how we are in social situations that derail us, and not the situation itself. Anchor in the moment and let these ruminations drift away. Finally, put your attention squarely on the other person – don't let your mind wander, and don't get distracted by your phone.

Exercise 4: Take care

This is an extension of the previous exercise. When you pause, you give yourself the chance to act deliberately rather than reactively. You stop being at the mercy of knee-jerk reactions and start to act consciously – congratulations, this is the beginning of that elusive quality called grace and poise! For example, if somebody says something that catches you off guard and embarrasses you a little, don't immediately blush and blurt out something that makes you sound defensive. Rather, pause and think, "how do I want to play this?" and then choose to laugh it off, deflect attention by saying something amusing or graciously thank the person for their comment, completely changing the energy of the interaction. But you can only do all this if you're aware enough to pause in the first place.

Here's a fun trick that may result in an unexpected boost of confidence: Remind yourself that *you don't have to react at all*. We can get flustered when something unexpected or unpleasant happens, but that doesn't mean we have to lose our equilibrium, give away our attention, or have our mood determined by something or someone else. We can always choose to simply not respond. Sometimes a pause is all it takes to switch you from the mindset of "Oh no, what should I do?" to "Never mind that, what do I *want* to do?" Remind yourself always that you don't have to decide what you think about every stimulus in your environment, form an opinion, engage, or even pay attention.

Every choice you make in a social interaction matters. Your body language, your tone of voice, your word choice, your facial expression. Rather than being intimidated by this fact, use it to your advantage – see all of these as colors on a palette to paint the image *you* want to paint. Don't leave anything to chance. Take care with how you dress, how you speak, and how you're holding yourself in conversations. Especially take care of what is happening with people around you and your effect on them. Again, we're in the realm of social control, which cannot be achieved without a degree of mindful awareness.

Pause before you respond – just a few seconds, and you'll seem more poised and put together. Instead of saying "um" simply keep quiet while thinking of what to say. If you are confident enough to take your time speaking, people will usually respond in kind and pay more attention to your words. Finally, be careful about your word choice, and consider your audience. It's always a good idea to match your tone, word choice, volume and pitch to theirs if you're unsure.

Howard Friedman's approach

University of California professor of psychology Howard Friedman has spent decades researching various social behaviors, particularly this elusive quality we call charisma. He developed the Affective Communication Test (appropriately called ACT), which he believed was a good indicator of people's emotional expressiveness, i.e., their overall charisma. Like Riggio, Friedman believed that there is something compelling and attractive about people who easily and comfortably **express** themselves. In a 1980 paper published in the *Journal of Personality and Social Psychology*, he and Riggio, together with two fellow researchers, found that nonverbal expressiveness plays a big role in social interactions.

Whichever form it takes, communicating with spiritedness, energy, passion, eloquence and vibrant gestures all make a person far more charismatic. Remembering that charisma is about impacting others emotionally, it's easy to see why expressiveness is so important – it allows us to more easily affect others, leading and captivating and inspiring them. Words matter, but when they're paired with *nonverbal* expression, they can be charismatic. It's as though charming people are fluent in two languages: the obvious superficial one and the more primal, unspoken and nonverbal one that captivates us more easily.

The ACT is pretty simple: there are ten statements that participants are asked to respond to, noting the extent to which they agree. You can try it yourself by seeing the degree to which the following statements apply to you (note that these are inspired by several different versions of the test):

When I hear good music, I can't help but move my body

When I laugh, it's jovial and buoyant, and everyone can hear me

When I'm on the phone, my mood and feelings come across loud and clear

In conversations with friends, I am tactile and easily touch or hug people

I don't mind when a group of people notice me or watch me

I usually have an obvious facial expression, and am seldom neutral

People often tell me I'd make a good actor or actress

I'm not shy and don't mind being the center of attention

I know how to look at people seductively if I want to

I've always been good at playing games like charades or miming

Strangers often think I'm younger than I am

The more strongly you agree to the above statements, the more likely you're perceived as charismatic. These statements essentially measure your nonverbal affective expressiveness. Let's look more closely at what this expressiveness actually looks like in the real world, and how you can go about cultivating some of it in yourself.

Kinesthetic responsiveness

People are drawn to and enthralled by displays of health, vigor, and liveliness in a very primal sense. Think of how people can't tear their eyes away from a talented performer, a passionate dancer or singer, or someone throwing their heart and soul into something special. We're attracted to people that seem to be filled to the brim with passion and energy – perhaps we hope that some of it will rub off on us!

Before human beings invented language, they communicated with their bodies. In fact, you could say that movement is a more primitive and immediate form of communication. Kinesthetic responsiveness is about expressing yourself emotionally through your body's movement. Boring and unengaging people seem to be dead from the neck down. They slump and appear stagnant – their bodies don't seem to extend or expand much into the space around them. In contrast, charismatic people are *embodied*, and their enthusiasm manifests in *all* of them. They move. They gesture. They shift in their seats, tilt their heads, or flap their hands around madly when telling an amusing story.

DO THIS: Stay in shape. No really! If you're healthy and physically active, you'll be more confident and at ease in your own skin, lighter on your feet and more mobile. As you speak to anyone, remember that your body is also constantly sending a message. Do you want that message to be "Zzzz, I'm half asleep…"? It's hard to communicate ease and confidence if you're unfit, uncomfortable, or physically struggling in some way.

Expressive and contagious laugh

A laugh is a powerful thing. It can make people fall in love, put them at ease, make them trust you… it can make *them* laugh. Why is a genuine, juicy laugh so infectious? Well, think about what a laugh is: a simple, direct expression of joy. It shows a person that, just for one unguarded moment, is genuinely expressing how they feel. Also, it's a potent communication that you're happy, resilient, healthy and able to enjoy yourself. People who are miserable, anxious or in the habit of denying themselves pleasure are not attractive, and they're not charismatic. But when you hear a person laugh from their core, something happens to you – you want to be a part of it! You're drawn in closer. All barriers and conventions temporarily fall away, and a moment of intimacy is possible.

DO THIS: Commit to never stifling a laugh. Be free and ebullient with your joy and let it overflow when you feel it, without a second thought for how you look or for social appropriateness (within reason, of course… bursting out laughing at a funeral is probably not a good idea). You could even practice by watching funny videos or comedy, and letting yourself laugh openly. The next time you're in company and want to laugh, don't force or fake anything: genuine and spontaneous joy is like charisma gold dust – don't hide it!

Expressive voice

Have you noticed how pets and other animals don't care about the words you say to them, but seem to respond only to the tone and pitch of your voice? Human animals are no different! Whether we're conscious of it or not, we all respond to the emotion we hear in other people's voices, regardless of the words they're using. If your words are saying one thing and your voice is communicating another, people will perceive the mismatch, and it will put them on edge; they may interpret the discrepancy as insincerity. This is why it's important to communicate with your whole body – and your voice is an especially important part of your body.

DO THIS: Never speak carelessly. Instead, think about the emotion you're trying to convey and make sure your voice expresses that. Through your tone of voice alone, let people know that you're excited to talk to them, that your conversation brings you pleasure, and that you're fascinated by what they're saying. An old trick for when you're on the phone: even though people can't see you, smile anyway. They will be able to hear it in your voice.

Expressive touching

When we communicate, we are reaching from our world out into the void to touch someone else's world. And the most obvious and concrete way to do this is to… literally touch them. Clearly, this comes with some caveats. Touch needs to be appropriate to work – lightly brushing someone's hand, upper arms or shoulder in the course of events can bridge distances, so to speak, and make the interaction feel more real and present. If touch is pushy or awkward, though, it can prove disastrous.

DO THIS: With people you don't know very well, communicate warmth and presence by touching them just once or twice in a conversation, on the shoulders, hands or lower arms. Naturally weave the touch into another expressive gesture, for example, a light touch when you are indicating "you" or a gentle nudge on the shoulder as you walk through a door to suggest they go first. The trick is to be casual and comfortable in yourself as you do so. If you can't touch without being stiff or uncomfortable, avoid it for a while.

DON'T DO THIS: A caveat here – touch will be received differently depending on whether a man or woman is toucher or touchee. As a rule, like it or not, men can get away with far less touch than women can, and it's usually better to touch someone of the same sex to avoid misunderstanding.

Relax into being in the limelight

If you're shy or an introvert, having all eyes turned on can feel pretty scary. But charismatic people soak up attention easily and with pleasure. Being put on the spot can be nerve-wracking, but even if you're not a natural performer, you can fake it somewhat. Protesting, being awkward or shyly trying to wriggle out of attention actually make things worse. A lot worse! So just relax. Something to remember is that when people turn their attention to you, their intentions are usually benign. Watch a nervous newbie comedian on stage for the first time. Usually, the crowd is generous with their laughs anyway – they *want* the performer to succeed and feel comfortable.

DO THIS: Use humor. You don't have to suddenly think of something witty to say on the spot. Just smile, relax, and breathe. Whatever you do, don't make a big deal of any awkwardness in the moment, or you'll amplify it. Maybe playfully make fun of yourself or the situation. If everyone has turned to look at you after a slip and fall, just get up, smile, take a bow and say, "ta da!" It's not original, it's not even all that funny, but it puts people at ease and will make them smile.

Communicate with your face

While you might find an inscrutable and mysterious person interesting for a little while, you'll soon get bored of how little they're revealing of themselves. Communication is about being engaged – people want to know that they're affecting you, that you have an opinion, and that you are alive and responsive. Think about being on a date; it's excruciating to be with an unreadable person, and not know how they feel about you. It's far more attractive to be with someone who is letting you know loud and clear where they are emotionally.

DO THIS: Speak less, and emote more. It could be as simple as smiling and nodding instead of saying "yes" or lifting a single eyebrow when someone asks your opinion of a movie. Expressing emotions via the face becomes easier the more you practice – look in the mirror and try to see how many different kinds of smiles you can make. Or, the next time you're in a conversation, replace "uh huh" sounds with expressions that mirror or respond to the speaker's.

Change your attitude to strangers

Public speaking coach Sims Wyeth did a survey and found that those who called themselves introverts actually prefer the company of extroverts. Trouble is, extroverts also prefer the company of extroverts! This suggests that it's simply easier and more fun to be with someone socially outgoing and expressive. While there's nothing wrong with being an introvert, the truth is that it can put further distance between you and others, and limit the closeness, engagement and presence required for charisma.

DO THIS: Make the first move. Say hello to strangers first. This may seem scary, but it actually puts you in the driver's seat and gives you more control over social interactions. Practice broaching the silence with new people, and you'll see that the *earlier* you break the ice, the easier the interaction tends to be.

Flirt a little

Friedman believed that charismatic people are experts at using a "seductive glance." While hard to describe, we all know this look when we see it! Sure, there is a strong link between being charismatic and being sexy, alluring or attractive to the opposite sex. But charismatic people are also masters at what could be called "platonic flirting." They flirt with everyone—if we broaden our definition of "flirt."

DO THIS: Practice platonic flirting – with family, friends, children, old people and people you don't even like. Think back to how much razer focus, warmth and sparkle you've brought to romantic dates in the past, and then bring that dazzling (non-sexual) version of yourself into the everyday. Be generous and sincere in the compliments you give. Smile at people often and praise them. Laugh at their jokes. Basically, demonstrate that just being around them *gives you pleasure*. This makes people feel like a million bucks, and like they're seen and appreciated. This kind of non-romantic "chemistry" is wonderful to see in action!

Ham it up

Finally, Friedman identified one form of emotional expressiveness that is the more fundamental precursor to body language: pantomime. Physically acting out a narrative is a brilliant and simple way to add color, life and dynamism to your stories, and to make you seem more relatable, more amusing and way more captivating. You can learn to do this by watching the pros: improv artists, comedians, clowns, impersonators and… two-year-olds, who are the reigning champions of the acting world.

DO THIS: The next time you're relating a story to someone, gradually try to incorporate gestures, actions, voices and movements to add dimension. This can be subtle; for example, if you're relating a discussion between two people, slightly move your position in space and change your voice and posture when you act out each person's part. Make liberal use of dramatic pauses, facial expressions and gestures. It may seem silly, but imagine you're telling the story to a group of excited toddlers and *exaggerate*.

Howard Friedman's approach to charisma homes in on the emotional expressiveness aspect of charisma, and judging by his research, this may be the most significant factor when it comes to charming and engaging people.

It's easy to imagine an emotionally expressive car salesman, stand-up comedian, preacher, politician or celebrity with a megawatt smile. But you may be starting to wonder: is there no room for those people who are quieter, calmer, more sophisticated, more refined, shy, reserved… or plain old timid?

A word on introversion
First, the bad news: charisma is about emotionally impacting others, and it's almost impossible to do that if you're not literally reaching out to others, taking the risk of showing yourself, and being interested in the people around you. Very few can manage to be aloof and dismissive of others and yet liked. So, if you consider yourself a naturally reclusive or introverted person, then there's no question: you will have to come out of your comfort zone and play a role that may not feel comfortable at first – if you want to increase your charisma, that is.

But the good news? Extroverts have to do this work too. Many shy people falsely assume that extroverts find all this easy. A few do, but if you ask most social butterflies, they'll tell you that they had to work on it. Sometimes constantly! Even the most confident and enigmatic person can sometimes feel vulnerable, crabby, unconfident, or socially terrified.

The difference is they understand there's no way around it: like anything in life, it takes consistent practice, humility and the willingness to learn.

There's more good news, though. You *don't* have to be an overbearing or fake loudmouth to be charismatic. You can keep your quiet, calm personality and still be alluring. "Extroverts sparkle, introverts glow." Being naturally less gregarious is no excuse for not mastering warmth, sensitivity, good communication, listening skills, tact and expressiveness. In fact, there are a few aspects of charisma that you may be *better* equipped to master than your extroverted brethren! In our next chapter, we'll look at two case studies that prove that charm comes in many flavors, and introversion/extroversion has very little to do with it.

Summary

- Olivia Fox Cabane explains how there are four charisma types according to the proportion of power, presence and warmth. The focused charismatic (who pays deep attention to others), the visionary charismatic (who communicates their infectious passion), the kind charismatic (who inspires with warmth and compassion) and the authoritative charismatic (who leads others with expertise and power).
- Depending on your goals, you can play up your natural charisma strengths or seek to balance out your weaknesses.
- To be socially and emotionally comfortable, plan ahead and make sure you're physically comfortable, which will remove barriers to charismatic connection.
- Use ritual and visualization as a "social warm up." Music, meditation, and affirmations can help you prepare.
- Build presence with mindfulness. Slow down, breathe and anchor in the senses. Pause before you respond, and take conscious care of every detail of the interaction, including your verbal and nonverbal expression, appearance, and behavior.
- Howard Friedman emphasized the affective, nonverbal expressiveness component of charisma.
- Communicate with *all* your body and laugh openly. Speak with a dynamic, varied voice that changes in pitch, tone and expression. Use touch to bridge distance and create warmth, aware that the rules differ for men and women.
- Speak less and emote more via facial expression. If you find yourself the center of attention, relax and don't draw attention to awkwardness, using humor to defuse tension. Use exaggerated, pantomime-like gestures and initiate contact with strangers. Finally, practice the art of "platonic flirting."
- Introverts *can* be charismatic, but they must do so on their own terms.

Chapter 3: Putting it all together

In chapters 1 and 2, we looked at several different models and theories that could help us better grasp the charisma phenomenon. We considered the researchers at the University of Toronto and their *General Charisma Inventory* outlining affability and influence aspects. We examined Riggio's model, which put expressiveness, sensitivity and control as the three tasks of charisma, whether applied to emotional aspects or social ones. We explored Olivia Fox Cabane's Power-Presence-Warmth trinity and looked at some of her practical exercises for visualization and ritual. Finally, we looked at Friedman's theory, which focused on "affective communication," and how charismatic people are those that express themselves nonverbally.

Well, that's a lot to take in! How can we pull all this together into something that will make a difference in our lives? Each of these theories is a blend of explanation, description of traits, and suggestions for practical exercises we can all try to become more charismatic. In this chapter, we synthesize the best of each theory and create our own meta-theory. Below we'll look at the *five traits most consistently associated with charisma*. Consider it a cheat sheet:

Trait 1: Likeability and warmth

Or "affability." Arguably the most important trait. If you can smile, put people at ease and accept others for who they are, you're already halfway there.

Challenge yourself to smile at a stranger every day. Compliment people. Show interest in their lives. Don't take yourself too seriously, but instead look for ways to laugh and be light-hearted. Commit right now to never being that person who gossips, criticizes or judges people in public. Forget about constant complaining and show gratitude instead. Make it a habit to genuinely learn what others can teach you in every interaction, and take it upon yourself to shine the light of your attention on others, so they feel seen, appreciated, and listened to.

Trait 2: Power and influence

The ability to convince and persuade others, and being perceived as competent and in control. The only chance you have of being an inspirational presence in people's lives, and to have them believe in you, is to start with belief in *yourself*. Tap into those things you know with all your heart, the skills you're a natural expert at, and the values that mean more than anything to you. Find your raw, sparkling passion and communicate it loud and clear to others – think of influence as the transmission of conviction from one person to another. But you must have that conviction in the first place! Constantly remind yourself what you're good at, what you care about, and what your job is in this world. Then give yourself permission to do that.

Trait 3: Emotional intelligence

Charisma is not about logic, intelligence, or being right. It's about emotions. Being emotionally intelligent means knowing how to perceive the emotions of others, as well as ensuring that your own are communicated. Charismatic people don't just rely on words – they can engage emotionally on nonverbal channels.

The single best way to ramp up your emotional intelligence is to get into your body. Use all of yourself to communicate, including your voice, posture, movement, and gesture. Likewise, watch closely how other people present themselves – all of themselves. Listening is about close conscious awareness, and the perception of patterns that go beyond the words people say. It goes without saying that the more emotionally literate you are with yourself, the better you'll be able to read other people.

Trait 4: Presence, awareness and self-control

Anxiety, distraction, assumption, expectation and getting stuck in our own heads… all of this take us out of the moment, and saps our charisma. Charm is something living and dynamic that unfolds in the moment; if we hope to master it, we need to be spontaneous, alive to the moment and responsive. This takes a degree of self-awareness. We can improve our ability to anchor in the moment and the person in front of us by using mindfulness techniques. Once we're routinely aware of ourselves, we can do the next thing: control ourselves.

Awareness paves the way for us to consciously choose how we want to appear, speak, and engage. What role do we want to play and why? What mask shall we wear, and what are the rules of the game we're playing?

Trait 5: Social intelligence and leadership

When we master ourselves in any social interaction, we earn the right to begin to steer things in the direction we want them to go. In other words, we become capable of leadership. In a way, the ability to lead is a culmination of all the charismatic traits, and is the intelligent synthesizing of all the social and emotional skills into one. If we have a vision, we can reach out to others, communicate it, and persuade them to help us build that vision.

Most of us want to be more charismatic because we just want people to like us. But charisma can also be applied – when we put energy, brilliance and warmth to work, what could we achieve and create? It's powerful stuff!

A prince and a queen – two case studies

In West Philadelphia, born and raised, this particular celebrity spent most of his days charming the pants off people. First busting onto the TV screen as the *Fresh Prince of Bel Air*, Will Smith has since won four Grammy Awards and been nominated for countless others. Will Smith is arguably one of the most recognizable and likeable actors (and rappers!) globally and has built his $250 million empire on one thing: his personality.

Will Smith is one charismatic guy. Picture him in your head right now – what do you see? Most likely, you envision a broad, easy smile. Smith is the quintessential "larger than life" personality and someone who can teach us a lot about thriving at the center of attention. How does Will measure up against our 5 ultra-charisma traits?

Likeability? Check. Emotional intelligence and presence? Check and check. In fact, Smith admirably demonstrates all these characteristics. His power and influence seem to come from his unapologetically being himself – and making it look so good that other people are inspired to imitate him!

Although the comedic actor gives off an easy-going aura, his success was *not* accidental. According to him, you need to be prepared. Take charge and decide how you want life to play out *before* it happens. "So if you stay ready, you ain't gotta get ready, and that is how I run my life. Just stay ready. Stay in shape and then you don't have to rush to train before the movie starts …And I'll show you my abs later because I'm in shape. But that idea, if you stay ready, you don't have to get ready." Will Smith is paying attention, he's being present, and he's committed to learning the rules of the game so that when it's time to play, he's ready to go. He's in control. Sure, he may play it cool and joke around, but deep down, there is a hard-nosed willingness to visualize what he wants, and to do the work required. "In my mind, I've always been an A-list Hollywood superstar. Y'all just didn't know yet."

Will Smith uses lashings of humor to keep things light and humble – and though it doesn't look like a fine art, it really is. "My daughter said, 'Daddy, are we rich?' I say, 'No, baby, you're broke. Daddy worked really hard. You don't even own them clothes. Mommy and daddy are going to teach you how to create a space where you have the life that you desire, but this is the life that mommy and daddy desired, and we worked really hard to create this life for ourselves, but you are going to have to create your own.'" See how he speaks to his passion and conviction, but never gets too serious or allows it to come across as arrogance? This is the power of well-placed humor.

Will Smith is off the charts when it comes to likeability. He's the kind of mega-celebrity you could imagine being friends with, and is frequently reported as being approachable and friendly to those who want autographs or pictures. Watch any recorded interviews with him, and you'll see that he takes the same relaxed, respectful and easy approach with everyone, no matter who they are. He looks them in the eyes, talks plainly and without airs, and keeps smiling. Because he is so at ease with himself, others feel relaxed around him. A little humor, open body language, a warm smile, and the occasional moment of deep sincerity all make for a pretty charming package. It's what makes Will Smith feel like something even better than a famous celebrity – that is, a genuinely awesome person.

So, where does this leave us? If you want to have superstar A-list energy and impressive charisma, do you have to start acting like Will Smith? *Absolutely not.*

Consider this: who else is like Will Smith? You may be able to think of a few people a bit like him (Eddie Murphy comes to mind), but Will Smith's personal brand is all his own. He took the way he looked, his personality, his accent, everything, and *owned* it. Can you imagine Will Smith before he was famous, trying to fake his way into celebrity by mimicking someone like Humphrey Bogart? Just picture it: Will Smith, speaking kind of like Frank Sinatra, wearing a suit and tie, and crooning in front of a big brass band. It doesn't even make sense, right?

Or picture Will Smith trying to be a dangerous "bad boy" and playing up his sex appeal like countless other celebrities he could have taken inspiration from. It just doesn't work. Instead, Will Smith took who he was and ran with it. His brand is "clean" and fun, and nobody does Will Smith better than he does! In a way, Smith made an exaggerated mask of his own personality, and played that role to perfection. He achieved levels of likeability and fame that he never would have if he merely imitated someone else.

If this inspires you, the lesson is to find your unique brand of charm, and play it up to the max. Being "larger than life" in *your* life may look nothing like it does for Will Smith, but it's still built on the same 5 charisma traits that he mastered.

So, that's our "prince" covered – who is our "queen"?

While Will Smith grabs the limelight with his bold, confident and in-your-face charisma, our next celebrity is a study in charisma that is more magnetic – i.e., it doesn't expand out into the world so much as invite other people to *come closer*.

Jane Fonda told the New York Times about the aura around Marilyn Monroe, who she had met in an acting class. Apparently, people at a party who were once waiting for Monroe to arrive were so excited that some were physically shaking. The actress purportedly told people she could switch her charm off and on, disappearing invisibly into a subway and not being noticed one moment, and behaving in such a way the next moment that people were falling over themselves to get a look at her.

Today, countless celebrities have been influenced by the original sex symbol, and one could argue her legacy is overplayed at this point. It's easy to forget, however, just how impressive Monroe's achievements were at the time – she literally transformed herself into a goddess of the screen, the likes of which nobody had ever seen before. If charisma was a skill, Marilyn Monroe was one of its first heavyweight geniuses.

Like Will Smith, her dazzling aura came down to the irresistible persona she portrayed. But that's where the similarities end. Whereas Smith is loud, confident and funny, Monroe was far more low-key. In interviews, she was gentle, soft-spoken, a little mysterious and flirtatious… even, bizarrely, conveying a fragile and vulnerable sense of innocence that somehow just seemed to make her more gorgeous. Monroe grew up poor, brunette and with crushingly low self-esteem that remained with her even after her mega-stardom. She suffered horribly from stage-fright and probably would not have considered herself an extrovert in the least.

And yet! Monroe didn't need to search for attention because it always seemed to find her. She was magnetic – she simply was her dazzling self, and people couldn't help but be drawn towards her. A reporter once said, "Amid a slowly gathering hush, she stood there, a blond apparition in a strapless cocktail gown, a little breathless as if she were Cinderella, just stepped from the pumpkin coach." No funny quips, no performance. She didn't *do* anything in particular. She just was.

So, what can we learn from Marilyn (especially those of us who want to create a quieter, more alluring magnetism)? Well, it probably doesn't hurt to be astoundingly beautiful. But other beautiful actresses surrounded Marilyn, and she still outshone them. Elizabeth Taylor, Audrey Hepburn and Sophia Loren were certainly formidable competition, but none had that ineffable star quality that Marilyn did. Why?

Marilyn was an actress, but her best role was off-screen, where she successfully created a dazzling sex-siren image. Like Will Smith, none of this was by accident. Marilyn Monroe wasn't born Marilyn Monroe. She spent enormous amounts of energy and time crafting her image; watch any of her gestures, idiosyncrasies and manners of speech in interviews – every inch of it is carefully considered, rehearsed and delivered with precision.

And she did it *without* being loud or larger than life. She was the queen of the seductive glance, the irresistible laugh, and dressing in such a way that you couldn't help but notice her. She used her sex appeal, yes, but it's interesting to note that Marilyn's biggest fans today are seemingly women, who are just as entranced by her vision of femininity, proving that raw sex appeal was only part of her charm.

If you can't see yourself cultivating an "out there" brand of charm like Will Smith, consider a more magnetic, passive charismatic such as Marilyn as your inspiration. Get people to come to you. One way to do this is to use your appearance – how can you immediately set yourself apart from other people without speaking a word? Ramp up your presence in a room by being *visually unusual*, in whatever way fits your personality best. It takes a little courage to be different, but many introverted or shy people find it easier to "express" themselves this way, since it doesn't require them to be brash and talkative. It may seem superficial to focus a lot on your appearance, but this is one of the most immediate and primal ways we communicate nonverbally.

Another thing we can learn from Marilyn is the power of crafting an image. The icon she created had very little to do with who she actually was as a person – reportedly a very intelligent, complex humanitarian. Marilyn played a role. Today, celebrities like Beyonce have admitted to doing the same thing, for example, when they get on stage, they are no longer themselves, but an alter ego. This is something that allows even painfully shy people to be terrific actors – when it's not *you* that you're putting out there, it's so much easier to take risks! You can do the same by creating your own alter-ego. Make this other person a kind of archetype, or a glamorous, brilliant version of yourself. Ask what they would do in a social interaction, then do it.

There's one final part of Marilyn Monroe's charm that it would be a mistake to leave out, which is her story's tragic element. Everyone knows that Marilyn was troubled, misunderstood, and haunted by her past—behind the glitz and glamor. There were suggestions of drug use, and her love life was tumultuous. She died young and in tragic and mysterious circumstances, and today people think wistfully about her legacy – who was the *real* Marilyn?

This is all to say that being charismatic doesn't necessarily mean that you are perfect, happy and uncomplicated. The fact that Marilyn's charming façade and her real self were at such odds doesn't detract from her appeal – it adds to it! In other words, we all find a little drama, mystery and darkness extremely enticing. She portrayed a beautiful, flawless image, but she is today loved for the fact that much of her life *wasn't* beautiful and flawless. People love Marilyn because she was vulnerable, imperfect and tragic. We feel touched that she suffered, not that her life was easy.

If you feel like you are too boring, flawed, insecure, or unhappy to be a truly charismatic person, think again. If you can consciously and deliberately show your vulnerability to others, you can come across as infinitely more human, more likeable and more real than if you had stayed completely cool and invincible. Especially for women, a degree of fragility can be extremely becoming. It's OK to be a little self-deprecating, or to humorously own up to your fears and weaknesses. Don't be afraid to show your soft side now and then. Done right, this can be incredibly charming!

Designing your unique charisma formula

Now, what about you?

You have your own, 100% unique form of charisma, just like our two case studies. Making that essence shine bright is just a matter of using the 5 traits we've identified. In a journal or word processor, answer the following questions:

Trait 1: Likeability and warmth

On a scale of 1 to 10, how warm and likeable are you, honestly?

What single behavior can you identify as an obstacle to you being more likable?

Think of times in the past where you've felt really warm, kind, and benevolent – what was happening, and what made it so easy to broadcast your friendliness in that moment?

Think about how you behave with your closest and best loved friends and family – what does your warmth look like?

Can you identify a single person who you could be warmer and kinder to? How?

Trait 2: Power and influence

Do you have a clear mission, passion or project in life you care deeply about?

If so, does everyone in your world clearly know about it?

Being honest, do you know your own value? Do other people? Why or why not?

What is holding you back from "speaking your truth" right now? What might be the costs of not speaking up about what you believe in?

Trait 3: Emotional intelligence

Think of the last time you felt you connected emotionally with someone. What were they doing, and what were you doing?

Thinking deeply, what is the thing you most want from others when you engage with them? Attention? Validation? Distraction? Stimulation?

What can you do *today* to gift this feeling to someone in your own world?

Trait 4: Presence, awareness and self-control

To what extent do you plan and prepare for social interactions?

According to your values and goals, how would you most like to come across to those around you?

Do you know how others see you? How could you find out?

What is the one thing you could do right now to communicate your ideal persona to others?

Trait 5: Social intelligence and leadership

What unique insights and abilities do you possess that nobody else does?

Are you conveying those to the world? If not, how could you start?

What would you like to create around you if you had infinite power and influence?

What small step can you take right now towards that vision?

Finally, to bring it all together:

What does your ultimate, supremely charismatic alter ego look like? What do they say, and how do they act?

What are your biggest flaws and weakness in social interactions? How would your alter ego deal with these?

Are you a larger-than-life extroverted and sparkly charismatic, or do you have a more a magnetic, alluring and introverted presence?

Think of the people you most admire for their charisma – what could you easily do right now to mimic some of their behavior?

Which questions were hardest to answer, and why do you think that is?

Finally, warmth, influence, presence, etc..... which aspects of charisma are most natural for you, and which are you happy to leave less developed?

To be frank, many of us have an internal picture of who we are and how we like to see ourselves, but this is often a lot more flattering than how other people actually see us! As you work at cultivating the kind of charismatic aura that fits you best, be prepared to be honest with yourself and admit when something isn't working. You could be a completely amazing person, but if you are not communicating that properly, it almost doesn't matter.

That said, remember that being charismatic is *not* about being perfect or invulnerable – far from it. You don't have to be the "best version of yourself." The singer Adele, for example, garnered staggering numbers of fans who rallied around her precisely because she was not some mega diva, but a relatable, ordinary woman who sang about heartbreak – and was overweight. After she lost weight, many fans liked her *less*, proving that what people found charismatic was not conventional attractiveness, but authenticity and imperfection. So, even if you have a "flaw," realize that this can be a part of your charm just as easily as any strong point.

It's our responsibility to know where we stand and to take steps to improve. The above questions are a good start, but they need to be made real in the world through concrete action. Today (right now, when you finish reading this chapter!), commit to taking one small step, whether that's smiling at someone in the street, striking up a conversation with a stranger, or hitting the gym, so you feel more comfortable and confident in your own body.

Summary

- We can condense the four theories of charisma into 5 distinct charismatic traits: likeability and warmth; power and influence; emotional intelligence; presence, awareness and self-control; and social intelligence and leadership. If we can consistently hit these five notes in our social interactions, we cannot help but boost our "charisma quotient."
- To be impactful, charisma has to be genuine to us. We need to take responsibility for honestly appraising our skills and taking concrete action to improve in real life. Whether we are extroverted or introverted, there is a unique charisma style that will work for us.
- Real life celebrities and historical figures can serve as examples and inspiration. Both Will Smith and Marilyn Monroe show how you can tick all 5 charisma boxes, but in completely different ways.
- Will Smith teaches us to be prepared, stay humble and work hard, and lead with positivity, humor, and good-naturedness. Though his social mask makes him appear easygoing and lighthearted, it conceals the effort, deliberation and hard work required to build the life and image you want.

- Marilyn Monroe teaches us that charisma can also be about magnetically drawing people towards you, rather than being loud and over the top to demand attention. Marilyn shows us the power of appearance, and how to craft a performing person down to the finest detail. She also shows us indirectly that perfection is not required, and that if you can lean honestly into your own vulnerability and fragility, people may love you all the more for it.
- You can design your own unique charisma formula by honestly rating how you perform in each of these five areas, and committing to taking action today to improve.

Part 2: Creating Charismatic Interactions

Chapter 4: The bedrock of good communication

In part 1, we looked at clear definitions for what charisma actually is, as well as explored four different models or theories about what charisma is made of, and how to increase each of these aspects in ourselves. With consistent practice smiling, being present, adjusting body language, conveying warmth, and so on, we can cultivate our own unique, charismatic aura that people can't help but feel when they're in our presence.

In part 2, we take this carefully cultivated aura and further extend it to others in social interactions. Just as we are in charge of the persona we broadcast to others, we also have a degree of control over how interactions play out. With a little know-how, we can learn to create moments, conversations, and connections that really sparkle. Charisma *in action* is not all that different from being a scintillating conversationalist, a good listener, a witty storyteller or an empathetic friend. In other words, it's impossible to be charismatic without exceptional communication skills.

In the following chapters, we'll look at simple and straightforward ways to be a better listener, master small talk, read people's emotions and engage authentically with people. But all of this stems from a more fundamental skill, without which none of it can happen: empathy.

Empathy is so, so much more than feeling for others when something bad happens to them. Empathy is really the only thing that allows human beings to reach out and connect to one another emotionally. Without empathy we cannot imagine another person's world, perspective, or emotions. Philosophers call this capacity to guess at the hidden inner world of people other than ourselves "theory of mind."

In imagining another's inner world, empathy is the *what*, and communication is the *how*. If we want to connect emotionally with others and share in their world, we need to understand how to communicate with them. If there isn't empathy, other people are nothing more than abstract entities to us, rather than living, breathing beings that we can *feel*.

There are actually two kinds of empathy: positive and negative. A charismatic person has both. Picture a woman who wins last place at a beauty pageant. She smiles broadly, hugs the winner and congratulates her. She revels in the winner's excitement and takes pleasure in her happiness, telling her how proud she is of her. It's a good look, right? This is what is called positive empathy – the ability to derive joy from other people's joy, and to feel good purely because they do. This is not even about social self-control, but genuine pleasure at other people's fortunes.

It's the opposite of jealousy, insecurity and selfishness, because it centers and finds satisfaction in someone else. The irony is that it ends up making the admirer so much more likeable, too! Charismatic people are never jealous (at least not outwardly...), and they don't compete in public or put themselves or others down. Watch any interview with the charismatic Dolly Parton, for example, and observe how she never puts down others in the industry, even those who criticize her. She playfully laughs off even insults with grace and humor. "I'm not offended by all the dumb blonde jokes because I know I'm not dumb – I also know I'm not blonde."

You can improve your own charisma by refusing to let other people's achievements threaten you, or their light undermine your own. Anxious people take the brilliance of others as a problem, perhaps because deep down, they doubt themselves and feel insecure. But if you get alongside those who are doing better than you, you elevate yourself and communicate a powerful message that you know how to generate your own value *that does not depend on others being smaller than you.*

When you feel that tinge of jealousy or envy, swallow your pride and praise or congratulate that person. Ask for their advice. Lavish them with compliments. Be their friend. See if you can genuinely find happiness for them. This not only makes you appear more magnanimous and mature as a person, but it will encourage you to think: why don't I do the same? Train yourself to see jealousy as an invitation to be better. Is there some potential going unfulfilled in you?

Negative empathy is the one most of us are familiar with, i.e., the ability to sympathize with and feel into the pain and suffering of others. Being able to help, support and comfort those in need is great, but it usually comes from a deeper ability to sincerely feel what others feel. Intellectually understanding the facts of someone's negative emotion is not the same as *feeling* that emotion along with them.

So, if we imagine that the second-place beauty queen is our friend, and she's feeling down about not winning, we can acknowledge her disappointment, validate it, comfort her, and let her know we've heard and understood the emotion she's communicating. Incidentally, real empathy can be difficult precisely because it's not about us – at all. So, even if we personally think that beauty pageants are nonsense, that our friend is beautiful and lovable just as she is, and that we can't understand why she's so upset, you still understand that it matters to her anyway, and have the compassion and humility to see the thing from *her* perspective, regardless of your own.

So how do we improve empathy? That's easy! Empathy is hard-wired in almost everybody; it's just a question of consciously bringing out this innate ability in every interaction. In a 2013 paper by Klimecki et al., researchers discovered that empathy is plastic, meaning it can literally be cultivated with effort. Even if you find empathy difficult or have trouble empathizing with particular people, it doesn't matter; there are still predictable patterns of empathetic conversation that anyone can learn to demonstrate. Fake it until you make it, in other words!

Strategy 1: Read

It might seem odd that this solitary activity would make you more socially charismatic and better in conversations – but it does! Reading puts you in someone else's shoes. You get to try on perspectives other than your own, inhabit someone else's narrative, see their values, and feel their interpretation of events. Think of it as an empathy training camp.

When you're with others, try to really grasp that from their point of view, they are the most important people in their worlds, in the same way that you feel that you are the center of your own. You begin to build real empathy when you understand that other people will always experience themselves as the protagonists of a story that may run on values and principles completely alien to you. And you can tailor and adjust your communication accordingly.

A kind and sympathetic person can think, "I feel for you, because I'd feel bad if that happened to *me*." But a truly empathetic person can think, "I feel for you, because I can see that it feels bad for *you*." Reading fiction helps you appreciate others, and see them not from your perspective, but see them how they see themselves, from their perspective. Make sure it's the right kind of reading though – mix up your authors and go for quality literary fiction from different eras, countries and styles to broaden your scope. Reading the same author constantly or flipping through *People* magazine doesn't count…

Strategy 2: Make an experience filter

You know how in kid's TV shows, the hero occasionally says something like, "now, if I were a lost walrus who escaped from a zoo, where is the first place I would go?" It sounds silly, but the ability to genuinely see life through the lens of someone (or some walrus) who isn't you is actually a sophisticated expression of empathy – and helps us be charismatic.

Try this right now: think of someone you're very close to, and then think of a current situation or issue in your own life. Now, ask yourself, "what would X think or feel about this situation?" Literally pretend you are them, with all their idiosyncrasies, beliefs, blind spots, goals and fears. When you do this, you create an "experience filter" that acts as a representation of that person in your mind. It's not the same as that person, no, but it is a stepping stone that helps you get into their world and empathize, as well as see the limits of your own perspective.

People react to life and interpret situations according to who they are. If you can really *see* this, you give yourself an edge in any social interaction. You can pitch your communication to them so that they actually hear it. For example, maybe you're a very emotional and verbally expressive person, but you know your mechanical engineer friend is more of a concrete, visual person who thinks in practical terms.

When you want to ask for their help, you don't get too focused on your vision of things, and instead frame your request as they would: you appeal to their logical side, and ask briefly for a clear and limited set of actions, focusing not on how grateful you'd be to get their help, but how it makes sense to ask them since they're the most knowledgeable, and the problem needs to be solved. When you hear people say about others that they "can talk to anyone," this is what they mean: a charismatic person doesn't just know how to speak, they know how to speak *other people's languages*.

Strategy 3: Deliberately practice theory of mind

Let's say you're at the post office and trying to get a package mailed, but the person behind the counter is being *really* unhelpful. You're in a rush and they're apparently not, and all you can focus on is the way the interaction feels to you: this person is standing in the way of the thing you want, and it's beginning to get annoying. Perhaps you look at their actions – the dawdling, the "attitude" or the refusal to quickly cut a few corners to speed things up – and from your perspective it looks like they're being obtuse and stubborn. You say rudely, "are you *trying* to make me angry?"

A little empathy could go a long way in a situation like this. Empathy could help us understand other people's behavior not in relation to our own interpretations, goals or values, but according to theirs. Empathy could make us peak out of our experience and into someone else's. It could help us notice, for example, that we are the last customer of the day, and that the post office was due to close 5 minutes ago. You might notice that the person is taking a long time because they have to boot the system back up again. What does the situation look like from their perspective? Just a few moments pondering this, and we'd have a novel insight: the person believes they're already doing us a favor after a long day by agreeing to serve us past closing time. From their point of view, *we* are the rude ones.

Theory of mind allows us to have the mature and grounding realization that we are not the only ones in the universe, and that our point of view is just that: a point of view, not reality itself. Everything other people say and do comes from a perfectly legitimate perspective informed by their background and their unique take on things. Our own thoughts, attitudes, expectations and interpretations might feel invisible to us, but they are no less arbitrary than anyone else's. Without theory of mind, we barge ahead on our own mission, insensitive to other people's realities. The result is usually conflict, misunderstanding or, even at the best of times, a failure to connect.

Deliberately practicing theory of mind doesn't mean focusing on other people's perspectives to the exclusion of your own. It simply means being aware that there are different viewpoints in the first place! Many of unconsciously place ourselves at the center of every conversation, and assume that others share our desires, know what we know, and think as we think. When you stop doing this, you naturally become more accepting and open-minded, because you no longer privilege your own experience as somehow more central or important than others'.

Here's a trick to try next time you find yourself thinking that someone is confusing, infuriating or plain old wrong. *Assume that their behavior makes total sense*. Take as a given that their words and actions completely align with their perspective, and then ask what that tells you about that perspective.

The way we ourselves act always makes sense to us because we know what is happening inside our own minds (usually!). But when someone behaves in a way that gets to us, it can be extremely useful to ask, "what does this behavior tell me about this person's perspective?" From that point on, you can talk to that perspective, rather than to a strawman or reflection of your own perspective. You're also likely to respect and accept that viewpoint, rather than seeing it as a problem simply because it's not like yours.

Strategy 4: Listen for facts versus interpretations

A great way to build more empathy and get into people's perspectives is to practice listening to what you're told, and discerning between fact and opinion. This is more difficult than it first seems. In conversations, perspective, interpretation, opinion and unique points of view are often presented mixed with concrete facts. The facts are just facts – the capital of Italy is

Rome, today is Tuesday, your car has four wheels – but everything else is up for discussion. When people talk, they're really offering you a sprinkle of fact... and a big mix of assumptions, interpretations, expectations, beliefs, anecdotal memories, arguments, value judgments and claims. This is where perspective lives. Change any of these, and the perspective changes, too.

Imagine someone says to you, "Last Tuesday, the guy at the post office lost his temper with me completely out of the blue." Let's look closely at this. What is fact here? Well, the person was at the post office last Tuesday. There was a guy there. And everything else? Not fact. That someone "lost their temper" is value judgment and interpretation. "Out of the blue" is an opinion and personal assessment.

Basically, there are many unknowns here, and only a few facts. Maybe it was *not* out of the blue, but completely warranted. Maybe no tempers were lost, but there was simply some mild irritation. And maybe the irritation was not directed at the person speaking, but the result of something entirely unrelated. By separating out fact from fiction this way, you are clearly identifying what the person's perspective is: from their point of view, this is the story. However, simply changing the words of the story allows you to realize this perspective is at play and then switch it up. "Lost his temper" could be reworded as "yelled at the top of his lungs" or "got a little impatient", each framing a different perspective.

The true value here is that you can read between the lines and understand their emotions and what it is that they are really trying to express. Usually, it's not the facts or logic, it's the emotions.

Anyone that has ever had an argument with a significant other can attest to this; logic will only get you so far because the reason there is an argument in the first place is almost always due to underlying emotions not being attended to or heard. When you know the difference between facts and interpretation, you will know what to focus on and make people feel glad that they told you something – because you can give them the reaction they were looking for instead of blindly focusing on pedantry.

All of this is to say that if you want to master perspective-switching and having the empathy needed for real charisma, you need to learn to identify the language of a perspective, as well as change that language to change perspective. Charismatic people know that words are like magic – when you change them, the whole world seems to change before your eyes. This understanding allows a charismatic person to say to the post office worker, "Gosh! You're such a lifesaver helping me out last minute like this. Thank you for being so quick!"

The postal worker feels seen, understood and maybe a little flattered. From their perspective, they also want to get things done as quickly as possible. They work as fast as they humanly can and are polite, too – which is not the outcome you'd get if you'd impatiently asked, "what's the hold up anyway?"

Likewise, if someone is telling you about a rude person they encountered at the post office on Tuesday, you will be spectacularly missing the point if you dwell on the fact that it was actually Wednesday, not Tuesday, and start grilling the person to find out who is exactly to blame. The person telling you this tale wants you to recognize the injustice and annoyance they suffered, and they are telling you a story in which they are unfairly the victim so that you will acknowledge this and respond accordingly. Again, a charismatic person sees beyond the words and looks at the intention and the emotion, and responds to that. Empathy lets you see perspective and interpretation beyond your own – and this elevates your communication ability to the next level.

The golden rule: make people feel important.

In later chapters, we're going to explore in more depth the various ways you can master conversations, optimize interactions, and create those powerful moments when you "click" with someone. Before we do that, let's consider one of our main jobs in any interaction – *making people feel as though they matter*. Imagine that everyone is walking around with a sign on their chest that reads, "I need to feel important." In the end, it doesn't matter how charming *you* are if the other person feels invisible or unappreciated.

The **SHR method** is a great way to constantly remind yourself of this golden rule. It stands for:

S – Seen

H – Heard

R – Remembered

This is how we should always strive to make people feel – and we can do that even before we open our mouths and say a word. Let's break it down.

For someone to feel that they have been seen, we need to... well, see them. *Truly* see them! As soon after you meet someone as possible, let them know that you have acknowledged their presence and are paying attention to them. People want to matter, and they want to feel like it makes a real difference when they are welcomed and appreciated for the unique people they are.

How do you do that?

Make eye contact. It's primal, and it communicates a strong message: "I see you." When it comes to eye contact, little and often is a good strategy. Try holding the gaze for a count of three before gently and casually relaxing and shifting your eyes to the side or down. Alternatively, use the triangle technique and flit your gaze from either eye to the mouth or chin to ensure you're not making too much eye contact. Avoid staring. A good rule of thumb is to match the level of eye contact they're sharing.

Give *strategic* compliments. There is something powerful in being witnessed by another human being who acknowledges who you really are and what you're trying to broadcast out into the world. But this only works if it's accurate – i.e., if you are seeing people how they want to be seen. For example, if someone has clearly made an effort by dressing up more than usual for an occasion, you would be seeing them by noticing and complimenting this effort. On the other hand, if you know that someone prides themselves on their intelligence, kindness, or sense of humor, compliment them in this area, rather than on their appearance. Try to avoid throwaway compliments that are not tailored to the individual and what they value – they can actually make people feel unseen and misunderstood.

Use the right metaphors and language. This one is a little more subtle, but try saying things like, "I *see* what you mean" or "I *hear* you." This will reflect that you are really perceiving the person in front of you. Most of the time, when people complain about not being seen, they are not talking about visually; rather, they feel that the other person has failed to understand their perspective or appreciate their unique point of view. Counteract this by using language that speaks to this perception. For example, reflect their own words to them or repeat their metaphors.

What about making people feel heard? Similar rules apply:

Be interested, not interesting. How can you show them that you are not only listening but actually absorbing and processing what they're saying? Nod, make encouraging noises, let your facial expressions mirror and match theirs, and ask questions that genuinely relate to what you're hearing. Demonstrate that you are being moved by what they say – it doesn't matter if you disagree, by the way, only that you have received the message! We'll look at strategies for great question-asking in the next section.

Finally, try to make people feel remembered.

Always remember people's names. A name is an identity. It's who you are. When people forget it, it's like they forget *you*… and only unimportant things are forgotten. Any little detail you remember about someone assures them, "This was so important to me that I paid attention and remembered it." It's easy to zone out when people are mentioning things like dates, family names, or little details, but if you remember these and mention them in later conversations, you will instantly make that person feel special.

Follow up. We all want to feel like we make a difference in the world. Have you ever met someone a second time and realized they didn't remember you or any part of the conversation you already had with them? It can feel really, really bad! But in the same way, people can feel invisible and unimportant if others keep asking the same questions (and not remembering the answers) or repeatedly forgetting key points of a story.

As you speak to someone, pay attention and carefully gather a few key facts about them and the interaction. The next time you meet, immediately lead in with these facts. "Oh, hello! It's so nice to see you again. It's been ages. Hey, I was wondering, how did it go, after all, at the doctor? Did you manage to sort everything out?" Not only does this convey the message that you were paying attention the first time around, but it will also create a feeling of trust, continuity, and familiarity. It's a great way to fill up awkward silences, too.

Summary

- Part 1 of this book is all about the charismatic presence. How might you wish for someone to describe you, and how much does that differ from reality? And then, how do you bridge the gap between these two versions of yourself? Part 1 is more theoretical and introspective, while Part 2 is all about action. How do you actually create the type of interactions that will draw people to you, regardless of your current personality?
- Unsurprisingly, it all starts with empathy. When you have empathy, you know what other people are thinking and feeling, or at least you can make a pretty darned good guess about it. And if we know what people are thinking and feeling, we can also make

a darned good guess as to what they want. And that's what will allow us to create charismatic interactions.
- The first is to simply read more. This is probably the best practice you can do without having someone in front of you, because it forces you to inhabit someone else's perspective and inner dialogue. You can see in the story that because X happened, Y and Z might happen. This seems simple, but it is not easy to practice in daily life. Having an experience filter is very similar, in that it forces you to step out of your perspective (which is necessarily limited) and really try to see someone else's. It might sound like we are only talking about empathy here, but the truth is that empathy and charisma are extremely, extremely related. Yes, deliberately practicing theory of mind is also more in the same direction of understanding another person's thoughts and emotions.
- Remember the SHR method and make sure that people feel seen, heard, and remembered. Eye contact, following up, listening, and compliments can make a person feel important and acknowledged.
- Finally, understanding the difference between facts and interpretation will help you know what you should respond to. Almost always, you should be trying to respond to people's interpretation because their emotions are buried within, and that's what will draw people to you.

Chapter 5: Engaging Fully

Questions – An Underrated Superpower

The physicist and theorist Heisenberg famously said, "What we observe is not nature itself, but nature exposed to our method of questioning." In the realm of conversation, we can take this to mean that what we see when we engage with other people is not how they really are, but how they look in relation to how we talk to them, and the questions we pose. To put it bluntly, if you ask boring questions, you get boring answers. If you don't ask *any* questions—well, the person in front of you starts to look like nothing more than a blank.

With all this focus on our own mindset, our preparedness and our ability to set the mood, we can forget that we always have at hand a very effective technique for reaching others—just ask them! Questions initiate and move conversations along particular paths. They give you some control and direction, they help you show interest, and they help you genuinely connect to and understand the person in front of you. In fact, questions are so important that it's hard to imagine anyone getting far in conversations without them.

Here, we'll focus on the *emotional* rather than *informational* impact of questions. You are not asking someone something because you literally don't know the answer and want them to tell you. That's what Google is for. In that sense, the answer can be important, sure, but it's not all that's important. Simply asking in the first place, and the way you ask, can also send a powerful message. This chapter is about participating fully in conversations, and the backbone of quality participation is to think like a scientist like Heisenberg, and *get curious*.

The first thing to understand: not all questions are created equally. We can group exchanges, and therefore questions, into three levels, according to their underlying purpose. The first is to exchange information (or learn), the second to exchange feelings and emotions (or get others to bond with and like us), and the third is to exchange values (ditto). It's worth knowing the difference, so you're clear on what kind of conversation you're having, and why. For example, the know-it-all from our first chapter makes a mistake in responding to other people's appeals for an exchange of emotion and feelings, by supplying factual information instead. This is the person who completely misses the point by focusing on the details and not shared emotional content.

The second thing to understand is that we need to master both the asking and the answering of questions, at the right level. Doing so makes us more likeable, more empathetic, and more successfully at connecting to others. In the remainder of the chapter, we'll be taking a closer look at how to frame and interpret questions, to use them to their best advantage.

But first: *just ask more*. Chances are, you're simply not asking enough questions. Even emotionally intelligent people can fail to show enough curiosity for others. Maybe you're too busy thinking of yourself or stressed about the interaction (still egocentric!) or maybe you genuinely don't care enough to know the answer. Maybe you think questions make you look nosy or worse, unsure of yourself. But the opposite is true.

Harvard research by Alison Wood Brooks and colleagues showed that when people were instructed to ask more questions in a conversation, people rated them as more likable than those who asked fewer questions. Speed daters were also found to agree more readily to a second date if their first date was filled with plenty of questions. So, this is pretty low-hanging fruit when it comes to increasing likeability!

Keep your questions open-ended and non-leading, and genuinely listen to the answers. Ask *why* more than you ask *who*, *where*, *when*, etc., and pose questions so that you are mining for information on an emotional human level, rather than just a factual one. Otherwise, you risk turning a conversation into a dry back-and-forth exchange where people dwell on the boring details of their jobs or where they live, without injecting any sense of why it matters or how they feel about any of it.

Don't be worried about coming off nosy if you ask too many questions; simply give enough space for the other person to answer, and intersperse your questions with a little information about yourself so it doesn't feel like disclosure is coming from one side only, or that you're interrogating them.

Questions unlock the next level of human connection, and may even be more powerful in situations where questions are *not* expected, such as job interviews. They show that you're paying attention, that you care, that you're engaging in the situation proactively, that you have your own values and expectations, that you appreciate the opinion of the other person (otherwise, you wouldn't be asking for it) and that you have been listening. Not bad for a single line!

The Socratic Method

The kind of questions and the way they're delivered matters, of course. And, unfortunately, it's not just up to you how well the conversation goes—the other party has to be on board, too. There might be a person who asks a lot of questions paired with someone who asks none, or a pair where both ask a lot, or a pair where neither do. Each of these dynamics is going to feel different.

The main reason is that each person may share different conversational goals. If both parties have the goal of connecting and getting something done together, the atmosphere will be cooperative. If one or both parties is using the conversation to gain an upper hand, wheedle out information or boast, the interaction becomes competitive. If one or both have very minimal goals for the conversation, it may just fizzle out, and so on.

Understanding that people are coming from different places when they talk to one another helps you in two ways: firstly, you can identify what kind of conversation you're in. If you're stuck with someone hellbent on competition and grandstanding, there may be little you can do but be polite and find a way to exit, or at the least refrain from sharing any information that would put you at a disadvantage. On the other hand, knowing the kind of exchange you *want* to be in can help you actively cerate it with others.

Use follow-up questions. Questions are good, but follow-up questions are better, because they show you were listening, and care enough to keep learning more. Good follow-up questions zone in on an important fact the other person has just shared—if you simply spout off a string of unconnected questions it may feel like an interrogation. But run with what's already been said and you tap into the conversation's momentum and flow. "Earlier on you mentioned spontaneously moving to Japan when you were younger. I'm so curious – what made you do that?"

Use open-ended questions. The idea is that you genuinely want to learn more, so don't go in with a very specific question that puts the other person on the spot or makes it seem like you're only after a particular response. Avoid yes/no questions or leading questions ("So, what do like best about our glorious leader?"). You don't want people to feel as though your questions are there simply to extract sensitive information out of you, since this will cause them to clam up or distrust you—rightly! It's a fine line, but try never to ask a question where it's clear what kind of answer you're hoping for. So for example, ask, "How did you two meet?" rather than, "So when's the wedding already?!"

Use questions to break the ice—gently. It may seem counterintuitive, but if you are curious about something, coming out and asking straight away can help cut through awkwardness faster than beating around the bush. You just have to do it right. No, you don't want to offend people or make them uncomfortable, but a well-pitched question can have an interesting effect—people may feel that you are so curious and interested in their answer that you are willing to gently bend social etiquette. Most people find this flattering! At the very least, you can mask potentially nosy seeming questions with a little humor. Another idea is to proceed your question with a bit of sharing on your part, as though to communicate nonverbally, "I'll show you mine if you show me yours!"

A sneaky way of boosting your likeability while at the same time dissolving awkwardness is to genuinely ask for someone's help or opinion on something. People *love* to share their opinion, and there's no faster way for people to feel comfortable around one another than to feel as though they are being helpful and cooperative. Imagine you are in a grocery store and a friendly-looking stranger asks which of two possible bouquets of flowers you think he should buy. You ask him who he's buying them for and proceed to have a genuinely pleasant conversation. Or someone you meet at a party tells you they're a professional dog walker teacher, so you tell them you're thinking of getting a dog and ask their advice on the best breed to pick.

Let's look at a few more examples of the right kind of questions in action. Picture a quick break room conversation with the new recruit at work. They're a little shy, but you push on and take your chance to start a conversation while you wait for your coffee to brew.

You: "Oh, hi there! You're the new hire in accounting, right?"

Them: "Yup. It's my first day."

You: "Oh, awesome. They're starting you off easy, I hope?" (A gentle question to gauge reaction only.)

Them: "Haha, yeah, I guess. I'm heading to IT right now to get my access code sorted out."

You: "Go on, be honest, what do you think about our state-of-the-art break room? I love working here but me and this microwave do *not* get on." (Breaking the ice, asking emotional/feeling questions rather than dwelling on the facts of what they're up to in the accounting department. Plus, a playful complaint is hard not to respond to.)

Them: "Oh, it's not so bad! You should see mine at home. I think its suicidal, actually."

You: "Ah, great, so you have experience with depressed appliances; you'll fit right in. So, you said you're on your way to IT. Have you met Rob yet?" (Follow-up question.)

Them: "Rob? I don't think so . . ."

You: "Rob's great, you'll love him. I've got to go, but good luck with your microwave! Hey, I should ask, do you live locally? The commute out here can be hell . . ." (Another follow-up question.)

Them: "Oh yeah, I'm just down the road, in [wherever]."

You: Oh, cool. You should come hang out with some of us on Fridays. We meet up at the bar on the corner . . ."

. . . and so on.

In this conversation, questions are helping everything flow more easily and comfortably. They all seem natural and good-natured, and likely make the new recruit feel respected and paid attention to. In just a two-minute exchange, a great impression is made.

When asking questions, be casual, take your lead from others, and pay attention to group dynamics. Mix up the kinds of questions you ask, but always be mindful about the match between you—are you sharing information, feelings, or values? Respond accordingly, or be prepared to gently try shift the frame with your question.

"Hey, how's it going?" (If said quickly and carelessly, not really a question, just polite conversational protocol—a similarly offhand question or response is probably enough.)

"So you were just released from prison?" (A request for information—possibly more, but this person likely wants to know the precise factual answer.)

"What do you think about the blue? The red looks better doesn't it?" (This is not a request for information—blue or red is irrelevant. The person is unsure which to choose and needs reassurance, or for you to share your own opinion. This is a request for an emotional response.)

"Where do you see our relationship going?" (A request not just for feelings, but broader values, such as whether marriage is important to them. If someone simply responds with how they're feeling right now, it's likely not going to be perceived as a satisfying or complete answer.)

What about when you respond to questions? As we've seen, it's a good idea to be open, and give more information than was asked for. Take your time in answering. Listen for what the person is actually looking for from you—are they just passing the time and being polite, or do they genuinely want to know more? Adjust your answer accordingly.

The Conversational Narcissism Ratio

Have you ever quietly waited for someone to stop speaking, thinking all the while about what you would say the moment they shut up? If so, you've likely been guilty of conversational narcissism! It is the inability to put aside your own internal monologue completely, and focus on what the other person is thinking or saying. It leads to the same outcome of dueling monologues, where conversation hasn't really happened at all—rather, you have two people talking *at* each other instead of *with* each other.

It's also a big reason why people fail to ask questions—or listen properly to their answers.

So, to start with, improve your listening skills by being vigilant about the ways in which craving attention can make you a worse conversationalist. This takes some conscious awareness and also a little honesty. We can ask what our true intentions and motivations are for entering into conversations, in general and specifically with people we know. Are we reaching out to others because we want the validation of their attention? Because we want the feeling of proving ourselves right and another wrong? Because we feel we have to for some reason?

Do we see conversation as a battle, or a game, or a dance? Perhaps we see conversation as an opportunity to show ourselves off, or share what interests us. Whatever your reasons are, though, you probably notice that they usually concern only *you* . . . and don't spare a thought for the other person sharing the conversation with you! How many of us can honestly say that our goal is to see and understand the other person, rather than just to have ourselves seen and understood?

The idea is not to always seek to turn attention to yourself. Conversations should be thought of not as a means to win attention, but to *share* it enjoyably with someone else. The goal is not competition for the floor, but cooperation with an ally. The purpose is to collaborate, not express solely. The aim is to learn, not teach, and so on. For some of us, this may require a complete re-tooling of what we seek when we want to be social.

After an ineffective conversation, people may feel depleted, bored, or even more alone. Good conversations, on the other hand, can be things of beauty, allowing both participants to create between them something bigger than the sum of its parts. One study even discovered that people valued being listened to and heard so much that, in an experiment, were actually willing to pay to enjoy the feeling. That's because that feeling of being acknowledged, heard and respected is incredibly valuable. Offering that feeling to someone else is just as rewarding, if not more so, than experiencing it for yourself. The truth is that if you prioritize the other person in this way, you often end up with a mutually fulfilling conversation anyway, without actually trying.

Listening well requires that you suspend your own self-interest and ego and gracefully allow someone else to shine.

It's now time to get self-conscious and introspective. Sociologist Charles Derber has studied this phenomenon extensively and believes that this form of conversational narcissism can occur without people even being aware it's going on. It can be easy to imagine that conversational narcissists are the stereotypical loudmouths who dominate conversation—but it's far subtler than this. It turns out that the situation can turn on a single word choice. He articulated what he called *support responses* and *shift responses*, and how they can subtly pervade our everyday vocabulary.

Derber explains what he calls "initiatives" in conversation—which can be *attention giving* or *attention seeking*, the latter of which can be further divided into active or passive. This is a little like our tennis analogy—in tennis, we are always either returning the ball or receiving it from the other player, enacting a give and take. In a conversation, what moves back and forth is awareness and attention. These can bounce between people, or pool on one side of the conversation. For our purposes, you can guess which kinds of behaviors we want to orient toward. Let's look at some examples of both in conversation.

Let's first look at support responses, which are what they sound like: words or behaviors that support the expression of the other person in the conversation. For the active, attention-giving variety, a *"support response"* maintains attention on the speaker and their topic—for example, asking a question about what's been said. Support responses can be simple acknowledgements ("Oh really?" "Uh huh."), positively supporting ("That's great!"), or in question form ("What did you say then?"). You can imagine the other person's story is a balloon that everyone else is trying to keep aloft, jumping in here and there to bounce it back up into the air. For instance:

"I love French films."

Response: "Which is your favorite?"

The above response only exists to maintain attention and awareness on the original speaker. The response doesn't interject any new information of its own, but encourages the flow of attention already unfolding. Obviously, this can make people feel, well, supported! This is a great way to validate your conversation partner, let them know you're listening, and send a strong message that you value what they're saying and want to hear more.

The *"shift response,"* however, is an active attention-seeking response that shifts the attention to the other person, in other words back to themselves. It's an act of grabbing the spotlight and pointing it in the opposite direction. With a shift response, the flow of attention and awareness is suddenly diverted elsewhere. What's going on when you see two people vying for attention and talking over one another? Their dialogue is made exclusively of aggressive shift responses!

"I love French films."

Response: "Yeah? I've never cared much about movies. The other day, actually, I saw this thing at the cinema . . ."

This isn't to say that shift responses are always wrong—in context, they can work, especially if the other person subtly reclaims attention again. Sometimes it might even behoove you to use more shift responses to grab some of the spotlight, or make your feelings known. But how much are you using them?

A shift response is a great idea if you want to move the chat along to another topic, or inject some fresh energy or ideas into the conversation. We acknowledged earlier in the book that being confident enough to disagree, to state your own opinion, or to be a little bold in what you share can increase charism and kickstart a flagging conversation. However, a shift response is a bad idea if you are simply trying to derail the existing conversation in your favor, so you can say what you want to say.

Many people get together and talk this way, each announcing a different personal anecdote that begins with a shift response. Even after hours, the conversation hasn't really gone anywhere, and both parties likely feel bored and unfulfilled. If you have two people with poor listening skills, and both are hell-bent on shift responses, you end up with a wrestling match for attention, rather than a conversation. Maybe both parties are satisfying their lust for expression, but their gas tanks for being heard are running on empty. You may not notice if you are locked in this type of battle, but from the outside looking in, observing this kind of interaction can be curious and confusing.

Moreover, if a bad conversationalist (someone who continually uses shift responses) is paired with a very empathetic listener (someone who continually uses support responses), one party may well feel as though they're having a good talk because the other person is consistently offering them support responses, while that person actually wants to jump off a bridge because the conversation is turning into an awkward pseudo-lecture on the other person's life and beliefs.

What about passive conversational narcissism? Naturally, some people are still quite aware of social norms and etiquette and so will vie for attention in subtler ways. One way of doing this is to fail to offer support responses, waiting till the other person's thread dies away and you can take the limelight. Here, you are hoping that the other person runs out of steam so you can finally get your word in. It is like sitting in a tree and waiting for the prey to get tired and go to sleep—you know it will happen eventually, so you passively bide your time.

Have you been part of a conversation where the other person didn't offer any support responses, even a quaint "Oh really?" or "Uh-huh"? You're not quite sure whether they've taken in what you've said, and that may be intentional on their part. It may have been a case of passive conversational narcissism. It's like letting that balloon drop to the floor. You don't have to do much to make someone else feel that what they're saying hasn't really "landed"!

Most of us are taught that it's polite to not ramble on, to take your turn and then rest, and to share space in conversations. Fine, this person will follow those basic rules. But they sure won't encourage their conversation partner to speak more, lest it cut into their own speaking time! A lack of (genuine!) feedback from the other person can quickly make someone feel they ought to stop speaking—and this is where the conversational narcissist steps back into the picture.

Though it's tempting to try to catch other people in the act of conversational narcissism, its far more productive to learn to notice it in *yourself* and guard against it. You can't control what others do, but you can control your actions and how good of a listener you are. After all, that is the goal of this book. For the other purpose, you may want to seek a book on persuasion or hypnosis.

The irony is it's often those who are able to listen well, to step aside, and to take a genuine interest in their conversation partners who become people we think of as most interesting, charismatic and worthy of our attention in the first place. So the purported goal of conversational narcissism (*making darn sure that people know things about you*) isn't even satisfied. Oops. Luckily, there are a few guidelines to battle these unconscious obstacles you'll undoubtedly face.

Balance your needs and desires with other people's.

To do this, you first need to be aware of your focus and where it's going. Pay attention to how the airtime is being distributed. Is one person doing all the talking? Is there a back-and-forth? This requires more than just playing at being interested in another person's life—you genuinely need to forget yourself for a moment and engage fully, and honestly, in what someone else is saying. Stop thinking about your response for the future, and pay attention to what someone is currently saying to you.

This means no rushing in to explain or frame what they've said so that it relates back to you again. Give more supportive responses, and guard against constantly referring every topic back to yourself. Ask questions to invite the other person to say more. If you take attention for a while, enjoy it—but volley it back again. Like we were taught as children: It's good to share!

"As you were talking, it made me think about this experience I had once, where XYZ. That made me wonder, did you find that XYZ was the case as well?" A person saying this demonstrates that they're willing to share the conversation, rather than hog it all for themselves. Another tactic is to actively look for ways to share opinions, perspectives, or opinions, or find connections between them. For example, "I'm going to guess we both share similar taste in movies! Like you, I love horrors, but what else do you watch?" Such a sentiment creates balance because it's no longer a question of them versus you at all – it's a way of including both of you at once.

Think about ego, power, self-esteem, and control.

Those who seem most boastful in a conversation, who jealously guard attention or speak over others, are often those who feel most insecure in themselves. Their need to control the conversation comes from a hunger for attention and approval. If you find yourself using conversations as a platform to boost your ego, feel better about yourself, or be witnessed and supported by others, your work may be to learn to be comfortable taking the back seat for a change. The paradox is that people who seem most likeable and confident are those who don't appear to be making frantic efforts to dominate others' attention.

The 30 Percent Rule
According to Charlie Houpert of *Charisma on Command*, the "30 percent rule" states that "we give ourselves just 30 percent of the time a listener would give us to fill a pause without things starting to feel uncomfortable."

Let's take a look at what this actually means. Imagine you're in a group setting and all eyes are on you as you relate an interesting story. Everyone is paying attention and listening to what you're saying, and you're confidently moving from one point to the next. Then, all at once, you kind of go blank. You forget what you were going to say next. There's a pause. The pause continues.

Awkward, right? As you try to think of what to say and get the flow going again, you might start to feel a little stressed and uncomfortable. You start to focus not on what you were talking about, but on your own discomfort. In this moment, a few milliseconds can feel like a painful eternity.

And then, things go downhill. You suddenly feel pressure to talk again and say something – anything. You might end up conveying this sense of discomfort or saying something you ordinarily wouldn't. But the trick here is that in reality you haven't actually paused for that long. It just *feels* like you have. According to Houpert's rule, you are only 30 percent of your way to an awkward pause, and the audience is not uncomfortable at all and has not even registered that there is an awkward silence. They are in fact willing to give you three times as much time to pause as you think they are.

So for example, you feel awkward and on-the-spot at around two to three seconds of silence, when other people are willing to listen attentively for up to six seconds or more. In other words, the audience is always more tolerant and patient than you give them credit for! They will take a much longer time to conclude that you are being awkward or that something has gone wrong with the conversation.

Try to notice other people and how they pause when talking, or watch recordings of natural conversation. Count the seconds of silence – you swill see that seven to ten seconds of silence is more than comfortably accommodated without it becoming awkward.

So what are we to make of this? First, relax. You are almost always less awkward than you think you are. If you are relaxed, you can focus on simply sharing your message. Typically, people who lack confidence can unconsciously feel that they have no real right to speak, and so when they do have people's attention, they rush to say their piece as quickly as possible. *This* is in fact the most awkward outcome, since you will tend to downplay, distort, or undermine your own message, not to mention come across as shy, anxious, or self-doubting.

Instead, make friends with pauses and silences. Take a moment to breathe as you speak – you don't have to hurry. Remember the rule and give yourself a good few seconds more than you think you should take. It's better to be quiet than to anxiously rush to fill in (what you think is) silence with meaningless chatter. If someone asks you a question, pause and take two seconds before you answer. Trust that they are listening. In reality, two seconds is not much time at all, but it will allow you to relax into what you're saying.

Finally, punctuate your speech with plenty of silences. These will help things flow and breathe – literally. Pause now and then to take a breath and your voice will come across smooth and natural. As you pause, make quick, unhurried eye contact. It will convey a strong sense of confidence and ease. When you are relaxed with yourself, others will be too. You may even find that once you stop speaking, they are silent and waiting, happy for you to continue and say more!

Obviously, there are some caveats to this rule. Bearing in mind everything we know about conversational narcissism, there is a big difference between confidently taking up space in a conversation, and hogging it. The 30 percent rule is for those people who feel uncomfortable when it genuinely is their turn to talk. Naturally, you should not butt in when it's someone else's turn to speak, or continue to drone on when you can tell that people are losing interest and trying to squeeze a word in.

Think of silences as *luxury*. They are what allow a conversation to expand, breathe, and relax. Don't rush. When you are asked a question, literally imagine yourself relaxing in your seat, breathing in, and then answering in a slow and calm manner. The irony is that if you speak in a measured, assertive, and self-assured way, people tend to want to give you plenty of airtime. If on the other hand you are rushed, breathless, apologetic, unsure, or anxious, people will be more ready to agree that your message is not important after all, and helpfully step in to relieve you of having to share it!

Instead, use pauses to convey a sense of power and relaxation. Study videos of influential people and how they speak in interviews. You'll notice they sit tall and take up space, they don't rush their speech, and yet they are not aimless, either. They neither need to dominate conversation nor be timid (both signs of insecurity). Instead, they hold themselves with a kind of regal, poised attitude that invites others to listen. They are comfortable, unrushed, and self-contained. They have nothing to prove.

This is a skill you, too, can practice, and much of it comes down to the artful use of pauses and silence. It's cheesy, but imagine that you are a very distinguished and important person being interviewed in exactly the same way. Practice a graceful, calm response that comfortably expands to fill the time available. How does it feel to slow down and be confident that people are listening? If you like, record yourself – you may be surprised to notice that you come across as far more hurried that you felt at the time! It's the 30 percent rule at work.

What Would Conan Do and Curiosity

Let's return to an idea we touched on earlier—the idea of playfulness and curiosity in conversation. Curiosity plays a huge role in the way we receive others and thus how they receive us. You can be the most charming, funniest person in the room, but if you aren't *interested and curious* about the person across from you, there simply won't be a connection. Why would there be? It's more like a one-man show than a conversation. Big surprise, it turns out that we care if the person across from us is engaged or scanning the room behind us and looking for someone better to talk to.

Staying curious is a difficult proposition because, at first glance, most people might seem uninteresting or unworthy of paying attention to. This is harsh, but it is in fact behind a lot of people's reason for "hating small talk." This is undoubtedly the biggest hurdle for most of us—even if you don't consciously think it, you subconsciously believe that someone is simply not worth being curious about. You think that even if you dig deeper you won't find anything worth your time, so why bother in the first place?

It's true that, at first glance, very few of us are compelling. You included. But acting on this impulse will limit your communication and keep you right where you are. We are cutting off people's *ability* to be interesting and compelling because we don't give them a chance. In the end, it doesn't particularly matter what you believe. Just start to build the habit of curiosity, and eventually it won't matter if you think people are worthy or not (they are). You'll be able to find the interesting aspects in just about anyone, and that's what counts.

To do so, I've found that the absolute best mindset to emulate is that of a talk show host—Jimmy Fallon, Jimmy Kimmel, Conan O'Brien, whoever your favorite is, they all do the same thing. Just ask yourself what they would do if you're struggling for what curiosity looks like and how you can wield it. Conan O'Brien happens to my favorite, so let's think about the traits he embodies in a conversation with a guest on his show.

Visualize his studio. He's got a big open space, and he is seated at a desk. His guest is seated at a chair adjacent to the desk, and it's literally like they exist in a world of their own. When Conan has a guest on his show, that guest is the center of his world for the next ten minutes. They are the most interesting person he has ever come across, everything they say is spellbinding, he is insatiably curious about their stories, and he reacts to anything they say with an uproarious laugh and an otherwise exaggerated reaction that they were seeking. He is charmingly positive and can always find a humorous spin on a negative aspect of a story.

His sole purpose is to make his guest comfortable on the show, encourage them to talk about themselves, and ultimately make them feel good and look good. In turn, this makes them share revealing things they might not otherwise share and create a connection and chemistry with him that is so important for a talk show. The viewers at home are desperate to learn about this celebrity guest, so Conan acts as a proxy for their curiosity. Also, the viewers can tell in an instant if either party is mailing it in or faking it, so Conan's job literally depends on his ability to use his curiosity to connect on a deeper level.

Even with grumpy or more quiet guests, he is able to elevate their energy levels and attitudes simply by being intensely interested in them (at an energy level slightly above theirs) and encouraging them by giving them the great reactions that they seek. It's almost as if he plays the game "How little can I say to get the most out of people?" It's a non-obvious talent that is worth its weight in gold—and it'll make the person receive this attention feel like solid gold!

Of course, in your life, you may be faced with those people that are like pulling teeth to talk to. A little bit of friendly encouragement and affirmation can make even the meekest clam open up. Numerous questions, directing the conversation toward them, and the feeling that you actually care are also integral. Imagine the relief you can create at dreaded networking events. People like those who like them, so when you react the way they want, it encourages them to be more outgoing and open with you.

Other talk show hosts would later go on the record lamenting how often they disliked his guests and how boring he found the actors and actresses that he would be forced to speak to. But the fact that this is never really detected is a testament to how highly trained his habit of curiosity was. He started by making a conscious decision to be curious, built the habit, and engaged his guests easily; do you think his guests could tell if he was interested or not? Never.

Curiosity allows people to feel comfortable enough to speak freely beyond a superficial level—because you are demonstrating that you care and that you will listen when they open up. People won't be inclined to reveal their secret thoughts if they think it will be met with apathy, after all. So whether you have to fake it till you make it, Conan O'Brien is who your mindset and attitude should feel like.

It's a banal and often-used quote, but for good reason. Dale Carnegie said it best: "You can make more friends in two months by becoming truly interested in other people than you can in two years by trying to get other people interested in you."

In case Conan O'Brien's curiosity still isn't coming naturally to you, here are some more specific patterns of thought you can use to improve your people skills.

I wonder what they are like? When you start to wonder about the other person, it changes your perspective on them completely. This is an inkling of curiosity. You start to care about them—not only about their shallow traits, such as their occupation or how their day is going, but what motivates them and what makes them act in the way they do.

Having a sense of wonder about someone is one of the most powerful mindsets you can have because it makes you want to scratch your itch. Scratching the itch of curiosity will become secondary to everything else because you simply want to know about the other person. Here, you don't have to *like* them, exactly—it goes deeper than that. Just perceive them, as much of them as you possibly can, and genuinely allow yourself to be amazed by that.

Suppose you had a sense of wonder about computers as a child. You were probably irritating with how many questions you asked anyone that seemed to have knowledge about computers. What kind of attention span are you going to devote to computers, and what kind of questions are you going to ask? You are going to skip the small talk interview questions and get right down to the details because it's what you care and wonder about.

Keeping the mindset of wonderment will completely change the way you interact with people because you will suddenly care, and much of the time, we don't notice that we don't care about the person we are talking to. You'll dig deeper and deeper until you can put together a picture of what you are wondering about.

It's important to note here that you need to be sincere about it. Conan is a pro who gets a salary from the job he does, but for the rest of us, it's so much better to foster a genuine interest in others rather than fake it. That boring person you're chatting to? Challenge yourself and your assumptions about them. They have a history, secrets, hopes, dreams, unexpected talents—what are they?

What can they teach me? Don't read this from the perspective of attempting to gain what you can from someone. Read it from the perspective of seeing others as being people worthy of your attention. Everyone has valuable knowledge, whether it applies to your life or not. Everyone is great at something, and everyone is a domain expert in something that you are not, no matter how small or obscure. People's perspectives have innate value, and just by learning about them, we are enriched.

The main point is to ignite an interest in the other person as opposed to an apathetic approach. Imagine if you were a huge skiing junkie and you met someone that used to be a professional skier. They may have even reached the Olympics in their prime.

What will follow? You'll be thrilled by what you can potentially learn and gain from the other person, and that will guide the entire interaction. Again, there will be a level of interest and engagement if you view others as worthy of talking to. But you'd never know unless you dug.

Whether we like to admit it or not, sometimes we feel some people are not worth our time. It's a bad habit, and this line of thinking is one of the first steps toward breaking it. *Everyone* is worth our time, but you won't be able to discover it if you don't put in the work. At the very least, most people have had interesting or noteworthy experiences in life. Become curious and you just may find that your grandma's Bungo friend was an exotic dancer during the war, that the friend you knew for twenty years has a secret passion for vintage magazines, and your work colleague actually used to be a missionary in the Congo before she had kids. Who knew!

What do we have in common? This is an investigation into the life experiences you share with someone. It instantly makes them more engaging and interesting—because we feel that they are more similar to us! It may sound a bit egotistical, but we are undoubtedly more captivated by people that share the same views and interests as us, and they us.

It may even *elevate* people, especially if we are surrounded by people different from us. For instance, if you discovered that a new stranger was born in the same hospital as you were, despite being in a different country, you would instantly feel more open to them. This person *must* share similar worldviews, values, and humor. You now have a positive bias toward them, actively seeking out more good in them. But you wouldn't have discovered that if you didn't make an attempt at digging.

You are going to be on a hunt, and you will ask the important questions that get you where you want to be. You might jump from topic to topic, or you might dive in and ask directly.

Perhaps it's just because you will have something to fixate on besides talking for talking's sake, but these attitudes will drastically change how you approach people. Curiosity can still be hard, which is why my final suggestion for creating curiosity is to make a game of it. Your goal is to learn as much about the other person as possible. Alternatively, assume there is something extremely thrilling and exciting about the other person and make it your quest to find it. Eventually, you'll find what you're looking for.

The next time you go out to a café or store, put these attitudes to the test with the captive audience of the baristas or cashiers you come across—the lucky few who are paid to be nice to you. Do you perceive these workers to be below you, or do you treat them differently than you would treat a good friend? Do you have a sense of wonderment and curiosity about them? What do you think they can teach you, and what do you have in common with them?

Do you tend to ask the baristas or cashiers about their day and actually care about their answer? If not, do you think you'll be able to simply "turn it on" when you're around people you care about? Practice your mindsets about the people around you. It's the easiest practice you'll have because you don't have to lift a finger, but it drastically transforms the quality of relationships you'll create.

Summary

- In order to interact and engage more fully in conversations, we need to work against our not-so-useful habits and learn better ones.
- A non-negotiable habit is becoming a master at using questions. The right questions help people feel closer to us, communicate our attention and care, share our competence, show that we're aware and paying attention, deepen intimacy, guide the conversation, and make us more trustworthy.
- All exchanges, and hence all questions, are typically on one of three possible levels: those exchanging factual information, those exchanging feelings and emotions, and those communicating deeper values. In social situations, you'll lean more heavily on the last two, but a good conversation works when people have similar conversational goals and are matched in the level they're interacting on.
- Conversational narcissism is an impediment to curiosity, engagement, and good question asking. Whether unconscious or conscious, this usually results from us placing something other than connection with the other person as our goal for conversation, i.e. to brag, to defend, to compete.
- We can reduce our own conversational narcissism by using questions. Follow-up questions are very effective, as are open-ended questions that don't make people uncomfortable, but may *gently* push on the barrier or normal etiquette.
- Just as a role model can be a guide and inspiration for your own behavior, a model can also help you stay curious when you talk to others. Talk show hosts are experts and placing their conversation partners front and center, so we can ask, what would they do? Usually, the answer is "treat my guest like the most interesting person in the whole universe."
- Remember the 30 percent rule and allow your silences to be longer. Relax and take your time.
- Curiosity needs to be genuine. We all have a bias against others sometimes, assuming they're not very interesting, but unless we ask, we won't learn about their more fascinating sides. Assume that everyone has something to teach you, and foster a genuine inquisitiveness into the details of their world. I guarantee you will not be disappointed.

Chapter 6: Subtly Charismatic

Humor and Misdirection

Phew! Time to lighten things up, wouldn't you say? Let's turn our attention to the surprisingly versatile skills of humor or its closely related cousin, misdirection. To put it simply, misdirection is when you say one thing and then proceed with an immediate opposite. For example, "It's a secret, but let me tell you immediately," or, "That show is great, except for everyone in it." It's not rolling-in-the-aisles funny, but it definitely captures attention, and gives conversation a kind of light playfulness that most people will be happy to call wit.

It seems confusing, but that confusion is precisely what makes the other person sit up a little and pay attention. It's playful and communicates a kind of wit and mental agility that is the calling card of a charming person. Luckily, it's not too hard to do, either: All you are doing is breaking a sentence into two parts.

You're stating something in the first part, then contradicting it immediately in the second. Ta da! Misdirection. People won't immediately be sure of what you mean, and part of the humor comes from this introduced confusion. You can have both positive and negative, or vice versa, in the same sentence.

Think of it as a little like a mini-joke, with a setup in the beginning and a punchline at the end. The second part of the sentence is the element that people will react to, while the first part is typically the setup. The second is your true sentiment on the topic.

This formula is the secret to the humor in such lines as George Jessel's, "The human brain is a wonderful organ. It starts to work as soon as you are born and doesn't stop until you get up to deliver a speech." Douglas Adams also used it when he said, "I love deadlines. I like the whooshing sound they make as they fly by." Here's another example: "I love dogs, but I hate seeing, hearing, and touching them," or, "This juice is awesome. Did it come from the garbage disposal?"

There's just such an appealing zing to statements like this. Setting up an expectation and then subverting it is subtly powerful… you can probably agree that this works, but *why* does it work?

Most of us try to be polite to people. We use euphemisms frequently, and we don't say what we really feel. Ordinary, conventional language, therefore, is a little dry and predictable. The first part of a misdirecting statement is what people expect—politeness. It's you following the same old tired expected script. But then surprise! You contradict yourself and give them a dose of reality, which sets up a humorous contrast since you have deviated from what most people expect and would say themselves. As you might have observed, ironic similes also make use of misdirection to derive comedic effect. The whole effect is to send a powerful message that you don't take yourself, or the topic at hand, all that seriously. Done right, misdirection can be amazingly charming and funny—it's a way to break the rules that works so well because you appear to be using the rules at first.

Last but not least, misdirection is simply a funny way to express your feelings on something. If you really feel X about a topic, then use misdirection! "Opposite of X, but actually X," will almost always be received far better than "Gosh, I hate X."

Sarcasm is a way for people to say things without saying them, and is the most common way we use misdirection.

Think about how Chandler Bing from the television show *Friends* talks. If he says something is wonderful, he says *it's wonnnnderful* in a tone that immediately lets you know that he thinks the opposite.

Sarcasm functions like a social cue—both are ways to express something without having to explicitly say it. In that way, it's a great device for handling uncomfortable topics or pointing out the elephant in the room without directly offending people (or pointing). It allows us to walk a tightrope, as long as we don't fall into the pit of passive-aggressiveness.

At some level, most of us can appreciate sarcasm because we know what is being accomplished. It can even be the basis for your own personal brand of humor. Standup comics often use it to great effect.

Chances are, you are already using sarcasm regularly without being fully aware of it. Sarcasm is mostly used as friendly banter with a friend or acquaintance with whom you are comfortable saying something negative. For example, consider that you've committed a minor gaffe at work, for example forgetting to return a borrowed file before it's due. If a close colleague teases you about it, you may reply with a sarcastic, "Oh yes, this is scandalous! This would for sure be in the headlines tomorrow!" But if it's your strict boss who sternly calls you out on it, you would not be likely to make a sarcastic announcement in response.

Sarcasm is usually used to poke fun at someone or something and is heavily context and audience dependent. If you are around somebody who enjoys wit and has a sarcastic sense of humor, it will be quite welcome. Sarcasm is also dynamite when used to make a playful jab at yourself—the irony is how it can have the effect of making you seem supremely confident, self-aware and intelligent. Someone might say, "Oh no, I think I've lost that twenty dollars I was holding on to . . ." and you quickly jump in with, "Oh no! What an idiot. I would never do something so thoughtless. When *I* lose money, I make sure I lose the whole wallet and everything with it."

But around others who don't share the same sense of humor, are less secure, or don't like you, it's too easy for them to interpret your attempts at sarcastic humor as a full-fledged insult. That's not what you're aiming for here. They might just think that you are an insulting jackass, or they're more inclined to listen to the first part of the misdirection than the second.

Using misdirection in the wrong context will cause people to think you lack empathy or, worse, get your jollies from hurting other people's feelings. There will be others who simply won't get the sarcasm, no matter how obvious you make it. They won't be insulted, just very confused. You'll want to avoid both outcomes. The only way to do that is to make sure you "know your audience" and start small, judge the reaction you've had, and go from there. If other people happily use sarcasm themselves, it's probably a sign that they'll appreciate yours.

Choose the correct context and sarcasm can make you more likeable and charming. It also makes you look intelligent and witty. In some social circles, appropriate levels of sarcasm are not only welcomed, but required—think of it as a refreshing antidote to humble bragging or complaining.

Now that you have a clearer idea about the proper context of sarcasm, the next step is to articulate the elements to make sure you don't just insult people left and right in your attempts at building rapport. If your annoying coworker understood sarcasm better, they might be as funny as they think they are.

For the most part, **sarcasm is saying the *opposite* of (1) an objective fact, (2) a subjective emotion, or (3) thought.**

It makes a contradictory statement about a situation to either emphasize or downplay its effect.

Objective fact: Bob plays Tetris at work constantly.

Sarcastic statement: *Bob, you are the busiest man I know.*

Subjective emotion or thought: It is hilarious that Bob plays Tetris at work constantly.

Sarcastic statement: *Bob deserves a medal for worker of the year.*

Here's another one.

Objective fact: There is a surprising amount of traffic lately.

Sarcastic statement: *What are we going to do when we get to our destination super early?*

Subjective emotion or thought: I hate traffic so much.

Sarcastic statement: *This traffic is the best part of my day.*

That's the first and most common use of sarcasm. Now let's lay out a framework for different types of sarcasm and exactly when and how you can use it. You'll be surprised how formulaic and methodical you can get with this, and subsequently with humor.

When someone says or does something very obvious, you respond by saying something equally obvious.

Bob: "That road is very long."

You: "You are very observant."

Bob: "It's so hot today!"

You: "I see you're a meteorologist in training."

Poor Bob: "This menu is huge!"

You: "Glad to see you've learned to read!"

The next application of sarcasm is when something good or bad happens. You say something about how that good or bad event reflects on the other person.

If it's good, you say that it reflects badly on them; if it's bad, you say it reflects well on them.

Bob: "I dropped my coffee mug."

You: "You've always been so graceful."

Bob: "I got an F on my math test."

You: "Now I know who to call when my calculator breaks."

You observe Poor Bob dropping a cup of coffee and state "You would make a great baseball catcher. Great hands!"

Proper delivery is crucial for sarcasm. This can mean the difference between people laughing at your sarcastic joke, or thinking that you're serious in your sentiment and branding you an overall jerk. Also keep in mind that sarcasm is perhaps the most overused technique to create humor. Use it sparingly, but effectively.

You have to make it clear that you're being sarcastic and give others a sign indicating so. Otherwise, people will feel uncomfortable at the uncertainty. Are you just being mean, or are you trying to be funny?

The most common way to do this is with a combination of a deadpan vocal tone and a wry smile or smirk. With deadpan delivery, you don't laugh while you're saying it; you appear completely serious. Then, you break into a smile to alleviate the tension and clue others in to your true intention. If paired with a genuinely nonsensical or over-the-top statement, people will put two and two together and see what you've done.

Now that you know when to deliver sarcastic remarks, it's also important to learn about how to receive them and be a good audience. Let's pretend that you are Poor Bob from earlier and insert a reply for him.

Bob: "That road is very long."

You: "You are very observant."

Bob: "You know it. I'm like an eagle."

Bob: "It's so hot today!"

You: "I see you're a meteorologist in training."

Bob: "I can feel it in my bones. It's my destiny."

Poor Bob: "This menu is huge!"

You: "Glad to see you've learned to read!"

Redeemed Bob: **"I can also count to ten."**

You need to amplify their statement and what they are implying. Does this look familiar? It's a self-deprecating remark + a witty comeback! If you can volley back a sarcastic comment without even blinking, the humor is basically guaranteed. You'll appear sharp and quick, as well as confident enough to not be flustered by an off-color remark. In fact, you signal that you're game for some witty banter, and are happy to have a bit of fun in the conversation.

When you respond to sarcasm this way, it creates a greater bond. And just as important, you don't come off as a bad sport or someone who can't take a joke. Everybody is comfortable, and you create a funny situation and potential for greater banter. This is how so many long-standing in-jokes get their start in life. If you can remember one of these witty remarks and call back to it later in the conversation, congratulations, you now have a shared conversational history with the other person—and that can be a very powerful thing.

However, there is a downside when dealing with sarcasm. A lot of people who rely on sarcastic humor, pretty much on an automatic basis, are actually masking passive-aggressive personalities. They're constantly using sarcasm as a defense mechanism to hide their true feelings. They use sarcasm to pass off their otherwise negative emotions. They might be doing this to you, so it's important to know how to sidestep their subconsciously vicious attacks.

In such cases, responding with sarcasm will only encourage them. It indicates that misusing sarcasm in that way is acceptable. If you find someone being overly sarcastic with you in ways that are passive-aggressive, approach them and politely convey that their sarcasm feels hostile, even if they didn't intend it to be so. With sarcasm, it's all about *intention*. Are you laughing *at* or *with* someone? Who is the butt of the joke, if anyone?

Next, we have irony. Irony is a type of humor that is very close to sarcasm, and often confused with it.

Here's the official definition from Dictionary.com, just because it's something that people can struggle with nailing down: "the expression of one's meaning by using language that normally signifies the opposite, typically for humorous or emphatic effect."

This is different from sarcasm in a few ways. First, irony is generally about situations and incidents, not about people. Something happens which is the opposite of what you expected. When you're presented with an irony, like a fire station burning down, it will quite obviously be ironic, and not sarcastic. However, sarcasm is usually more derogatory in nature. You're saying things you don't mean. The definition of sarcasm is "the use of irony to mock or convey contempt." Thus, you can see how saying, "You are very observant," when someone says, "This road is very long," is sarcasm, not irony, because of the element of mockery inherent in the former remark. (Naturally, you'll be using sarcasm not to insult or convey contempt, but to create humor, which will hopefully build rapport and connection.)

Ironic humor is when something that is the exact opposite of what you might expect occurs. Another way to define irony is when you say something but mean the exact opposite of what you expect.

In other words, the words that come from your mouth are the opposite of the emotion you are feeling. If you're starving, an ironic statement might be something like, "I'm so full I need to unbuckle my belt. It's like Thanksgiving in July."

Ironic humor draws its power from contrasts. There is a contrast between literal truth and perceived truth. In many cases, ironic humor stems from frustration or disappointment with our ideals. The way we imagine the world should be produces comedy when it clashes with how the world actually is.

Ironic humor is usually used to make a funny point about something or to point something out. For example, when you see a big a sign that says, "No signs allowed," that's ironic humor. The sign bans signs but is itself a sign. The expectation that the sign ensures there will be no signs in the vicinity failed.

Another example is when you see a car with a logo on the door saying, "Municipal Traffic Reduction Committee," and the car, along with everybody else, is stuck in two hours of bumper-to-bumper traffic. There is a profound ironic comedy there, as you would expect the traffic management planning committee would do a better job so they wouldn't be stuck in traffic themselves. It's like someone ordering a diet soda after they've just ordered three double cheeseburgers and fries or someone else crashing into a "thank you for not speeding" sign.

Irony is all about finding contrast and drawing some interesting and creative judgment out of it. As the examples indicate, ironic humor is more a matter of observation than one of spontaneity or creativity. You're more likely to find and point out things that are ironic than come up with something that is.

Ironic humor, on the other hand, is when you intentionally imply the opposite meaning of what you say. When we think about how to use irony conversationally, what we're really asking is what ways can we convey two messages at one time? So, your boss tells everyone to attend a meeting to discuss some issues with people being tardy to work and you slyly quip, "Sorry, Bev, is it all right if I'm ten minutes late?" with a big cheesy smile. (This, of course, depends on whether Bev is likely to find this funny or not . . .)

The Power of Improv

Let's turn our attention to a group of people who have made good banter and wit their business: improvisers and stand-up comedians.

The Rule of Improv Comedy: Great improv is a result of the creativity in spontaneous situations, and set agendas and outlines put a very low ceiling on that.

Improv comedy performances are, guess what, improvised!

The performers may occasionally work with a set theme that has been decided on beforehand, but there will always be large portions of an improv performance that involve taking direction from the crowd or audience. They can't predict what a crowd will give them to work with, so it's out of necessity that they can't have a strict agenda or outline.

That's part of the fun in attending an improv performance: you feel that you are a part of the outcome and have contributed to the show.

Obviously, these are situations where the performers have to think on their feet as quickly as possible, so they don't get tongue-tied and silent while everyone in the room is waiting. But overall, we have the perfect arena where we can watch spontaneity, curiosity, and good humor play out.

As an improv performer, you have to process what was said to you, try to project where you want the scene to go, and then predict what others might also say in response. And you have to do it all knowing that your plans might need to completely change when the other players switch things up. You have to read people's body language, try to determine if there is any ulterior message, and actively provide detail that other people can work with.

Improv comedy is collaborative in nature, but it's impossible to know what your teammates are thinking. In a split second, you need to perform a full analysis of the entire scene and spit out words that will enhance the most important aspects of it. Oh, and you're in front of a crowd of people, and there is a team of people on stage waiting on your response.

That might be the very definition of thinking on your feet (or hell on earth, if you're prone to anxiety!).

How does all of this make you a better conversationalist?

Recall that improv performances and conversations have the exact same goal—a flowing, entertaining interaction. If we look at some of the ways that improv performers are able to think fast and approach this unpredictability, we'll be able to improve our conversation skills immensely. *Without* trying too hard!

Don't Hold on Too Tightly

Imagine you're in a business meeting where you have an agenda to address a certain outstanding issue. Conversation centers around this issue, but soon morphs into a discussion about a separate but related issue. You didn't plan for it, and you're annoyed because you wanted to get through all your slides and say your speech. Plus, you're not quite prepared to talk about this other issue and don't have all the answers at hand, so you keep valiantly trying to steer the conversation back to the previous issue. You succeed! You force everyone to pay attention to your slides again… but now instead of it seeming like everything is back on track, everyone is bored and the whole thing feels a little lifeless. Why?

The first step to lively conversation is, without a doubt, to let go of any preconceived notion of how and where you want your conversation to go. Be "outcome independent." Professional improv players are able to create a fluid, dynamic, and witty interplay with their audience members because they are flexible and open to any possibility and direction. They are not stubborn or rigid—they understand that conversations *emerge* from the collaboration of the group and cannot be predicted or controlled too closely.

Yes, it can definitely be scary to go into a conversation with a completely blank slate, so to speak, especially if you are the type to plan and scheme. But planning and scheming has probably not gotten you too far in social conversations, so it's time to open up and let go of the talking points or agendas you want to take into your conversations with you.

Don't worry. You never need to enter conversations unprepared—you just won't be using set agendas. When it comes to "agendas," this can mean goals, talking points, or objectives that people want to achieve or gain from a conversation. Your conversational resume? In the next section we're going to uncover some tools to help you *structure* conversation in the moment. But these are temporary training wheels, and they're there to help natural conversation, not replace it.

When you talk to other people, the focus of the conversation should be about the conversation. The point is to connect and engage – not to play out some predefined idea of what you've already decided connection and engagement look like! Holding on too tightly is a big reason some people's attempts to seduce and flirt fail so spectacularly. Rather than letting things unfold in a playful, loose, and exciting way, such a person may unconsciously have a very limited view of the potential of the encounter, and try to force it – and nothing is less sexy than pressure and desperation, right? Instead, it's almost always better to let go of your expectations of what the conversation should look like – or how you or the other person should be – and get into the mindset that you are having a conversation *in order to find these things out*.

Each conversation is its own animal, with its own inherent flow and natural rhythm. It should not be about you or what you are trying to get out of the other person or people. It shouldn't be forced to resemble a great conversation you've had before or some idea of how you think perfect conversations go. Why restrict yourself that way? If you want to be in perfect control, have a monologue (perhaps, that's why people do!). If you want to encounter another human being and see what happens, then realize that they are *co-creating* the dialogue with you, and that means anything can happen.

The moment other people are able to perceive your agenda, guess what happens? They will shut you out. You become somebody worthy of suspicion and skepticism. So, you might convince your colleagues to pay attention to your pre-prepared slides, but you can't make them care, and they won't. If you are trying to sell something, it makes it all that much harder once people feel that you have an ulterior motive. It's difficult to overcome the feeling that someone wants something from you. The same goes if you're trying to impress someone, to convince them of something, to get them to do this or that, to force them to pay attention to you. People want to feel like conversations are natural, fun, and something they do because they want to. Nobody wants to feel manipulated, right?

If you are approaching a conversation with an agenda, even an unconscious one, first it becomes exceedingly clear that you are only waiting for your turn to speak, and not actually listening to people. You aren't present and you aren't listening.

People might say something to you, and you might not even acknowledge their statement and just continue along with yours. You are telling them that you don't care about where the conversation is naturally heading—your agenda is more important. Another sneaky way this can happen is when the conversation is gradually shifting and evolving… but then you say something that takes it back a few steps (usually, right back to the last point *you* made…). It will feel like you're throttling the conversation and slowing it down, not to mention disregarding other people's input:

Person C: I think such and such about XYZ.

Person A: Observation about XYZ.

Person B: Support response – Tell us more specifically about Y?

Person A: Okay, sure. Here's something about Y.

Person B: Fascinating. I know about Y, too. It connects to ABC, don't you think?

Person A: Definitely. Person C, do you ABC?

Person C: Well I have an anecdote about XYZ.

Person C's contribution here is like a speedbump that takes all the momentum out of the conversation – and strongly hints that they haven't even listened to the other speakers. Now, the conversation may be forced to go back to XYZ… but at the loss of the vitality of the conversation. Person C may well feel satisfied that the topic is once more the thing they most care about, but it's a hollow success.

Others will notice your patterns sooner than you think. What are they getting out of a conversation like that?

Second, agendas leave people unready to adapt. Unless you are going to drop a speech on an audience, things will never go exactly as you plan.

When you create an agenda, you memorize it and become reliant on it. The more often that happens, the more uncomfortable we are with the unpredictability of thinking on our feet. You are essentially acting form fear—or reacting. What happens when you deviate and can't find a good place to step back into your agenda? You're left utterly unprepared for the rest of the interaction because of your reliance on what you've planned. You're no longer alive and authentic. You're like an actor on a stage who's forgotten their lines.

This is why it is extremely important to constantly listen to other people and acknowledge them. You might even go with *their* agenda. That's okay, because your goal here is to build rapport, and that will do it. Not holding on too tightly to an agenda sems scary until you realize that an agenda only gives you the illusion of control. That once you abandon it and just be in the moment, the real interesting stuff happens!

People can sometimes fall back on agendas or fixed plans out of fear or lack of confidence. They want to avoid that embarrassing moment when they're tongue-tied and awkward, unable to think of what to say next. But actually, it's those very moments that keep a conversation alive and interesting. And really, what's so wrong with finding yourself in an unexpected situation? Is it really the end of the world if you are not perfectly in control?

If you can trust yourself a little and surrender to the conversation rather than try to steer it, you give yourself opportunities to learn to become comfortable with that crucial moment, when all eyes are on you and it's time to say something. At the very least, don't underestimate the power of self-deprecating humor or a little disarming honesty:

Person A tells a witty joke, and you laugh, but suddenly feel at a loss for words and can't think of an equally funny thing to say. So, you shrug and say what you're really thinking: "You know, that's exactly the kind of brilliant joke that I could come up with, but you'll have to wait until three a.m. tomorrow morning for me to suddenly think of it..." In other words, you've made a witty joke… about not being able to make a witty joke. Congratulations, you've thought on your feet!

On the other hand, conversation is not about performance. If you can't think of anything to say, it's also a valid move to just pass the ball to someone else. Keep it going, whether all you do is ask a question, reiterate what's just happened, or use something unexpected to put the limelight back on someone else.

Learn to Make Quick Connections
Let people feel that the conversation is a two-way street. It actually becomes a two-way street when you stop, listen, and interrupt your own thoughts for theirs.

Up to this point in the chapter, we've discussed the negatives of over-preparing for conversations and coming in with outlines of what you want to discuss. Being able to rely solely on your ability to improvise is incredibly important, but just as frightening for some. So, how can we increase our capacity for quick thought?

There's no way other than through intentional practice. No, no rehearsing a script or churning out lines. But practice.

The first method is to turn on your favorite quick-witted television show with your remote in hand, because you'll be pausing constantly. For example, *30 Rock*, *Gilmore Girls*, or even *Saturday Night Live*. These are all good shows to use because there is a lot of witty banter, and direct and indirect jokes. They have the type of dialogue we want to be able to create ourselves. (Actually, for our purposes, you don't even need to watch a show you find particularly funny. It's still useful just to watch how those jokes unfold, and how energy moves between the players).

Now, pretend that you are one of the characters on the screen. It doesn't matter who you are, as long as they have a lot of interaction with other characters. Then, when other characters reply to your character on screen, pause the show and construct your own reply. Play the show again and compare your responses. What do you notice? This is going to train your ability to think through different circumstances and come up with responses.

It's not going to be easy at first. You'll probably be blank a lot of the time and not know what to say. However, if you can do this for at least fifteen minutes a day for a week, you'll eventually become quicker with your replies. It'll start to feel more comfortable, even second nature. You can also practice this exercise with podcasts and radio interviews. What you're doing is putting yourself in a position to think quickly. You can then hear what your character or avatar actually said, and you can get immediate feedback on what you could have said given the circumstances. You get to do all this at your own pace, and with the gift of being able to pause the conversation. Every piece of feedback is going to help hone your ability to come up with wit in record time.

The second method is to play free association with words and phrases. Free association is when you hear a word, then you come up with another word that the first word makes you think of. The second word can be anything, and the goal is to do this instantaneously.

For example, cat:dog, dog:puppy, puppy:paws, paws:fur, fur:allergies, allergies:medicine, medicine:nurses, nurses:doctors, doctors:plastic surgeon, plastic surgeon:fake lips, and so on. That was a free association word chain that began simply with the word cat.

How do you train this? Pick a word at random from a dictionary, and list out fifteen words in a free association word chain as quickly as possible. Then, do it again and again—verbally, because that will require the quickest thinking. The trick here is not to try too hard. Don't think about it, literally just say what pops into your head, without censorship or mulling over it.

After you grow more comfortable with random free association with words, you can take the next step and choose two random words from a dictionary and pretend they are the name of a company. Then, create a short story about what that company does, as quickly as possible.

For example, the two random words you pick are: bottle, Africa. The short story I would construct about a company named "Africa Bottle" is that they import African homemade liquors. Sure, you'll probably come up with a few doozies as you practice this, but keep your judgment at bay—your only goal is to practice being swift and relaxed making associations.

The final step of this set of free association exercises is to choose five random words from the dictionary and make up a story that involves all of the words, as quickly as possible. Let's say you choose *hiccup, elevator, heat, president,* and *fern*. Then you quickly envisage a skit where the president once got overheated in an elevator in Hawaii and thus developed hiccups, which meant he had to postpone his media conference for ten minutes while one of the aides attempted to scare him again and again behind some fern bushes in the lobby. By showing him his latest approval ratings. In a way, this is not dissimilar from what you did with the R part of SBR, or the M part of HPM.

Again, these exercises train you to think quickly and be creative, so it's imperative that you do these exercises at "full speed," so you don't have the time to step in and start second-guessing yourself. They'll be tough, and at first, your responses might be terrible. But imagine how big the difference will be between your first day and your tenth day, for example. That's the power of free association, and practice.

If you also care to analyze the similarities between free association and conversation, you might find that they are virtually the same. In conversation, you'll reply to someone on a topic, a slightly related topic, or a new topic. That's exactly the type of thought process that free association takes. In a sense, you are training yourself to come up with conversation topics quickly. In another sense, you are training yourself to trust these first impulses and not self-censor—you may be surprised, in other words, at just how creative you can be when you simply get out of your own way!

The third method is to come up with a simple structure for yourself when you're backed into a corner. For example, an easy response structure you can use for just about anything is to (1) restate what was said, (2) state an emotion, and (3) ask a question.

Here's how that looks in practice:

"So, then I punched him in the face and all was well."

 "You punched him in the face? That must have been satisfying. How did it feel after?"

"Did you like the coffee?"

"Did I like the coffee? Well, I'm in a great mood now, so I guess I did. What kind was it?"

"I hear the zoos here are amazing."

"The zoos are amazing? That would make me so happy to see one. Do you want to go tomorrow?"

It's an easy template that allows you to respond to anything, even if your mind is blank, because it literally tells you what to say. So, relax; even if you're in the pickliest of pickles, getting out of it can often be as simple as that. Skip a beat and don't sweat it—you'll be witty on the next one.

Have a Little Faith

What really makes confident people feel confident? So much of the beauty in our lives is unplanned. This occurs because we are able to step outside of the boxes and limits in our heads and explore things we wouldn't have otherwise. And what results is often amazing. Confidence could be called the belief in this truth.

Over-planning and preparing is like a straitjacket for your conversation and rapport. The irony is that holding things with lightness takes far less effort than trying to force and control them, and always leads to better results. In a way, it's about committing to having better conversations rather than becoming a better conversationalist—once you get your ego out of the picture, you can actually start to let things flow. But you have to take that first step, and that takes trust.

When you remove the possibility of spontaneity from your conversations, you might feel like you are safe from spectacular failure, but you also limit the potential of how high your conversation can soar. In other words, it's safe but boring.

The most memorable moments do not typically come because somebody planned them that way. In fact, it's usually the opposite.

Here's a quick thought experiment that will bolster your sense of confidence in the face of unpredictability. Hopefully it will help you realize that you don't need an agenda, and that your worst-case scenario is not really that bad.

Pick five topics that you know absolutely nothing about. Bring them up one by one with a friend. Commit to talking about each topic for at least five minutes. See the various angles and routes you can go to make a topic interesting. Grasp for straws on how to keep a dialogue going. Notably, see how you can relate it to other topics, and see how easy it is to get sidetracked onto something else. There's not much to fear, is there? You might convince yourself of something interesting: that the content of a conversation is only secondary, and your attitude and energy play a much, much bigger role.

The 1:1:1 Method of Storytelling

On the theme of simplifying storytelling, we've been talking about how we can use a mini story in many ways. You may be wondering what the difference is between a *mini* story and a *full-fledged* story.

To me, not much. As I mentioned, many people like to complicate storytelling as if they were composing an impromptu Greek tragedy. Does there have to be an introduction, middle, struggle, then resolution? You may have read that great stories are about X, Y, and Z; that you need a beginning, middle, and ending; that you should use as much descriptive detail as possible; or how important pauses are. That's one way of doing it, but certainly not the easiest or most practical.

My method of storytelling in conversation is to prioritize the discussion afterward—similar to what you saw with the fallback stories in an earlier chapter. This means that the story itself doesn't need to be that in-depth or long. It can and should contain specific details that people can relate to and latch on to, but it doesn't need to have parts or stages. It can be *mini* by nature. That's why it's called the *1:1:1 method*.

It stands for a story that (1) has one action, (2) can be summed up in one sentence, and (3) evokes one primary emotion in the listener. You can see why they're short and snappy. They also tend to make sure that you know your point before starting and have a very low chance of verbally wandering for minutes and alienating your listeners.

For a story to consist of *one action* means only one thing is happening. The story is about one occurrence. It should be direct and straightforward. Anything else just confuses the point and makes you liable to ramble.

A story should be able to be *summed up* in one sentence because, otherwise, you are trying to convey too much. This step actually takes practice, because you are forced to think about which aspects matter and which don't add anything to your action. It's a skill to be able to distill your thoughts into one sentence and still be thorough—often, you won't realize what you want to say unless you can do this.

Finally, a story should focus on one primary emotion to be evoked in the listener. And you should be able to name it! Keep in mind that evoking an emotion ensures that your story actually has a point, and it will color what details you carefully choose to emphasize that emotion. For our purposes here, there really aren't that many emotions you might want to evoke in others from a story. You might have humor, shock, awe, envy, happiness, anger, or annoyance. Those are the majority of reasons we relate our experiences to others.

Keep in mind that it's just my method for conveying my experiences to others. Whether people hear two sentences about a dog attack or they hear ten sentences doesn't change the impact of the story. The reason I abbreviate stories is so the conversation can move forward and we can then focus on the listener's impact and reaction. So what does this so-called story sound like?

"I was attacked by a dog and I was so frightened I nearly wet my pants." It's one sentence, there is one action, and the bit about wetting the pants is to emphasize the fact that the emotion you want to convey is fear and shock.

You could include more detail about the dog and the circumstances, but chances are people are going to ask about that immediately, so let them guide what they want to hear about your story. Invite them to participate! Very few people want to sit and listen to a monologue, most of which is told poorly and in a scattered manner. Therefore, keep the essentials but cut your story short, and let the conversation continue as a shared experience rather than you monopolizing the airspace. Make it a shared experience rather than all about you.

The 1:1:1 method can be summed up as starting a story as close to the end as possible. Most stories end before they get to the end, in terms of impact on the listener, their attention span, and the energy that you have to tell it. In other words, many stories tend to drone on because people try to adhere to these rules or because they simply lose the plot and are trying to find it again through talking. Above all else, a long preamble is not necessary. What's important is that people pay attention, care, and will react in some (preferably) emotional manner.

Ask for Stories

Most of the focus with stories is usually on telling them—but what about soliciting them from others and allowing them to feel as good as you do when a story lands well? What about stepping aside and giving other people the spotlight? Well, it's just a matter of how you ask for them.

When you watch sports, one of the most illogical parts is the post-game or post-match interview. These athletes are still caught in the throes of adrenaline, out of breath, and occasionally drip sweat on to the reporters.

Yet when you are watching a broadcaster interview an athlete, does anything odd strike you about the questions they ask? The interviewers are put into an impossible situation and usually walk away with decent soundbites—at the very least, not audio disasters. Their duty is to elicit a coherent answer from someone who is mentally incoherent at the moment. How do they do that?

They'll ask questions like: "So tell me about that moment in the second quarter. What did you feel about it and how did the coach turn it around then?" as opposed to: "How'd you guys win?" or: "How did you turn this match around, come back, and pull out all the stops to grab the victory at the very end?" as opposed to: "How was the comeback?"

The key? They ask for a story rather than an answer. They phrase their inquiry in a way that can only be answered with a story, in fact.

Detail, context, and boundaries are given for the athletes to set them up to talk as much as possible instead of providing a breathless one-word answer. It's almost as if they provide the athletes with an outline of what they want to hear and how they can proceed. They make it easy for them to tell a story and simply engage. It's like if someone asks you a question but, in the question, tells you exactly what they want to hear as hints.

Sometimes we think we are doing the heavy lifting in a conversation and the other party isn't giving us much to work with. But that's a massive cop-out. They might not be giving you much, but you also might be asking them the wrong questions, which is making them give you terrible responses. In fact, if you think you are shouldering the burden, you are definitely asking the wrong questions.

Conversation can be much more pleasant for everyone involved if you provide fertile ground for people to work in. Don't set the other person up to fail and be a poor conversationalist; that will only make you invest and care less and cause the conversation to die out.

When people ask me low-effort, vague questions, I know they probably aren't interested in the answer. They're just filling the time and silence. To create win-win conversations and better circumstances for all, ask for stories the way the sports broadcasters do. Ask questions in a way that makes people want to share.

Stories are personal, emotional, and compelling. There is a thought process and narrative that necessarily exists. They are what show your personality and are how you can learn about someone. They show people's emotions and how they think. Last but not least, they show what you care about.

Compare this with simply asking for closed-ended answers. Answers are often too boring and routine for people to care. They will still answer your questions but in a very literal way, and the level of engagement won't be there. Peppering people with shallow questions puts people in a position to fail conversationally.

It's the difference between asking, "What was the best part of your day so far? Tell me how you got that parking space so close!" instead of just, "How are you?"

When you ask somebody the second question, you're asking for a quick, uninvolved answer. You're being lazy and either don't care about their answer or want them to carry the conversational burden. When you ask somebody one of the first two questions, you're inviting them to tell a specific story about their day. You are inviting them to narrate the series of events that made their day great or not. And it can't really be answered with a one-word answer.

Another example is "What is the most exciting part of your job? How does it feel to make a difference like that?" instead of simply asking them the generic "What do you do?" When you only ask somebody what they do for a living, you know exactly how the rest of the conversation will go: "Oh, I do X. What about you?"

A final example is: "How did you feel about your weekend? What was the best part? It was so nice outside," instead of just: "How was your weekend?"

Prompting others for stories instead of simple answers gives them a chance to speak in such a way that they feel emotionally invested. This increases the sense of meaning they get from the conversation you're having with them. It also makes them feel you are genuinely interested in hearing their answer because your question doesn't sound generic.

Consider the following guidelines when asking a question:

1. Ask for a story
2. Be broad but with specific directions or prompts
3. Ask about feelings and emotions
4. Give the other person a direction to expand their answer into, and give them multiple prompts, hints, and possibilities
5. If all else fails, directly ask "Tell me the story about..."

Imagine that you want the other person to inform your curiosity. Other examples include the following:

1. "Tell me about the time you . . ." versus "How was that?"
2. "Did you like that . . ." versus "How was it?"
3. "You look focused. What happened in your morning . . ." versus "How are you?"

Let's think about what happens when you elicit (and provide) personal stories instead of the old, tired automatic replies.

You say hello to your co-worker on Monday morning and you ask how his weekend was. At this point, you have cataloged what you will say in case he asks you the same. Remember, they probably don't care about the actual answer ("good" or "okay"), but they *would* like to hear something interesting. But you never get the chance, because you ask him "How was your weekend? Tell me about the most interesting part—I know you didn't just watch a movie at home!"

He opens up and begins to tell you about his Saturday night when he separately and involuntarily visited a strip joint, a funeral, and a child's birthday party. That's a conversation that can take off and get interesting, and you've successfully bypassed the unnecessary and boring small talk that plagues so many of us.

Most people love talking about themselves. Use this fact to your advantage. Once someone takes your cue and starts sharing a story, make sure you are aware of how you're responding to that person through your facial expressions, gestures, body language, and other nonverbal signals. Since there is always at least one exciting thing in any story, focus on that exciting point and don't be afraid to show that you're engaged.

One quick tip to show that you're engaged and even willing to add is something I call *pinning the tail on the donkey*. There is probably a better name for it, but my vocabulary was severely lacking at the time. The donkey is the story from someone else, while the tail is your addition to it. It allows you to feel like you're contributing, it makes other people know you're listening, and it turns into something you've created together.

People will actually love you for it because, when you do this, your mindset becomes focused on assisting people's stories and letting them have the floor.

Bob's story: "I went to the bank and tripped and spilled all my cash, making it rain inadvertently."

Tail: **"Did you think you were Scrooge McDuck for a second?"**

When you make a tail, try to home in on the primary emotion the story was conveying, then add a comment that amplifies it. The story was about how Bob felt rich, and Scrooge McDuck is a duck who swims in pools of gold doubloons, so it adds to the story and doesn't steal Bob's thunder. Get into the habit of assisting other people's stories. It's easy, witty, and extremely likable because you are helping them out.

Conversational diversity
Hypotheticals

A hypothetical is a classic conversational diversification tactic. Okay, that's a fancy term for what really amounts to, "Hey, what would you do if . . ." and "What do you think about . . ."

But here's what happens when you throw a hypothetical into your conversation. You inject exponentially the amount of variability and unpredictability possible because it's likely something your conversation partner has never considered, and the hypothetical you pose will be something that has no clear or correct answer. Instead, something hopefully exciting comes out of it and you get to discuss something that would never have come up otherwise.

Use hypotheticals to see how people react and how their minds work. You'll learn something about them from how they answer, and you can treat the hypothetical itself like an inkblot test—how they answer probably says something about them. In the end, wherever it goes will probably be more interesting than an interview!

The easiest way to make a conversation awkward or to introduce dead space is to ask questions that can easily be answered by a simple yes or no. Open-ended questions allow for creativity. They allow people to dig into their memory banks, come up with random associations, or otherwise trigger their imagination. With that said, your hypothetical question should be challenging enough so that the recipient actually needs to be a bit creative in answering the question. What's more, it can inject a much-needed jolt of life and playfulness into a flagging conversation that has become a little too stale and predictable. Think about two people on a date in a restaurant and one says, "Hey, if you had a magic carpet and could travel anywhere in the world right now, and we could have a date there, where would you go?" It's not just cute and romantic, it creates an engaging moment of possibility – and who knows what might happen next?

The secret to hypotheticals is to make them appear spontaneous. Ask for their opinion on something out of curiosity, for example. Be genuine. You don't want to come off as contrived or like you're reading from a script, or else it might make you look ingenuous. You don't want to seem as if you have some sort of agenda. Adding a one- to two-sentence backstory as to why this thought "spontaneously" popped into your mind tends to help.

Finally, keep in mind that when you use these, you must also have an answer prepared for the hypothetical you ask. You can step in with your answer while they are formulating theirs—and you should have thought about this answer beforehand so you can be prepared and rehearse it if necessary. Picture the dating couple again, and the person answers the question but then returns it – where would *they* like the magic carpet to take them? They answer, "Maybe it will sound cheesy, but now that I think of it, I wouldn't want to be anywhere else right now but here. With you."

Whatever happens, don't be in a situation where you don't know the answer to your own hypothetical. You don't need a definitive answer, but you at least need a stance or opinion. There's nothing worse than your conversation partner saying, "I don't know," and you also saying, "I don't know." Nothing else will fill that space besides awkward silence.

Here are some examples of hypothetical questions you can toss into your conversations like a grenade. It's a good rule of thumb to have a few prepared and up your sleeve for when you sense you are falling into some type of routine or pattern. It's a good idea to try to tailor them to the situation at hand, but they'll still work even if they're completely out of the blue!

Type #1: What would you do if . . .

Example: What would you do if the waiter from lunch screamed at you to give him a bigger tip?

Type #2: Would you rather have this or that?

Example: Would you rather be four inches shorter or sixteen inches taller?

Type #3: My friend just did/said this . . . What would you have done?

Example: My friend just called out his boss for working too much. Can you imagine that? What would you have done?

Type #4: What if you were in this situation . . . ?

Example: What if your co-worker was stealing your food from the fridge every day? How would you handle that?

Type #5: Which of the following . . . ?

Example: Which do you think is better: super cold winters or hot summers?

Type #6: Who do you think . . . ?

Example: Which of us do you think got the best grades in school? Or the worst?

Think Out Loud

This is a rather simplistic way of phrasing it, but thinking out loud can introduce quite a bit of conversational diversity. We filter ourselves far too much, and while it's called for sometimes, it doesn't always help.

If we just voice our inner monologue about what we're thinking about during our day, this can be quite an icebreaker. Share your thoughts about your surroundings or what you observe around you. Share what you are doing, what you are seeing, what you are thinking, and what you are wondering. Thinking out loud can also just be voicing your feelings, such as, "I'm so happy with the sunshine right now," or, "I can't believe the coffee here is so expensive!"

This will lead to a more open flow of communication. Others will feel less guarded around you and that can lead to a higher level a mutual comfort. It's also bound to be more interesting than filling the silence with a question that no one cares about.

Just say what's on your mind and you are inviting others to speak, but it's not a demand.

The added benefit is you'll probably end up being that person who says what everyone is thinking but is afraid to say. Maybe they're just shy or want to seem polite. Whatever it is, they are thinking it, but they feel it's not proper to voice their thoughts aloud. If you become that person who is the first to say what everyone is thinking, you break the ice.

People will feel they can trust you and be comfortable around you because you actually have the guts to say what they wanted to say. At least you'll bring up some common ground that others can comment on.

Summary

- Lightness, humor and playfulness are the life blood of good conversation, and there are ways to develop them for yourself.
- One quick technique is misdirection, where a statement has two parts: the first is expected and ordinary, the second contradicts it with unexpected and comedic results. Sarcasm can be powerful but is best when directed at yourself and used with those you are more familiar with. Ironic humor is similar to sarcasm, but more focused on the observation of the contrast between the expected and the actual.
- The world of improv has a lot to teach us about good conversational chemistry. One improv rule is not to hold on to any outcome too tightly, and be ready to follow the emerging flow of the conversation.
- Another rule is to rely on quick connections to make sure you always have something to say. This can be practiced by free associating one, two, or five words. Good improv is about having faith in the conversation's direction, and your ability to be okay with where it goes.
- The 1:1:1 method of storytelling is a mini story technique that relies on one action, summarized in one sentence, that evokes one main emotion in the listener. This keeps your stories engaging, short, and effective. Alternatively, you can ask for other people's stories.
- Conversational diversity is about having as many different tools in your toolkit as possible. Hypothetical questions are one such tool. These kinds of "what if...?" questions inject some excitement, creativity, and unpredictability, while showing something interesting about the person giving the answer.

- Finally, thinking out loud can be a way to turn monologues into dialogues. If we speak freely and without self-censoring, we break the ice, share ourselves honestly, and invite (rather than demand) others to join us.

Summary Guide

CHAPTER 1: SO, WHAT IS CHARISMA ANYWAY?

- Charming people may seem to possess a mysterious quality nobody else does, but charisma is a knowable set of social and emotional behaviors that anyone can learn.
- Charisma can be defined as a blend of likeability and influence. Charismatics have presence in a room, can impact and persuade others, can lead, but also know how to put people at ease, are warm, smile often, and get along with anyone.
- Practice taking up more space in a room, and examine any core beliefs that may negatively impact your posture and expression. Believe deep down that other people are not a threat and that you have something worthwhile to communicate.
- Speak openly about your passions, and when you address others, speak to their highest selves. Smile often and remember the details of what people tell you.
- Don't interrupt, judge, complain, gossip or express negativity. Instead, express gratitude and optimism.
- Ronald Riggio broke charisma into 3 social and emotional functions: expressiveness, sensitivity to other people's expressiveness, and self-control.
- To be more charismatic, express yourself emotionally with colorful language and dynamic facial expressions. Pay attention to people's nonverbal expression, but don't be afraid to ask directly about how others feel.
- To improve emotional control, slow down, breathe and become present, rather than reacting mindlessly.
- Acting and improv can help you improve social skills, and the ability to consciously wear a social mask. Pay attention to how you're physically presenting yourself and dress with care and deliberation.
- Finally, learn to "people watch" and get into the habit of asking more questions instead of talking about yourself in conversations.

CHAPTER 2: BUILDING REAL-WORLD CHARISMA

- Olivia Fox Cabane explains how there are four charisma types according to the proportion of power, presence and warmth. The focused charismatic (who pays deep attention to others), the visionary charismatic (who communicates their infectious passion), the kind charismatic (who inspires with warmth and compassion) and the authoritative charismatic (who leads others with expertise and power).
- Depending on your goals, you can play up your natural charisma strengths or seek to balance out your weaknesses.
- To be socially and emotionally comfortable, plan ahead and make sure you're physically comfortable, which will remove barriers to charismatic connection.
- Use ritual and visualization as a "social warm up." Music, meditation, and affirmations can help you prepare.
- Build presence with mindfulness. Slow down, breathe and anchor in the senses. Pause before you respond, and take conscious care of every detail of the interaction, including your verbal and nonverbal expression, appearance, and behavior.
- Howard Friedman emphasized the affective, nonverbal expressiveness component of charisma.

- Communicate with *all* your body and laugh openly. Speak with a dynamic, varied voice that changes in pitch, tone and expression. Use touch to bridge distance and create warmth, aware that the rules differ for men and women.
- Speak less and emote more via facial expression. If you find yourself the center of attention, relax and don't draw attention to awkwardness, using humor to defuse tension. Use exaggerated, pantomime-like gestures and initiate contact with strangers. Finally, practice the art of "platonic flirting."
- Introverts *can* be charismatic, but they must do so on their own terms.

CHAPTER 3: PUTTING IT ALL TOGETHER

- We can condense the four theories of charisma into 5 distinct charismatic traits: likeability and warmth; power and influence; emotional intelligence; presence, awareness and self-control; and social intelligence and leadership. If we can consistently hit these five notes in our social interactions, we cannot help but boost our "charisma quotient."
- To be impactful, charisma has to be genuine to us. We need to take responsibility for honestly appraising our skills and taking concrete action to improve in real life. Whether we are extroverted or introverted, there is a unique charisma style that will work for us.
- Real life celebrities and historical figures can serve as examples and inspiration. Both Will Smith and Marilyn Monroe show how you can tick all 5 charisma boxes, but in completely different ways.
- Will Smith teaches us to be prepared, stay humble and work hard, and lead with positivity, humor, and good-naturedness. Though his social mask makes him appear easygoing and lighthearted, it conceals the effort, deliberation and hard work required to build the life and image you want.
- Marilyn Monroe teaches us that charisma can also be about magnetically drawing people towards you, rather than being loud and over the top to demand attention. Marilyn shows us the power of appearance, and how to craft a performing person down to the finest detail. She also shows us indirectly that perfection is not required, and that if you can lean honestly into your own vulnerability and fragility, people may love you all the more for it.
- You can design your own unique charisma formula by honestly rating how you perform in each of these five areas, and committing to taking action today to improve.

CHAPTER 4: THE BEDROCK OF GOOD COMMUNICATION

- Part 1 of this book is all about the charismatic presence. How might you wish for someone to describe you, and how much does that differ from reality? And then, how do you bridge the gap between these two versions of yourself? Part 1 is more theoretical and introspective, while Part 2 is all about action. How do you actually create the type of interactions that will draw people to you, regardless of your current personality?

- Unsurprisingly, it all starts with empathy. When you have empathy, you know what other people are thinking and feeling, or at least you can make a pretty darned good guess about it. And if we know what people are thinking and feeling, we can also make a darned good guess as to what they want. And that's what will allow us to create charismatic interactions.
- The first is to simply read more. This is probably the best practice you can do without having someone in front of you, because it forces you to inhabit someone else's perspective and inner dialogue. You can see in the story that because X happened, Y and Z might happen. This seems simple, but it is not easy to practice in daily life. Having an experience filter is very similar, in that it forces you to step out of your perspective (which is necessarily limited) and really try to see someone else's. It might sound like we are only talking about empathy here, but the truth is that empathy and charisma are extremely, extremely related. Yes, deliberately practicing theory of mind is also more in the same direction of understanding another person's thoughts and emotions.
- Finally, understanding the difference between facts and interpretation will help you know what you should respond to. Almost always, you should be trying to respond to people's interpretation because their emotions are buried within, and that's what will draw people to you.

CHAPTER 5: ENGAGING FULLY

- In order to interact and engage more fully in conversations, we need to work against our not-so-useful habits and learn better ones.
- A non-negotiable habit is becoming a master at using questions. The right questions help people feel closer to us, communicate our attention and care, share our competence, show that we're aware and paying attention, deepen intimacy, guide the conversation, and make us more trustworthy.
- All exchanges, and hence all questions, are typically on one of three possible levels: those exchanging factual information, those exchanging feelings and emotions, and those communicating deeper values. In social situations, you'll lean more heavily on the last two, but a good conversation works when people have similar conversational goals and are matched in the level they're interacting on.
- Conversational narcissism is an impediment to curiosity, engagement, and good question asking. Whether unconscious or conscious, this usually results from us placing something other than connection with the other person as our goal for conversation, i.e. to brag, to defend, to compete.
- We can reduce our own conversational narcissism by using questions. Follow-up questions are very effective, as are open-ended questions that don't make people uncomfortable, but may *gently* push on the barrier or normal etiquette.
- Just as a role model can be a guide and inspiration for your own behavior, a model can also help you stay curious when you talk to others. Talk show hosts are experts and placing their conversation partners front and center, so we can ask, what would they do? Usually, the answer is "treat my guest like the most interesting person in the whole universe."
- Curiosity needs to be genuine. We all have a bias against others sometimes, assuming they're not very interesting, but unless we ask, we won't learn about their more fascinating sides. Assume that everyone has something to teach you, and foster a genuine inquisitiveness into the details of their world. I guarantee you will not be disappointed.

Chapter 6: Subtly Charismatic

- Lightness, humor and playfulness are the life blood of good conversation, and there are ways to develop them for yourself.
- One quick technique is misdirection, where a statement has two parts: the first is expected and ordinary, the second contradicts it with unexpected and comedic results. Sarcasm can be powerful but is best when directed at yourself and used with those you are more familiar with. Ironic humor is similar to sarcasm, but more focused on the observation of the contrast between the expected and the actual.
- The world of improv has a lot to teach us about good conversational chemistry. One improv rule is not to hold on to any outcome too tightly, and be ready to follow the emerging flow of the conversation.
- Another rule is to rely on quick connections to make sure you always have something to say. This can be practiced by free associating one, two, or five words. Good improv is about having faith in the conversation's direction, and your ability to be okay with where it goes.
- The 1:1:1 method of storytelling is a mini story technique that relies on one action, summarized in one sentence, that evokes one main emotion in the listener. This keeps your stories engaging, short, and effective. Alternatively, you can ask for other people's stories.
- Conversational diversity is about having as many different tools in your toolkit as possible. Hypothetical questions are one such tool. These kinds of "what if…?" questions inject some excitement, creativity, and unpredictability, while showing something interesting about the person giving the answer.
- Finally, thinking out loud can be a way to turn monologues into dialogues. If we speak freely and without self-censoring, we break the ice, share ourselves honestly, and invite (rather than demand) others to join us.

BOOK 2: The Science of Reading People:
How to Understand What People Are Really Saying and Why

Section 1

Chapter 1: What Stops Us from Accurately Perceiving Others?

The first step to really reading a person? Pay attention!

You'd be surprised how much you can see if you only look. But by the same token, many of us don't see what is right in front of us because there is something in the way of our perception. "Perceptual barriers" interfere with our accurate perception of others. This seems obvious, but it's a point worth laboring—if you only perceive what you want to, it's as good as not perceiving at all. That means that **if you can remove bias, expectation, assumption, ego, prejudice, interpretation, judgment—in short, as much of your subjectivity as possible—then the better you will be at reading people.**

Here are some of the things you may not realize are undermining your ability to really understand other people.

Perceptual Selectivity

Simply, this is the tendency to choose certain objects from the environment while ignoring others. An individual's pre-existing beliefs, values, and needs determine which objects are focused on. Being selective means that your perception is more influenced by your own attitudes, interests, and background than by the stimulus itself. To really see what is in front of them, a person must screen out most stimuli and focus on only a few—but *how* they do this makes a world of difference.

Importantly, being selective is not a huge problem—we all do it. Rather, we need to be aware of when it's happening so we don't confuse our own conclusions with reality. For example, let's say we are in an ambiguous situation. Someone is suddenly upset. We think, "Must be that time of the month," and congratulate ourselves for being great at reading between the lines.

Can you see the problem? Your selective focus on one aspect of the situation (the person being female), combined with your own beliefs and assumptions, has led you to make a guess about someone that is probably distorted. In this case, you are more accurately perceiving your own intellectual shortcuts rather than something objectively in your environment.

Attribution

Attribution is what we do when we try to explain why people behave as they do. For example, we see a child having a tantrum and think, "He's deliberately trying to push my buttons." We've made a guess as to the cause and motivation of the behavior. It's normal to draw conclusions about the factors that influence people, or try to make meaning of their behavior. We all like to feel that the world makes a certain sense and that we can reliably predict the behavior of others. But again, in this way, our own bias may creep in and obscure what is actually happening. We are too busy seeing what we know is there that we cannot see what *is* there!

Imagine this example. You are talking to a person from Japan. They have made a mistake. You've brought it to their attention, and now they are grinning at you and nodding furiously. If you did this yourself, it would mean one thing only: You didn't take the situation seriously and were even laughing rudely at the other person. So you ask yourself the question, "Why are they behaving this way?" But you answer the question as though you were answering for *yourself*: "Because they don't take this seriously." In fact, it's just a cultural difference. The Japanese often smile in awkward situations in order to defuse tension—it is the opposite of rudeness!

Stereotyping

That is, judging someone based on what you think about the group to which they belong. It is a basic human trait to see a person as part of a single group or class, and then to give that person positive or negative traits based on what most people think about that group as a whole. It's one of the ways we simplify our world and make it easier to understand. It's also a surefire way to distort our perception of how people actually are— and they're usually a lot more complex than stereotypes would suggest.

Have you ever been really surprised to learn that a person you thought you knew was actually quite different from what you first thought? It's a great opportunity to ask why your expectations were so subverted. **Stereotypes don't have to be full-blown prejudices to distort perception**. In fact, our perception can be most disturbed by those assumptions we have that are usually true. For example, a drug-trafficking operation could work precisely because it employs the help of unassuming elderly women to transport packages. The stereotype that little old ladies don't smuggle heroin is pretty accurate—but believing it will allow you to miss the truth.

The Halo Effect

Speaking of little old ladies, **the "halo effect" is the tendency to judge people based on a single trait, whether that trait is good or bad**. The halo effect is very similar to stereotyping. However, in stereotyping, a person is judged by the group they belong to, while with the halo effect, they are judged by a single trait they possess.

We sometimes judge a person based on the first thing we see or hear about them. For instance, if someone is kind, they may also be seen as trustworthy, competent, hardworking, and so on. If someone is beautiful, we might wrongly assume that they are also healthy or intelligent, or if rich we might imagine they are materialistic or have good taste. We might see a tech billionaire with an interest in economics, politics, or social issues, and wrongly assume that if they possess a certain business acumen, they must somehow also be adept in other areas.

In real life and with real people, these traits sometimes go together, and sometimes they don't. A celebrity may have something relevant to share about animal rights or the best diet for children, but they may also be just as ignorant as the next person. By the same token, there is nothing to say that a doctor who goes to prison for assault suddenly knows any less about medicine than he did before (let's call it a "devil horns" effect!) or that people who are color blind can't be good artists. In either case, if we take one observation and over-extrapolate it, we stop perceiving what is actually happening in front of us.

Projection

Sometimes, we perceive not what somebody is, but what *we* are—we project onto them the same way a film projector puts its image onto a screen. This idea originally comes from the theories of Carl Jung, who explained how people might disidentify with some unwanted traits, and then seem to discover them in other people.

But projection doesn't have to be a serious psychological phenomenon involving shadows and unconscious material. Sometimes it simply occurs because **people lazily assume that others are more like themselves than they really are**.

Have you ever been surprised to find that someone you knew actually had very different religious or political opinions than you originally believed? You might have enjoyed their company and simply assumed that what they thought was the same as what you thought. So there is some stimulus in the environment and you wrongly assume what their response will be. Or you observe some behavior in them and automatically conclude a cause for this behavior that is more accurately a cause for *your* behavior, not theirs.

Perceptual Set

A perceptual set is a group of beliefs about how others see and understand certain situations. For example, a manager may come to believe and act as if workers are lazy and just want to get as much as they can from the organization without giving their best. This is a mix of different assumptions, preconceptions, and ideas—it's a set. Another example is when a family has a perceptual set for one child that includes a whole narrative about them being special, unique, and precious, while the perceptual set for the other child revolves around their being difficult and troubled.

You can tell a perceptual set is in play because it tends to distort neutral stimuli so that it fits the set, rather than realizing that the set is inaccurate. For example, the "black sheep" described in the family above may often behave in intelligent, kind, and unexpected ways, but this behavior will be interpreted so that it *always supports the pre-existing perceptual set*. The parents might perceive this behavior, but say, "Every once in a while, he does stunts like this just to show off. He's always been egotistical like that. He's just looking for attention, as usual."

Implicit Personality Theory

When judging and making assumptions about other people, a person's thoughts are affected by **how he thinks certain human traits are linked to each other**. This is something you might never have given a second thought—but can you be sure that the "rules" you assume control the way personality traits cluster are actually accurate?

Later, we'll see that personality theories have been a perennial fascination for social theorists, psychologists, and lay people-readers since time began. But an *implicit* personality theory is the (often unexamined, unconscious, and inaccurate) model of what personalities are and how they are formed.

For example, hard work is often linked to being honest. People think that anyone who works hard must be honest. Have you ever made this implicit association? If someone told you that someone at work had been stealing petty cash, wouldn't you tend to suspect the lazier members of the team over the workaholics and "Type A" people? It's because you're working with a model that assumes the traits go together.

But if you examine this association, you'll see that there's no reason at all that one implies the other. If you don't believe it's possible for someone to share *both* traits, or neither, then you stop being able to accurately perceive that person when they cross your path.

Expectancy

Expectation is the tendency to see people, things, and events based on how we thought they would be in the first place. Imagine you're about to be introduced to someone you are told is a priest. You know very little about priests and have no experience with them, but you immediately start assuming things: They're stern, maybe a bit of a killjoy, upright, softly spoken, middle-aged, kind of boring, morally superior, compassionate, or perhaps they are hiding a terrible secret.

When you actually meet the priest, your expectations mean you are unconsciously looking for confirmation of all this. You discount all the things that don't line up with the picture you already have in your head. The things that do line up, you focus on and even encourage. This situation is why this is sometimes also called a "self-fulfilling prophecy."

Let's say you believe that priests are all compassionate and non-judgmental. When you meet, you start confessing all your personal troubles. The priest sees that someone needs his attention, and politely gives it. You think, "See? Priests are compassionate." However, if you hadn't led the priest down that path by confessing so much, you might have discovered that he would have preferred to talk about Formula One racing.

Perceptual Defense

One final thing to consider is that **we may not be able to accurately perceive people simply because what they are or what they are saying are actually too threatening to acknowledge fully.** Here, "threatening" can encompass a broad range of ideas. It can mean subtle but culturally unacceptable ideas that your mind unconsciously chooses not to see. Have you ever noticed that some people can be very obviously gay, and yet many people around them seem oblivious to the fact? Their eyes work; it's just that they don't really want to see!

It can go the other way, too. If someone is very anxious and suspicious, anything their partner does may be perceived as strange and troubling. In the first example, the defense is not to perceive fully; in the second example, the defense is to see things that aren't actually there. In both cases, the perception is not accurate. A little perceptual defense is only human, and sometimes it's necessary. For example, we don't tell little kids that it's impossible for them to become astronauts—a little modification of a harsh truth is sometimes necessary!

Improving Your Perceptual Accuracy

As you can see, one thing continually gets in the way of accurate perception: ourselves! **All the above share something in common: We prioritize our idea about reality over reality itself.** Anytime we do this, we undermine our powers of perception. So how do we get better?

1. **Know thyself**

Knowing who you are is a powerful way to avoid perceptual distortions. It lets you know what is *your* stuff, and what is *their* stuff. What values, beliefs, and blind spots do you bring to the table? To be a good people-reader, you don't have to completely remove these blind spots—you just need to be honest about the fact that they are there.

Overwhelmingly, people usually see others wrong because they don't see themselves right. The better a person knows himself, the better he can understand other people. Importantly, don't just flesh out your idea of who you *want* to be, or focus only on the good. Instead, be clear about all that other stuff, too—prejudices, fears, bad habits, and so on.

A good question to ask yourself is, what are your most recurrent personal biases and prejudices? If you say "none," then there is work to do! We all have them. Know what yours are. For example, if you are aware that you tend to assume that everyone is less intelligent than you are, be honest about how this skews your perception. What can you routinely do to offset this tendency?

2. Cultivate empathy

We tend to think of empathy and kindness as more or less the same thing. But empathy has a perceptual and cognitive component. It means not merely caring about how others feel, but actually understanding it and being able to perceive it. After all, how can you care and be kind if you don't even know what is happening, or why?

Empathy is a natural trait, but it's also a skill one can develop over time with the help of a good feedback system and genuine interactions with others. Don't simply assume you are already empathetic enough. Constantly check that your perceptions about others are actually true—or else you risk becoming one of those people who crows about being an "empath" but who really, really isn't!

Something to try: Get into the habit of *asking, not assuming*. For example, if you're worried one day that you've offended someone, don't just take it as a given that you have. Don't just assume that your guess about their inner perception is 100 percent accurate. Confirm your reading of the situation by asking them. Empathy is not all about mind-reading—sometimes good old-fashioned communication leads to far more understanding!

3. Be positive

Perceptions are strongly and long-lastingly affected by how people feel. When we have a bad opinion of someone or something, our view of that person or thing will be skewed. Furthermore, if we have a bad opinion of *ourselves* or of life in general, that cannot help but color the way we see the person in front of us.

"Positive" here doesn't mean rose-colored glasses, but rather a kind of gentle, curious, open-minded optimism that is secure enough to allow us to abandon our own preferences so we can more clearly see the way things really are. It's the wholesome attitude of, "Hm, here is a new person I know nothing about. I wonder what I'm going to learn about them?"

A good habit to practice: When dealing with someone you find difficult, routinely ask yourself "What is working right now?" This will train you to see possibility, options, solutions, and avenues you hadn't considered. Be willing to learn. If someone says something that seems totally wrong, ask what is right about it. Assume there *is* something. Ask how their perspective is enriching you. Ask what you can learn from any difference between you. Ask what that potential friction could be showing you about your own limitations.

4. Postpone Impression Formation

People have a natural tendency to quickly form strong opinions about things or people. Just from one or two meetings, we can figure out what someone is like. Though this is an understandable part of human nature, we often sacrifice accuracy for speed and ease. But just remind yourself of how annoying it is to be pigeon-holed by others based on just one or two of your traits. **Deliberately make the effort to just *wait*—you don't have to form an opinion about everything!** Let people show you who they are. It takes time.

Here's a great habit to cultivate: Change statements to questions. This will keep you curious and open-minded and will improve your perception. The moment you form a conclusion about someone, your perception is out of the game and you go into *assumption* instead! For example, notice yourself wanting to say "She's a snob," and turn it into a question. "Is she a snob?" This simple shift allows you to notice the possibility that you could interpret her behavior in some other way. It helps you notice what is happening, rather than you focusing on your premature *theory* about what is happening.

5. **Practice open communication**

Many misunderstandings are caused by poor or one-way communication. Or, let's be honest, a complete lack of communication. A whole world of perceptual distortions can appear in a conversation if we are not conscious of how we send and receive information.

One good idea: don't ask leading questions. Instead, ask with a genuinely open and curious mind and truly listen to what you're told. Imagine that you are not asking questions to confirm or disprove a running hypothesis, but are genuinely wanting to learn something . . . and perhaps even be surprised.

To run with the previous example, you might ask the woman who always insists on wearing cashmere, wool, and silk to tell you more about why she does this. You learn that she's not a snob at all, but has a skin allergy that makes wearing synthetic fabrics impossible.

6. **Verify your perceptions by comparing them with others**

One way to reduce perceptual errors is to compare how you see something to how someone else sees it. You may have already done this in the past and were shocked at the discrepancy! By talking about how we see things, we learn about different points of view and may be able to understand the situation much better.

That said, comparing our perceptions with others doesn't mean they're right and we're wrong; rather, it's an exercise in perspective taking. In the same way that certain colors tend to change depending on what colors they appear next to, comparison can bring to light certain assumptions we didn't know we were making.

Chapter 2: The Art of Perspective Taking

Perspective taking is the ability to imagine another person's psychological viewpoint. When we are very young children, we actually don't know how to do this—it is a human skill that needs to be learned like any other. It requires stepping outside one's self-centeredness to genuinely see things from another's perspective. Not see that person's situation through your own eyes, but see their situation as *they* would see it, through their eyes.

Empathy is about imagining what a person perceives, thinks, and feels as themselves. Perspective taking naturally leads to imagining what another person would *do*. We can predict their behavior because we more thoroughly understand their motivations. **"Theory of mind" is the ability to imagine someone else's mental state, even if it differs from our own.**

The fashion designer Oscar de la Renta is said to have once advised women: "Walk like there are three men walking behind you." From his point of view, he imagined what it was like to be a woman and concluded that if there were three men walking behind you, you would probably walk in a sexier way. But women were quick to point out that when they heard this advice, they were confused. If three men were walking behind them, they said, they might not be feeling sexy but cautious and alert. They'd walk faster or even cross to the other side of the road.

De la Renta illustrates here a common blind spot—he was not imagining what it would be like to be a woman, but rather imagining what it would be like for him, as a man, to be a woman... big difference! Perhaps he had seen women in the street, thought they were sexy, then concluded that this experience of them as sexy was identical to what they were experiencing. His perception on the entire thing was distorted. He was unable to genuinely abandon his perspective and take up another.

Everybody *thinks* they have empathy, the ability to perspective-switch and find true understanding, but in truth they seldom do. Our insistence that we can properly see others actually prevents us from doing so! But here are some ways to sincerely practice walking in another person's shoes—and not in the way that Oscar de la Renta does!

Tip 1: Watch a movie or TV show

Getting into movies or TV shows is a great way to learn how to see things from other people's points of view. Many believe reading fiction helps you really get into other people's feelings and see events from their points of view, but the same thing can be done with film—literally you are forced to take a certain angle on a situation.

When you want to see something from someone else's point of view, pick a movie or TV show and choose a character's point of view. You can even begin with a character who reminds you of yourself. As you get better at putting yourself in other people's shoes, try to ask yourself certain questions as you watch:

- What are they thinking, and why?
- Why are they behaving as they are?
- What are they trying to achieve?
- What emotions are they experiencing, and why?
- How are they explaining the situation to themselves?
- What aspects of the situation are most salient for them?

One of the problems with studying people this way is that it can be tricky to know if you've missed the mark or not. But a few questions can help you assess your reading:

- Were you able to understand the events on screen in a deeper way? In other words, could you more easily predict the ending or understand the character's choices? Did you feel like the story and the character "made sense"?
- Could you clearly see and articulate the reasons the character did what he or she did?
- Could you feel the emotions the character portrayed and point to where they came from?

Another problem is that not all film and TV is created equal. Practice this often enough and you may find your tastes changing because you more frequently spot a poorly developed character!

Tip 2: Use your (social) imagination

Imagining hypothetical situations, like one does in role-play, is another good way to think about things from different points of view. The key is to really inject yourself into different roles and fully inhabit them. Little children do this when they play with dolls, alternatively speaking for each one. Practice a similar exercise and you can develop your social imagination.

Find a picture of people engaging in a dynamic scene—look at magazines, photos, movie stills, etc. Look closely at the image and try to imagine a dramatic story to accompany it. What came before, and what will come after? What's going on and how do each of the people feel about it?

For example, if one person in the story is holding a gun, ask yourself how they feel and try to really imagine being them in that moment. Are they scared, angry? How do the other people seem to this person? What are they focusing most on in the scene? What are they trying to achieve, and how?

Now switch and inhabit the point of view of another person in the image. How does their perspective compare? What do they think of the person with the gun? As you can see, there are many layers to this—not just comprehending other people's emotions, but their assessment of the emotions of people around them, and so on. We'll explore this more deeply in the next chapter.

Tip 3: Switch perspectives in your own life

Take a moment to recall a recent misunderstanding, argument, or conflict. In the same way as you did above, try to hold a snapshot of this in your mind's eye, then deliberately switch between points of view, almost like you were changing radio stations. What does the problem look like from the other person's perspective? How do you appear to them? If you're finding this exercise difficult, don't worry—it *is* difficult! Try answering these questions to deepen your insight:

- What has objectively happened?
- What has each person focused on in this situation?
- What is everyone's motivation?
- How do you think everyone feels?
- How is each person making sense of what is going on? How do they explain it?
- What do they think about *your* role—is it accurate?
- How does each person frame the issue?

Though perspective taking is great for improving communication and helping smooth over conflict, it can be applied to improving our people-reading skills, too. The idea is that if we can fully understand *how a person sees things*, we understand more about them on a fundamental level. The reverse is true, also—if we know who they are, we can more accurately understand how things will appear to them.

Chapter 3: The Four Personality Types and "Perceptual Positions"

When trying to read and analyze people, it's human nature to simplify things and set out to understand what "kind" of person we are looking at. What category do they belong to? Centuries ago, in medieval times, people spoke about how the "humors" of the body determined personality (some people could be "choleric" or "sanguine," etc., according to the functions of their dominant organs), and in ancient Ayurveda, a person's physiological constitution also told you a lot about their attitude, intelligence, and emotions.

To this day, people continue to be captivated by the idea of what makes each of us unique—by putting us in groups with others who are similar! We also seem to be interested in where our psychological traits come from and how they're grouped, not just so we understand others better, but also so we understand ourselves.

More recently, the Myers-Briggs Type Indicator (MBTI) and the Enneagram have become the personality assessment frameworks that capture the modern desire to put people in categories. Typically, some fundamental human characteristics are identified and then combined in a matrix that yields a limited set of possible types.

One notable personality theory to understand is what's called the Big Five, or the OCEAN model. This is a long-standing framework in personality assessment that is used by psychologists the world over. A person can score high or low on each of these main factors:

Openness – Your natural curiosity and readiness to learn and experience new things.
Conscientiousness – How thoughtful, considerate, or dependable you are.
Extraversion – How outgoing, sociable, and assertive you are in social situations.
Agreeableness – Your willingness to be sympathetic, accommodating, and cooperative with other people, and your broad concern/sympathy for them.
Neuroticism – Your emotional style and the likeliness of emotional instability, mood swings, depression, loneliness, anger, or sadness.

Whichever model you use, though, the idea is that if you know a person's type, you immediately have deeper insight into what makes them tick.

But it's worth remembering that personality theories and frameworks of this kind are just that—models. That means that they are necessarily limited. We continue to propose new frameworks, however. In 2018, Northwestern University's Luis Amaral and colleagues conducted a worldwide survey. Participant data on personalities and traits were collected from all around the world using a questionnaire, and the results were synthesized in the research.

The researchers then looked at the data of more than 1.5 million people who'd taken part in personality tests, and started plotting where they scored on each of the Big Five factors. Examining the patterns in their data, they managed to identify four main personality types, i.e., the most recurrent patterns of scoring on the Big Five factors—**"average," "reserved," "self-centered," and "role model."** Their new personality types look like this:

Average
- The most common personality type
- High scores in both neuroticism and extraversion—these people tend to be more sociable and assertive, but also fairly pessimistic and oversensitive
- Low scores in openness—they're likely to be more routine-based, suspicious, conventional, and less open to abstraction
- These people tend to seek attention, but are not overly intellectually curious
- More likely to be women

Reserved
- Higher scores of agreeableness and conscientiousness—these are people who tend to be more trusting, sensitive, well-liked, and reliable
- Lower scores for both openness and neuroticism—this means they are not as open-minded and curious, but once on a path, they stay the course with confidence and reliability
- Low neuroticism also means they're more emotionally stable and get on well with others
- Somewhat extroverted, but not overly so

Role Models
- High scores in extraversion, openness, agreeableness, and conscientiousness—these are the people who tend to exhibit qualities that evoke respect and admired leadership, and which allow them to cultivate good relationships with others
- Low scores in neuroticism—they are fairly confident and brave, taking calculated risks
- High conscientiousness and openness means they are dependable and open to new ideas
- They tend to be strong leaders
- More likely to be women

Self-Centered
- High scores in extraversion—such personalities are often very socially confident, energetic, and outgoing
- Low scores in openness, agreeableness, and conscientiousness—so they may be impulsive, headstrong, bad-tempered, rude/insensitive, and fixed to their routines
- Typically a self-serving attitude at the expense of others

The findings for the above four groups were published in the journal *Nature Human Behavior*. The researchers' claim was that the four types clustered predictably in the way they ranked the five different OCEAN traits. That means that the data consistently suggested that there were four recurrent ways in which people scored on the different aspects—rather than it being completely random.

So, what does that mean for the person who wants to master their people-reading skills? Well, simple: it means that your job suddenly got a whole lot easier!

Consider an example. You meet someone for the first time, and you notice a few things about them:

- It's a woman
- She mentions interacting with her family and friends a lot (i.e., seems close to them and therefore pretty sociable and extroverted) but always in the context of some sort of drama or dilemma (i.e., pretty high on neuroticism, too)
- When you mention something she says she's never heard about before, you notice that she shows no subsequent interest in it, preferring to steer the conversation back to familiar things instead of asking questions (i.e., low openness)
- You notice her make a little joke about pretending to be ill to get out of work (i.e., potentially low or average on conscientiousness)

Now, if you looked at all the above clues and came to the conclusion that you were dealing with an "average" personality type, would it be guaranteed that you were correct? Of course not. But as the evidence mounts, your hypothesis certainly becomes stronger. You may be dealing with the sort of person who has a rare blend of scores on each of the five traits. But it's not *likely*.

The researchers who proposed these four personality types were making probability claims—they used computational methods to analyze the data of 1.5 million people, and they found stable trends. That means that their findings can help you identify the most *likely* outcome—but never with 100 percent accuracy. But these four personality types are a great starting point.

If you identify one, you can always use that as your "working model" and continue to observe in order to learn more about the person in front of you. If this woman suddenly tells you that she actually used to be a UN goodwill ambassador and that she founded her own charity, you might adjust your assessment and look for further clues that she is actually closer to the "role model" type.

As you read and observe people, you are not just coming to conclusions and piecing clues together, you are also eliminating possibilities. For example, the researchers claim that teenage boys tend to be more highly represented in the "self-centered" category, and less so in the "role model" category. If you one day meet a teenage boy who is extremely low in agreeableness, then you can find out more about who he is by seeing who he *isn't*: Being low in agreeableness rules out the "role model" and "reserved" categories, leaving only "average" or "self-centered." Let's say that, due to him being a teenage boy, you *temporarily* assume he is in the "self-centered" category. But this is only temporary—when you get more data, you can rule out either one and be left with the most likely category.

You could still be completely wrong. But you are probably closer to the truth!

The researchers for this study also point out that even though they've identified some stable patterns in personality clusters, this doesn't mean that personality itself is static—i.e., that it never changes over the course of human development. The teenager above may find that puberty makes him temporarily less agreeable and conscientious, and his youth may make him more extroverted and energetic. But, in twenty years' time, he may morph into an enviable "role model" type. Likewise, he may be far more neurotic at school, but less so at home, where he is more comfortable. His personality didn't change, exactly; it just shifted a little given the change in environment. Finally, a person may enhance or downplay certain aspects of their character simply because they are in our company. We can all imagine that a teenage boy would find himself being a little more agreeable and conscientious if he was in the company of a girl he had a crush on and wanted to impress!

We don't need to worry too much about this, however. All we can ever do is perceive the information in front of us in whatever moment we find ourselves in. The next time you are trying to read and understand a person from scratch, ask yourself a few of the following questions to narrow things down a bit:

- Are they generally high in everything except openness? They're probably **average**.
- If they're high in everything, low in openness but don't seem to be neurotic—they're probably **reserved**.
- Do they seem not very open-minded but neither extroverted nor introverted? Again **reserved**—don't let the ordinary meaning of "reserved" fool you!
- Do they appear high in everything but unusually calm, content, and stable emotionally? A clear sign they are **role models**.
- Do they seem low in everything except extraversion? Probably **self-centered**.
- Do they seem kind of average in everything? They might be **reserved** (*not* average, which scores quite high on most traits).
- Do they seem kind of volatile and emotional (awkward, cynical, fearful, unconfident, insecure, and defensive)? They're probably **average** (interesting, isn't it, that high scores on neuroticism are actually most common?).
- Not extroverted? They're likely **reserved**—the only ones who consistently score low on extraversion.
- Are they open-minded and willing to experience new things? They're **role models**—again, the only category that consistently scores high on this trait. If you see it, it's a sure sign you're talking to a role model.

One final word on these traits: despite the impression the categories may give, there are no strict "good" traits or "bad" ones. For example, if you are extremely agreeable, you might find yourself being a bit of a doormat or a people-pleaser, or having poor boundaries. Being too open to experience may make you a little naïve and open for deception and manipulation. Being too conscientious can lead to stress, guilt, or weird codependent dynamics with others (i.e., those who are extremely low on conscientiousness!). By the same token, a little "neuroticism" is great if it allows us to properly assess risk, speak our truth, and assert our healthy boundaries.

But there's another reason it's important to remember not to make value judgments when we observe and read others: We risk distorting our perception. For example, if we personally think that extroverts are kind of annoying and superficial, we might notice this in someone and develop a "perceptual set," stereotype, or expectation about them that colors everything else we perceive. If we have an unconscious preference for introversion or think that this is the "right" way to be, then we are jeopardizing our people-reading accuracy.

Perceptual Positions
Let's see if we can combine what we know about personality types with what we know about perspective taking.

The perceptual positions framework is a basic method for understanding another person's viewpoint. Perceptual positions are a form of modeling that allows us to step into somebody else's shoes, see what they see, hear what they hear, and feel what they feel.

The technique comes from NLP—neurolinguistic programing—and has plenty of uses, including defusing conflict, fostering empathy, learning more about yourself, communicating well, and, of course, reading and analyzing people more effectively. If we combine it with a good personality theory, we can rapidly learn a lot about a person.

There are three perceptual positions: the first, the second, and the third (also called the observer or meta-position). Your task is to analyze or read a situation *from these different positions*. Doing so gives you so much more information (and empathy) and brings extra dimension to the entire encounter. Importantly, you are not just thinking about the things when in any position—you are engaging *all* your senses, so that you are considering what you smell, see, touch, etc. Let's look more closely.

First Position

This is like the "I" frame. It's the world as you see it through your own perceptual filters—a natural place to start. To flesh out this position, though, consider your perceptions on all five senses and become fully associated and embodied here. You'd be surprised at just how much you can learn about others in a situation when you more clearly understand where *you* are in the interaction.

Second Position

Also thought of as "the other" position. It's the ability to see the same situation that is seen by the person in the first position, but through their personal filters. This is a natural place to be for therapists and coaches, but also salespeople and those trying to persuade or motivate. Here, we are not associated, but dissociated and imagining someone else's perceptions.

Third Position

This is where we see the world through the "observer" filter, like a fly on the wall observing the interaction from outside the interaction. We are objective here and pass no judgment. This position is not actually involved in the unfolding story—i.e., the bigger but more neutral perspective. We are not associated or dissociated, but entirely independent.

Now, all this may seem pretty abstract until it's taken and put into context. It's nothing more complicated than a way to switch lenses as you view reality. Let's look at an example to show how the model can be applied.

Step 1

Think about a situation, problem, or conversation. Look at this situation from your own point of view. Flesh out your perspective and associate with it fully, on all five senses. It can be useful to describe the entire experience in one word.

For example, you are having an issue with a brother—you have invited him to stay, he's invited a friend you neither know well nor particularly like, and now things are awkward. You begin by fully inhabiting your own perspective: You see the intrusion of this unexpected person, feel an obligation to play host, but definitely realize that you'd prefer that the friend weren't there. One word: put upon (Okay, that's two words, but you get the picture).

Step 2

Look at the very same situation but from someone else's viewpoint. Do this *as them*—not as yourself imagining them. Big difference! If you were talking to a child, for example, and you were taking the second position and imagining their perception, literally picture what it's like to be small and look up at a taller adult—you. Find a single word to describe the experience from this perspective too.

In our example, you might do this both for your brother's point of view and for their friend. You do this as fully and genuinely as you can. In your brother's shoes, you feel fine—you like this person, so why wouldn't other people?

You are happy to see your brother, and you're relieved you get to have a friend nearby to keep you company (yup, you're feeling a little anxious and need backup!). One word: cautious. From the friend's point of view, you feel kind of nervous but unsure. You're happy to be with your friend but know nothing about his brother. You're there to give moral support, but the last thing you want to do is cause any trouble. One word: supportive.

Step 3

Now imagine that you are the independent, neutral third-party observer outside of this situation, and see what you perceive. Notice how the behaviors of all parties interact and compare with one another. Notice the overall atmosphere, energy, outcome. Pick one word to describe it.

In this example, you see that a simple miscommunication is unfolding. One brother assumed the meeting would be just the two of them. The other didn't, and brought along a friend for company, not realizing it would create awkwardness. One word: mismatch.

Step 4

Now is the time to reflect. Go back to second position and look again at the facts, seeing if anything has changed. Finish by returning to first position, your perspective, and see if anything has changed there. Is there any new information you possess? New insight?

You can probably already see the value of this perspective switching. If you had merely stayed in first position, you would have dwelt on the inconvenience you felt, and even felt hurt. But by changing positions, you can appreciate that no hurt was intended, and what things look like from both your brother and his friend's point of view. Can you see how this approach will lead you to behave completely differently from the way you might have without switching perspectives?

As you can see, the above technique is a brilliant way to generate real empathy for people and situations and figure out how to really connect and communicate with them. But we can also use this approach when we are trying to more deeply understand the world they live in and their frame of mind within that world—i.e., it's a powerful tool for analyzing people, too.

Let's say you notice your brother bringing along a friend. What does this say about him or the friend? If you can put aside your own perceptual position for a moment, you allow yourself the opportunity to read these actions rather than simply react to them from your own limited position.

Depending on the rest of the context, you may determine a world of information about your brother's discomfort with intimacy, the friendship between him and his friend, and even the friend and his level of conscientiousness or openness. Gradually, you start to develop a working model of other people's personality and position, which are constantly interrelated. It's wonderful to think that, with the right mindset, conflict and misunderstanding are actually nothing more than fascinating data points to feed into the big people-reading machine!

Summary:

- If you can remove bias, expectation, assumption, ego, prejudice, interpretation, and judgment, the better you will be at reading people.
- Distortions and biases (what we think we see) can get in the way of actually seeing. These biases include perceptual selectivity, attribution errors, stereotyping, the halo effect, projection or assuming others are just like us, holding a "perceptual set," using implicit personality theories, expectation, and perceptual defense that causes us to deny or distort what we are seeing if it's perceived as a threat.
- To improve your perceptual accuracy, work hard to know yourself and then cultivate genuine empathy for others; confirm your perceptions are true and compare them against others'; be curious, open-minded, and non-judgmental; ask open-ended questions; and delay forming an opinion about people.
- Perspective taking is the ability to imagine another person's psychological viewpoint—not their life through our eyes, but their life through their eyes. Some ways to cultivate this skill include trying to understand the perspectives of characters in film and literature. You can also practice switching perspectives to gain insight into conflicts or relationships and understand other people's roles.
- The perceptual positions framework is a basic method for understanding another person's viewpoint. There are three—first, second, and third—and switching between them allows you a richer and more dynamic insight into any situation.
- Personality categories can help us simplify human behavior. One notable theory is the Big Five, or the OCEAN model, which rates people on openness to experience, conscientiousness, extraversion, agreeableness, and neuroticism. Luis Amaral and colleagues have suggested four personality types based on how the Big Five traits usually cluster: "average," "reserved," "self-centered," and "role model."

Section 2

Chapter 4: The Four Functions of Behavior

In the previous chapter, we set about trying to understand what people are like—are they open-minded or more uncurious? Are they "neurotic" or more emotionally even? But what you might notice from this model is that it is not dynamic in any way—it's about what people *are*, not what they *do*.

Especially as outsiders looking in, **we can gain real insights into people's characters by observing their behavior, their choices, and the way they behave.** After all, how do we know that someone is conscientious? We look at their behavior. Someone who merely felt they were conscientious in some vague internal way wouldn't quite make the grade!

In the previous model, we observed behavior and made some inferences about what that means for the person acting that way. For example, we see them talking loudly and animatedly to a big group of people and conclude they are extroverted. In this chapter, we'll consider a model of human behavior that approaches things from the other direction. It asks:

1. How are people behaving?
2. *Why* are they behaving that way (and why do they keep behaving that way)?

This theoretical shift is about seeing personality as a **functional** quality—i.e., as something that we have because it's useful to us in some way. **Understand the function that certain behaviors serve for a person, and you understand who they are**. But before we leap into an explanation of the "four functions," let's take a moment to understand exactly what we're trying to achieve.

Imagine you see a person at a party who is laughing and talking loudly with a big group of people, regaling them with stories. What does it mean? Well, we could say it's proof that the person is outgoing and gregarious, or that they enjoy people. We might get carried away telling ourselves a complicated story about why that person is this way, what it means, and so on . . . but the story may be completely biased. That's because we don't really know what is going on in the head of the person we're observing.

How on earth could we measure their internal state at that moment? We might say "they're extroverted," but the person might actually be acting this way because they're nervous in social situations, and the only way they can reduce that anxiety is to fiercely control the situation—i.e., by dominating socially. They're not extroverts at all; their coping mechanism just makes it look that way!

This explains why some theorists have argued for the use of a "functional behavioral analysis" (FBA) instead of merely telling stories about observed external behavior. **FBA is about formulating a theory about the functional relationship between a person's behavior and their environment.** It's not about the static, standalone personality traits but about how that person responds to stimuli in their environment. One way to think about this is to imagine a trait like extraversion. Can one stand alone, by themselves, and *be* extroverted? No! Extraversion is something you *do*, and it's a dynamic response to the environment—which in this case also includes other people.

In the previous model, we assumed that people behave the way they do because that's just the way they are. But with this model, people behave the way they do because something in the environment instigates and supports that action. In fact, every time their action is supported this way, it's reinforced—no personality required, just habit!

While personality assessments and profiles might be useful when you're working on your own personal development and self-awareness, it can be tricky when trying to apply to other people because we cannot see into their heads. What we can do, though, is observe the behavior and its environment.

Let's imagine that there are **four functions of behavior**—access, escape, attention, and sensory.

Access – This includes mainly tangible things—items you can literally see and interact with via your five senses.

Attention – This is an interaction, praise, or any kind of feedback or signal from others. This could be anything from a slight increase in awareness and attention from other people to a full-blown reaction from them, or even their subsequent actions and conversations.

Escape – This is about removing an unpleasant item, event, or stimulus from the situation—especially one that has been previously punished and discouraged. An obvious example is the behavior of pulling your hand away from a hot fire. A less obvious example is turning down invitations from people who make you feel bad in subtle ways.

Sensory – This function has no connection to outside factors at all, but rather refers to internal rewards within the body itself. The pleasure of a hug, for example, or the satisfaction of having solved a difficult puzzle.

Furthermore, we can take note of:
1. The antecedent (what comes before the behavior)
2. The behavior (what the behavior is)
3. The consequence or outcome (what the new situation was after the behavior occurred)

Setting things out this way, we can see that behavior can be rewarded or punished, i.e., reinforced or discouraged. Behavior always has an effect on the environment—after all, that's why we do it! Understand all this, and you gain a deeper, functional awareness not just of the person or of the environment, but of their interactive relationship.

All behaviors follow the A-B-C shape, but they will each be maintained by different functions—or a combination of functions. Returning to our example, we can imagine that someone might choose to behave in a gregarious and extroverted way because the behavior serves two broad functions:

1. Escape – taking charge of social situations allows them to escape the anxiety that comes from other people potentially asking intrusive questions, steering the conversation, or making a big deal out of noticing that they are quiet and putting them on the spot.
2. Attention – When this person behaves in this way, people tend to respond in predictable and comfortable ways. The attention they give is a lot easier to deal with than the awkwardness of being asked, "Why are you so quiet?" all the time.

Is the above person extroverted? Yes, in a way. But using functional behavioral analysis allows you to understand the **why** and **how** of the behavior, not merely **what**. Many standup comedians and famous entertainers surprise their fans when they claim to be deeply insecure, private, or introverted individuals. That's because, just as in this example, those fans were only looking at the behavior and not considering what this behavior meant and *why* it was being used.

Let's zoom out and think about how we can use the insights from this kind of behavioral analysis to improve our people-reading skills. The principles are as follows:

- Every action has a reason for happening, so ask yourself what the reward or positive outcome is to see why it's in that person's interest to keep behaving that way. This tells you a lot about them.
- We behave because of how that behavior feels, because of the response we get from our environment, because it gets us something we want, or because it helps us to get away from something we don't want. Try to understand the function of the behavior you're looking at and you will instantly understand it better.
- Personality theories can only go so far. Certain behaviors may be identical in two people who are nevertheless behaving that way for completely different reasons. That's why you shouldn't consider people in a vacuum or separate their behavior from their environment.

How to Read People Using the ABC Model
Step 1: Identify the behavior

First, just take note of what you're looking at and try to see it without telling any stories about it or making any assumptions—or else self-confirmation bias will creep in. So, instead of noting that "he's extroverted," just note the behavior: "he is talking more loudly and more often than anybody else. He is steering the conversation. He is positioning himself in the center of the group . . ."

Step 2: Collect data to help you establish the antecedent and consequence of this behavior

Now, in our example, if you had never met the person before, you would have much less data to work with. But if you knew them, you could gather plenty of data and combine it with what you know about their behavior at all parties or with other people in general. You could notice how people respond to the loud, excited talking and storytelling. You might notice that the more stressful the situation, the more animated this person becomes. You could even notice that a few years ago, this person was quieter, and people responded to him differently back then.

Step 3: Infer the function of the behavior

Now you put all this data together and make an educated guess about *why* this pattern exists. You could even make a hypothesis and test it. Your hypothesis could be "he behaves in an outgoing and extroverted way so he can cope with and control anxiety-provoking situations." Maybe you decide to test this by seeing how he behaves in less stressful situations, or with smaller groups. You might combine all your guesses with other observations and come to the same conclusion about how the behavior is functioning.

The ABC model is often used by counselors and psychologists to help people get a handle on their own (maladaptive) behaviors. But understanding what triggers and what sustains unwanted behaviors, they give themselves the chance to change things. But you can also use the model in a more open-ended way—**by observing any one of the three components, you can make guesses about the other components, as well as gain insight into the person making those choices.**

Here are a few more common and straightforward examples to show how you can begin using functional behavioral analysis yourself when observing and reading others.

Example 1:

A five-year-old is cheeky and frequently interrupts the adults' conversation.

Antecedent: The adults are not paying her any attention.

Behavior: She does something silly or butts into the conversation.

Consequence: The adults laugh and smile and say things like, "She's such a little character, isn't she?"

Your hypothesis for the function of this behavior: **attention**. The five-year-old reliably wins praise and positive attention from the adults when behaving this way.

Example 2:

Joe is meant to be coming out with you for an early morning run, but instead he's at home in bed, snoozing.

Antecedent: He stayed up late the night before. He's currently in a lovely warm bed.

Behavior: He . . . continues to stay in the lovely warm bed instead of waking up to go run outside in the cold.

Consequence: His running mates are annoyed with him. But also, he gets to stay a few more hours in the lovely warm bed.

Your hypothesis for the function of the behavior: **sensory**. It's not rocket science. Joe is doing what he is doing because it feels good.

Example 3:

Nicky does come along with you on the run that day. In fact, she seems completely jazzed up and ready to go.

Antecedent: Nicky has been having marriage difficulties with Joe, and the two can barely stand to be in the house together these days.

Behavior: She started the running group herself and has worked hard to motivate everyone to the cause.

Consequence: She is grinning from ear to ear after the run, and as soon as it's over, she starts talking about tomorrow's run.

Your hypothesis for the function of the behavior: **escape**. Nicky might want to literally escape her bad marriage, but the running may also serve as a way to escape feelings of frustration, helplessness, and anger, and to give her a sense of purpose when life feels difficult.

If you had only relied on static personality analysis for any of the above examples, you would not have grasped the full situation. That's because it might be the case that the five-year-old is not especially outgoing, Joe is not lazier than average, and Nicky is not a particularly energetic or motivated person, either. Rather, each of their actions is a direct result of their interaction with the environment—and not with their abstract personality or character.

If you've ever found it difficult to read people because they tend *not* to follow patterns, this could be why. **All of us will act against our normal baseline or in ways we're not accustomed to if it serves our purposes in any particular moment.** That's why we need to consider not just the person in front of us or their behavior, but how they and their behavior are embedded into the environment. If we bump into Nicky five years later and she tells us she never kept up her running routine, we won't be too surprised to also hear that she has gotten divorced!

Even in cases where you don't know people well and cannot guess at what came before or what will happen later, you can still get a handle on their behavior by asking what function it serves. Begin by assuming that **people make sense—they behave as they do because, in some way or another, it's working for them**. Yes, even those behaviors that seem completely self-destructive or illogical!

Imagine you have a colleague at work who constantly second-guesses you and checks your work. You do the "perceptual positions" exercise described in the previous chapter, but you're still having a hard time empathizing, and you're beginning to get annoyed. Start by assuming that in his own way, your colleague's behavior makes perfect sense to him, even if not to you. All you have to do is figure out what is triggering that behavior and what is maintaining it. Not only will this give you some insight into what's going on, it might hint at a possible way out of the dynamic once and for all.

Antecedent – You are your colleague's superior, so you're often given more challenging or complex jobs. You also know this colleague would like to advance in their role someday but is new at the company and finding it challenging to distinguish themselves.

Behavior – They stick their nose into your tasks, offering their "help" and "advice" even when it isn't requested.

Consequence – When the task is finished, you typically submit it and get the praise, satisfaction, or reward that comes with it. You also notice that the colleague tends to hover around when you're receiving feedback on these tasks, and once or twice has said, "We did a good job!"

Are you beginning to get a sense of the function of this behavior? It may be a question of **attention**. When behaving this way, your colleague gets to indirectly participate in feelings of having done good work on a job that he does not strictly have access to. This might satisfy a whole host of his needs, such as feeling relevant or convincing himself that he is learning and advancing, even if his actual job title doesn't reflect it.

Two things emerge from this analysis. First, you realize that this colleague must be feeling some sort of insecurity about his position and is perhaps frustrated in his work. Is he struggling to get promoted? Does he not feel recognized in his own tasks, or are they not challenging enough? Second, you start to see a solution to your problem (or a way to test your hypothesis). You simply ask your boss to deliver feedback to you privately. If your theory is correct, the colleague will soon stop the behavior because there will no longer be the same consequence reinforcing it.

Let's say you do receive private feedback . . . and the behavior continues. Now what? You throw away your hypothesis and make a new one. Could there be a more internal sense of satisfaction that is driving this person (i.e., a sensory function)? Could they perhaps be trying to impress you directly (attention function, but in a different way than you first thought)? Either way, you are closer to understanding their real motivations than if you merely looked at the problem through the "personality type" lens.

Chapter 5: Learning to Read Emotions

Let's change gear once more and consider another rich and nuanced channel of data that we can mine when we observe our fellow humans: emotions.

Nonverbal communication and expression provide us a world of information about a person. What's more, emotion and behavior are linked. Everything we do that's visible is behavior—and that also includes things like facial expressions, gestures, tone of voice, and body posture. Learning to read body language is kind of like learning to read the behavioral component of emotion—our physical attitude in the world is an expression of our internal emotional state.

Now, this may seem like a very obvious point to labor. Is it really so earth-shattering to suggest that people's emotions influence their behavior? Well, yes, when we consider how often we all ignore this kind of information in favor of listening to the words people say, or simply assuming that what they think and feel is more or less the same as what we think and feel. Never underestimate the power of bias and assumption to spoil the most obvious observations!

The great thing about reading body language is that it reveals emotions in a spontaneous, unconscious, and unintentional way—that means you can trust it. And it also means that if what you observe in someone's nonverbal expression differs from what they're communicating verbally, you can read this mismatch itself as a point of interest. It can reveal deception, ambivalence, or a desire to conceal, among other things. Again, context matters; if someone sees something funny during a funeral but does their best to keep a straight face anyway, this is obviously not a question of deception but plain etiquette.

One way to think about body language and emotions is to imagine that human beings only ever express themselves on a single broad continuum, which you can understand loosely as **open or closed**. Broad, expansive gestures suggest confidence, excitement, happiness, trust. Compacted, tight, tense, retreating, and cowering postures suggest disgust, fear, sadness, and so on. Simply being aware of the patterns of relaxation and tenseness in people will already clue you in to the more subtle emotions they may be feeling.

In fact, some theorists (Schutz, 1958) go so far as to suggest that persistent patterns of psychological tension or relaxation actually settle and calcify in the body. So, the person who is constantly angry, critical, or suspicious ends up earning a literal line across their forehead or between their eyes—sustained emotion, in other words, can become a fixed part of the physical body. Think about that next time you see someone who is chronically stooped in posture, has an eternally tight neck and shoulder muscles, or has a face full of smile lines.

Let's take a look at some common behaviors that are expressions not of people's behaviors or personalities, but of how they are feeling in that moment.

Withdrawal, fidgeting, and plenty of small, unnecessary movements suggest **inhibition and anxiety**.

Slow, sparing movements that lack energy and don't seem designed to reach out or connect in any way suggest **depression or exhaustion**.

Fast, expensive, spontaneous, energetic movements and plenty of assertive, confident, and even affected (i.e., almost faked) gestures suggest **elation, joy, self-assuredness**.

Fiddling with hair and skin, wrangling and twisting hands over themselves or holding them in tight fists, or plucking at clothing, eyebrows or objects suggest **stress, repressed anger, or irritation.**

A bent and collapsed body, a slight pout, angled shoulders, and a general vibe of slouching suggests **sadness, defeat, and worry**.

Recoiling slightly, lifting the upper lip, wrinkling the nose, and raising the shoulders suggest **disgust or fear**.

Of course, all of this is relative and context dependent. Wringing your hands and shaking your head at a ball game is totally different from at someone's death bed. One clever trick for reading facial and body expressions is simply to try mimicking the gesture yourself and seeing what emotion it invokes. Try it right now: Gently touch the fingers of both hands to your lips, raise your eyebrows, and let your mouth open a little. What emotion do you feel? If you said "surprise" or even shock or horror, then congratulations, you may be more emotionally literate than you think!

Cultivating "Emotional Granularity"

Pretty much everyone knows that someone who is screaming and holding their hands to either side of their face is probably terrified. But to be masterful at people-reading, you need a little more nuance, i.e., you **need to have a broad and deep knowledge of many different shades of emotion, plus the ability to distinguish between them.**

The trick is that being able to read all the subtleties of emotion in other people requires us to be fairly emotionally literate ourselves. It's about going further than "sadness," and learning to identify the rich palette of emotions that include despair, apathy, misery, resentment, sorrow, grief, disappointment, uneasiness, dismay, anguish, cynicism, or gloom . . .

It's true that some people are simply better equipped to understand emotions, but that absolutely does not mean it's something that can't be learned. What's more, the real skill comes in learning to interpret certain expressions and gestures in context. For example, we saw above that someone behaving in an outgoing and extroverted way doesn't mean that this is simply their personality. Rather, in that example, it was a coping mechanism that served a particular function. Similarly, a smile doesn't always mean happiness, and tears don't always mean sadness. But, noticing these things adds one more data point and, taken together with all your other observations, brings you one step closer to understanding people.

Here are a few ways to train your emotional granularity and expand your emotional vocabulary:

- Read or listen to thought-proving content that uses specific terms to describe feelings. Keep track of your own responses to various stimuli, both verbal and nonverbal.
- Learn the differences between similar words. You might know that there is a subtle difference but wouldn't know how to pinpoint it when you experience it. One surprising way to do this is to try new and unusual foods. Have you ever noticed how rich the vocabulary is for describing wine? It's the same skill!
- Research words in other languages that could apply to the way you feel right now. By learning new words, you can give your brain more options for predicting and perceiving emotions.
- Think of emotions as occurring on a continuum. If one day you feel, say, bored, try to imagine what that feeling would be if you dialed it up one notch, then another. It might turn into "frustration" or even, at the very high end, something like "resentment." Can you discern the difference all along the scale?
- Make friends with a thesaurus. It seems strange, but looking at synonyms for emotions in a thesaurus can give a finer grasp on the subtle differences. Let's say you're talking to someone one day, and then pause to try to put a word to their emotion. You choose "pensive." You see that some synonyms include "thoughtful" and "contemplative." This is true, but you also sense a certain distraction in the person. You search around further and settle on different words like "distant" and "detached." Just by fleshing out the various possible adjectives, you're getting a deeper sense of a person's experience—while improving your vocabulary!
- Finally, read fiction and watch movies. Pick a character and challenge yourself to describe how they feel in five words. See if you can track that character's emotions as the story develops.

The Real Way to Read Body Language
Gestures are the body's "emotions."

It makes good sense to look to the body any time you want to understand what someone is feeling. However, most body language advice out there is very one-dimensional. You may see it claimed that if a woman plays with her hair, for example, she is being flirty, or if someone crosses their arms, it means they're standoffish or stubborn.

But if we're using the "X always means Y" approach to reading body language, we won't get very far. The woman may be nervous and distracted; someone may cross their arms because they're cold or trying to hide a stain on their shirt. In other words, it's not that these observations are *wrong*, just that they only really "mean" anything when considered as part of a more complex whole.

You are never merely reading an individual, but reading that individual's behavior and orientation within their environment. A few easy examples: if someone is sitting with their legs sprawled wide on the chair and their belly hanging out, it means two very different things if they behave that way alone in their own living rooms, or on a subway train crowded with people. Looking at your watch when you're standing waiting for the bus means one thing, but a totally different thing when you do it seated at a restaurant with a date. Frowning denotes one thing when you do it during a difficult exam, and another thing when you're listening to someone ask you a big favor. Basically, what a thing ever "means" depends heavily on who is doing it, when, how, and where.

So, just as we considered functional behavior a more illuminating thing to observe than static character traits, let's think about expression and gesture as contextual. Here are a few questions to ask to help you gain more insight into the nonverbal expressions you observe in others.

How does their expression compare to everyone else's?

In a group social setting, notice a person's expression relative to the consensus group expression. Is someone talking much louder than everyone else, adopting a posture much more subdued, dressed in a very different manner, or speaking in a way that doesn't match or mirror those around them? Pay attention to any discrepancies of this kind because they will tell you a lot about what is going on with that person.

Combine your observations with any insights about the function of their behavior. For example, if someone is being way more polite and deferential than everyone else and is smiling a lot more, this may signal an intention to win approval, escape criticism, keep the peace, or else slip beneath the radar. You might confirm this hypothesis if you also see them constantly fretting to offer people drinks or using plenty of defensive and protective body language (for example, shrugging the shoulders as though to lower and hide the self while extending the hands outward, palms open, as though to say "I come in peace!"). By making these observations, you're not only noticing how this person probably feels right now (nervous, vigilant, conciliatory) but also the role they play in this group or in life in general.

Another example: imagine you see a family out and about. Mom, Dad, and two of the children are smiling and laughing, and they have open, relaxed postures and expressions. One child, though, is unsmiling and has tense muscles around their forehead and mouth. This discrepancy tells you that there is something on which this child disagrees with the rest of their family. What is it? Notice what else is going on, and try to find the source of the difference. If the unsmiling child is the eldest teenager, dressed in goth clothing, you can begin to piece together a puzzle about the role this child is presently playing—not to mention the way the other family members are responding to it.

How is their nonverbal expression as a response to stimuli in the environment?

People seldom stand in an empty room and have an emotion. The emotion is almost always in response to something. The way people react to things in their environment tells you a lot about them. Again, it's not rocket science, and we can infer a lot simply by considering the degree of openness or closedness, tension or relaxation.

For example, what can you infer about a person who makes fists and tucks away their hands when someone teases them and puts them on the spot? They are probably not enjoying the challenge/attention. What about when someone leans in to whisper something in another person's ear, and that person responds by touching their neck to pull them in even closer? They are probably feeling (more than) happy with the escalation of intimacy the original gesture symbolized.

"People-watching" is a great way to fine tune this skill. Simply pay attention to people walking, shopping, eating in cafés. Pick someone and see how they respond to other people, to everyday tasks, and so on (politely and unobtrusively, of course!). Try to guess what they are feeling given the way they react to things around them.

You can do this in a smaller, more controlled way every time you converse with someone. Make a small change in the interaction, then watch closely to see how the other person responds to it. For example, touch them lightly on the forearm, change the topic, or ask a slightly more personal question. Then watch for changes in them. For example, if you tell a little joke in which you reveal some harmless but embarrassing detail about yourself, but you notice that the other person remains stoically unchanging in their expression (i.e., they don't laugh, act shocked, or share a similar story of their own), you might guess that they are not interested in the slight escalation of intimacy this move suggests. When you later lean back, adopt a more formal tone, and lessen eye contact, you note they become more relaxed and even start smiling. More evidence for your hypothesis!

How is their nonverbal expression unusual or mismatched?

Often, the most noteworthy aspects of a person's experience are those that are unusual, heightened, or unexpected somehow. Pay attention if someone's responses to something seem (to you, anyway) mismatched. Are they very relaxed in a stressful situation? Smiling whilst getting reprimanded? Look more closely and see what you can infer from this.

People will often respond in overexaggerated ways when the matter is something they are ashamed, confused, or angry about. Defensiveness in general suggests a lack of confidence or feeling of vulnerability. On the other hand, people who seem to show too little emotion may communicate loud and clear all the same.

Imagine that you notice that someone is getting extremely flustered and stressed while trying to save a phone number on their mobile phone. You watch them and notice that they get irritable and clumsy, and then almost give up when their first attempt doesn't work. They're blushing, almost angry. Considering other observations (they are an older person, unfashionably dressed, retired, and soft-spoken), you assume that this total overreaction to the annoyances of technology says something about their discomfort and resentment of modern life.

Perhaps they are embarrassed by their lack of ability, or perhaps you can infer that they have never bothered with certain material trappings because they prioritize other values. Perhaps their reaction tells you something about their attitude toward *you*—do they worry you will think they're just a foolish old person and will get annoyed and impatient with them? Whatever it is, this little detail about the phone is a gem and can help you build a rich and nuanced picture of the person in front of you.

You can also stay alert not just to over- or under-reactions, but to reactions that just seem odd, unusual, or unexpected. For example, you may be with someone when you both experience a sudden frightening situation—let's say an attempted mugging or a mild earthquake. You notice that not only is the other person *not* frightened, but they seem to actually be enjoying it! What could this tell you?

You might conclude that this person is a thrill seeker, a little bored in their own life, or even that their tolerance of risk, danger, and novelty is unusually high. On the other hand, if the person leaves the situation completely distraught and talking nonstop about what *they* experienced and how traumatized *they* are, you can guess they are pretty self-focused or like to imagine themselves as victims!

Why You Can't Always Trust Facial Expressions

Way back in 1972, with the publication of *The Expressions of the Emotions in Man and Animals*, Darwin first suggested that human emotions map onto distinct facial expressions. The trouble with humans, though, is that we may be in situations where we wish to conceal our emotions, or else appear to be feeling ones we aren't.

Richard Restak is the author of *Mozart's Brain and the Fighter Pilot: Unleashing Your Brain's Potential*, and he provides a simple exercise designed to improve your ability to read other people's emotions. Restak claims that "when a person pretends an emotion, he or she activates the same brain areas that would be activated in circumstances when the emotions are naturally and spontaneously expressed."

Try this exercise. Get a trusted friend and position yourself around three feet away from one another. Get your friend to close their eyes. Gaze at your friend's face and ask them to think about the saddest memory they have of their life, but also instruct them that they shouldn't respond in any way—for example, by sighing or frowning. Watch their face and see if you can note any subtle changes.

Next, ask your friend to completely clear their mind and think of nothing. Again, watch and see what you can see. Now ask your friend to open their eyes and look at you, again thinking about the saddest moment in their life, followed by a completely neutral experience, say, buying milk at the store. Finally, ask the friend to imagine the happiest moment of their lives. Throughout, keep a close watch on their face, especially the eyes. In particular, notice what happens in the moments when one emotion *shifts* to another.

The exercise is also illuminating when you switch roles. What did you both notice? Is there anything you're especially surprised by?

You may find that what your friend tells you they were thinking about and what you perceived in their facial expression were totally at odds. For example, from your perspective, they might have seemed totally serene and confident, but they tell you they were at that moment recalling the distressing moment they learned their grandmother had died. You'll notice this the other way around, too, and be surprised at how badly wrong your friend read your expressions. Sure, in hindsight you may be able to read certain subtleties in an entirely different way. But what if you were *only* relying on your reading of their facial expression?

The point of this exercise is not to show you that facial expressions are meaningless and that it's not worth paying attention to them. Rather, **it's to show just how hidden people's true emotions can actually be.** The exercise shows you how well people can conceal their actual emotions, even when you think you may be seeing something in the movement of an eyebrow or the twitch of a lip.

Something else you might notice is that the transitions themselves provide more information than any single facial movement or gesture. In other words, what you might be discerning is the *effort* someone is making to conceal their emotions, or else the change from one emotion to another. Even if someone is doing their best to hide their true feelings, you can still infer something when a stimulus gets some kind of rise out of them. What does it mean? Well, the rest of the context and all your other observations will help you find the answer.

Consider this example. You're having a disagreement with a family member because you strongly suspect them of lying to you. Let's say you're having a discussion, and their facial features are lively and animated. Then you bring up the issue of the lie, and this suddenly changes. Their face goes blank. They start making simple, clear, concise statements and repeating themselves. What does their facial expression tell you? Well, nothing. But the sudden change from expressive to non-expressive tells a big story. Even though the topic is distressing and you're unhappy, they don't mirror this or respond in a normal way to it.

What you are noticing is actually the lack of expression or, more accurately, the effort being made to create that impression. What does it mean? There is an attempt to minimize or hide something, or else to de-escalate the situation. This person may not be outright lying to you, but they are definitely trying to avoid showing you *something*. We will explore this issue of lie detection in a later chapter, but first, we need to consider a very important concept in the art of people-reading.

Chapter 6: Baselining

Picture this. You meet someone new for the first time, and they are grinning ear to ear. They immediately start gushing about how much they love your shoes, and when you start talking, they listen with rapt attention, laughing (loudly) at all your jokes and telling you afterward that they have never met anyone quite so interesting as you. When you part ways, they make a big deal about getting your contact details and invite you to their house, but not before giving you an enormous hug to say goodbye.

What do you think about such a person? You probably assume that they really, really like you. They seem ultra-friendly and positive and like they really enjoyed your company. Maybe other observations make you think that they might be a bit lonely and hungry for company, or even that they're coming onto you. That is, until you meet this person again, this time in a group. You see that they treat *everyone* this way. You suddenly realize that they don't think you're especially great—that's just what they're like with everyone!

The behavior, in a vacuum, usually does indicate someone who is interested, positive, happy, etc. But these in-a-vacuum observations don't tell you how common this behavior is *compared to that person's own tendencies.* Perhaps, after watching them interact with other people for a while, you actually realize that they are a little less warm and friendly to you than they normally are in general.

It's important to consider any single behavior not just as it compares to other people or to the environment itself, but to the person behaving that way. In other words, is this behavior common or uncommon *for them*?

We can't make any conclusions about the information we gather if we don't have something to compare it to. What seems normal to you might not be normal to them, and so on. **A baseline is a set of nonverbal behaviors (like posture, movement, and gestures) that a person usually uses when they are comfortable and relaxed**. It's like a default setting.

When you read body language, you are looking at expression in absolute terms, but also relative terms. You decide whether something is noteworthy according to how far from the baseline it is. If the person above meets someone and you observe them being polite and kind, but very much less so than normal, you can probably conclude they don't like that person—even if their behavior is objectively friendlier than the average.

Body language experts agree that you should pay attention to the subtleties and *changes* in a person's body language to know when it's been activated or triggered during a normal conversation. Notice all the ways in which they are behaving differently from what's normal for them.

The first step, if you can, is to establish a baseline. Here are things to look for:

- Blink rate
- Eye contact—how frequent and duration
- Breathing—both rate and depth
- Body movement speed and fluidity
- Facial expressions
- Gestures used
- Cadence, pitch, volume, articulation, and rhythm of voice
- Overall posture—open or closed, tense or relaxed

Note, of course, that the above all need to be considered **in context**. So, someone's baseline when they are at work doing their teaching job may be completely different from their baseline on the weekend when they're with friends and doing a hobby.

It's difficult to establish a baseline for someone the first time you meet—you will typically need to spend more time with them in different contexts to begin to notice any stable patterns. That said, you can still use the principle of baselining even if you only engage with a person for a short time. For example, during the course of a twenty-minute conversation, you might establish a baseline *for that conversation*, and this allows you to detect when something suddenly changes. In fact, being aware of how people change over the course of a single interaction is also what will allow you to gracefully end the conversation at the right time.

Using Baselines to Detect Deception

The baseline approach is especially useful for one type of people-reading: catching liars.

Many people believe all sorts of myths about how you can catch a liar red-handed (they look up and to the left, they bite their lip, etc.), but these will seldom help you. **A better way to find out if someone is lying is to identify "leakage," which is unintentional and inconsistent communication across multiple channels like:**

- Facial expressions
- Gestures and body language
- Voice
- Communication style
- Verbal statements

A leak can be anything—but it is always something different from the baseline, something that was intended to be concealed but wasn't. Spot it, and you can infer a bigger concealment that may be underway. Let's take a look at how this may play out in real life.

Step 1: Gather information

Everyone has a "norm," which is a basic preferred setting for how they act when they are under normal amounts of stress. This can be anything from how often or quickly they blink, to the words they usually use. A person often has a "tic," or a sign that they are uncomfortable, just like they have a "norm." You've seen these expressions on your family and friends: a quick smirk or frown when you say something they don't agree with, or a tendency to suddenly muddle words. But even if you see a "tic," keep looking. A tic doesn't automatically mean a lie. But it does tell you something—what you continue to observe will help clarify what that something is.

Try to answer the questions:

What is normal for this person?
How does this change when they are experiencing stress?
When and where are the most dramatic differences?

You may gather this information all at once in a single conversation, or you may need to really get to know a person well first.

Step 2: Establish rapport

Now, if you were an FBI agent trying to uncover deception, you might need to quickly establish rapport to build on. Since you're probably not an FBI agent, just apply this step in whatever way suits your situation. It goes without saying that if you have just met someone or don't know them well, your chances of finding out the truth will be greater if you can establish some kind of shared understanding and connection with them first. This will put them at ease (without stress, you can more easily establish their baseline) and also put you at ease, making you more observant.

Even if you already have an established relationship with the person, the way that you talk to them will make a big difference to how they communicate with you. Of course, at no point should you give any hint that you are trying to uncover deception. Be relaxed, make eye contact but not too much, be warm and steady, and invite them to tell their stories by listening with relaxed and respectful empathy. If you are unguarded, they will be too. Ask open-ended questions rather than leading immediately by grilling them with what you want to know, and don't come across as too forceful or determined. One good way to subtly promote rapport is to mirror them in small ways—adopt the same posture, tone of voice, expression, or even verbal idiosyncrasies to show that you're on the same wavelength.

Step 3: Run through the baseline checklist

The following five-part checklist is about making as thorough an observation as possible, in as short a time period as you can. While you're making your observations, though, remind yourself that what you don't observe can be as important as what you do! The general rule is to start your way at the top of the person and work your way down:

1. First, observe the face

- What is the position of their head and how are they holding it?
- Are they touching their face? How and where? How often?
- Watch the eyes—where are they looking? How fast are they blinking?
- Can you notice any tension or looseness in the mouth?

2. Next, listen to the voice

- What is the tone or character of the voice? Smooth, jerky, wavering, clear, monotone?
- Is the pitch low, medium, or high?
- Listen for both kinds of volume—loud or soft, but also how much talking they're doing.

- How fast or slow are they talking? Is their pace consistent or all over the place?

3. Listen to the words they're saying

- Do they use verbal fillers (um, ah, like)? How often?
- Are they being formal or causal? Swearing?
- Do they use full sentences? Are the sentences unusually long or short?
- How is their grammar? For example, do they frame things in passive voice or state everything as a question?
- Do they use a lot of "I" and "me"?

4. Notice how they're holding their body

- How much space are they taking up? Are they spreading out or collapsing? Rigid or yielding?
- Is their posture generally open or more closed? Tight or loose?
- Do they seem to be advancing or retreating?
- Notice their gestures—are they wide and expansive or small, nervous, and useless?

5. Finally, take note of the fidget factor

- Are there lots of unnecessary and pointless gestures? What kind?
- What do they do in a relaxed position?
- Is their overall impression one of movement or stillness? Calm or agitation?

Okay, great. Now that you've gathered all this data, what do you do with it?

Your main goal as a deception-detector is to look for stress signals that alert you to an inner state of effort, anxiety, or dissonance.

What does this mean? Think about what it's like to lie. If your brain is a computer, then lying represents an additional computational burden that asks your brain to work far harder than it would have to if it was just recounting the truth. In the same way that a CPU that is hard at work will sometimes make loud noises or start to get hot, you can learn to look for the human "stress signals" that tell you that some additional work is underway—potentially a lie.

Right away, you can see the first problem with using this approach—i.e., someone may be burdened with extra thinking not because they're lying but because they're unhappy for another reason, or simply nervous (perhaps because they sense you're interrogating them!). Again, the only way out of this dilemma is to continually observe the whole and consider what you're observing, even making allowances for the fact that someone might be nervous for some other reason.

You always want to take into account:

Social norms
The impact of the context and environment
The social role that person is currently playing
What they may be trying to achieve with their behavior in general
The nature of your relationship

Their normal personal baseline
Any other potential sources of stress
The unique way their expression changes in response to stress

Once you've gathered information and established a baseline, your next move is to **watch very closely for anything that does not fit that baseline.** The logic is that if you are familiar with how a person behaves when relaxed, then you can clearly notice when they are stressed and outside that range—i.e., might be telling a lie. That's why every attempt to uncover an untruth always begins with establishing a connection, rather than jumping in with accusations, threats, or targeted questions—these will naturally just make the person clam up. Even worse, when they start behaving in a stressed way, you won't know if this is because they're genuinely lying, or just because it's stressful to be accused this way!

Once you have established rapport and observed them in their relaxed and calm state, and you pose a meaningful question, *then* their sudden change in behavior will tell you something useful. Though you don't need to practice this skill in the way that professional interrogators do, the principles are actually the same. Let's look at an example.

Let's say you are interviewing a candidate for a role in your company, but you have reason to believe they're not being especially truthful on their resume. Now, you're not too concerned about the white lie—it's rather small—but you are concerned about the overall trustworthiness of the candidate and bluntly want to see how good they are at hiding the truth! Either way, you will learn something interesting about them.

You begin with two simple questions: What's normal for this person? How do they behave when they're stressed out?

You prepare for the interview by reading up on them as much as you can beforehand, and try to make inferences based on their age, where they grew up, education, social media use, background, etc. This can only take you so far, though. You look at the way they've compiled their resume. You see what they are emphasizing (their degree and awards) and what is de-emphasized or not mentioned at all (a gap of two years, their exact job title at a previous position, etc.). This tells you a lot about how this person wants to present themselves. What *aren't* they showing, and why?

In the interview, you simply begin by getting to know them. You keep things very warm and relaxed and even make out that you're not a seasoned interviewer and don't intend to take the process all that seriously. You do what you can to put them at ease—smiling, eye contact, offering to make them a coffee, leaning in close, and making friendly small talk about relatable things.

But all the while this is happening, you are watching them. You are paying attention to those five areas of observation to establish the baseline. Now, you already know that an interview is a naturally stressful situation, so all you are doing is looking for what the baseline level of stress is before the "real interview" begins. You notice:

Lots of eye contact and smiling
Leaning forward in the chair
Voice medium loud, strong, even
Fidgety hands
Lots of "I" statements

Lots of nodding along
Tight but active overall posture; impression of alertness and energy

Great. So this is what the candidate looks like under the normal conditions of interview stress. Once you're sure that rapport has been established and you have a baseline (i.e., run through the five-point checklist in your head), then you can start pressing on what you believe to be the deception. You first ask about something that you know is true, and observe the response.

"So you went to Harvard."
"Yeah, I did."
"This was in . . . 2019? Okay, so I also see you took an extra year to complete your degree."
"Yeah, that's right. I was in quite a bad car crash and so I graduated a little later."
"I'm sorry to hear that. But it says here that you went straight from that into your position with the first startup, is that right?"
"Yeah, that's correct. Spring of 2020, I began work with *Real Time*."

While on the surface all this seems pretty run-of-the-mill, you are actually hard at work noticing the way the candidate responds to questions when it's the truth: short, to-the-point answers, frequently beginning with "yeah" and accompanied by an energetic nod, eye contact, and an alert posture. **This is what the truth looks like for this person in this context.** Let's move on.

"Well, we've been looking for developers like you for ages, so it would be great to have you on board. But I'm curious, it seems like your last role would have been more your speed, salary-wise at least. Why the change?" Now, you play it cool and watch. You notice these things:

The candidate keeps smiling and making eye contact, but all at once, they lean back in the chair and fold their hands firmly in their lap. Their voice drops in volume and pitch, and their posture seems to spread and loosen a little.

"There are a lot of reasons for that, the primary one being issues with their initial stages of funding. The company was bought out, but there was a lack of overall interest from investors. Long story short, I'm looking for a little more security regarding pay."

What to make of this answer? Let's say that you happen to *know* that this is a white lie. You know the founders of *Real Time* and know that although financing was tight at first, this particular employee was fired for completely unrelated reasons. It's not a big deal, but you make a note of this. **This is what this person looks like when they're lying**—or at least bending the truth! Let's move on again.

You ask them some more questions, keep them at ease, and then you finally ask the question you are most interested in.
"If we offered you this role, do you see yourself remaining on for the foreseeable future? At this stage, we are really looking ahead at the long term, and we want to start bringing in people who can grow with us. Does that align with what you're after?"

Let's say the candidate does this: They lean back even further and give another formal, long-winded answer, some of it in passive voice and delivered in a kind of low-energy way compared to their previous answers. They assure you they are very committed to the role.

You ask some further questions, and their demeanor changes again, back to what you have already registered as the baseline.

So, does this mean they were lying about wanting to stay in the role for the long term? It's not *conclusive* . . . but the evidence strongly suggests it! Crucially, if you had simply followed ordinary body language (i.e., fidgeting and nervous, tight posture equals lying), then you would have completely gotten this wrong. You would have assumed that the calm, relaxed-looking person who was speaking clearly and articulately was telling the truth. But for this person, whose natural state was more energetic and excitable, this relaxed body language was, ironically, a "stress signal" hinting at deception.

As you can imagine, learning to spot liars is more like a dark art that requires years of practice to master. At first, try not to think of it as "catching a liar." Rather, just become aware of people's patterns and shifting energies in any interaction or conversation. Become good at noticing changes and shifts. Learn to see the switch from normal to unusual. Yes, this will help you become better at spotting lies, but it will more generally help you become a brilliant people-reader.

Chapter 7: Watch Wardrobe, Walk, and Food

"The clothes maketh the man," says the old proverb. It turns out that not only does a person's wardrobe tell you a lot about them, but so does the way they walk, the shoes they wear, and what and how they eat. However, all the same rules about perception and non-verbal expression apply, and we need to learn to regard people with genuinely fresh eyes.

Clothing Speaks
Jennifer Baumgartner, a clinical psychologist and author, has always been interested in the "psychology of dress." In her fascinating book, *You Are What You Wear: What Your Clothes Say About You*, she explores this complex relationship: not only how **psychology affects our clothing choices, but also how our clothing choices in turn can impact our psychology**. On a personal level, understanding how you are portraying yourself aesthetically is, she claims, as important as understanding your biases, beliefs, and communication style—in fact, clothing *is* a communication style!

Northwestern University recently explored the concept they called "enclothed cognition" in a study. In their report, researchers define it as "the systematic effect that clothes have on the psychological processes of the wearer." This means what your clothes say to you, not about you, and how you feel about them. But for our purposes as budding people-readers, we can see that clothing is also a brilliant window into a person's current state of mind. Let's imagine that we are extending our understanding of body language (gesture, voice, posture, facial expression) to include the choices a person makes every time they get dressed in the morning—let's call it fine-tuning our "enclothed perception."

Both Baumgartner and the researchers at Northwestern University would suggest that you don't dress based on how you feel, but based on how you *want* to feel. Want to feel strong, sexy, serious, in control, or relaxed? Then dress that way. However, we are also interested in the fact that people do tend to pick clothing that mirrors their emotional state. Look at the clothes and you see the emotion.

As you can guess, however, there are some caveats (and they're not that different from the caveats we keep in mind when reading body language in general).

- Context matters—if people have to wear something as a part of their job or social role, it implies much less about them, for example.
- Age, gender, ethnicity, social class, and background all play a role too—what is considered daring for one group may be conservative for another. What is expensive-looking in one country may be casual in another.
- Historical period—obviously, our shared cultural understanding of what the vocabulary of fashion means will change over time!

Baumgartner also explains how it's not just the clothing itself, but the way a person wears that clothing. The messages are quite obvious when you stop to pay close attention to them. For example:

A person who keeps everything they own, never throwing anything away, or else a person who is still wearing things from decades prior may be clinging to the past.

A person who wears neutrals only, "basics," and no accessories may be stuck in a rut, too comfortable, complacent.

A person wearing clothing that's too big for them may have yet to update to a smaller body size from their past, or they might desire to hide something.

Someone who consistently dresses to emphasize sex appeal is very culture dependent, but likely either craves attention from the opposite sex and envisions their identity primarily in these terms, or else they are insecure in this area and are trying to encourage others to see them this way. Occasionally, this style can suggest that a person is playing what they feel is the role they've been assigned.

Dressing too "young" or too "old" hints at the age that the person feels themselves to be, or either what they wish to convey to others. This style may point to signals around maturity, sex appeal, professionalism, or class.

A person who basically only wears work clothes—obviously, their "uniform" tells you the role they are most commonly inhabiting. Whether in a good or bad way, work is a big part of their identity.

A person who is always wearing designer logos or expensive status markers wants you to treat them well. They want to be seen as winners or in a special category above others. They may be very goal driven and seek external validation and approval, basing their aspirations on conventional symbols of wealth and prestige.

The person forever in jeans/tights and a relaxed hoodie or sweatshirt—unless they are literally coming back from the gym or a walk, assume this person has put their own vanity on the back burner and is focusing on something else, such as parenthood. It may signal low self-worth, exhaustion, or a lack of purpose.

A person deliberately wearing a symbol that connects them to a certain group—be it a band T-shirt, a religious necklace, a hat with a political slogan, or a tattoo of a meme—sees themselves as one of the group, but also that they wish for others to recognize that fact.

Just as we do with every other behavioral observation, we need to interpret clothing **in context**. For example, you might have met someone wearing a torn T blouse with shoulder pads, a tulle skirt, high top sneakers, and a crocheted handbag made out of seashells. Her hair was full of untidy clips and bows, and she was wearing bright-red lipstick and horn-rimmed glasses.

Now, if the woman were eighty years old and wearing all this to her granddaughter's graduation, we might think that her choices signaled a kind of nostalgia, lack of connection to current trends, or else an endearing disregard for other people's opinions. But if the woman were twenty-three years old and wearing this to a job interview, we would conclude something entirely different. We might wonder why she was so eager to communicate that she was different from the norm. Was she a very dramatic person? Insecure? Flamboyant? Genuinely unconventional and artistic? A bit self-absorbed? Your other observations will help you decide.

As with other body language, it's worth watching for changes from the baseline, or clothing that is out of sync with others, unexpected, or exaggerated in some way. If you have gone on several dates with a person, every time with them turning up super well-dressed and groomed, ask yourself what it means if they show up to date number seven wearing tracksuit bottoms and an old gym shirt. They may suddenly be feeling more comfortable around you, or else they have unofficially abandoned "the chase" and decided that, for whatever reason, it was no longer necessary to impress you.

It's not just clothing. A 2012 study investigated how well people are able to make character judgments about others just by looking at the shoes they wear most of the time. They concluded that a snapshot of a person's favorite footwear *can* reveal a lot about them, including their age, income, and even attachment anxiety. On their own, shoes reveal a tiny amount of information about the wearer, but this information can be quite useful. According to Gillath et al., shoes are a pretty accurate thing to look at for good first impressions. Consider:

Flat shoes indicate a humble person who gets things done without requiring supervision or praise.
High heels can signal confidence, deliberation, ambition, and perhaps a need for attention.
Flashy shoes can, naturally, hint that a person is an extrovert and likes to stand out.
Flip flops point to a relaxed, easygoing attitude that may tend to laziness.
Shoes that are always squeaky clean and polished suggest the desire to make a good first impression and someone who takes care of their life and themselves.
High-heeled black ankle boots or "Chelsea" boots may suggest confidence or even aggression. Often worn by people who know *exactly* what they want in life. On the other hand, tan or brown cowboy-style ankle boots are typically worn by more relaxed, arty types.
Shoes that are in poor repair or constantly dirty may suggest this person doesn't take care of themselves, either.
Formal lace-ups or expensive loafers, especially if not in a professional context, are somber-looking "classic" shoes that suggest someone wants to be taken seriously and that they value tact, discipline, and order.
Sports shoes could symbolize being goal-oriented and active, but if they're more like ordinary sneakers or street shoes, the person may be versatile and energetic and find it easy to get along with everyone. On the other hand, if those sneakers cost two hundred dollars, then the story they tell is a little different . . .
"Sensible" footwear suggests that people are secure in themselves and internally motivated. Birkenstocks, for example, suggest someone loves comfort, the outdoors, and quality things—and that they prioritize comfort over style.
Barefoot—well! Depending on the context, you could be dealing with a rugged outdoor type, a dedicated rebel, or a toddler . . .

Naturally, shoe choices will take on different meanings depending on time and place. In some parts of the world, at some points in history, red shoes were associated with prostitutes. Of course, if you saw red shoes on the pope (a centuries-old papal fashion), you would not make that association! That's why observing shoe type is not enough on its own. Notice how people take care of their shoes—or not. Do they insist on wearing light-colored or delicate shoes that require constant cleaning? See if you can notice signs of perfectionism, competitiveness, or obsessiveness in the rest of their behavior.

Do they regularly toss their shoes to the side when they take them off, allow them to get dirty and broken, walk freely through dirt and water, or insist on wearing shoes that are ugly, inappropriate, or ill-fitting? Look for other signs of either a free spirit or a general air of self-negligence. Do they constantly wear shoes that do not match the occasion? Become curious about what they value instead. Do they prioritize fashion over conformity or comfort? Would they rather be cold than ugly?

Remember, though, that you need to think about the type of shoes that people wear most often. Consider also that a person who has an enormous wardrobe of very different shoes may value novelty and choice more than a person who literally wears the same pair every single day. Finally, shoes have a way of telling you about the person someone wishes they could be. If you can, peek into someone's closet and notice if there's a difference between what the person wears everyday and what they tend to buy again and again. A woman who lives in worn-out ballet flats but keeps on buying sparkly stilettos is telling you something about how she sees herself—and what she is aspiring to. It's a point worth bearing in mind: not everyone sees themselves accurately!

It's in the Way You Walk

Werner Wolff, a German-born psychologist, did one of the first studies examining the connection between gait (the way people walk) and personality. How a person walks, including their speed and stride length, can speak volumes. Everyone is different, and so is the way they walk. It's even been suggested that the way a person walks can give clues about what they are trying to hide from the world. Again, none of this is rocket science, but it does require us to pause and pay attention and carefully analyze what we are observing.

If someone is a fast walker, they may be a hardworking, outgoing person. Fast walkers tend to be open-minded, extroverted, and conscientious. Go-getters and risk-takers walk fast. They will be bolder than usual, energetic, and detail-oriented. They may also be more stressed!

If someone walks slowly and takes short steps, it's more likely they're an introvert. People who have a slow-walker personality tend to turn inward more often, are more contemplative, and keep to themselves. Most of the time, people who walk this way are calm and happy when they are by themselves. When there are a lot of people in a room, you might notice them move into the background or away from the center of attention.

If someone's walking style is loose and relaxed, it shows that they like to live life on their own terms and at their own speed. They're not in a hurry to be anywhere but here and now. They're also not in a hurry to take orders. They're calm, happy, and sure of themselves inside and out, but won't fight for the spotlight or stay ahead of the crowd.

If someone usually takes long, quick strides, they probably have a healthy attitude about life. Covering a lot of ground when walking suggests competitiveness, focus, and a desire to get things done. People still like them even if they sometimes come off as a little cold.

If someone is always dragging their feet, it suggests an anxious personality prone to worry. People who walk this way are usually upset or sad. They can't pull away from things or thoughts that make them feel bad. They can't stay in the present moment very often. They keep dragging around their past or worry about losing things or people they care about.

But once again, context and baseline make all the difference. Notice how a person is walking *relative to* others in group or compared to how they normally walk. Notice if they always want to walk side by side with others, dawdle, or want to be in front. As with other body language, look for the openness or closedness of the body, look for dynamism (suggesting confidence, joy, etc.) and gesture. **One way to think of walking is that it is like a visual representation of the way a person thinks**. Describe their walk and you have described their cognitive processes. Are they confident, relaxed, and easy thinkers? Are they always going somewhere rather than just stretching their legs? Are they walking like a queen or scuttling nervously along like a crab?

Observe a Person's Food Choices

Juliet Boghossian is a food behavior expert in Los Angeles and founder of the food behavior research firm Food-ology. According to her, a person's eating habits can tell you enormous amounts about their personality, priorities, values, and identity. And why wouldn't it be that way, considering that what and how we eat probably represents dozens of choices we each make every day?

Observe people's behavior around food and drink and you can infer a lot about their state of mind and the way they think of themselves and the world. According to Boghossian:

If someone eats slowly, they tend to like to be in charge, and they know how to savor life. They are also usually sure of themselves, in control, and calm.

If someone eats quickly, they tend to be ambitious, goal-oriented, and open to new experiences, but they may also have a tendency to be impatient. Eating quickly can also suggests distraction and anxiety, so watch for other context clues.

If someone loves to try new food, then you can safely assume that they are open-minded and curious types, and they may be a lot less judgmental than the average person. This willingness to move out of a comfort zone can signal creativity, maturity, a joyful disposition, or perhaps a tendency toward boredom.

If someone is picky about what they eat, it generally suggests discomfort and anxiety of some kind or other. It's no coincidence that picky eating is most commonly associated with children, who are still developing their sense of discipline, adventurousness, and trust in the world. A fussy eater may demonstrate fearfulness or lack of maturity in other areas of life, or they may be signaling a pronounced desire to control the external environment in an attempt to moderate themselves internally.

On the other hand, a limited palette can also be a simple question of habit and background. So much of what we enjoy eating comes down to how we have been raised, our culture, our income, what is available to us, and what brings us the most joy. What can you infer about an adult who won't eat their vegetables or who only ever wants to eat cheese pizza? It could be poor discipline, bad habit, or a more serious aversion . . . or all of these. Gather more data and you will get a clearer picture!

If someone likes to eat one food at a time, they are the so-called "isolationists." These people eat all of one food before moving on to the next, and so on around the plate. They pay a lot of attention to details and always give things a lot of thought. Predictably, they may like to do only one task at a time. They may be conscientious, a little anxious, disciplined, but possibly "control freaks" who would prefer if life stayed neat and orderly.

As you're making your observations, become curious about *everything* you see:

- How are their table manners? Slurping and talking with their mouth full, or taking pains to be neat and delicate?
- Are they comfortable eating in front of others?

- Are they very certain about their preferences, or do they find making a decision difficult?
- Do they order the same thing everyone else does?
- Do they order the cheapest or most expensive thing on the menu?
- Do they avoid complaining if given the wrong food?
- How do they treat the waiter?
- Do they offer to pay, or do they wait coyly for you to do it?
- Are they snobby and disparaging about the food?
- Are they consciously dieting and talking about food in combative terms?
- Do they whip out their phone for Instagram pics while their food gets cold?
- Do they take food off your plate, offer you a taste of theirs, or happily chat to the people at the next table?

As you can see, it's all grist for the people-reading mill. Perhaps now you can see the wisdom of businesspeople inviting one another out to lunch for meetings. It's not a social occasion, but an opportunity to mine the rich data that comes from observing people doing ordinary things like wear clothes, walk, and eat. In just a ten-minute snack break, you can observe:

How a person walks
Their voice—pace, pitch, timbre, volume, etc.
Their body language and facial expression
Their clothing choice
Their posture, gestures, and way they move
The language they employ
The literal words they say

It's a lot of information, but all this data really starts to mean something when it's put all together and embedded properly in the environment from which it emerged. Importantly, when making your observations, try to keep your own assumptions and values out of the picture. **What you are trying to understand is what a certain food behavior means to them, not to you.** They may tell you that they are a vegetarian, and you maya assume this is because they care about animal welfare, and then start telling yourself a story about how compassionate and conscientious they are. In fact, they are vegetarian for the health benefits only, and primarily because it's doctor's orders—that paints a very different picture!

A big caveat here: humans are judgmental. Yes, even us! At any one time there is a whole world of signs and symbols out there, most of them attached to a "good" or "bad" label. But it's only when we drop this value judgment and become genuinely curious that we can start to understand what we're actually looking at. The deeper you go, the more thorough your understanding. If you are lazy and simply think, "That guy makes tea in the microwave. I bet he's some kind of psychopath," then you are missing out on a whole universe of valuable information.

Summary:
- We can gain real insights into people's characters by observing their behavior, their choices, and the way they behave, plus the function of this behavior. Functional behavioral analysis is about formulating a theory about the functional relationship between a person's behavior and their environment, and not just static personality traits. Their behavior function may be access, attention, escape, or sensory. We can

- also observe the antecedents and consequences of behavior to see what triggers and sustains it.
- Nonverbal communication provides us a world of information about a person, and emotion and behavior are linked. Body language reveals emotions in a spontaneous, unconscious, and unintentional way. Don't just read an individual, but that individual's behavior and orientation within their environment. Look for unusual, mismatched expressions and how people respond to those around them.
- Develop emotional granularity, which is a broad and deep knowledge of many different shades of emotion, plus the ability to distinguish between them. Remember that emotions can be concealed; watching for transitions and responses may be more illuminating.
- A baseline is a set of nonverbal behaviors that a person shows when relaxed. Pay attention to different-for-them behavior and consider context. Baselining can also help you identify lies and deception. Establish a baseline when relaxed, add stress and observe, then ask the relevant question and watch what happens.
- Finally, consider clothing, shoes, gait, and food choices as an extension of body language. The way a person walks can tell you about how they think and their level of ambition and stress, clothing can signal identity and intention, and food choices tell you a lot about a person's values and background.

Section 3

Chapter 8: NLP and People's Meta-Programming

In NLP, or neurolinguistic programming, **meta-programs are basically our "maps of reality."** These maps describe our style of thinking, feeling, sorting, valuing, and choosing information and perceptions, and consequently they affect how we behave. It can be fascinating to learn more about your own mental models of the world, but meta-programs can also offer us a rich insight into how *other* people tick.

So how do meta-programs work?

Whenever a person encounters something in the world, they form an internal representation of that event (i.e., a program) within their own minds. *How* they do this depends very much on a larger organizing principle, i.e., their meta-programs. The brain is a pattern-making machine and loves to make shortcuts and models of what it experiences. But the key is that brains are completely unique in the patterns they see (and don't see!), the meaning they make, the things they find most important, and the shortcuts they create.

Luckily, these internal models, though invisible, reveal themselves in countless ways as a person interfaces with other people and the world at large. **To fully understand someone's meta-program, we need only pay attention to their words, body language, and actions**—these are reflections of the kind of mental representation that person is working with.

For a quick example, imagine that you are riding a rollercoaster with three new friends. As you round the corner, you are surprised by a scary fake monster that jumps out at you. Everyone screams (you included), but you notice with interest that their reactions beyond this are quite different. One friend then immediately breaks out into laughter, a second friend gets a little angry and defensive, and the third starts mocking and teasing the second for being a big baby.

It's a small observation, but this difference in the way your new friends react to *the same stimulus* can tell you a lot about the internal mental maps they are working from. You notice how they talk about this moment the next day. The first friend talks about the group and how much fun "we" had and how everyone enjoyed themselves. The second friend complains about the surprise being sprung on them with no warning and talks at length about how unfair it is and how doubly unfair it is that the third friend is being mean to them. The third friend says how they can't wait to go back to test to see if it's as scary the second time round.

These differences in reaction are interesting because they reveal something about the hidden worldviews from which they sprang. The first friend is showing you that they think of the world as a largely happy, non-threatening place, but also that they aren't that good at noticing when other people's experience is not the same as theirs. The second friend is showing you that they think of themselves as something of a victim and have chosen to focus on those parts of a situation that they see as unfair or unjust. The third friend seems to enjoy being a rebel and different from the rest of the group. Instead of being amused or insulted by the rollercoaster surprise, he's curious and seems to want to return to master the situation.

Kinds of Meta-Programs

People are complicated. Though there may be predictable patterns, **most of us are complex and usually show a blend of different meta-programs**. The program can adapt depending on context, stress levels, and stage of life.

Nevertheless, the more we understand how other people make sense of their world, the more we understand them. This means we can communicate with them more easily, work with them, and speak their language in such a way as to get around any potential conflict or misunderstanding. Whether you want to create better rapport or simply adapt and adjust so you work around people, this NLP theory can help.

A meta-program is not exactly the same as a personality type, but it's close! That's because the mental program someone is running is precisely what allows them to form their own beliefs, perspectives, and opinions, and decides how they will organize meaning around their actions, their circumstances, and other people they encounter.

Here's an important thing to note: A meta-program is never "good" or "bad." It's neutral. It answers the question of what a person is going to focus on and what they filter out of awareness—none of us is omniscient, and simply by being alive, we apply mental filters to the world (you included). You could say that a person's way of doing this is unique to them and a prime determiner of their character. The only judgment we can apply here is whether this frame of reference is helping or hindering the person from achieving their stated aims (and again, their aims will be determined by their values, not necessarily yours).

Let's look at five common meta-programs used by NLP practitioners (there are seven, but we'll only consider the most common ones here) so we can better understand how to identify and work with each.

NLP Meta Program 1—Toward or Away

This is a question of "pain or gain." Does the person move *toward* something positive or *away* from something negative?

Tony Robbins, a popular NLP proponent, says,

> *"All human behavior revolves around the urge to gain pleasure or avoid pain. You pull away from a lighted match in order to avoid the pain of burning your hand. You sit and watch a beautiful sunset because you get pleasure from the glorious celestial show as day glides into night."*

"Toward" people are goal-oriented. They prioritize well and know what they want in life, as well as how to put that want front and center. They are motivated to always move toward something out there, in the future. Possibilities are imagined to be positive—however, there is sometimes so much positivity that critical thinking can take a back seat.

"Away" people are also motivated, but to get away from something. They're not crystal-clear on what they want, but they know very well what they *don't* want! Their focus on problems and potential obstacles makes them a bit of a stick in the mud, but on the other hand, they are more likely to anticipate snags and think more clearly and pragmatically about the future.

How can you tell the difference between them? Listen closely when people get very passionate about something. Are they excitedly talking about what they want and are striving for? Or are they passionately positioning themselves *against* something else? Let's say a person wants to lose weight. Notice how they talk about this goal. Is it "I'm going to look so hot when I reach my goal weight," or is it "If I don't turn my bad habits around, I'm going to kill myself"?

The difference can be subtle. Someone might *say* they're goal-oriented, but listen closely to how those goals are worded. "I want to not be fat anymore" is an *away* goal, whereas "I want to be thin" is a *toward* goal.

To connect with a toward person, you need to get on their wavelength and talk in such a way that centers their goal. If you're trying to convince them of something, focus on the long-term benefits and positive outcomes of what you're talking about, use expansive, inclusive body language, and look upward as though toward a bright future. To smooth over conflict with them, talk about the future and how things will be better then, and downplay what's already happened.

To connect with an away person, you need to frankly acknowledge the problem and, if you wish to motivate them, even hold them responsible for fixing it. If there's conflict, focus on what you're going to do to escape that conflict, rather than trying to smile and minimize—this might actually inspire them to dig their heels in!

Remember that no program is better than another—it's just a question of perspective. To talk to an away person, elaborate on the kind of situation you want to avoid, on risk, and on body language gestures that suggest exclusion. The key with this type of person is to mobilize their focus on the problem. Don't let them get diverted by crises, but ask what can be done to fix things.

Imagine that you yourself are primarily a toward person but you're talking to an away person. Because you understand this, you don't get frustrated with them being a stick in the mud about an exciting holiday you're planning together. When they keep homing in on potential disasters while you'd like to enjoy picturing how much fun you'll have, you decide that you won't argue with them or say things like "Don't be so negative! It'll never happen." Instead, you say, "Hm, maybe you're right about getting better travel insurance. Not having good coverage could be a nightmare. Could you shop around and find the best option for us?"

NLP Meta Program 2—External or Internal Frame of Reference

This "sort" basically depends on whether a person bases their standards on themselves or on others.

Internal frame-of-reference people are perceptive and self-centered. Here, the term isn't meant as an insult, but rather to show that such a person makes choices based on their own emotions and ideas. They process the world from the inside out. They must feel *personally* satisfied with their work or choice or they don't consider it valuable. Frequently, they give preference to their own intuitions and gut feeling over what others say they should think.

On the other hand, external frame-of-reference people concentrate on others and the value they imbue into things. They value other people's opinions because, for them, agreement, harmony, and consensus are precisely what give choices their value. This is the kind of person who is largely unclear about their thoughts, beliefs, and behaviors until they know what other people's are. They can easily imagine making a choice that is favored by the group whilst not necessarily valuing it themselves.

Robbins claims,

> "Ask someone else how he knows when he's done a good job. For some people, the proof comes from the outside. The boss pats you on the back and says your work is great. You get a raise. You win a big award. Your work is noticed and applauded by your peers.
>
> When you get that sort of external approval, you know your work is good. That's an external frame of reference. For others, the proof comes from inside. They 'just know inside' when they've done well."

To tell who you are dealing with, simply ask someone what their opinion is on a slightly contentious topic. You are listening not for what their answer is, but how they arrive at and justify that answer. Do they say "Well, I was raised Catholic, and we were taught X," or do they say "You'd be an idiot not to believe X"? Both these answers suggest they may be external. If they say "Well, a lot of people have different ideas" or "My personal feeling is X," then they may be more internal. While the body language for an internal type will be tight, closed, and focused on the self, the external type will be broader, more open, and less focused on the person.

Importantly, people can be internal or external while varying considerably in how much they actually conform to society's expectations, so don't let that fool you. For example, a person may do what their family/work/culture tells them, but resent the fact and see their actions as valueless. On the other hand, someone might appear to be a rebel or a black sheep, but deep down really crave societal approval—they're just bad at getting it! So, don't look at actions alone, but at the way people express themselves. Their choices matter, but *how they explain and justify those choices* matters more.

To connect with the internal type, the way is clear: Bear in mind that their source of value and meaning is internal. That means you speak about their experiences, wants, desires, needs, opinions, and so on. Frame the picture with them in the center, and there will seldom be any conflict. You make it so that they are deciding for themselves independently. These people have their own internally driven criteria—understand what they are and speak to them by framing your speech in terms of "I" and "you" and saying things like "personally . . ." or "that's your choice."

To connect with the external type, you must do the opposite: Introduce your own ideas or discuss others' ideas and how they might be useful. You are painting a harmonious picture and suggesting how they ought to fit into that. For example, you might invoke ideas such as duty or obligation, convention, law, tradition, authority, or even just fashion.

Think about a teacher who is trying to support the learning of two very different students. The first one he knows is an internal type, so when he gives feedback, he frames the student's performance in individualistic terms and refers to goals the student has set and to *their* values and principles. Where something is a problem, the teacher frames this problem as a violation of the student's own ethical code (even if the teacher doesn't agree with this code in the least).

However, in talking to another student who he knows is more external, he refers to their performance in relation to others in the class, to the teacher's own expectations or disappointments, and to the commonly held grade standards that determine that student's accomplishment. In dealing with more serious problems, the teacher might even mention the fact that the student's parents have paid a lot of money for school fees and will be upset that their child is not performing.

NLP Meta Program 3—Options or Procedures

Does the person enjoy choosing from many options or do they want to follow the set path already determined by the rules? In other words, what degree of autonomy does this person prefer?

The options type will actively seek out novelty and will value thinking outside the box. They want to be spontaneous and improvise.

The procedures type is not that thrilled with this approach and prefers to just use a tried-and-true method that has already been established. They value efficiency and productivity above being creative.

To connect with an options person, you need to . . . give them more options! Keep questions open-ended so you are always inspiring them to think about how they would create their own procedure. If you can, try to throw something unexpected into the mix—these people can be good problem-solvers if you gently direct their enthusiasm to all the possibilities around a current problem. Lean into their desire to sink their teeth into a complex problem.

For the procedure person, your focus in communication with them will always be on the HOW and not the WHY. They don't necessarily want to reinvent the wheel for every project; simply give them clear instructions that will help them get the task done as quickly as possible. Don't bother trying to convey the broader implications or get them enthusiastic—their lack of enthusiasm does *not* mean they won't work hard or well.

To tell the difference between an options person and a procedure person, pay attention to how they react to being given any type of task. Do they immediately start "playing" and trying to invent something new and different? Do they start trying to make something new or "explore the space"? They're an options thinker ("What can I do?").

Do they diligently get on with it and produce an efficient (if conventional) result? Do they ask what is ordinarily done and what has been done before? They're a procedures person ("What do I do?").

Imagine you're planning Christmas with family. Some of your family members are options people, so you know that when you talk with them about what they'll contribute to festivities, you inspire them by asking for fresh ideas or something new and different they can create ("Maybe we could do something totally different with the tree this year? Why don't you come up with something unconventional?").

With procedures people, you do none of this; you choose the quickest, most straightforward thing, then give them clear instructions for how to achieve that ("So you're in charge of Christmas Eve dinner, which is traditionally fish pie. I'll send you a recipe.") You probably can see that procedures people are often external, too.

NLP Meta Program 4—Matcher or Mismatcher

This key difference is about whether you focus on differences in relationships (mismatcher) or similarities (matcher).

Matchers are optimistic and approving and look for *commonalities* in conversations. They're all about harmony and cohesion. Thus, they base their decisions on similarities in others, circumstances, and life in general. They are always looking for the common denominator and value harmony and cooperation—which they may seek even to a fault.

The mismatchers take a different strategy and often prefer to rebel. Their tendency to be oppositional can sometimes manifest as creativity, quirkiness, or insightful critical reasoning, but just as often it comes out as fault-finding and general disagreeableness. This is the kind of person who will automatically argue with you in a heated conversation . . . even if they don't actually have a strong opinion either way.

Tony Robbins believes there are two subtypes of mismatchers:

> "One type looks at the world and sees how things are different . . . The other kind of mis-matcher sees differences with exceptions."

Here, it's a question of what is seen first: Some people start with all the ways things are different, and then they build on to that the similarities. Others start with what is common and then look for exceptions.

In both cases, the way to determine which type someone may be is to pay attention to how they classify and perceive objects. For example, a matcher might look at a series of different-sized circles and notice one pertinent fact about them: "They're all circles." A mismatcher, however, will focus mainly on what is different: "They're all different sizes." Listen carefully if a person uses a lot of words that suggest difference: *but, although, however*. They may also be away people, constantly defining themselves and their needs in opposition: "I'm *not* a conservative, I *don't* agree, I *can't* imagine that . . ."

With a little practice, you can hear this difference of orientation in the way people speak. Try to notice if their attention is always on what is the same or what is different. Are they always zooming in on the one tiny thing you two don't agree on? Or are they quite quick to round everybody up into the same category and look for common ground—even if there may be very little?

To connect with the matching type, lean into their tendency to find connections, and let them do the work—it's easy to find rapport with such a person since they will default to seeing you as similar to themselves. You can amplify that by mirroring—use similar language, spoken metaphors, gestures, etc. to cement your harmony. ("What are we going to do about this?"—the use of *we* comfortably implies similarity and cooperation.)

If you try to do this with a mismatcher, though, you will actually inspire the opposite reaction in them. That's what they're all about—opposites! Like many parents of rebellious teenagers know, you can go a long way with a little reverse psychology. If it's a given that they'll push against and disagree with whatever you propose, then propose the opposite of what you want them to do or see. ("Now, I'm pretty sure you're going to shoot this idea down, but what about if we . . .?" Here, you are working with the mismatcher's tendency to immediately respond, "You're actually wrong on that. I wouldn't shoot it down. In fact, I think it's a great idea.")

NLP Meta Program 5—Necessity or Possibility

Finally, notice whether someone makes decisions based on maximizing or simply satisfying. According to Robbins,

> "[Necessity people] are not pulled to take action by what is possible. They're not looking for infinite varieties of experience.
>
> They go through life taking what comes and what is available. When they need a new job or a new house or a new car or even a new spouse, they go out and accept what is available.
>
> Others are motivated to look for possibilities. They're motivated less by what they have to do than by what they want to do. They seek options, experiences, choices, paths."

For those more focused on necessity, there is a lot of value in "settling." They are happy to avoid the bad thing, and don't necessarily value looking around for alternatives and variety. For them, comfort and consolidation provide a lot of satisfaction. The irony is that such a person is more likely to be satisfied with life and better positioned to maximize on the opportunities that are actually in their world, instead of entertaining a bunch of pie-in-the-sky dreams. However, they may just as easily fail to peak out of their comfort zones, with underwhelming results.

For those more focused on possibility, there is a lot of excitement to be had in variety and opportunities for things to be different. They would prefer to pursue something enticing and unknown than to settle for the default. They take chances. These carry risks and costs, *sometimes enormous ones*, but also occasionally result in growth, which they highly prize.

To connect with a necessity person, remember that it's useless to focus on "what if"—this is not exciting for such a person. It may even be intimidating or unsettling. Instead, look at what actually *already is* and focus on the positives that are there. The idea is to amplify feelings of familiarity, security, ease, and safety. Find reasons for why the choice already made was a good one, rather than asking what choices could be made in the future.

A possibility person has a completely different motivation, so when you are attempting to communicate with them, you need to more heavily favor what could be rather than what is. In a way, the split between necessity and possibility is the divide between conservative and progressive (in the psychological, not the political sense). Because possibility is about growth, development, exploration, and novelty, you would do well to frame any course of action in terms of its potential. Focusing on the benefits of staying the same (i.e., conserving) will leave possibility people uninspired and unconvinced. Alternatively, focus on the idea of challenge and encourage them to weigh up risk and reward and to chart a course into the future.

How can you tell which one a person is? Ask them some kind of "why" question. For example, "Why did you take this current job?" or "Why did you choose to live in this neighborhood?" Then listen to the kind of answer you're given (important—not the content of the answer, but the way this content is framed). If they frequently use language along the lines of "need" and "have to," then they are operating from necessity—"We had to be near the school" or "I needed the money!" If they answer with language more to do with "want," then they are more likely running the possibility meta-program—"We wanted to be closer to nature" or "I wanted to challenge myself in a new role." Listen for other meta-programs—this one overlaps predictably with the away and toward meta-program.

Now, knowing all this about each of the meta-programs, it's worth bearing in mind that it takes some skill to identify these models in others. Not least because you have a meta-program, too, and will be seeing them through *your* filter!

Always remember that meta-programs depend on context, are stress-related, and may change over time. So, don't notice one event and assume you know everything about the person. Instead, notice stable and recurring patterns. Another thing to be cognizant of is what your intentions are. If you are merely seeking to understand another person, then do so by **working with their meta-program**, not opposing it. If you are trying to communicate well and establish rapport, then it is not your job to challenge, diagnose, or convince. Understanding your own meta-program will help you make changes, but unless you're a therapist or a motivational speaker, there's seldom a need to enter social interactions with the agenda of changing people's fundamental perspectives.

Finally, keep in mind that **this theory is also best understood contextually and relatively.** People do not exist in a vacuum, and their mental models are not static. Notice how they are interacting with their environment and with other people, and how their meta-programs are actually functioning. In other words, if you want to quickly understand how someone ticks, ask what function their mental model is actually serving. **They think that way for a reason. What's the reason?** Look at the way they respond to other people, to challenges, to opportunities, to ambiguity, etc. This will tell you a lot about the invisible mental programming they're running.

Summary:

- Meta programs are our mental maps or representations of reality. To better read people, fully understand we need only pay attention to their words, body language, and actions and infer the meta-programs they are running. Most people show a blend of different programs and can change over time.
- Identify the meta-program and then work with it to create harmony and understanding, remembering that meta-programs are contextual, relative, and influenced by stress.
- One program is whether they move *toward* something positive or *away* from something negative. Observe what people are passionate about and how they frame their motivations.
- Another program is *external* versus *Internal* frame of reference—i.e., whether a person bases their standards on themselves or on others. To test this, ask questions about the person's source of value or satisfaction, or ask their opinion on a slightly contentious topic, and observe how they justify and explain their choice.
- Discern between *options* versus *procedure* thinking—i.e., the degree of novelty, autonomy, and spontaneity a person prefers. To tell the difference, pay attention to how a person reacts to being given a task.
- Discern between *matchers* and *mismatchers*—i.e., whether someone focuses on similarities or differences. Observe the way they classify and group objects—according to similarity or difference?
- Finally, discern between *necessity* or *possibility* mindsets—i.e., maximizing or simply satisfying. Ask a "why" question and listen for "need to" versus "have to" clues.

Chapter 9: Keep Your Ears Pricked for Word Clues

If you want to know who people are, simply listen—they will *tell* you!

No, they will seldom spell it out directly, but if you know how to "listen between the lines," there is a whole world of insight you can glean from a person's ordinary speech.

Some particular word choices reveal things about the person who chose them. John Schafer, an FBI behavior analyst, called these especially revealing words Word Clues. By looking at the words people use when they talk or write, Word Clues help you understand what motivates people, predict how they will behave, and get a deeper understanding of how they see their world.

Of course, Word Clues can't tell you *everything* about a person's personality, but they can give you a starting point. Word Clues are a great way to come up with an initial hypothesis about someone. With more in-depth observations, you can then test this hypothesis and gradually confirm your original hunches. All you have to do is listen carefully, identify certain words, and then make educated guesses about what these word choices suggest.

A key part of Schafer's theory is that **when people think, they do so using only verbs and nouns. Other parts of speech—adjectives and adverbs, especially—are added on purpose after the fact.** *Why* **they are added reveals something about the speaker** and what they are trying to achieve and why. If you simply notice adjectives and adverbs in everyday speech, you will more readily notice this form of bias that people can't help but reveal. As an example everyone will understand immediately, imagine someone tells you, "A black man killed that beautiful young woman." You'd instantly wonder *why* the adjectives "black," "young," and "beautiful" were included.

For a more subtle example, imagine someone is telling you an anecdote, and they say at some point, "I walked quickly." You notice this word "quickly" and how it's not really an integral part of the meaning of the story. The person is telling a story about something else entirely, but they add in this tiny detail about how quickly they walked to get to the train and arrive at a meeting. "Quickly" becomes a Word Clue for you. It gives a sense of urgency, but it doesn't explain *why* the urgency is there. But you can guess: You might walk quickly because you're afraid of being late to a meeting you're going to and of the disappointment of breaking a social norm or expectation.

Perhaps, given the context and what you know of this person, it might suggest that they wish to be thought of as reliable and trustworthy. They want to live up to expectations. Or, another interpretation still is that the word implies a more general sense of anxiety and heightened tension. "Quickly" can suggest haste, even a tiny bit of fear. Either way, the fact that the person has included it in a story that isn't actually about their being on time at all tells you something.

What does it tell you? Well, the rest of the conversation will help you decide. But what's important is that your observation is a *clue*—not a full-blown conclusion about anything, just a clue. A hint. A suggestion. If you find several other such hints and suggestions in the person's speech, you gradually get to confirm one of your original hypotheses. For example, if the person uses lots of other adverbs to suggest promptness, correctness, and reliability, even when these details are not crucial to the story at hand, then you can be sure that you are dealing with someone who is conscientious, eager to please, and observant of social etiquette.

The next time you're talking with someone, tune out the content for a moment and listen to the word choice they are making.

1. Identify the core, necessary parts of speech—verbs and nouns
2. Identify everything else
3. Then ask what this "everything else" means—why was it chosen and not something else?

For a very basic example, imagine that your aunt arrives at your house unannounced one day. She says to you, "Oh, I'm sorry. I was in the neighborhood, so I thought I'd just come over for a teeny tiny visit. Hopefully you still like almond cookies, right?"

The core of this piece of communication is: "I came to visit."

Everything else is extra:

The fact that she is sorry (i.e., aware that you won't like her coming unannounced).

The fact that she feels it necessary to justify her visit (being in the neighborhood).

She *just* came over for a *teeny tiny* visit (this adverb and adjective combination suggests she doesn't want to intrude, but downplays the inconvenience she might be causing).

She has brought cookies expressly for you (the "hopefully" suggesting that they are a kind of offering to offset showing up unannounced, and the "still" carrying all sorts of connotations—it implies that she has known you for a long time, that she is familiar with your tastes, but that she won't assume they have stayed the same, etc.).

Can you see how the bulk of what your aunt is really saying is *outside* of the main components of the message itself? All you need to do to confirm this is to change these extra details while still keeping the central message intact, noticing how much it changes everything:

"I've brought you some almond cookies. Well, are you going to invite me in? Or is the place a mess?"

Or what about:

"Hello, hello, hello! It's your favorite aunt! Surprise! You are going to just die when you see what I've brought for you."

Of course, you'd be exhausted if you had to analyze every sentence out of every person's mouth, but it is good to remember that nothing that people say or do is ever really neutral. Remind yourself that people are often in the position of being able to say absolutely anything at all, but they choose one specific thing. *Why?* Answering that question gives you a glimpse into their world.

Let's look at a few more examples.

"I won another award."

The Word Clue "another" not only makes the point that the speaker won previous awards, but also that they wish to draw your attention to this fact. This person wanted to ensure that other people know that he or she won at least one other award, thus bolstering his or her self-image. If you notice other corroborating Word Clues of this kind, you can safely conclude that this person needs or enjoys the adulation of others to reinforce their self-esteem.

Observers could exploit this vulnerability by using flattery and other ego-enhancing comments; alternatively, you can connect more deeply with such a person knowing that their self-worth is a tender point and a potential inroad to more authenticity in future communication with them.

"I worked hard to achieve my goal."

All achievements require work. But if someone emphasizes the *hardness* of the work, what does it imply? The Word Clue "hard" may suggest this person values goals that are difficult to achieve, precisely because of their difficulty. They may relish a challenge, seeing its difficulty as proof of the value of any action.

But you could read other things in this word, too. Someone who not just works, but works hard, wants to emphasize not just the fact of their having competed a task, but of how much they deserve that outcome. This Word Clue can suggest pride or even a sense of entitlement or defensiveness. You can almost imagine it following the unspoken sentence "I know others get things in life for free, but . . . I worked *hard* for it."

Finally, listen for other Word Clues, since other interpretations are possible. For example, someone may say this a few times specifically to emphasize that it was not luck or talent that won, but sheer grunt work. They may have a strong desire to be recognized for their work, or even for others to admire them or acknowledge the sacrifices they made. Compare the following two pairs of statements and notice how, in context, the Word Clue "hard" suggests different interpretations.

"Growing up, I had none of the support you kids have today. I worked hard to achieve my goal."

"I know some people find a bachelor's degree a walk in the park, but I don't care. I worked hard to achieve my goal."

See the difference context makes?

"I patiently sat through the lecture."

Another adverb that tells a story.

The Word Clue "patiently" presents several hypotheses. Perhaps this person is bored with the lecture. Maybe they don't think very highly of the lecturer, or maybe they think very highly of their own mastery of the subject. Regardless of the reason, this person is preoccupied with something other than the content of the lecture . . . and yet chose to stay in the lecture. Furthermore, they want to *tell* you about this discrepancy. Note, they don't say "I went to the lecture." They are communicating something additional with the Word Clue "patiently." What could it be?

Perhaps this is a person who adheres to social norms and etiquette but doesn't especially like doing so and wants you to know that while they'll follow certain rules, that doesn't mean they like them! After all, a person who doesn't care about social rules will just leave a lecture if they're not enjoying it. They will not present this action as something out of the ordinary, either.

So what does it mean if a person does frame a situation this way? Let's say you form the hypothesis: "this person is externally motivated. They're fair and law abiding, but a little passive." Later, you notice again that they complain a few times about things they're uncomfortable with, but you also notice they make no efforts to improve the situation or get away from it in any way. This kind of thing is subtle but powerful—you are noticing that this person has a very external locus of control.

So what? Well, people with external loci of control are those who tend not to take responsibility for their own lives, but who see occurrences, good or bad, as always stemming from other people or circumstances, and not their own volition. This is a pretty good thing to know when it comes to choosing a running partner to keep you accountable to your fitness commitments, right? You can predict that this is the kind of person who will avoid a workout and then blame something or someone else.

"I decided to buy that model."

On the other hand, here is a person who is telling you, with this Word Clue "decided," that they are the autonomous, active agents in their lives and that things are happening because they *choose* for them to happen. While someone could simply tell you what they bought, here is a person who wants to emphasize the fact that this outcome was deliberately created by themselves. Why?

The word indicates that this person weighed various options prior to the purchase. Perhaps they struggled to some degree before deciding. They may want to communicate that this was not some haphazard thing, but a process of careful deliberation. Combined with other clues, this might suggest you are talking to someone who is not impulsive. Unlike, for example, the person who says "I just bought this model." "Just" strongly communicates impulsivity, indifference, or spontaneity. The action is not something they value or focus on.

"I did the right thing."

The Word Clue "right" suggests that this person struggled with a legal, moral, or ethical dilemma and overcame some level of internal or external opposition to make a fair and just decision. You are speaking to someone with a pronounced sense of right and wrong. They frame their actions in terms of some objective measure of truth. Compare this, for example, with someone who says, "I did the best thing for me," or even, "I did what I was supposed to." The meaning could not be more different, right?

A person who litters their speech with reference to goodness and rightness is, obviously, sending a message not just that they hold personal values, but that they believe in some higher, objective ethical standards, and more than that, they wish to align themselves with that. In other words, you're dealing with a pretty trustworthy and scrupulous person!

"It was done . . ."

Listen for people who frequently use passive voice when they speak, rather than active voice. To quickly explain:

The dog bit Johnny (active).

Johnny was bitten (passive).

The way that people order the subject and the object in a sentence tells you a lot about how they view culpability, agency, and choice. You can immediately see in the example above that the first sentence centers the dog and very clearly identifies it as the agent who did an action—biting. The second sentence, however, puts Johnny in the center, and the dog becomes less important, or even invisible. What matters more is that someone was bitten, and not *who* did the biting.

With this in mind, it's easy to read certain implications in someone's claim "I'm sorry you were hurt," when they could have just as easily said "I'm sorry I hurt you." If people suddenly switch to passive voice, ask why. Are they trying to downplay someone's agency—likely their own? They may be running an external reference meta-program and don't truly see themselves as responsible or to blame. This distinction goes beyond just the grammatical fact of passive voice, though. For example, compare the difference between "we arrived at the party" and "I took us to the party." The latter is more concerned with the agency and actions of one specific person than the action itself. If a person is repeatedly talking about themselves this way, you can infer that they see themselves in the driver's seat (in this case, literally!) and that this is the most salient feature of this situation for them.

A final word of warning here: While FBI agents and interrogators have to come to life-or-death conclusions based on very little information, you can give yourself a bit more leeway. No single Word Clue is enough on its own. Rather, look for **recurring patterns of words** and ask what broader meaning these choices convey about the person who chose them and not some other words.

Listening to Tone of Voice
As the old saying goes, it's not what you do, it's the way that you do it. Or to put it another way, it's not what you say, it's the way that you say it.

A person's tone of voice may be one of the most meaningful components of what they're communicating to you. Consciously or unconsciously, people convey enormous amounts of information in the timbre, speed, clarity, tone, volume and projection of their voice—no matter what particular words they are or aren't saying!

If a dozen people all say the same sentence, they'll each do it completely uniquely, and their different tones of voice will tell you a lot about their different psychological states (not to mention the facts that their accents and voice "age" will tell you loads, too—but that's for another chapter).

The Laboratory of Instrumental Analysis of Communication at the Autonomous University of Barcelona conducted a research study investigating tone of voice and perception. Their findings were fascinating. They discovered that deeper voices were associated with maturity, while higher tones were perceived to carry less credibility. However, extremely deep ones could go too far and convey something more sinister. Talking very quietly was perceived as weak or unconfident.

The big question here is, if we perceive these things to be true, does that mean they're *actually* true? While there probably are socialized and arbitrary elements (for example, it wouldn't be fair to say that women, who have naturally higher-pitched voices, are all uniformly less credible than men, who have naturally lower voices), we can nevertheless make some educated guesses about the variations in voice that are *not* genetic and unchangeable.

Breath

When you think about it, the voice is made out of breath. How someone speaks comes down to their mastery and regulation of air flow from the lungs over the vocal cords. If someone's voice is calm and even, then it's likely they feel calm and even, too. A person who speaks as though they're constantly running out of air is telling you that they are nervous, unsure, or rushed.

Volume

How loud we speak conveys plenty of information about how much "aural space" we are comfortable taking up. People who talk loudly or even over others (or screaming babies, for that matter) are conveying that they feel confident and even entitled to dominate the airwaves in such a way.

A person talking quietly, though, isn't always telling you that they're timid. In certain contexts, speaking quietly can convey an extremely strong and self-assured sense of confidence, or else can even be seductive; when someone whispers, they may be deliberately drawing us in closer to them so we can hear—it's a power move.

Articulation

Think of vocal expression in terms of agility. Is the person talking with clarity, ease, and control, moving with precision and proficiency? Or is their speech chaotic, imprecise, stumbling, inelegant, or filled with "ums" and "likes"? Vocal mastery is almost always a reflection of some other form of mastery. They may be intelligent, knowledgeable, experienced, well organized, or on the ball in some other way (or, at the very least, they *think* of themselves in this way!).

Speed

Speed of speech tells you a lot about emotional state and degree of excitement. If the speed is slow and ponderous, there's a lack of interest there, or even a disconnect (it's important to see the source of this indifference, though—is it the topic being discussed, the audience, or life in general? Do they just not like you?). A rapid speed can suggest excitement, but also tension or a feeling of being rushed. An irregular speed suggests confusion on the part of the speaker, or that communication breakdown is occurring.

Pitch

Research by the University of Göttingen published in the *Journal of Research in Personality* suggests that a lower-pitched voice is associated with people who are more dominant, extroverted, or higher in "sociosexuality" (which means more interested in casual sex or sex outside a relationship). They claimed these findings were true for both men and women.

The researchers asked two thousand people to complete personality tests, and then analyzed recordings of their voices so that pitch could be measured objectively by computers.

According to research lead Dr. Julia Stern,

> "Even if we just hear someone's voice without any visual clues—for instance, on the phone—we know pretty soon whether we're talking to a man, a woman, a child, or an older person. We can pick up on whether the person sounds interested, friendly, sad, nervous, or whether they have an attractive voice. We also start to make assumptions about trust and dominance."

Stern's research shows that we may be right to make these assumptions after all!

An easy tip to learning to read people's tone of voice is to simply become more aware of your own. After all, you always know how you feel in situations; pay attention to how this manifests in your voice. What is true for you is probably true for others.

A fun exercise to try is to watch movies, but in a language foreign to you. Listen closely to how the actors and actresses are speaking, and try to glean as much information from this as possible. If you like, to train yourself to focus on the sound alone, you could even close your eyes and completely remove the visual element. What can you guess about the way they are feeling just from the quality of their voice?

Understand Function Words

Can pronoun use tell you anything about a person? According to James Pennebaker's research in the 90s, yes. He helped develop software that analyzed various texts, including student essays, IMs, press conference transcripts, and more. This research revealed that "function words" (words like pronouns, articles, prepositions, conjunctions, and auxiliary verbs) give more important clues to a person's emotional state than do "content words" (i.e., the ordinary nouns, adverbs, verbs, etc.).

According to Pennebaker,

> "Function words help shape and shortcut language. People require social skills to use and understand function words, and they're processed in the brain differently. They are the key to understanding relationships between speakers, objects, and other people. When we analyze people's use of function words, we can get a sense of their emotional state and personality, and their age and social class."

Pronouns tell us where we have put our focus. Imagine you ask someone what the weather is. Consider these two possible answers:

1. It's hot.
2. I think it's hot.

That little extra pronoun in the second option seems small, but it makes a big difference. It shows a focus on the self. If you had a hunch that the person you were talking to had an internal frame of reference, this would certainly be a clue to support that hypothesis. Interestingly, Pennebaker found that depressed people use "I" more often than non-depressed people. Now that's something to listen out for!

Pennebaker also believes that people who are lying tend to use "we" more often or avoid first-person pronouns, almost as an unconscious bid to rope you in on the reality they're trying to sell you. Those intending to deceive or obscure their culpability will often make generalized statements that include everyone else. For example, they won't say, "I didn't take the money" but something like, "These days, everyone knows you can't just leave money lying around like that." On the other hand, repeated use of "we" in certain contexts could indicate a strong social bond—or the desire for or assumption of one.

People who heavily use articles (like "a," "an," and "the") are communicating a concrete style of thinking, i.e., they tend to see ideas, situations, and even people as things or objects in their field. Conversely, people who tend to refer to things and situations in relational terms are telling you that they predominantly focus on relationships and dynamics between people. Compare, for example, the difference between saying "I'll bring my wife" versus "I'll bring the wife."

It's important to state here that these findings were made using computer software to analyze very small differences in speech—in other words, variations that were too tiny to be perceived in ordinary interactions. In addition, they applied to populations, not individuals. That doesn't mean you can't use their insights in your own life to better read people; it just means that you will need to clock many more **repeated instances** of a particular language clue before you can conclude anything meaningful.

How Language Reflects a Person's Meta-Program

You've probably noticed that there is significant overlap in how we interpret Word Clues, tone of voice, and function words, and how we analyze the meta-program a person is running. Let's say you're trying to determine if a person is using the NLP meta-program of internal or external reference. You listen closely and the person drops Word Clues:

"I chose to do XYZ because . . ."
"I decided to . . ."
"I married him . . ."

You notice that the person has a tendency to choose words that reflect their own agency, volition, and choice. Totally an internal reference! What's more, you suspect they may be more oriented toward options than they are to procedures because they tend to focus on the available possibilities and what they personally wish to do with those options. You notice loads of "I" statements (for example, this person doesn't say "we got married" or "he married me," but "*I* married *him*"), showing you that they have an internal, individual focus.

Imagine now that all of this is delivered in a tone of voice that is quiet, high pitched, and rapid. Sentences are long and complex but rushed, without you being able to get a word in. Are you beginning to get a richer sense of who this person is? You might hypothesize that this person is dominant, a little self-absorbed, and highly energetic, but that at their core, they are slightly insecure and in a hurry to prove something.

Luckily for you, you can build on this hypothesis with every conversation, and with focused listening and careful inference-making, you can begin to see deeply inside this person's head and at things they themselves might not even be aware of! But you don't have to do all this guesswork in the dark. There is one very obvious way to directly test and refine your hypotheses, and that's to ask questions.

Summary:

- People think in verbs and nouns with other parts of speech added after the fact. These additional word choices reveal a lot about a person and can be considered Word Clues. Pay attention to adverb use and the story they tell about how the person sees themselves and others. Notice what is emphasized and what is ignored, and especially pay attention to recurring patterns of words.
- Tone of voice is a part of body language and may be one of the most meaningful components of what a person is communicating. Notice breath (fast and shallow suggest excitement or anxiety), volume (loud suggests confidence or aggression), articulation (correlates with clarity and organization of thought), speed, and pitch.
- "Function words" (such as pronouns, articles, prepositions, conjunctions, and auxiliary verbs) give more important clues to a person's mindset than do "content words." They tell you about the way the speaker understands relationships, objects, and the world in general, as well as all about their emotional state, personality, age, and social class. High personal pronoun use suggests a focus on the self, liars tend to focus on "we," and heavy article use (a, the) suggests a concrete thinking style.
- There is significant overlap in Word Clues, tone of voice and function words, and the meta-program a person is running. Listen carefully for words that signal things like internal or external frame of reference, necessity of possibility thinking, or matching versus mismatching focus.

Chapter 10: The Art of Asking the Right Questions

You can tell a lot about somebody by reading their body language and looking at their clothing, their posture, their accent, the words they use, the things they *don't* say, and their facial expressions. But at some point, you're going to need to go a little deeper and get more detailed information. And sometimes, the only way to get that information is to come out and ask. However, **there are a million ways to ask a question, and sometimes the best ones are those that get us the information we want while appearing on the surface to be completely unrelated.**

Let's take a closer look at how to ask questions that really help you learn the most you can about people.

The Kipling Method

In general, the 5W1H is a way to ask questions and solve problems and is meant to help you see ideas and problems from different points of view. It helps you get to the bottom of a problem and figure out how to fix it. It's pretty straightforward: the acronym stands for what, where, when, why, and who, with the letter H standing in for how.

5W1H is also called the Kipling method after the British author and poet Rudyard Kipling, who came up with it. Kipling used five W questions in his poem "The Elephant's Child," which is the story of an extremely curious elephant who is interested in everything around him. It may sound obvious, but in reading and analyzing people, we can use the Kipling method to help us structure our efforts to gather information that will help us understand a person better.

What

We often ask "What" to seek things that are and will be. We can use this when we are interested to know something specific about a person.

Examples:

- What do you intend to do?
- What do you enjoy doing?
- What pisses you off?

Why

When you ask "why," you are looking for links between causes and effects. This question word probes for a far more sophisticated depth of understanding. Knowing what someone has done doesn't always give you insight into their reasons and motivations. But if you know *why* people have done something, you can begin to understand the world of meaning they have constructed for themselves in their own heads.

Examples:

- Why did you do that?
- Why did that happen?
- Why is it important for us to try it again?

When

When looks for a place in time and can mean two different things—either a point in time that has passed or one that might still come. When can be used to ask for a single specific time, like when someone will arrive at a certain place or when something will be done.

Examples:

- When will you be finished?
- When should we meet?
- When did you give me the money?

How

How is a question that asks for "verbs of process." In other words, the answer is usually an adverb. Knowing what we know about how adverbs are almost always powerful Word Clues, we can ask how to dig deeper into what has happened or what will happen.

Examples:

- How did you do that?
- How did you get everybody's attention?
- How are you finding this project?

Where

Where tries to locate an action or event in three-dimensional space. This can be a simple space, such as on, above, under, or below, or something like a country, a building, a type of location, or even a vague context or environment. When a person answers this kind of question, they are giving you valuable information about how they contextualize and locate certain ideas.

Examples:

- Where did you get that bubbly personality?
- Where did you study?
- Where is this relationship going?

Who

Who brings people into the picture and links them to actions and things. It's a question that directly inquires about the relational human aspects to any situation. The most interesting people in any scenario tend to be the ones who are causing an action, or else deriving a benefit or penalty from that action.

Examples:

- Who is this work for?
- Who will benefit most from what you propose?
- Who else would be interested?

Though the above might seem pretty elementary, we can sometimes forget that **the questions we ask play a major role in the type of information we're likely to extract from someone.** Let's imagine that we're talking to the woman we introduced in the previous section—the one who says "I married him" rather than "he married me." Let's say that, given all your observations, you make a hypothesis about her motivation as a person: You guess that she is very goal-oriented and independent.

So you ask her some questions and notice that almost all of her answers begin with "I think" or "I feel." When you ask a *how* question, she answers with statements about how she achieved something, what she wanted, what she chose, and what she thought of the outcome. When you ask her a *why* question, you notice that she doesn't attribute many outcomes to random chance or the actions of others, but rather to her own actions. Incidentally, you also notice that she appears to quite enjoy being asked questions of this kind and is happy to talk about herself . . .

Bit by bit, your questions mine for data that you use to strengthen and refine the working model you have of her. All questions will yield interesting information, but *why* and *how* questions tend to be more open-ended and invite more colorful responses. These are the ones most likely to give you an insight into how a person thinks.

On the other hand, pay attention to the kind of questions the person is asking you. When you bear in mind that it's recurrent patterns that matter and never just a single question, it's obvious that a person's question shows you what they're most interested in.

Who? This is a person who is interested in relationships and people.
What? The details matter to them.
Where, when? They have a more procedural view and want to construct a narrative in a time and place.
Why? This person is interested in cause and effect, motivations, meaning, and bigger-picture ideas.
How? As above, but the person is asking for more explanation, detail, and nuance.

The questions a person chooses to ask can tell you what they see as the most important element of a situation. For example:

"I got a C minus in math again."
"What?! Who is your teacher?"

Assumptive Questions

Imagine there is an ad in a beauty magazine. The ad copy says *stop wasting money on harsh drying toners* and *we love simplicity as much as you do*.

The ad has made certain forceful assumptions—namely that you are the kind of person who not only knows what toner is, but uses it, spends a lot of money on it, and is dissatisfied with it, finding it dry and harsh. You are also assumed to be a lover of simplicity. The conclusion is that you are like the people writing the ad, and so ought to buy whatever they're selling.

While marketers use assumptions like this to artificially create the kind of consumer they want for their product and generate the sort of desire that results in profit, the same technique can be used to confirm your own hypotheses about people and to sneakily pose a statement as a question.

Consider these examples, which all *look* like questions, but aren't. In order to answer them, you have to accept the hidden assumption within:

- How much do you care? (Assumption: you do care)
- How will you persuade her? (Assumption: you want to persuade her and are going to do it, it's possible to persuade her in the first place, and perhaps there are many different ways to choose between).
- Where do you buy your cheese? (Assumption: you buy cheese!)
- What are you avoiding admitting to yourself? (Assumption: there is something you are avoiding, you know what it is, and the person asking the question is entitled to be told all about it).

Simply by framing a question a certain way, we are implying something about the possibilities for the form the answer will take. The way the other person chooses to respond to these implications can speak volumes. Let's imagine you ask the woman in our example, "So what do you think your biggest flaws are?" and you notice that she can't quite answer the question, or says something like, "I guess people can find my confidence a little intimidating…" This tells you that the hidden assumption (i.e., that she has flaws) is actually not something she acknowledges—that is not part of her own mental model. But if you had asked outright, "Are you a little arrogant?" you would not have received such a revealing answer!

On the other hand, the questions that people ask *you* can also reveal their own assumptions, biases, and preconceptions. If someone asks, "So, was his proposal really romantic?" they are not just assuming that there was a proposal, but conveying a whole world of value judgments and expectations. They are asking you about the thing that *they* are focused on and value. Even though they are asking the questions and you are answering, you are actually gleaning information about their values, priorities, and meta-programs! Consider this exchange and see what the question implies about the asker's values and frame of reference:

A: I've gone vegan. It's been six months now!
B: Oh my God, good on you! Tell me, how much weight have you lost? Do you find your skin is much clearer?

Chunking Up and Chunking Down

"Chunking" is the act of putting together or breaking up information or data into bigger or smaller pieces. In conversation, it's a way to ask questions or organize ideas in such a way as to reach an agreement or gain clarification. But the way that people use chunking in their own speech can tell you interesting things about them as people—if you pay attention!

"Chunking up" is when you move from specific and detailed information to more general or abstract information. How and why questions tend to lead to chunking up.

"Chunking down" goes the other way and happens whenever we move from broad generalizations and abstractions down to finer specifics. Where, what, when, and who questions tend to lead to chunking down.

When you chunk up, it is as though you are zooming out of the conversation to gain a broad, top-down overview of it, or as though you were getting a more general but larger "map" of the terrain of the conversation. When you chunk down, it's like taking a deep dive or getting stuck back into the nitty-gritty level, filling in the inevitable gaps you have on a more abstract overview.

Understanding how chunking works can help you in three ways:

1. It can help you structure your own questions so that you zoom in and out of the topic appropriately, helping you gain a detailed but also broad understanding of what the other person is trying to share with you.
2. It can help you understand how the other person is using chunking, and what this implies about how they're structuring their own mental maps.
3. It can help you identify differences in chunking styles—typically, misunderstandings and conflicts arise from a mismatch of chunking styles. Making sure that chunking styles are balanced and aligned can smooth over conversational difficulties.

So how do you use chunking in a conversation where you're trying to learn more about a person?

First, chunking up questions will help you zoom out and find commonality, look for themes, or help you summarize what you've been told so you can reflect it, showing that you understand and are paying attention.

A: So after we lived in Puerto Rico for a while, we found ourselves back in Italy, but within just two months, because of work, we found ourselves pulling the kids out of school again and doing a year-long stint in France. We wanted to come back to Puerto Rico, but . . . oh well, long story short, we're here in New Zealand instead!

B: Wow, what a whirlwind! So overall you moved, what, four times in one year?!

A: Pretty much.

B: What toll do you think all that had on you?

A: Well, it was hard, but we all learned a lot, I will say that.

Speaker B above has asked two chunking up questions. The first more or less summarizes the key theme of the story ("a whirlwind!"), and the second probes a little for bigger overarching themes that connected all these disparate travel experiences. The question itself is looking for a broader, more abstract analysis, rather than any tiny details about what happened in each particular country, or the exact dates they went there.

If Speaker B continues asking these kinds of chunking up questions, eventually the pair might find themselves having a very detached and abstracted conversation, indeed, about how humankind has always been nomadic, the resilience of children, globalization, the philosophical and political implications of being dislocated from the land, etc.

If A and B are enjoying this, it *may* be a good conversation, but it probably won't be a conversation in which they learn much about one another as people!

Adding some chunking down questions will not only make for a more balanced and comfortable conversation, it will allow more personal and detailed information to come through. The devil is in the details, but so are people's more interesting idiosyncrasies. A good rule of thumb is to stick to no more than three questions of one type in a row. If you ask three chunking up questions, switch to a chunking down question to drill down a little more deeply into a specific idea or detail. But don't stay there too long or you'll risk getting "caught in the weeds." Come up for air after a few chunking down questions to get a breather and a bird's-eye view:

B: What toll do you think all that had on you?

A: Well, it was hard, but we all learned a lot, I will say that.

B: So be honest, which country was your favorite?

A: Hm . . . honestly? I thought I'd love France, but it was nothing like I'd imagined. I'm really loving New Zealand, which I never expected to.

B: What surprised you most about France?

You can almost imagine zooming in on the mental map, from countries to favorite countries to France to something specific about France. But if Speaker A had said, "You know what, they all drink too much!" and Speaker B had another fifty questions about what kind of wine, the conversation would not only stall, but they'd stop gaining further insight into Speaker A.

Here are some examples of chunking-up-style questions (importantly, these are not necessarily verbatim):

What do you think that means?
Why did that happen?
So in the bigger picture . . . ?
Is that connected to . . . ?
What do you think that says about . . . ?
How do all these things connect?
What do you think of . . . ?
How do you make sense of . . . ?

Here are some examples of chunking-down-style questions:

How did you like that?
What happened?
What happened next?
When . . . ?

Who did that?
Tell me more about . . .

So, if you make sure to balance the ratio of chunking up and chunking down questions in any conversation, you'll likely keep things moving along at an enjoyable and balanced pace. But pay attention to learn more about your conversation party.

Do they continually ask chunking up questions themselves and respond most enthusiastically to chunking up questions from you? This could mean a few things. Organizing, analytical, and pattern-seeking activity typically show intelligence, awareness, and mastery of a topic, but it can also hint at a desire to be personally and emotionally distant from a certain topic. If you're having a heated conversation with someone and they suddenly seem to retreat into lofty abstractions about nobody in particular, ask whether you've struck a nerve and if chunking up is serving as an evasive maneuver.

Do they continually ask chunking down questions or respond most enthusiastically to yours? This could indicate a narrow, focused, or even enthusiastic sense of attention to concrete matters, but it can also signal a lack of insight and critical thinking. People most comfortable continually chunking down could be read as running the procedural meta-program and may feel bored or lost in a conversation that doesn't anchor directly onto something in their literal lives in that moment. On the other hand, someone asking chunking down questions could be signaling that they are interested not in the topic at hand, but in *you*. You'll notice that people who flirt, for example, are seldom having a deep and meaningful conversation!

Finally, if you do notice that someone prefers chunking down, pay attention to the kind of questions they ask to gain insight into what they're primarily focused on. Are they more interested in people, places, what happened, the prices of things, family connections, the sequence of events? If you're talking very generally, notice what triggers people to dive deeper into detail. They are communicating what inspires and excites them. By the same token, someone who repeatedly chunks up while you're trying to chunk down might be telling you that they don't find that particular topic very interesting!

You may be wondering if every question is potentially a chunking up or chunking down question. The answer is yes! That said, there are also questions you could ask that act to keep the conversation at more or less the same level of depth—i.e., they neither chunk up or down but stay at that level of focus.

At the end of the day, it's not any particular question itself that will yield greater or lesser insight into someone's character. Rather, it's how that question is used. This is why it's important to create hypotheses in your mind to explain your perceptions and observations. That way, you "test" that observation through targeted questions. At the same time, you listen to their questions, what they are probing for, what they are focusing on, and what that tells you about their motivations, priorities, and thinking style. The methods we've discussed (listening for Word Clues, meta-programs, and overall language use) are relatively weak on their own, but become incredibly powerful when combined. You can use these methods strategically, focusing and targeting your questions to confirm or disprove certain working hypotheses.

Have you ever heard people say that they've spoken to someone for hours, or even known them for years, and yet they actually know nothing about them? That's because their conversation lacked strategy and focus. With a little practice and awareness, though, you can be the opposite—you will be able to talk to people for an astonishingly short amount of time and yet see more clearly into the depths of who they are as a person.

Here are a few last hints and tips for asking questions that will help you fine-tune your people-reading skills:

- As a rule, begin with open-ended questions and lead to more closed ones once the flow of conversation is established. This neatly maps on to asking more chunking up questions first, and then after you've gained an overview (and the person is more comfortable with you), you can drill a little deeper with a closed question that probes for a specific, detailed answer.
- Be careful not to ask too many questions (of any kind). It will feel like an interview or interrogation, and the person will definitely register that the exchange of information is imbalanced.
- Try posing some questions as statements—for example, "You're one of those super smart people, so I bet you learned all sorts of amazing things while living there." Such statements act as questions since they spur conversation and inspire the other person to tell you what you want to know. Extra points if you can be a little unexpected or controversial—the way people jump in to respond tells you a lot about where they are psychologically: "Smart!? Well, I certainly didn't feel that way at the time. Quite the opposite, actually . . ."

Finally, one tip is to work on the delivery of questions. When you ask, use a friendly, relaxed tone of voice, without eye contact, and then once you've asked the question, pause and make eye contact—this body language acts like a nonverbal invitation for them to speak, and communicates your respectful interest in their answer, without being pushy. Likewise, pay attention to their eye contact. Avoiding your gaze or looking away may suggest their wanting to avoid that question!

Summary:

- A great way to get information about a person is to ask targeted questions. The best questions are those that appear on the surface to be asking about something unrelated.
- We can use the Kipling method (5W1H—who, what, where, when, why, and how) to help us structure our efforts to gather information that will help us understand a person better.
- An assumptive question is one that forces certain assumptions and thus implies something about the form the answer could take. The way someone responds to these implications can speak volumes, so notice what they focus on and what they dismiss. The questions that people ask *you* can also reveal their own assumptions, biases, and preconceptions.
- "Chunking" is the way information is grouped into bigger or smaller pieces. The way people use chunking in their own speech or respond to your chunking can tell you interesting things about them.
- "Chunking up" is moving from specific and detailed information to more general or abstract information and can signal detachment or critical thinking, while "chunking down" inquires about details and specifics and can signal interest or more concrete thinking. Notice the person's chunking style and how they respond to yours.

- Keep questions open-ended and varied and don't ask too many. Try to pose some questions as statements and note the response. Ask with a friendly tone and maintain eye contact, leaving enough space for an answer.

BOOK 3: Make Friends Easily:
How to Charm and Connect in Record Time

Chapter 1: Getting to Know You . . .

Loneliness is an epidemic. More than half of Americans report that they feel lonely (Cigna Loneliness Report, 2020), and despite living in one of the world's densest cities, fifty-five percent of London residents say they feel isolated (City Index Survey, 2016), and sixty-two percent of young Australian adults report the same (APS, 2022). With the fallout from Covid lockdowns all over the world, it's no surprise that millions of people in the world now claim they have no friends and that socializing is harder than ever before (Roots of Loneliness Project).

Do you feel the same?

This book is for you if you'd like to:

- connect more with others, and connect more authentically
- make new friends
- improve the friendships you already have
- become more comfortable and confident in social situations
- become a better conversationalist
- get out of your comfort zone
- become a dazzling, ultra-charming social butterfly

Well, that last one may be an exaggeration! Nevertheless, the hope is that by the end of this book, you'll see that becoming a charming, likeable, and confident social butterfly is not as unachievable as you might first think.

Let's be honest: Our world is becoming a strange, fractured place with an increasing sense of division between people. Life is busy. Even those of us who consider ourselves friendly extroverts may find that certain periods in life pose challenges to building a healthy support network. With the rise in certain technologies and lifestyles, you could be forgiven for thinking that the art of conversation and friendship-making is in massive decline . . .

But all is not lost! Making friends is *not* some mysterious dark art, but something that anyone (yes, even you!) can learn to do, no matter where you're starting from.

In the chapters that follow, we'll be looking at how people become friends in the first place, and how to engineer those circumstances yourself. We'll consider ways to create your own personal "aura" of confidence and likeability using simple techniques you can practice immediately. We'll explore how to ask questions, listen actively, tell stories, create witty banter, and reveal more about yourself in just the right way and at the right time. You'll learn more about why previous friendship-making efforts may have failed, and how to make sure you're removing any future obstacles to real connection so you can build rapport with others quickly and reliably.

One caveat, however: there won't be any of the old conventional advice in these pages, like suggestions to join a Meetup group or try to find the love of your life at a community pottery class. The truth is, your life circumstances are completely unique to you, and no book could ever claim to tell you exactly where to meet your future friends, or what they will look like. Most of us already know the standard advice to join an interest group, get involved in your community, sign up to volunteer, or join a church, parents' group, singles club, or the like. This is good advice (and it works best when you actually do it!).

But for many of us, meeting people is just the first step—it's what happens next that's difficult, right? That's where this book comes in. The principles and techniques discussed here will help you take those first crucial moments of meeting someone new and nurture them so that you gradually work your way up to being closer friends one great conversation at a time.

Please don't let reading this book be the *only* thing you do. Learning new techniques and approaches is a necessary but not sufficient condition for making real change in your life, and none of it will make much of a difference unless you have the magic ingredient: ACTION.

The ideas discussed in these pages are not meant to be interesting intellectual musings, but prompts to get out there and literally try something new. How do these concepts look when applied to your unique life circumstances? There's only one way to find out!

Real experience in the world is what creates change. That's why at the end of each section, you'll be encouraged to get out there and experiment. Some of the material and exercises will seem really obvious to you . . . until you try them for yourself. The magic happens in the consistent application and practice of an idea, not in how well you can grasp it intellectually.

Who are you going to practice on? If you are socially anxious or shy or have difficulty with people, relax. You don't need to make quantum leaps overnight. Wherever you are, just start there. If needed, you can always make short, brief connections with shop assistants, people standing in lines, random acquaintances. Take a look at your social circle and identify the people in the periphery—you only need the smallest of connections to build on. And small connections are everywhere!

All you need is an open mind, the willingness to step a little out of your comfort zone, and some genuine curiosity of the world and the people who live in it. We're all different, and we all have our own obstacles and blind spots. But remember that **human beings are built for connection**. You know more than you think you do!

THE FRIENDSHIP FORMULA
Haley remembers her best friend from first grade, Kitty. The two first met when they were seated next to one another in homeroom, and they spent every weekday together at school . . . and soon every weekend, too. They'd talk for hours or just do homework together in silence or walk home together from afterschool activities. Haley remembers how her friend had been like a lifeline to her. She had just moved to the neighborhood, her parents had just gotten a divorce, and everything in life was upside down—except Kitty. With her she could talk about anything. In fact, the two became so close that they considered themselves inseparable, better than sisters, and swore they'd be best friends forever.

Kitty is still in Haley's life, although they now live on opposite ends of the world. Haley is now thirty-four and discovering that making friends as an adult is . . . different. Haley considers herself a kind, friendly person who makes an effort to meet new people. So she doesn't understand why, years after moving to a new area, she doesn't feel like she really knows anybody.

A woman she really wanted to be friends with, Alex, is the wife of someone she met in painting class. Though Haley felt like they had made a connection, Alex just seemed to drift off, their text messages became strained, and nothing really took off. Haley's world, in fact, seems full of awkward meetups, promising connections that quickly fizzle, and "friendships" that revolve around drinks every four months. Soon Haley is sick of hearing the phrases "so busy" and "sure, let's get a coffee or something . . ."

Why was it so easy to make such a strong connection in first grade, and why is it so difficult now?

Dr. Jack Schafer, former FBI agent and author of *The Like Switch*, has a theory that might have the answer. Schafer is a behavioral expert who first introduced the concept of "the friendship formula." According to him, clicking with a person and becoming their friend is not some random bit of magic, but follows a predictable pattern. The formula goes like this:

Friendship = Proximity + Frequency + Duration + Intensity

In other words, friendship will develop most quickly and most firmly when all four factors are strongly present. Without them, friendship cannot emerge. Let's take a look at each in turn and see how they apply to Haley's friendships.

Proximity
This is the distance between you and the other person. When you think about it, **building friendships is simply a matter of fostering increasing *closeness***—and that closeness is not just metaphorical. The closer you are physically, and the more context you share, the better your chances of striking up a friendship.

Haley and Kitty sat right next to each other for hours, every day, for all of first grade. That's a lot of time! Compare that with her friend-of-a-friend Alex, who she will only see if she makes a concerted effort to arrange a meetup.

The psychology of this is straightforward. **Human beings tend to like what they are already familiar with.** If you are spending a lot of time with someone, they become familiar to you. Sure, constantly being in someone's space doesn't *necessarily* mean they will like you (siblings all across the world can attest to this!), but it does mean that you will increase your exposure to that person, and if there is a potential for friendship, all that exposure will help you make something of that potential.

Alex and Haley, on the other hand, are simply not in each other's world. They each have completely separate, different lives, and to find room in that life for someone else takes an active effort—an effort that people are sadly not too ready to make.

Frequency
You can probably already see how Kitty and Haley's friendship was based on greater frequency than most adult friendships are. **Greater frequency means a stronger chance**

of friendship developing. Even if you can't spend a lot of time with someone, it's still worth something to *frequently* spend time with them.

Consider a long-distance marriage where the couple spends only one day a month together. Now consider a different long-distance couple who only spends twelve days in a year together, all at once. Which couple do you imagine has the greater chance of staying connected?

Both spend the same *amount* of time with one another, but the latter couple has more frequent contact, and this naturally leads to a stronger sense of bonding. It comes back to repetition and familiarity. **The more frequently you engage with someone, the more they feel like part of your world.** There are simply a greater number of opportunities to share, to communicate, to become a part of one another's experience.

You might wave hello and say one or two sentences to your neighbor every single day for years, and genuinely come to think of them as a kind of friend. One day you might meet a person and have a deep and meaningful conversation with them for hours, but never see them again. The connection with this latter person is definitely deeper and more satisfying . . . but you probably don't consider them a *friend*.

Duration
As we've seen, friendships can be formed in short, frequent bursts, but all the better if they have the luxury of time on their side. If you add up the total time that Haley and Kitty spent together, it probably borders on thousands of hours. If you add up the total time Haley and Alex spent together . . . it's probably around thirty minutes. Even though Haley and Kitty were joined at the hip, even *they* weren't that interested in one another after only thirty minutes! **Friendship takes time to build.**

You're probably wondering if this is a catch-22 situation: People only spend time with those they're already friends with, but how can you make friends with someone until you've spent a lot of time with them? It's true that adult friendships are plagued by this very problem, but understanding this snag means you're best positioned to get around it as quickly as possible (which is exactly what we'll be doing through the rest of the book).

Intensity
The final variable in the equation is how well you are able to satisfy another person's needs during any social interaction. The more you can, the better the chance of striking up a friendship. Siblings are a great example of how even people with high duration, frequency, and proximity in their interactions don't necessarily become friends—they may not meet one another's emotional needs (in fact, they may actively get in the way of them!).

Siblings who get on well, on the other hand, often do so because they have a connection based on mutual support through a shared challenge, or else they have come to help one another with their respective needs—i.e., they have intensity. Haley and Kitty found a safe haven with one another. They had long, intense talks about their secret feelings and helped one another through the tough times. Compare that to Haley and Alex—both are independent, self-sufficient adults with husbands, children, and fulfilling jobs. Their lives are full. To put it bluntly, the mutual emotional *need* for that connection is simply not as strong.

Incidentally, flagging intensity is a big reason for the failure of already established friendships and relationships. It is the reason a couple complain of lack of connection when they spend every day together: because when they are together, they're both distracted, staring at their phones, or occupied with low-level chit chat. As they lose intensity, they lose connection.

To return to the equation, you can see that **friendships will develop according to the sum of all these four elements.** That means that one element can be relatively weak if another compensates by being extra strong. Consider these examples:

- Two colleagues work together and happen to spend a lot of time doing the same hobby, too. There's not much intensity, but they make up for it with plenty of proximity, duration, and frequency, and consider one another good friends.
- Two old college friends have long since moved to different countries and now only see one another yearly for a long Christmas vacation together. They spend a full two weeks together, catching up—they lack proximity and frequency, but they have plenty of intensity and spend hours together, just all at one time. This has kept their friendship going for decades.
- Two people live on the same block and over time have come to an arrangement—they collect one another's packages if they're out, and they pass on messages or check in on the houseplants if the other one goes away for a few days. Despite being two completely different people who move in different circles, they have become friends. They have very low duration (they have seldom chatted for longer than five minutes at a time), but high intensity and frequency since they regularly meet one another's needs.

Though all sorts of combinations can and do come together to make a friendship, naturally there are lower limits, and **if the total package comes below a certain threshold, a friendship simply cannot develop.** This is what has happened with Haley and Alex: They have low proximity, low duration, low intensity, and low frequency. Haley thinks, "I don't understand. We got on so well together, and we both really wanted to get to know each other better!" But Dr. Schafer would say that friendship has very little to do with how much people like one another or how similar they are.

He might point out, in fact, that many good friendships can form even if people are quite different or annoy each other sometimes or come from wildly different backgrounds. You can probably prove this to yourself by thinking back to your own childhood friends—how many of them were genuinely great matches for you as a person, and how many simply took root in your life because they were there, they were familiar, and you both went through the same experiences together?

How to Use Schafer's Formula to Your Benefit

Many people who struggle to make friends start out by asking the wrong questions.

How can I be more likeable?

What's wrong with me? Am I not interesting/funny/smart enough?

Why don't they like me?

Instead, take Schafer's advice and **deliberately find ways to increase proximity, and the duration, intensity, and frequency of your interactions with people.** Here's how.

1. Start by increasing proximity. Your goal is just to get them comfortable with you being around so that you start to feel more and more familiar. The big caveat here is to do this slowly—if you push yourself on people, they'll perceive you as a threat.
2. Once proximity is established, gradually increase the amount of time you spend with that person. At the same time, slowly increase frequency, too.
3. Only after you've done the above can you start ramping up the intensity by talking about more in-depth things or revealing a little more about yourself.
4. If the intensity part goes well, the cycle should repeat, with both of you seeking out more proximity. Over time, a friendship is established, and the same four factors help to maintain it over time.

Granted, this seems like a pretty easy process, and it is. It can take **time**, however, and the biggest reason for failure along the way is impatience. Imagine you meet someone interesting at a party, and you immediately click and start talking. Even though it's the first time you've ever met, you soon notice yourself sharing personal details, ranting about politics and other heavy topics, and probing them for answers to all life's deep and meaningful questions.

Now, whether the other person reciprocates or not, you may find that after the conversation is over, a sudden awkwardness sets in. By skipping the parts where you build proximity, frequency, and duration, you risk going too far too soon. If you've ever formed an intense connection with an "instant friend" who then disappeared after a month of knowing you, this might be the reason why.

On the other hand, it's not enough to *only* increase proximity and so on. The old advice to find friends at shared interest groups or hobbies is good advice—but it's just a starting point. If you are regularly spending hours every week with people but you never increase intensity or ask them to hang out outside of those scheduled times, chances are the friendship won't properly launch.

In the remaining chapters of this book, we'll be looking at plenty of different techniques for better listening, asking questions, telling a great story, and building rapport. But all these techniques are best when embedded in a firm understanding of this overall timeline of a developing friendship. Even the wittiest banter and charming conversation won't help if you're only at the first stage of gently increasing proximity with a potential new friend.

The rule is: go slow. Take your time and build up each successive interaction on the previous one.

Put it into practice: Look around your social network and identify one person who is an acquaintance—i.e., someone you know but don't know very well. How often do you spend time with this person, and for how long? Do you meet one another's needs in any way?

Once you've quickly appraised the current status of the relationship, decide on what you need to do next in order to create more closeness. You will probably need to increase proximity or frequency first. How could you do that? This is not necessarily about inviting them out somewhere or conspicuously asking them to be your friend (although if this feels right to you, you can do this!). Instead, become curious about how you might start gently building value in one of the four variables. You don't need to commit to a lifelong relationship, either—just take action and see what happens.

CREATE YOUR OWN REALITY DISTORTION FIELD

Right now, try to think about the people you've been drawn to in your life, perhaps even attracted to. Think about how you first perceived them and what made you single them out in a world filled with other people. Why did you decide you liked *them* especially and wanted to know them better, even when they were still relative strangers?

Bestselling author and self-help guru Tim Ferriss claims that certain people in the public eye have what he calls a "reality distortion field." Sounds impressive, huh? In less flashy language, he's referring to none other than that irresistible combination of charm, charisma, confidence, and ability to persuade. In other words, that quality that makes other people flock around you and want to be your friend.

Luckily, says Ferriss, this quality is not one hundred percent innate but something you can develop and cultivate—in fact, when it's all broken down, the skill of charming people is made of astonishingly simple parts:

Make (Brief) Eye Contact

Most people tend to go about their daily business with only cursory glances at the world around them, other people included. **But brief eye contact with strangers is simultaneously the easiest and most powerful way to quickly convey connection, confidence, and a little sprinkle of charm.**

It's simple: For less than a second, glance into the eyes of people you walk past, then look away again. That's it! The key is to keep it as brief as possible. The fact is, people, even complete strangers, will not mind or see it as an intrusion, but with that flicker of eye contact, you actually create a strong sense of presence that most other people are probably not creating.

While you make eye contact, keep your gaze soft and neutral. You don't want to be staring at someone or making them think that you're looking for something, trying to flirt, or making a point of any kind. If this trick seems too simple to actually work, then try it for yourself. The next time you're out in public, challenge yourself to make fleeting eye contact with five or ten people in this way. Then notice not only how you feel, but how others respond to you. Prepare to be surprised!

Be Very Aware of Personal Space

Charismatic, confident people have a way of being very physically present, without it feeling imposing or threatening. It's all about proximity again: "Closeness" is not just a physical feeling, but a function of many subtle psychological experiences. There's a reason they call it eye "contact," for example—looking at someone psychologically brings you closer to them, even if the space between you remains the same.

There are other ways to create this perception of closeness without literally getting in someone's face. For example, you could face them head on, use touch (sparingly), raise or project your voice, or talk to or even about them. You can imagine that if someone enters a room, makes eye contact, greets you at a fairly loud volume, and then comes over, gently touching your elbow as they shake your hand, you'd feel they were extremely present without impinging on your personal space. It's this conscious use of physical proximity that allows charismatic people to command attention while staying friendly and respectful.

Ferriss claims that Bill Clinton was such a man. A friend of Ferriss's claimed to dislike Clinton, but by chance got to meet him at a party one day. Ferriss explains,

> "In that moment, face-to-face, all of my friend's personal animosity toward Clinton disappeared, in one instant. As they were shaking hands, Clinton made eye contact with my friend in a way so powerful and intimate, my friend felt as though the two of them were the only people in the room."

Two things are fascinating about this: The first is that charisma is so powerful it can completely remove and reverse any active biases a person may have, and the second is that all of this can be done with small, simple tools—just eye contact and a handshake.

Stay Present
It sounds kind of obvious, but if you want *presence*, you need to actually be present!

That means that **you cannot be distracted by your own anxieties about socializing, you cannot be thinking about what you're going to say next, and you can't be quietly judging the other person or worrying that they're judging you**. The moment you go off in your own head and abandon the real, unfolding moment right in front of you, you lose some of your raw power and potential magnetism. You're elsewhere . . . and other people can feel it.

We all know what it's like to talk to a person who is only half listening, looking past us, or distracted by a nearby screen. But it's worth remembering that you can make others feel invisible or unheard even without being this obvious. It's possible for somebody to be looking right at you and yet not really see you, and it's possible for someone to say "uh huh" and repeat what you just said, even though you know deep down that they haven't *really* heard you.

Sadly, in today's information-soaked world, we're all in something of an attention deficit. The good news is that by pausing, by being present, and by actually paying total attention to the person in front of you, you will instantly stand out from the crowd and elevate that interaction to something special. It is one small way that we can build the intensity we spoke about in the previous chapter.

The simple reason is that eye contact fulfils a very primal and real need in every human: the need to be acknowledged. Consider again what Ferriss's friend said about Clinton: that he made it feel like they were the "only people in the room." What this tells us is that Clinton's eye contact made people feel important. They were not there in a crowd, clamoring for attention. They were seen and heard. The person looking at them treated them as though they were genuinely interesting. What could be more magnetic than that?

Here's another example. In a now famous 1977 interview Barbara Walters did with Dolly Parton, we can see all three of the above play out beautifully. It's worth watching a clip of this interview if you can, simply because it's a perfect masterclass in what a "reality distortion field" actually is, and just how powerful it can be when done right.

What's fantastic about the interview is that it also dispels the myths many of us have about what charm looks like. Look at any win-friends-and-influence-people-style material, and you could be forgiven for thinking that "charisma" is something reserved for businessmen in power suits in the eighties; you could come to the conclusion that presence and gravitas were about domination, power, and "crushing your opponent."

However, Dolly Parton proves that this has nothing to do with it. In the interview, Barbara Walters is pretty obviously going for the kill and posing questions deliberately designed to throw Dolly off, embarrass her, or get her flustered. But watch how Dolly reacts. She does a few key things:

- She is perfectly, almost serenely calm in herself. She doesn't rush, she isn't tense, and she doesn't for a second behave as though she doesn't have the right to speak freely. She is self-assured, calm, composed.
- She maintains deep, sincere, and frequent eye contact with Walters, even as the questions are obviously hostile. Dolly *knows* exactly what is going on but doesn't descend to that level. She smiles, she's amiable, and she consistently pulls the conversation in the direction she wants it to go, never taking any bait or reacting. She responds to intrusive and insulting questions in a thoughtful, mature way that consistently elevates the conversation to where she wants it to be. She doesn't get angry or defensive—she maintains her frame in the way she wants it, and sweetly, easily dismisses Walter's attempts to create drama or tension.
- She is fully, one hundred percent present in the interview, in herself, and in her body. She leans forward and listens closely to Walters. She takes up space. In fact, a big part of Dolly Parton's legendary charisma comes from this ability to expand so visibly into her surroundings—her body is big, her smile is big, her hair is big! She makes no apologies and simply, comfortably takes up this space for herself. The message is communicated on a primal level: *I'm here. I'm in the present. I'm comfortable.* Note, however, that this is a quiet but firm resolve, rather than arrogance, pushiness, or aggression.

Dolly Parton won hearts and minds precisely because she could control situations in this way. She looked like a blonde bimbo (Walters even insultingly asks whether she's a "hillbilly"), but that's only to the untrained eye that cannot see the social genius of working with eye contact, presence, body language, and energy. Barbara Walters, a skilled and experienced broadcast journalist, is left looking petty and transparent—because she lacks the charisma that Dolly has in abundance.

When Barbara takes a snipe at Dolly's outrageous fashion sense, insinuating that she "doesn't have to look like that" in a condescending tone, Dolly answers not with her words, but with her demeanor. She laughs and replies, with a charming, totally relaxed smile, that no, she doesn't have to dress as she does . . . but chooses to because she wants to. "I would never stoop so low to be fashionable; that's the easiest thing in the world to do." In this way, she communicates beautifully that she doesn't play the games Barbara does, and that she is way above being provoked using so trivial a tactic.

Not only does she put Walters in her place, she actually manages to do it with kindness, civility, and a degree of grace that is far more than the rudeness of the interview deserved. Barbara went into the interview with the intention to show up Parton as a ditz and an airhead; Parton saw it all coming and disarmed it to perfection.

When you watch the recording of the interview, you realize Parton achieves all this with *nothing more than her physical presence, her eye contact, and the way she carries herself.* That's all. She doesn't have any "wit" or clever "clap backs." She doesn't attack or get angry. She certainly doesn't make intelligent arguments. She conquers the interaction solely because she is in perfect, total control of herself. And her "reality distortion field" blows everything out of the water.

Can you learn to do this for yourself? Absolutely. **But take a page from Dolly's book and realize that the biggest impact you make on people does not come from what you** *say*—**it's from how you** *are.* In the interview Dolly said,

> "Oh, I know they make fun of me, but all these years the people have thought the joke was on me, but it's actually on them. I am sure of myself as a person. I am sure of my talent. I'm sure of my love for life and that sort of thing. I am very content. I like the kind of person that I am. So, I can afford to piddle around and do-diddle around with makeup and clothes and stuff because I am secure with myself."

Put it into practice: The next time you're interacting with someone, **try to hold the frame of yourself as secure, worthy, and perfectly calm in yourself.** If you like, you can temporarily imagine that you are someone else that you admire, and then behave as you imagine they would behave. What would you say, do, and think if you knew deep down that you had intrinsic worth, and so did everyone else? How might that change the way you approach every interaction?

Note how your mindset instantly alters the way you hold other people's gazes, how you take up space, how you move. Notice what it does to the reality around you. Is there anything you'd like to keep on doing?

RECIPROCAL CURIOSITY

Picture this. You're at a party and get to chatting with a person you don't know, and they seem interesting. They ask what you're up to at the moment, what you do for work, and so on. You answer them, but each question and answer seem to go a little like this:

You: "I'm ready to start growing the business at this point, but I'm kind of not sure exactly what that will look like, so it's like being in limbo. I know there needs to be a next step, but I haven't quite figured it out yet..."
Them: "Uh huh, sure. Tell me about it. I know how that goes. You're just scared. I went through the same thing last year."

Then later...

You: "My wife and I seldom come to these things, but we had a free weekend, so we decided we'd—"
Them (interrupting): "Oh, totally, yeah, you decided you'd give it a shot. That's cool. You have to force yourself to get out there."

And then again...

You: "Man, my back's been killing me, though."
Them: "Let me give you the number of my chiropractor. He's the best, hands down."

Now, looking at the above, you wouldn't say there is anything *wrong* with these interactions, right? And yet somehow you leave the conversation feeling a mixture of boredom and irritation. The other person was polite and you talked well enough, so why did something feel so "off"?

The reason may be a simple one: They lacked curiosity.

If you go back and read the interactions again, you'll see that the other person has an attitude of *already knowing* who you are and what you're saying. To put it bluntly, they're not really interested. **They do not view the interaction as a possible way to learn something new or encounter something they aren't already familiar with.** They don't ask any questions or listen to the answers because, on some level, they don't believe that you as a person have anything new or interesting or valuable to give them.

Sounds extreme, but imagine having another conversation later on at the same party, and saying all the same things again, except it goes like this:

You: "I'm ready to start growing the business at this point, but I'm kind of not sure exactly what that will look like, so it's like being in limbo. I know there needs to be a next step, but I haven't quite figured it out yet..."
Them: "So, you're basically an independent publisher? Have I got that right?"

Or...

You: "My wife and I seldom come to these things, but we had a free weekend, so we decided we'd take a look, you know, try something new."
Them: "Oh yeah? Sounds great. Who was playing the last time you were here? This is my first time, so I have no clue what to expect!"

And then . . .

You: "Man, my back's been killing me, though."
Them: "Oh no, don't tell me you've got back pain, too! Do you think we're all getting old or something? You're the third person to tell me about back pain this week . . ."

Bearing in mind the idea of curiosity, can you see the difference between the first person's approach and the second person's?

Social skill experts often tell people to **ask more questions**. But it's worth understanding *why* they give this advice so often. The fact is that the best conversations are real, spontaneous, respectful ones. They're conversations in which we are fully present, open-minded, and receptive to whatever new thing we might learn about the fascinating person in front of us. Questions are good because they keep us curious—and curiosity is the secret sauce.

The worst conversations are those where we're not really paying attention, where we make assumptions that we don't bother to confirm the truth of, where we judge the other person or simply go through the motions rather than have a living, breathing conversation in the present moment.

Curiosity makes all the difference. It's the lifeblood of a genuine, authentic interaction. You can spend your whole life talking to people, being polite, being "interesting," etc. But if you are genuinely not curious about them, or about the potential for your interaction as it unfolds in that moment, then your interactions will always feel a little small, hollow, and flat.

Be honest with yourself: Do you find people interesting? Do you genuinely enjoy learning about them and having them show you their unique new ways of looking at the world? Do you let them change your mind or steer the conversation in the ways only they can? Do you *like* them? Do they inspire or comfort or teach or entertain you? Do you leave interactions feeling honored that you got to peek into their special world for a brief moment?

If truth be told, **most of us are more interested in convincing others how fascinating we are than finding what is truly fascinating about them**. But think about the last time you really enjoyed someone's company. Did you enjoy them because they said all the right things and were clever and impressive? Or did it simply feel good to roll with the moment as it came, learn something new, and uncover something unexpected? Something real?

A good conversation is a thing of beauty, and it's about reciprocal curiosity. When the first person at the party says, "Uh huh, sure. Tell me about it. I know how that goes. You're just scared. I went through the same thing last year," what they are doing is making sure that you think they are interesting. They want you to know that they are smart and experienced and know what you're talking about. They've seen it all before and have the answers. They're clever.

This is an understandable human impulse, but it misses the fact that it doesn't feel good from the other person's perspective. To them, it sounds like: "You are nothing special or interesting. I'm not really that interested in hearing about you. You're not unique. Your situation doesn't really grab me or warrant any further investigation." When you say "you're just scared," you are closing the potential of the conversation down. You don't care to learn more about the other person, because you think you already know what they're going to say.

When you ask a question and instead say, "Do you think you're scared?" then suddenly everything is different. You are opening the conversation and allowing it to be what it is. You're curious. And the more curious you are, the more alive your conversations will be—and the more people will like having them with you!

The first person at the party was essentially in a monologue. The second one was letting you know that they wanted the conversation to be a collaborative effort.

The best conversations are co-creations. They are mutually steered by both parties, and neither of them knows exactly where it's going to lead—that's the fun part, right? A boring conversation is where both people are uninterested and inflexible. They stand next to one another and take turns telling the other person what they know, while the other person waits for their turn to do the same. Boring, huh?

How to Build Curiosity

Curiosity means connection and authenticity. **Unless something is connected to the other person, or connected to the present moment, it's not really alive**.

Curiosity, like the quality of charisma we've already explored, is something you *are* rather than something you *do*. The most important thing, then, is to first make the mindset shift and genuinely want to know and connect with people. This is a massive hurdle! But unless you cross that hurdle, your attempts to "seem" curious will always fall flat and be inauthentic.

From there, consider these simple rules for maintaining a frame of curiosity in your conversations:

1. Listen deeply
2. Never assume
3. Focus on the person, not the story

Listen Deeply

Listening is a profound act. When we listen, we open ourselves receptively to learn something new. **We're not just gathering data when we listen. We're suspending ourselves and paying close attention to someone else—their world, their experiences, their system of meaning.** We're prepared to be surprised.

The golden rule is: **listen to understand, not to respond.**

You've probably been in a conversation with someone before and could *feel* that they were just waiting for you to stop speaking so they could jump in and argue with you or add their two cents. They were listening, yes, but only enough so they could insert themselves into the conversation. It's invalidating, and it quickly turns conversations into competitions, or, as we saw above, parallel monologues.

When you sit down to talk to someone, be an alien who has never talked to anyone before. Pretend you know absolutely nothing, and listen attentively for the other person to tell you.

Listen for nuance. Even if you think you're familiar with what they're saying, be humble enough to imagine that the way they're expressing it may be completely novel to you. You might catch your brain wandering off and trying to tell its own story about the details its hearing—pull it back when it does that and remind it to listen to the other person's story about what is happening. *That* is what you're listening for.

Another good rule of thumb is to **listen for emotion, not fact**.

Person A might tell Person B a long list of everything that has bothered them that day, listing a broken-down car to an irate customer at work to a mother-in-law who made a mean snipe for no reason. Person B could latch on to one of these details—let's say the broken car—and start to "help" by suggesting solutions for fixing the car.

The problem? They've listened . . . but not really. Person A is communicating one overall message: I'm stressed and overwhelmed today and need to vent. Person B pays attention to the details but misses this bigger point. Person B is not listening to the *emotion* behind all these separate little facts—frustration, annoyance, etc. They're also not "hearing" the reason Person A is talking to them in the first place—i.e., Person A wants someone to hear them and acknowledge their emotion. Person B could instead say, "Wow, sounds like you've had a day from hell! Let's get a drink and you can tell me all about it." It would then feel like they had truly listened.

Good listeners are great at noticing patterns, and they pay attention to things that stand out. They notice when someone keeps mentioning the same phrase or word over and over, for example, and they use that word themselves, or paraphrase it when trying to demonstrate that they've heard and understood. They notice body language and speech patterns and infer the overall context of what's being communicated. They're not just listening to the words spoken, but to everything around those words.

Assume Nothing

This is basically the same as being curious. If you find people boring, it's usually not that they themselves are boring, but rather that the categories you've put them in are too narrow and limited.

So, you see a teenage boy in front of you and make the kneejerk assumption that he's probably immature, that he spends too much time gaming, or that he's a little awkward or untidy at home. But if you hold on to this stereotype too tightly, it may stop you from seeing the genuine human being in front of you: That teenage boy may be incredibly mature, self-controlled, creative, sensitive, thoughtful, and unconventional. The only way you will see all that, though, is to drop your assumptions.

When you listen to such a boy, then, you are not listening to confirm what you already think of him. When you perceive him without bias, assumptions, and filters, you are also "listening" on a deep level. **You are willing to *discover* who he is, rather than to come to a lazy conclusion that's based on nothing.** After all, wouldn't you want people to approach you in the very same way?

It's human to "fill in the details." We see a middle-aged woman in tweed carrying a briefcase on a university campus and we assume she's a lecturer or professor. Chances are, she is—but what about all the times she isn't? Our mental shortcuts and assumptions are fine when we are aware that we're using them, but we need to be able to ditch them when faced with a real person, not a stereotype.

Another way that assumptions can creep in and spoil connection is when we are too hasty to interpret a situation according to our frame of reference, forgetting about the other person. Someone announces a pregnancy and you say to them, "You must be so excited." But must they be? In being so quick to assume that excitement is the only response to a pregnancy, you've lost sight of the other person and their unique experience.

Your goal with listening is not to guess things accurately or come up with some compelling theory or explanation to feed back to the other person. **Your goal is simply to be there as a witness to the experience they are sharing**. Give yourself this permission and you will notice how much easier conversations are—for you as well!

Person, Not Story

This is an extension of the last rule, which is to focus on the person behind the story and not so much on the story itself. **The details are beside the point—what's interesting is how they experience those details.** What do the details look like to them, in their world, from their frame of reference? What does it all mean to them?

Imagine a conversation where someone is telling a friend a story where they feel persecuted unfairly at work. If the friend goes into Private Investigator mode and immediately starts trying to figure out who is "really to blame," they have missed the point entirely. It doesn't matter how they make sense of the story, or how others would. That's irrelevant. What matters is how the first person has experienced the story.

A good friend will say something like, "How are you feeling about the whole thing?" or, "What do you think you want to do now?" rather than, "Oh, I'm sure you've just misunderstood. You're being too sensitive." Conversation is not about finding out who's right; it's about support, connection, and understanding.

So, instead of having a conversation about whether a colleague was or wasn't rude, you simply focus on the fact that the person in front of you believes they were. Internet forums often have sections devoted to people asking the anonymous public if, in some personal situation, they were being unreasonable or were in the wrong. But this kind of conversation is never satisfying, for obvious reasons. Conflict is never resolved when people find out what is rationally "true" or "reasonable." And someone's hurt feelings don't go away just because everyone else feels like they shouldn't feel that way. The fact is they do. So, instead of focusing on who is right and who is wrong, forget the story and look at the people underneath. How do they feel? Does someone feel guilty? Ignored? Confused? Misunderstood?

Never mind about what you think of the situation, or what anyone else does. What do THEY think of it? Follow that thread and it will lead you to richer, more real connections.

You Go First

Before we close this chapter, let's look at **one unexpected way you can show that you're willing to really listen to people: Disclose something about yourself.**

This may seem counterintuitive, but it's really about emphasizing the *reciprocal* in *reciprocal curiosity*. If one person repeatedly feels called on to self-disclose while the other person doesn't, it can feel unbalanced and create weird power dynamics. Especially if someone feels like they're already on the back foot, asking too many questions while you reveal nothing of yourself can actually make the situation worse.

Taking the initiative to disclose something real about yourself can be a way to correct this and almost invite the other person to do the same. It creates trust and sets the tone.

Take another look at this interaction from the second person at the party:

You: "Man, my back's been killing me, though."
Them: "Oh no, don't tell me you've got back pain, too! Do you think we're all getting old or something? You're the third person to tell me about back pain this week . . ."

Notice the very subtle self-disclosure and how they are creating a sense of shared experience and trust by this little word "we." There is a teeny tiny gesture of vulnerability in there. The self-disclosure, no matter how small, is paired with a question and an invitation for the other person to disclose—it's balanced. Questions are great. Too many questions without any personal disclosure from you will feel intrusive and disempowering.

The trick with self-disclosure is to use it sparingly, use it wisely, and be sincere. If you don't really know how someone feels, for example, then don't say "I know how you feel"!

Put it into practice: In your next conversation, imagine that you are switching out your normal ears for "emotion ears" that can only detect emotional content. Without making any assumptions, ask yourself why this person is telling you what they're telling you. There's no need to necessarily act on what you "hear" with these ears, but practice turning them on in social interactions and notice how different the situation appears to you when you take in this stream of information, rather than perceive only the verbal and factual.

Summary:

- Dr. Jack Schafer's "friendship formula" is as follows: Friendship = Proximity + Frequency + Duration + Intensity. Friendship will develop according to the sum of all these four elements. That means that one element can be relatively weak if another compensates by being extra strong.
- Building friendships is about fostering increasing closeness—i.e., proximity. Greater frequency also means a stronger chance of friendship developing. The more frequently you engage with someone, the more they feel like part of your world. Friendship takes time to build, so greater duration of time spent together means greater chance of friendship. Finally, it matters how well you're able to satisfy another person's needs during any social interaction. The more you can, the better the chance of striking up a friendship.
- When making friends, deliberately find ways to increase proximity and the duration, frequency, and intensity of your interactions with people, in that order. Go slow!
- To create a reality distortion field, you will need to increase eye contact, be aware of your personal space, and stay present and open-minded in conversations. Charismatic, confident people are physically present, without being imposing or threatening, and their eye contact is natural. They do not let judgment, anxiety, or distraction undermine

their presence in the moment. The key is to acknowledge people and make them feel important.
- The biggest impact you make on people does not come from what you *say*, but from how you *are*.
- Maintain reciprocal curiosity and the mindset that you can always learn something new from others. Be fully present, open-minded, and receptive rather than approaching with bias, judgment, or distraction. Instead of trying to convince others how fascinating you are, find what is fascinating about others. Conversations are co-creations!
- Genuinely connect to others by listening deeply, focusing on the person and not their story, and never making judgments or assumptions. Listen to understand, not to respond; listen primarily for emotion, not just fact. One way you can show that you're willing to really listen to people is self-disclosure.

Chapter 2: The Friendship Mindset

THE ART OF ACTIVE LISTENING
Do you know someone who is a really bad listener?

Sadly, the modern world is full to bursting with them, so chances are you do! Think about them right now and try to recall conversations with them. When did you most feel unheard in their presence? Why? What were they doing, and importantly, what *weren't* they doing?

Let's look at a story of the kind of person you might have encountered in your own life. We'll call him Jez.

Jez is a great guy and considers himself a "people person." In fact, he believes he's better than average when it comes to understanding what makes people tick, and is something of an armchair psychologist. He tells people, "I'm a great listener. People are always asking my advice." Jez genuinely thinks he's an empathic person.

The trouble is . . . he's not. Take a look at the following conversation and see if you can spot why.

Friend: "Well, I don't know, we'll see how it goes with the new guy, but it's the early days and so—"
Jez: "Uh huh. Uh huh. I'm listening."
Friend: "I'm just keeping things open-ended for now, you know? I didn't even want a new boyfriend a month ago, so."
Jez: "Uh huh. I completely understand."
Friend: "Anyway, we were out yesterday and he said to me—"
Jez: "Sometimes when we've been hurt in the past, we can keep people at arm's length to protect ourselves. I get it."
Friend: "Well . . . yeah, I guess. I'm not really keeping him at arm's length, I don't think. More like taking it nice and relaxed. Last time I rushed into a new relationship, but this time—"
Jez: "Oh, I know exactly what you mean. This time you're not willing to open yourself up again because you can't really trust people. Have you ever considered that you actually may have PTSD? It's more common than you think."
Friend: "PTSD? No way!"
Jez: "Look, you don't have to be ashamed at all, don't worry. It's all so *complicated*, isn't it? Getting involved with a new person?"
Friend: "Well, uh . . ."

Obviously, reading the above, nobody would say that Jez is a good listener! You can probably notice his astounding lack of curiosity, but it goes further than this:

- He interrupts. Instead of listening to how his friend feels, he's *telling* her how she feels (we'll be taking a much closer look at interruption later in the book).
- He offers her an interpretation of events, rather than asking her about her interpretation ("you can't trust people").
- He gives advice and makes diagnoses (which, even if they *were* accurate, are not wanted).
- He's not paying attention to the actual emotional content of the conversation.
- He's using the conversation to play at being "good with people"—and ignoring the person in front of him.
- He's using labels to describe his friend's experience that she herself does not use ("PTSD," "complicated").
- He is reacting inappropriately and disproportionately. The friend is having a relaxed, lighthearted conversation, and Jez is treating it like a soul-baring deep-and-meaningful therapy session—it isn't.

Basically, it's very clear what this conversation is all about: Jez. Everything else is coming a distant second!

I've included this example because **sometimes the worst listeners among us are those who have actually become distracted by the very idea of being good listeners**. It's precisely because they are so attached to their *idea* of being empathetic that they fail to properly hear and see other people. In other words, Jez is actually letting his own desire to be a good listener stop him from being a good listener. Note how he interrupts his friend . . . to tell her he is listening. Oops!

If you're even a little bit like Jez, then don't worry—we've all been there. Active listening is harder than it looks, and few people are good at it without taking the time to really be mindful and *practice*. It's a skill worth developing, however, because it can single-handedly transform all your relationships—whether they're personal or professional. What's more, knowing how to properly listen can spare you a lot of awkwardness, misunderstanding, or outright conflict.

Here are five basic techniques that naturally skillful listeners tend to use every time they're with another person. The important thing is to not be like Jez—remember that you're not trying to *give the appearance* of a person who is good at listening, you're really being that person!

Pay Close Attention

Imagine that someone has told you that you're about to go into a lecture hall to hear a very important talk. Hidden somewhere in what the lecturer says is a clue that will tell you where one million dollars is hidden. If you blink, if you lose focus for one second, you could miss that clue. Now, imagine the degree of focus you would carry with you into that lecture hall! Could you bring that same degree of utter rapt attention to every person you meet?

Concentrate all your awareness and interest on them. There is so much to take in when you really look. Don't just listen to what they're saying, but read their body language, their tone of voice, their facial expression . . . even think about what they're not saying. If people seem a little boring to you, it's only because you're not paying attention. If you look with the right eyes, every human being can seem like a bottomless mystery (well, okay, maybe not *every* human—but it's worth giving the benefit of the doubt whenever you can!).

Give the gift of your solid, respectful attention. Act like a million-dollar clue might fall from that person's lips at any moment—it could. Listen generously, as though you are prepared to hear the value, the sense, and the meaning in what you hear.

- Eye contact is again important here.
- Turn your body to face them, lean in a little, and adopt a posture that communicates "this conversation is the most important thing I'm doing right now."
- Whatever you do, get off your phone. Not even a little glance, nothing. Just put it away, on silent, and be in the moment. The same goes for clocks, TV screens, and so on.
- In the same way, park all your busy thoughts and internal distractions. Think of it this way—they'll still be there waiting for you later. Just pay attention to the other person. You might find it's actually quite relaxing to forget about yourself now and then . . .
- If you catch yourself thinking of your reply, gently let it go and turn your attention back to what is currently being said.
- If you had an amazing point to make but the opportunity is passing by, let it pass. You don't have to say everything you're thinking. Let the conversation be what it is, and don't be tempted to drag the topic back to where it was ten minutes ago—your conversational partner will rightly think you simply don't care about everything they've said in the meantime.

Be Mindful of the Little Things

Listening is great—but you also need to make sure that the other person can *see* that listening. Make sure you're actively showing them, and remember that people can't read your mind. If, for example, someone has been talking for a few minutes, and you're listening closely but silently, they may wonder if you are actually listening. Let them know you are with little gestures that accompany conversation, but are not strictly a part of it:

Give a little nod—it says "I understand that" or "That makes sense. Got it."

Slightly mirror their facial expression—"I understand the emotional content of what you're saying."

Adopt a comfortable posture—"I'm not going anywhere. I'm here and I'm interested."

Give little encouraging sounds as they speak—"I'm here to support what you're expressing. I hear you."

Make small comments ("What, really?" or "That's amazing")—"Your story matters and is important to me."

Of course, if you do too much of this, or if you're not sincere, you will come across like Jez. This will give people the wrong impression entirely, and they will only feel the effort you're making to connect with them, rather than the connection itself.

Help People Think Out Loud

When Jez launched into unsolicited psychotherapy with his friend, what he was doing was imposing his own assumptions, filters, beliefs, judgments, and systems of meaning on her, and disregarding hers. While Jez is an extreme example, **it's actually very easy to allow your own perspective to impair your ability to understand somebody else's.** This interferes with communication on the most fundamental level possible and is an enormous barrier to genuine connection and understanding.

The first thing is to recognize that unless you know someone very well, or you're very similar to them, it's unlikely that you will truly understand the nuances of their worldview and perspective. You will need to *actively* find this out for yourself—in fact, this is what communication is for. Instead of assumptions (the biggest assumption being that other people are more or less the same as you are), try to **start from a position of ignorance and work your way up to real understanding.**

Take an example:

Jez's friend says, "I'm just keeping things with my new boyfriend open-ended for now. It's the early days."

Now, ask yourself, what does she *mean*? There are a few possible interpretations, even of this quite basic statement. Maybe she means that she's not taking the relationship seriously. Maybe she *is* taking it seriously, but is trying to play it cool for fear of jeopardizing things. Maybe what she feels is uncertainty right now, so she can't actually say what's happening with any accuracy. Maybe she's bored of talking about it and is subtly wanting to move the topic along to something else (i.e., "it's none of your business, Jez!").

If you enter into a conversation carrying your own unexamined and unacknowledged biases, you might pick any of the above interpretations according to your own needs and perceptions. If you're Jez, you might hear something that isn't even there, and launch off in that direction. But, if you're a good listener, you will not assume anything, and ask more questions to help you understand better. You'll remain curious. Every step of the way, you'll want to *confirm* that what you're hearing is actually aligned with the speaker's intention.

Have a look at the same conversation with someone who is genuinely a good listener:

Friend: "Well, I don't know, we'll see how it goes with the new guy, but it's the early days and so I don't know. I'm not sure."
Good listener: "Yeah? Like, you're not sure about how you feel about him or . . .?"
Friend: "Well, yes. Partly. I mean, I do like him, but I didn't even want a new boyfriend a month ago, so . . . maybe I'm just keeping things open-ended for now."
GL: "Hm, that makes sense. You like him, but it's only been a month, and before that you were thinking that you didn't want to get involved with anyone."
Friend: "Exactly! So it's not like things aren't good between us, I'm just . . . cautious."
GL: "Yeah, cautious. Maybe you want to go slow with it?"
Friend: "I think so, yes. But I think it's best for me right now. I've got a lot of other stuff going on, that's all."
GL: "Seems like you're not saying no to it or anything, just that it's not quite what you had planned, seeing as you have all these other priorities."
Friend: "Yes, that's exactly right. It is all about priorities right now. I like him, but he's not my priority."
GL: "Nothing wrong with that!"
Friend: "No, I guess not. You know what, you're a really good listener."

When a conversation is flowing well and someone is truly listening, they almost become part of the speaker's thought process—**it's as though by listening, they are helping the other person to hear themselves, to think through their thoughts and emotions, and to arrive at some conclusion**. But if you read the conversation again, you will see that the good listener hasn't done anything special—in fact, he's barely introduced any new information at all. What he has done is:

- Directly restate what he is told
- Paraphrase what he's told—i.e., put it in slightly different words
- Summarize what he's hearing
- Reframe the content of the story
- Gently suggest something new

Let's take a closer look, with examples from the same conversation.

Restate
Simply repeat what you have just been told using the exact words or else words that are very similar.

Friend: "Well, I don't know, we'll see how it goes with the new guy, but it's the early days and so I don't know. **I'm not sure.**"
Good listener: "Yeah? Like, **you're not sure** about how you feel about him or . . . ?"

Paraphrase
Restate what you have been told but use your own words to demonstrate that you have grasped the meaning behind them. You could also use terms like "It seems like . . ." or "If I understand correctly . . ." and then offer your interpretation to signal that you are in fact paraphrasing.

Friend: "Well, yes. Partly. I mean, I do like him, but **I didn't even want a new boyfriend a month ago**, so . . . maybe I'm just keeping things open-ended for now."
GL: "Hm, that makes sense. You like him, but it's only been a month, and before that you were thinking that **you didn't want to get involved with anyone**."

Summarize
Paraphrase what has been said but in condensed form so you reflect the essence of the overall message you're hearing. Summarizing in particular is great for "helping people think aloud," and it also shows attention and empathy since you are not just hearing facts but synthesizing the bigger picture.

GL: "Seems like you're not saying no to it or anything, just that it's not quite what you had planned, seeing as you have all these other priorities."

Sometimes, all that's needed to summarize a person's message is to accurately label the emotion behind the details they're expressing. The Good Listener could also say something like, "It sounds like you're a little hesitant."

Reframe
This is different from the other active listening skills because you are inserting something of your own interpretation into the mix. The Good Listener in our example does this subtly, first by introducing the frame of "priorities," which is something the friend had not really considered before but seems to latch on to. Later on, the Good Listener also introduces another frame:

Friend: "Yes, that's exactly right. It is all about priorities right now. I like him, but he's not my priority."
*GL: "**Nothing wrong with that**!"*

At the beginning of the exchange, the friend is speaking in a way that suggests she's conflicted and almost a little defensive, as though she's worried that how she feels about her situation is not quite reasonable or doesn't make sense. The Good Listener here deploys some very subtle listening skills and picks up on this hesitancy and doubt—and gently reframes it. They suggest, instead, that the way the friend feels is perfectly normal, and there's nothing wrong with it. The friend thus moves very slightly from one frame of mind to the another and ends up feeling like "Yeah, actually this *is* what I feel and what's so bad about that?"

If the conversation continued, the Good Listener could start to reframe things even further. Rather than focusing on what the new boyfriend *isn't*, he could ask the friend to tell him more about everything else that's interesting and exciting in her world. Thus, it's not a frame of "You're only lukewarm about your new boyfriend" but "You're really fascinated by a new project at work right now."

This ability to shift frames is the single thing that allows for problem-solving, creativity, and conflict resolution. Incidentally, it's what people really mean when they say that someone is good at giving "advice"—they are not talking about being told what to think but being helped to discover what *they* themselves think. Big difference!

While this is all extremely subtle, the same dynamics can play out in all kinds of conversations, big and small. Do this in conversation and you will quickly earn a reputation for being genuinely "good with people." In fact, these four skills alone will make you a better listener and friend than ninety percent of the human population!

Put it into practice: Time to test drive these ideas with a real live human again! Whatever your next conversation is, agree with yourself that you are entering it only to listen. Play a game with yourself where you introduce zero new information and only reflect, summarize, rephrase, or restate what the other person is feeding into the interaction. Keep this going for as long as is comfortable, and notice how it changes things. How do people respond when you really, truly listen? Have you really been listening in the past?

QUESTION-ASKING

We've explored *why* it's so important to ask questions, but in this section, let's take a closer look at exactly *how* to do it.

First, imagine a hypothetical situation. You're at a work event and meeting lots of new people:

Person A is witty and tells you a fascinating and entertaining story.
Person B asks thoughtful questions about how you ended up in your line of work.
Person C tells you about the new software products they're launching.

Let's say that each of these people is genuinely polite and intelligent, and each of your brief conversations with them is pleasant enough.

Now ask yourself, which one do you would *like* more?

Research by a team of Harvard psychological scientists suggests that the most likeable will be Person B because they ask questions. The likeability, they claim, increases even more if the person asks follow-up questions that show they listened to and cared about the answers you gave to the first questions.

Karen Huang and colleagues concluded from their research that **talking about yourself is always going to make you a little less likeable, while asking questions makes you a little more likeable**. Even if you are talking about yourself in an inspiring, interesting, useful, or amusing way . . . you're still talking about yourself.

Remember Bill Clinton and how he made people feel like he was looking right at them, and that they were the only two people in the room? Being a president almost certainly makes you a fascinating personality . . . but even in that case people would still rather have you notice, acknowledge, and engage with *them*.

Huang's research found that people who asked open-ended questions showed the greatest relationship to likability. And yet, in new and unfamiliar situations, people tend to get nervous and do the opposite. In a bid to get people to like you—you end up doing the opposite:

> "The tendency to focus on the self when trying to impress others is misguided, as verbal behaviors that focus on the self, such as redirecting the topic of conversation to oneself, bragging, boasting, or dominating the conversation, tend to decrease liking. In contrast, verbal behaviors that focus on the other person, such as mirroring the other person's mannerisms, affirming the other's statements, or coaxing information from the other person, have been shown to increase liking."

In a 2015 study published in *Psychological Science*, Duffy and Chartrand put study participants in groups, with each part of the pair being told to ask a certain number of questions. Neither party was aware of the instructions the other side had received. After a fifteen-minute chat, everyone was asked how much they liked their conversational partner, and the results were unsurprising: Those who asked more questions were rated as more likeable because they appeared more responsive.

It's active listening again: **We like those people we genuinely feel are hearing us, seeing us, and reacting to us**. The researchers further explained that "follow-up questions are particularly likely to increase liking because they require responsiveness from the question-asker, and signal responsiveness to the question-asker's partner."

The researchers also concluded that extroverts were rated as more likable than introverts. However, this is NOT because extroverts are loud mouths who talk about themselves, but because they were better at asking questions. So, if you are a more introverted person, relax: You can still be ultra-likable, just as long as you allow yourself to get out of your head and engage with the person in front of you!

So, a rule of thumb that will never let you down: when in doubt, ask an open-ended question. If you can, ask a meaningful follow-up question. Of course, asking too many questions can backfire, especially if they are closed, repetitive, unimaginative, and intrusive. Generally, though, most people are asking too few questions, not too many.

Chunking Up and Down

Okay, so asking questions is important, and we should all be asking more of them. Open-ended follow-up questions are best. But let's explore a few more considerations for getting questions right.

The concept of "chunking" was introduced by Harvard psychologist George A. Miller. He was the man who popularized the concept of "The Magical Number Seven, Plus or Minus Two." His research in working memory found that human beings are able at best to retain around seven pieces of information, plus or minus two. That means if you tell them ten pieces of information, it will be too much and some won't be absorbed. However, he also discovered that if you organize some of those bits of information into groups, more could be remembered.

For example, the phone number 555 987 2323 has ten numbers, which would be hard to memorize individually (it's greater than the human limit of seven, even adding an extra two at a push!). However, if you chunk the numbers, the 555 becomes one chunk, and the final 2323 becomes two bits of information, not four (two lots of 23). Chunking the whole number into six pieces of information suddenly makes it easier to remember.

Miller applied this to higher order types of information, too. He found that the way you present information greatly influences the way people receive it, and this has far-reaching consequences for communication. **Today, the concept of chunking is used as a way to vary the degree of detail at which we present or absorb information**.

Learning how to chunk can improve the way you negotiate with others, explain yourself, or ask for what you want. It can help you "meet people where they are" and resolve conflict, as well as create a quicker sense of rapport. Yet most people are completely unaware of the option to vary the way they chunk information according to the needs of the conversation—instead they let the conversation run where it will, for better or worse.

We can chunk up or chunk down. Broadly:

Chunking up means to "zoom out" and go up a level of abstraction.
Chunking down means to "zoom in" and explore a smaller, more concrete detail or specific instance.

To really understand the role these two functions play, let's look at some examples where chunking is *not* being properly used—and how it undermines connection and communication.

Example 1

A: "You were late again this morning."
B: "Really? I don't think I was. Maybe like one or two minutes, but I don't think that counts as late."
A: "It was more like ten minutes, actually."
B: "No, that's not what I remember at all. I remember walking in and it was like, 2:05 or something."
A: "Okay, so it was more than one or two minutes, like I said. And you were late yesterday as well."
B: "I didn't even come in yesterday."
A: "Sorry, I meant the day before yesterday."
B: "The day before yesterday I was on time. Or does being on time also count as late in your book?"
A: "Well, why not? Everyone else was here and ready to start at 2 p.m."
B: "So I wasn't actually late. I was there at 2 p.m. You're now saying that you want me to be there *before* that? You're asking me to be early, not to be on time. I was on time."
A: "But that's not what I'm saying . . ."

And on and on, you get the picture! Before we comment on this exchange, let's look at another one.

Example 2

A: "So, what do you think you're really looking for in a partner?"
B: "Oh, you know, the same thing everyone else is, I guess! I really value honesty. At this point in my life, I'm looking for more authenticity, more realness."
A: "Oh, cool. I can totally relate to that. You seem like a pretty straightforward person to talk to, in fact. I like that."
B: "Yeah, I just feel like society has just become so fake, you know? Everyone's wearing masks all the time."
A: "Oh, I agree. I hope . . . well, I hope I'm getting to see the real you? I'll show you mine if you show me yours, haha!"
B: "Yeah, it's definitely about vulnerability, isn't it? I read this article the other day about how the internet has rewired the way people connect with one another, and how everyone has become kind of passive and demanding. Like, we're all used to this kind of browsing mode and have no patience for each other anymore."
A: "Yeah . . . but I'm liking talking to you right now . . ."
B: "Do you know about Lacan? He was a psychoanalyst who had some cool theories about how humans form their identities, and the role that desire plays and blah, blah, blah . . ."
A: (Screams internally.)

Hopefully, you can see that both these interactions could be better. Let's look at each in turn and see why they went wrong and how chunking could have improved things.

In example 1, the trouble is that both people are getting "stuck in the weeds"—they are allowing themselves to be bogged down in irrelevant detail. They're quibbling about whether it was one minute or five, or what the definition of "late" is and of exactly when this event happened or didn't happen. As a result, no progress is made, no understanding is found, and these two are likely to go on arguing pretty much forever.

They are both repeatedly chunking down—drilling down to details and hashing over them while losing sight of the bigger, more abstract organizing principles that could pull these details together. Speaker A never zooms out enough to say what is really behind every little gripe of theirs: "People in the team are feeling like you don't take them or their work seriously."

Likewise, Speaker B is defending themselves on each little accusation while never seeing the bigger pattern all these little data points form: "I know I'm tardy sometimes, but I don't agree with your assessment that I don't care. I do care. I'm hurt that you think that a few minutes here and there mean I don't care, considering all the hard work I do put in." Chunking up could have saved this conversation and brought A and B to a real resolution. Instead, they stay trapped on one level, arguing.

So, does that mean chunking down is always a bad thing, and chunking up is what makes you a good communicator? Nope! Example 2 is the proof. In that conversation, the problem is that Speaker A and Speaker B are pulling in opposite directions: A is attempting to chunk down, B is continually responding by chunking up instead. In this example, A is trying to have a flirty, personal, and specific conversation. But B is abstracting and depersonalizing this at every turn, talking vaguely about "people" and "society" rather than "you and me."

B launches off into interesting but sterile musings on vulnerability, Lacanian theory and mask-wearing—all the while not noticing A's attempts to remain in that *specific* conversation, in the here and now. A keeps talking about B directly; B responds by talking about ideas and concepts, in a removed and detached way. A is trying to make a connection, B is *talking about* connection in an abstract sense. It's the opposite problem from Example 1—**the conversation is all very lofty and high-minded, but it lacks detail and specificity.**

What both these examples show us, then, is that **it's not chunking up or down that is important. Rather, it's about balance, variety, and matching the other person.**

When you are asking questions, keep this in mind. Some questions will chunk up, some will chunk down (a few will keep you where you are). **As a general rule, try not to ask more than three of one type of question in a row.** If you ask three chunking up questions (or make three chunking up comments), then zoom in again and ask a chunking down question. Mix things up. Listen to hear where the other person is and try not to pitch your comments or questions too far from where theirs are in terms of specificity.

Here's how to chunk up:

Look at some of the details being discussed, and ask what they could be an example of.

Example: If you like football and they like tennis, notice that they're both examples of sports.

Ask about the deeper connections between seemingly disparate ideas.

Example: What's common to both these sports? What "bigger picture" is that a part of?

Ask about overarching patterns, themes, or underlying purposes that connect things.

Example: They're British and love football; you're French and love tennis. What does this say about how culture influences the sport you like?

Ask about the meaning or purpose of things.

Example: Why do they like tennis? Why do you like football? What's the point?

Here's how to chunk down:

Look at the overall principle and become curious about specific instances of that.

Example: They love cooking, so you ask them: What type of cooking do they like? What ingredients? What specific stores? What recipes?

Ask about the facts—what, when, where, who (note, this does not include the question why—that's a chunking up question).

Example: Who taught them to cook so well? Was this when they were younger? How old? Where did this happen?

Ask about differences and distinguishing features.

Example: They like spicy food, but do they prefer Mexican spicy or Indian spicy? What's the difference? Are there actually many different types of Mexican cuisine?

Basically, chunking down means to look at the "pixels" of the conversation, whereas chunking up is about looking at the overall picture those pixels make.

Once you know all this, it will become obvious that the most effective communication happens when chunking is varied and appropriate. You want to continually zoom in and out, getting both a detailed view of the conversational landscape, as well as being able to zoom out and check on the bigger picture now and then. Again, remember that neither is better than the other; instead, they are both very different tools. Let's look at how and when to use each tool.

When to Chunk Up

- When you want to depersonalize—let's say in a professional context, or in a confusing or emotional argument where a little psychological distance could allow everyone to "step back."
- When you want to summarize what has been done or what will be done. Chunking up is reminding yourself of your overall strategy and intention of the conversation. It's a way to check in and see if you're on course.
- When you want to solve problems, but solve them by thinking outside the box or working at a higher level of abstraction.

- When you are trying to resolve conflict and want to move away from the details of the problem and start thinking of a way forward (like the people in the first conversation).
- When you are making a theory or trying to learn.
- When you are considering meaning and purpose.

When to Chunk Down

- When you want to create more closeness, intimacy, and rapport. Specificity equals intimacy. It's here and now.
- When you want to keep things light and inoffensive—this is the domain of small talk. Asking about details maintains conversational connection without much emotional risk.
- When you want to demonstrate active listening and show that you're paying close attention. Asking questions can often lead to someone sharing more and more detail, and this can be an opportunity for validation and empathy.
- When you want to solve a problem, but on a very practical, specific, and pragmatic basis.
- When you're fact-finding and trying to gather data (you then use chunking up questions to analyze and synthesize that data). This is the rule about "listen to understand, not to respond."

In the real world, of course, things can't be so easily divided into "chunking up" or "chunking down," but you may be surprised at what you notice when you use this framework in your own conversations. In time you can become more skilled at not just asking more questions but asking the right *kind* of questions.

Both chunking up and chunking down can make you more likeable, more charismatic, more empathetic, and more interesting. If a conversation is stalling or feeling too superficial, it's time to ask a chunking down question and get more personal. If you notice that one or both of you are getting lost in pointless detail, zoom out, take a breath, and see if you can inject life into it by making a comment about a broader pattern or theme. Then, you can drill down again later in some new, fresh topic.

Put it into practice: Time to find a conversation guinea pig again. In fact, this exercise can be done on anyone you encounter today. Simply become mindful of the level of abstraction/specificity they are functioning at. Notice where *you* are in relation to them. Do you notice certain people who have a consistent tendency to be one way or another? Do you tend to default to more chunking up or chunking down questions and comments? If there is someone who you repeatedly feel awkward around, ask if part of the mismatch could be in the way you organize information.

ACTIVE AND CONSTRUCTIVE RESPONDING
You've paid close attention and listened to the other person—check.
You've taken care to ask plenty of questions and kept an eye on the way information is organized—check.

In the rest of this chapter, we're going to spend a little more time on **responses**. Consider the following situation. You've just been nominated for an award at work that you never in a million years thought you'd be eligible for. You're over the moon, and by the time you get home that evening, you're bursting with excitement.

Your roommate is already home, and you excitedly tell them the good news, with plenty of expansive and energetic body language, big smiles, and rapid talking. Maybe you even make a few excited squeals or do an impromptu happy dance in the kitchen!

Your roommate sees all of this from their spot on the couch, and says, without looking up from the old *Law and Order* episodes they're rewatching, "You go, girl, that is so amazing. Proud of you. Did I tell you the toilet's blocked again, by the way?"

Let's take a closer look at the roommate's response. They clearly have listened, and they obviously have detected that you're excited and want acknowledgement of your good news. They say all the right things, but . . . the response is just one hundred percent wrong, isn't it? Why?

Much of the advice out there on how to be a good friend and make better conversation is geared around how to be compassionate and nonjudgmental to people who may be sharing sensitive or unhappy information with you. But what about when people share their *good* news? It turns out that your responses to that are just as important, if not more so.

Psychologist Shelly Gable coined the term "active and constructive responding"—and it's something that was entirely absent from the fictional roommate's response to someone else's good news. **She explains how there are two main variables when it comes to responding to someone's good news:**

1. **How active versus passive**
2. **How constructive versus destructive**

These two variables create a matrix of four possible reaction types. Let's look at each in turn and see if you can identify which one matches the roommate's response.

Passive and Destructive Response

A: "Oh my God! I won the lottery! Woohoo!"
B: "Huh. And here I am worrying about how to make rent next month."

A: "Well, thank God, I've finished work for today and have the afternoon off!"
B: "Uh huh" (looks at phone).

Passive here means not just low energy and effort, but also a kind of failure to match the energy of the news being shared. Destructive refers to the damage done to the connection between A and B—after such a response, the conversation is likely to rupture or fizzle out.

Whether the "news" is that big of a deal or not, it's about the level of energy and enthusiasm being shared, and how much of that is being acknowledged and mirrored by the listener.

This kind of response is characterized by a tendency to ignore or avoid the speaker and what they're saying, or to focus on the self rather than the speaker.

Active and Destructive Response

A: "Oh my God! I won the lottery! Woohoo!"
B: "Wow, way to brag about it. Are you trying to make other people feel bad or what?"

A: "Well, thank God, I've finished work for today and have the afternoon off!"
B: "Big deal."

This kind of response is also destructive, but it does even more damage because it is actively, deliberately, and forcefully so. This is a person who either intends to show hostility or has unintentionally revealed their negative feelings about what's been shared. Either way, the effect is to make the speaker feel dismissed, demeaned, and undermined. It's the opposite of support and validation.

Occasionally an active destructive response masquerades as "concern" or helpful "advice." If someone excitedly tells you they won the lottery, for example, and you immediately launch into warnings about how they mustn't ruin their lives with the money, and to watch out for scammers and greedy friends, they are actually responding to the good news as though it were bad news . . . and this response is just as actively destructive.

Passive and Constructive Response

A: "Oh my God! I won the lottery! Woohoo!"
B: "Good for you. That's nice" (then says nothing further).

A: "Well, thank God, I've finished work for today and have the afternoon off!"
B: (distracted with something)
A: "I think I might head out to the pool later."
B: "Oh yeah, cool. Good idea."

This response type is a lot better than the previous two because it is constructive—i.e., it acknowledges and supports the positive content of what is being shared. What's missing, however, is a reflection of the emotion and energy behind what's being shared. These responses are generally "nice" but lack energy and enthusiasm and may be too quiet, subdued, or delayed to feel good for the speaker.

Active and Constructive Response

A: "Oh my God! I won the lottery! Woohoo!"
B: "WHAT!? I can't believe it! Amazing."

A: "Well, thank God, I've finished work for today and have the afternoon off!"
B: "Oh, you lucky devil. I'm so jealous. Any plans?"

This response is the ideal one because it actively matches the energy level of the speaker, but also offers constructive, supportive listening that will make the speaker feel seen and heard. Note in the first example above that B responds with plenty of enthusiasm, while in the second the response is still positive but somewhat less enthusiastic.

Both of them, however, are constructive, active responses because they are pitched at the same level as the speaker. In the first example, the speaker is really excited—and the listener reciprocates. In the second example, the speaker is pleased with the situation but not ecstatic; again the listener acknowledges and reflects this.

This raises a subtle but related point: A response that is more active than the speaker's own expression is not as supportive.

A: "Well, thank God, I've finished work for today and have the afternoon off!"
B: "WHAT!? I can't believe it! Amazing."

The effect is a little like what happens when overly enthusiastic family members go a little overboard in their praise for someone's achievement, much to their embarrassment. It's worth being careful about this and paying attention not merely to the content of the message and what you think of it, but of the feeling and energy behind the message and what the speaker thinks of it.

If someone pulls you aside and says with a slight frown, "Okay, don't tell anyone, but I've won a tiny bit of money in the lottery," then a supportive and active response might be to whisper back, "You have? Oh, wow. Tell me more."

Now, reading the above four types of responses, you can probably guess that the roommate from the very first example was using a passive, constructive approach—not great! It would have been far better for them to communicate that they had seen and understood your excitement by showing genuine interest, excitement, or even pride at what you'd told them.

Shelly Gable's big contribution to this discussion is perhaps the fact that **active listening and question-asking do not necessarily show support or compassion.**

Most conversations usually unfold at several levels at once. On one level, there is body language. On another, there is the factual content in the words you're speaking and the information you're sharing. On another level still, there's nonverbal information that comes from the feeling, intention, and meaning of the facts being communicated.

The more literal-minded among us might fail to see that when a person shares good news, they are not conveying information in the ordinary sense. **They are usually sharing information in a conscious or unconscious bid for you to recognize and affirm how they're feeling.** Most people share good news because they want others to confirm and validate those good feelings, reflect them, or perhaps even praise and support them. If you fail to recognize that this is the unspoken request being made of you, you might inadvertently disappoint or even offend someone.

Sometimes, adults can take this position with their children and forget to actively praise or support their efforts. If a child announces an achievement they've made at school, for example, there could be a range of invalidating responses.

"Great. Now eat your dinner, please." (Passive destructive.)
"So you got ninety out of hundred? Where did the other ten marks go?" (Active destructive.)
"Aw, well done, honey." (Said on autopilot while distracted—passive constructive.)

So much damage to relationships of all kinds exists not because people are genuinely hostile to one another, or because they're bad people. Instead, it's often nothing more than a lack of awareness and not being mindful of the subtler nonverbal purpose of certain kinds of communication. A child may announce they've made the team, and in response the parent starts complaining immediately about how they'll arrange lifts to practice or how much the sports uniform might cost.

It's not enough to just *feel* pleased and happy for someone in an abstract way—you need to actively communicate that. If someone's good news doesn't in fact make you happy, then the compassionate and mature thing to do is suspend your own perspective for a moment and focus on theirs. Your focus should be on maintaining rapport and connection. Celebrate with them to the extent you can, and separate any of your own negative feelings and shelve them for another time.

Finally, it's worth noting here that our responses should never be solely verbal, either. A truly active and constructive response makes use of body language, posture, voice, and gesture:

1. Smile
2. Make eye contact
3. Use open, friendly body language angled toward the speaker
4. Match their voice and vocal expression (if their pitch is high and they're talking rapidly, do the same)

The Perfect Compliment

Unlike the common wisdom tells us, flattery can indeed get you everywhere!

Every human being alive loves to be seen, heard, and validated. And there isn't a person on this planet who doesn't love hearing a genuine and thoughtful compliment. But you can probably agree that somebody muttering "You go, girl, you're amazing" on autopilot is not going to have this effect!

Compliments are like magic gold dust that supercharge connection and rapport—if they're done right. A good compliment has three key features:

1. It's genuine
2. It's specific
3. It's appropriate

On the first point, this should be obvious—a fake compliment is worse than useless and can actually undermine connection. This is why, even if you genuinely mean it, you should avoid saying cliché things like "You've got this" or "I'm proud of you!" They will not be heard as genuine. Nobody benefits if you are perceived to be handing out a compliment just for the sake of it, or worse, using it to get your way.

That's why a good rule of thumb is to use compliments—but rarely. Try not to offer more than one per interaction, and only say what you sincerely mean. Also, avoid offering a compliment immediately after someone gives you one, or else it will naturally appear transactional and not spontaneous.

The specificity of a compliment matters most. The golden rule is: **compliment people on what they themselves will find most meaningful.** You'll have to pay attention to context and listen carefully to figure out exactly what they do find meaningful and what they are proud of.

Always avoid giving people compliments on things they actually had no part in creating. For example, saying that someone is beautiful/attractive/handsome may seem like a nice thing to say, but the truth is that someone's attractiveness is largely a genetic accident out of their control. That means praising it is not really praising them and will always be felt as a little hollow. What's more, you might give the subtle impression that their value as a person comes from this completely random and arbitrary feature of theirs—even if they don't acknowledge it consciously to themselves, they may think, "Well, people are nice to me and like me . . . as long as I'm beautiful/attractive/handsome."

It would be far better to give these compliments instead:

"Wow, you have the most amazing taste in jewelry."
"Has anyone ever told you that you have really lovely eyes? Your kindness just shines through."
"You have such a good eye for fashion. I love the outfits you put together."

It's not the case that you can't compliment people on appearances—the above examples do just that, but they do so in a way that acknowledges the person's deeper qualities, their values, skills, talents, and deliberate choices. For example, their eyes are pretty—but because they show how kind the person is. Their jewelry and clothes are great because they show their excellent taste, and so on. This is likely to be far more meaningful and memorable.

If you notice someone takes pride in their home, compliment them on how clean and tidy everything is. If someone clearly sees their intelligence and work ethic as a big part of their identity, compliment them on how well organized and persuasive their arguments are. If someone has given plenty of clues that they value family more than anything in the world, compliment them on how well-adjusted and happy their kids seem. The last thing you want to do is compliment someone on something they don't care about—or actively devalue.

Finally, consider context and appropriateness. You might genuinely believe someone is sexy and have reason to think they value being seen this way, but if that person is a subordinate at work, for example, you'd be crazy to give them that kind of compliment! Here are a few more compliment faux pas to avoid:

- Unless you know the person well, avoid asking where they bought something or where it comes from.
- Avoid bringing money into things, and don't say things like "Oh, it looks so expensive" or "I love your shoes. How much did they cost?"
- Don't ask if something is real or genuine (especially not body parts!).
- Just don't mention weight or body size at all. It's a minefield. Instead of saying "You look great. Have you lost weight?" just say "You look great!" The same thing goes for age—i.e., don't assume that someone will be flattered if you tell them they look younger than they are.
- Avoid underhanded compliments—i.e., "Wow, your quiche is surprisingly good, actually!"
- Don't put yourself down in order to compliment others—it will diminish the perceived value and truth of what you're saying and is a subtle way of making things about you. So, for example, don't say "Oh, wow, you look amazing in that suit . . .

makes me feel like a dog's breakfast," but just say "You look amazing in that suit," and leave it at that.

What about receiving compliments? Well, there's an art to that too. Get into the habit of pausing, smiling warmly, making eye contact, and saying simply "Thank you." That's all you need to do. Avoid the temptation to argue, to be demure, or to rush in and say something nice about them. Likewise, there's no need to start boasting or start elaborating on the compliment. Without being overly modest *or* arrogant, gracefully accept and move on.

Summary:

- Give the gift of solid, respectful attention at all times. Listen generously, as though you are prepared to hear the value, the sense, and the meaning in everything you hear. Don't let your desire to seem like a good listener get in the way of actually being one. Let people know you are listening with small verbal and nonverbal gestures.
- Try not to let your own perspective impair your ability to understand somebody else's. Start from a position of ignorance and work your way up to real understanding, rather than making assumptions about what other people's experiences mean.
- To be a good listener, practice restating what you are told, paraphrase that content in your own words, summarize what you're hearing in a useful way (or else condense things by labeling the core emotion), then potentially reframe the story or gently suggest something new if this might help solve a problem or create an emotional resolution. Do this without assumptions, biases, or interpretations, but with a mind to truly understand the other person's point of view.
- Your response to someone's good news can vary, being passive or active, constructive or destructive. Aim for active, constructive responses that acknowledge and reflect the emotion and energy in a speaker's message.
- Give compliments—but keep them rare, sincere, specific, and appropriate.
- Avoid giving advice. Problem-solving, creativity, and conflict resolution are best achieved with a gentler frame shift and helping people discover what *they* themselves think, rather than telling them.
- Research suggests that talking about yourself makes you a little less likeable, while asking questions makes you a little more likeable. Open-ended and follow-up questions especially showed the greatest relationship to likability. People like those they believe are genuinely hearing them, seeing them, and reacting to them.
- Questions that chunk up or down allow you to vary the degree of detail at which you present or request information. Both approaches have their uses, but it's about balance, variety, and aligning with the other person. Become curious about where a current conversation is and whether it might need more chunking up or chunking down.

Chapter 3: Turning on the Charm

STORYTELLING IN CONVERSATIONS

If you can apply the friendship formula, create your own "reality distortion field," and communicate an attitude of curiosity by asking questions and genuinely listening, then you are already well on your way to being a likeable, trustworthy, charming person. Many people spend their entire lives not quite mastering these basic steps, so take a moment to appreciate any little progress you've made!

That said, there will come a time where presence, eye contact, questions, and so on are not quite enough. You may be wondering "What do I actually *say* when I'm talking?" In this chapter, we'll be looking at how to tell engaging stories, dish out witty banter, and piece together a fun, lively conversation that draws people to you.

Whatever you do, however, don't forget the real foundations of a good conversation: humility, curiosity, open-mindedness. Don't forget that you travel most of the way with good eye contact, open posture, well-timed questions, and genuine listening. Only once all these things are established is it worth thinking about how you're going to talk, tell stories, or make jokes. Stories and anecdotes are like the icing on the cake—but you really do need that cake!

Okay, so, let's start with an obvious question. Are you a good storyteller?

Perhaps you've heard an amazing joke that made you die with laughter, and yet, when *you* told it, the whole thing fell flat. Maybe you find that people always seem bored and distracted when you're relating a story, or that you're frequently interrupted. Perhaps you've just stopped trying to tell jokes at all, certain that you'll only mess them up.

Let's get one thing straight: Anyone can be a good storyteller. Including you! You do not need to be the most fascinating person in the room, a standup comedian, or an extrovert. You don't need to be funny or a rock star or fake. But, telling a good story is an art, and it seldom happens by accident. Here are the elements that every good story has to have: a hook, brevity, a point, and plenty of feeling.

Why Stories Matter

Author and programmer Scott Young recounts this charming story on his blog:

> It had finally happened. Scientists traveled from around the globe to marvel at it. We had finally created a computer that was as powerful as the human brain. It could

calculate numbers at a blurring rate and engage in human dialog. There was just one question remaining. Was it just a big calculator or could it actually be conscious?

The scientists decided the best test would be to ask the computer itself, "Are you conscious?" Upon receiving the request the computer processed continuously for hours. Hours became days, but after an entire week the computer had arrived at an answer. The scientists huddled around the screen to see the reply.

In bright green letters on the screen, the computer wrote, *"You know? That reminds me of a story..."*

This is kind of a fun meta-anecdote—a story about stories. It tells us that there is something fundamentally human about storytelling, that it characterizes our consciousness and ability to think. What's more, it's *relational*—a story is about communication, connection, understanding.

A story is something we tell; it's a path we follow ourselves and invite others to follow. Unless someone else is coming along with you for that journey, you're not telling a story but monologuing. That's why it's important to remember that **your story's value is in how it lands and how it's perceived.** It's never just about the content, but the style in which that content is delivered, to whom, and for what purpose.

Four Elements of a Good Story

A Hook

Writers of all stripes know that a reader's attention is not a given—they have to catch it. It needs to be earned and then maintained. A hook is simply a reason for your audience to pay attention. A hook is something sharp and interesting that snags their awareness. It might not feel fair, but other people are not naturally inclined to listen to you; you need to give them a reason first.

Brevity

The best stories are short. Only try to remember what it's like to listen to someone drone on for fifteen minutes telling a story that could have been conveyed in two minutes and you'll know why being concise is so important. Sometimes, people can get nervous and try to fill up empty space or keep talking so that others will keep listening. It backfires. If you tell a story littered with unimportant details, you can't blame your audience for assuming that only some of what you say will be interesting, and that they can safely ignore you half the time!

Don't fall into this trap. If you have a funny anecdote that happened at a ski lodge, there's no need to begin the story with the reason you were there in the first place, or how much your flights cost.

Precision

Do you have a point?

This may sound strange, but many people open their mouths to speak and share a story with very little understanding of what they're ultimately trying to say. It's a very quick way to bore, alienate, or even offend people.

If our contribution doesn't add anything and people can't see how it connects, they'll assume something unflattering: that you only spoke to hear yourself speak. Your story doesn't need to be a perfectly outlined essay, but it does need to have a main point. It needs to have a reason for being told, and that reason needs to be clear and obvious to everyone who hears the story. There needs to be a clear payoff, and this needs to connect somehow to the flow of the rest of the conversation.

This ties in to the previous section—one surefire way of taking too long to tell a story is to not really know what your story is about. Nobody likes listening to someone for five minutes only for them to forget the punch line or lose track of what they were saying. Similarly, nobody wants to stop the flow of the conversation so you can tell a tale that doesn't relate to anything that came before it.

Feeling

What's the purpose of a good story?

In conversation, a story is meant to create connection and rapport. And the way it does that is through emotion. Without feeling, it's not a story—it's just data. When you share something, your goal should be to create an emotional impact for the listeners. Everything else comes second—the concrete facts are not as important as the feeling they create in the listener.

For many stories, the main point is the emotion created—whether that be the absurd and hilarious punchline, the shock of an unexpected situation, or the feeling of validation that comes with hearing a story that confirms what you already suspect to be true. Just make sure that you're not just rattling off a list of facts. Tell your listeners *why* it matters. Make them experience the story emotionally with you.

That said, one word of warning: don't react more to your own story than the audience does. You want them to have the experience, not watch as you have it!

If you go back and read the short story earlier in this section, you'll see how neatly it ticks all four of these boxes.

Be Natural . . . But Have a Plan
You already know that it's important that conversation remain open-ended, natural, curious. You want to remain alert and alive to possibilities as they evolve in a conversation. At the same time, however, there is some skill required to tell good stories. It may take a little preparation and forethought at first, but practice makes it more automatic.

Step 1: Build a library of stories

The way to make sure you have a good story to tell is to have a big collection ready to go. Then you can pick something that fits the occasion, without it seeming like you rehearsed ahead of time. Don't doubt people's ability to spot a pre-prepared tale that you've tried to wedge in!

If you're super organized and want to be methodical, you could even keep a written record of these stories in a spreadsheet. In one column, note down interesting experiences you've had that you think others can relate to. You probably have dozens of them—for example, moving house or taking a gap year after high school. In the next column, brainstorm some specific examples that illustrate your experience. Think of a crazy story that happened on moving day or about an unusual place you took your gap year.

In a third column, think carefully about what these stories might say about you as a person, and how you might like to tailor them to send a particular message. For example, you might like to run with a story about how you went to Mongolia when you were nineteen because your stories from that time paint you as a spirited young person who was up for adventure.

In a final column, boil down the essence of what makes each of these stories special and meaningful. How has your Mongolian adventure influenced you today? You might find yourself in a conversation with someone at a networking event, and they start talking about taking risks in a new business. You practice all your usual conversational skills, but you also deliver a quick, one-minute story about your time in Mongolia. In just that minute, you let the other person know you heard them, but also shared something of yourself and cultivated a particular image of how you'd like them to see you—for example, brave, daring, and unconventional. If you've ever wondered why some people just "click" socially, often it comes down to a powerful, well-placed story just like this.

Taking time to think about these aspects will also make sure you are never telling stories over and over again without a good idea of the point or the overall emotional impact. With this library prepared, you are ready to contribute *meaningfully* to a conversation. People who are bad at this tend to have a library as well, but it's not properly organized. You've probably noticed how some people look for any opportunity to launch into a favorite old yarn of theirs, whether it fits or not. One final caveat: try to keep tabs on who you've told the story to, or just ensure that you're keeping things fresh and never getting stuck on the same one.

Step 2: Use natural transition phrases

With good friends, stories flow naturally and easily. With people you're less familiar with, you might need a little help to ease things along. Use a transitional phrase to help you introduce the fact that you're about to tell a story. For example:

- "You know, that reminds me of . . ."
- "I remember when . . ."
- "That makes me think of this one time when . . ."

Here we see one good reason to listen—it tells you when there's a natural space to introduce your story. You don't have to make a big deal of connecting what you're about to say to what's come before, but make a cursory connection so that people don't feel you've just abruptly changed the topic to speak about yourself.

Step 3: Keep practicing

It takes time to become a natural, confident storyteller. You need daily practice out in the real world. The trick here is to remain open-minded and curious and to not let nerves or lack of confidence get in the way of you putting yourself out there. Think like a scientist and try out different stories and ways of telling them, and then see what happens. Adjust as you go along.

- Notice people's body language and facial expressions—it's very obvious when people are enjoying your story and when they aren't.
- When in doubt, be shorter and more concise. You could even tease with an outrageous statement or a half-story and have other people so curious that they *demand* you tell them the rest of it. In fact, some of the best storytellers do precisely this and deliver something odd, surprising, or hilarious as their hook. They are then guaranteed of people's interest as they explain further.
- If someone says "You've told me this before," then *stop the story*. Consider this valuable feedback.
- Watch comedians and the way they deliver stories. Note how they take their time, how they present the most important pieces of information, and how they use their bodies, facial expressions, and voices to convey the meaning. A good storyteller can describe a whole world of meaning with a lifted eyebrow or a telling pause. That's because they're paying attention to the audience's responses and playing off them in real time. Just because your story is fixed and semi-rehearsed, it doesn't mean that you can't adapt it in the moment to suit the occasion. **Telling a story should still be a conversation!**
- Don't interrupt someone else's story, especially to tell your own. Don't follow up on someone else's story by essentially telling the same one yourself. Does your story move the conversation forward somehow? Or is it just a way for you to say "Me too! That also happened to me"? If so, save the story for a time when it can really shine.
- It goes without saying, but avoid stories that make other people look bad, boastful stories, or stories that may make people feel uncomfortable for any reason.
- Be aware of your audience. Your creepy ghost story is the perfect thing for a casual night in with close friends, but completely the wrong choice for a more professional get-together with people you don't really know.
- Finally, realize that you don't have to tell stories at all. Remember that rapport can be achieved perfectly without it. If you don't yet feel comfortable, or if you notice you become inauthentic, just shelve storytelling for a while. Anyone can learn to be funny and entertaining, but you don't *need* to be to make friends or have amazing conversations.

USING WITTY BANTER IN BUILDING RAPPORT

When was the last time you really "clicked" with someone? Maybe you had a good vibe going, or maybe there was even some flirtatious energy. Things felt alive and exciting and lots of fun.

What was actually going on for you in that moment? And can it be recreated at will?

Call it witty banter, chemistry, connection, or rapport, but in this chapter we're looking at the special quality that makes some conversations feel like they're sizzling and popping. With wit, humor, and relaxation, you can disarm people, ease tricky or awkward situations, and come across to others as majorly likeable and charming.

Witty banter is that playful, clever, amusing type of conversation that feels like it supercharges interactions and speeds up rapport. In other words, it's magic gold dust that **creates intimacy and closeness very rapidly**. Not only does the connection feel fantastic, but you will seem to shine in the other person's eyes. That's because witty banter conveys a sense of relaxation, confidence, ease, strength, and resilience. It's the habit of people who are healthy, self-possessed, in control, and interesting. It's potent stuff!

If you think that this kind of charisma is something you have to be born with, take heart. You *can* learn. While it's true that banter is an art that takes practice, it's something that will only improve the more you work with it. There are clear techniques that you can use consciously:

Platonically "flirting"
Being mildly sarcastic (within reason)
Being self-deprecating
Saying something goofy or unexpected
Teasing in a lighthearted way
Laughing at a situation
Being playfully self-referential (more on this one later)

However, all of the above can flop spectacularly if they are pitched incorrectly. Light sarcasm can become hurtful sarcasm, goofy can become weird, self-deprecating can become a bit sad, and so on. That's why there are a few golden rules of banter:

1. Start small and build
2. Banter WITH someone, not AT them
3. A little goes a long way

Technique 1: Self-Deprecating Humor

When you poke fun at yourself, it's like you let all the anxiety out of an interaction. **Deliberately dropping your ego a little shows strength and maturity and puts people at ease.** Not taking yourself too seriously is ironically a display of poise and self-possession, and people trust and like it when it's genuine.

What's *genuine*, you ask? Well, if you're really insecure about something, don't try to make a joke about it or people will rightly feel uncomfortable and wonder if you're fishing for compliments. The best way to laugh at yourself is to be obviously, hilariously over the top.

In an old episode of *The Tonight Show*, Conan O'Brien makes fun of himself in front of his guest Andy Richter, saying, "I think on TV I come across as a mean little punk, but in real life, I'm actually very large, tell them, very attractive." He then playfully gestures for Andy to confirm his ridiculous claim, and Andy picks up the thread and runs with it, starting a conversation in which they both playfully tease and insult one another.

Self-deprecation works here because while it's slightly rooted in reality, it's also quite obviously overblown. When you self-deprecate, try to:

- Keep it brief—going on and on can start to seem strange
- Exaggerate and be very, very obvious—for example, "Man, even the cockroaches are telling me to clean up my flat already" is pretty funny, but "My poor mental health makes basic hygiene difficult at the moment" is just awkward and sad!
- If you can, use self-deprecation to remove some tension from the situation. For example, when a clearly stressed-out job interviewer asks you, "Where do you see yourself in five years?" you could quickly quip, "Well, I would say my biggest weakness is listening." It's unexpected but pretty disarming . . .
- Make a self-deprecating joke, *then wait*. See how it's received. If people aren't really enjoying it or extending the joke, don't make another.

Technique 2: Use the Element of Surprise

Charming conversation feels special because it's so different from the boring same ol' same ol' that most of us go through in rote conversations. **Be unexpected and you immediately grab people's attention and create a little moment of spontaneity—and in that moment you could light a little spark of connection and intimacy.**

With self-deprecating humor, exaggeration is a great tool, but you can also distort things by inverting them or connecting two seemingly unrelated ideas to create something fresh and even amusing. The effect is to make you seem intelligent, funny, and switched on.

In a speech by former US president Barack Obama, he makes a point about the complexities of the different governmental agencies, but does so by associating two things that aren't usually connected, and in an unexpected way:

Obama: "Twelve different agencies deal with exports. There are at least five different agencies that deal with housing policy [. . .] Then there's my favorite example. The Interior Department is in charge of salmon in freshwater, but the Commerce Department handles them when they're in saltwater [pause]. I hear it gets even more complicated once they're smoked" (the crowd laughs).

Technique 3: Sarcasm

Sarcasm is defined as "the use of irony to mock or convey contempt." **However, when used in witty banter, sarcasm is not at all intended to convey contempt, but rather to issue an invitation for the other person to play.** On the face of it, you can be sarcastic simply by saying the opposite of what you mean, or the opposite of what is clearly the case. It's a form of exaggeration, and it also employs the unexpected because it playfully flaunts typical conversational rules. If you're known for being a chocoholic, for example, say, "Oh, you know me, I can't stand the stuff." If you're freezing to death, say, "Hey, can we open that window a little wider, please? That howling gale outside is really so lovely and refreshing." If someone is asking you a question, say with a deeply sincere expression, "I cannot tell a lie . . ." and then proceed to tell a very obvious and ridiculous lie.

The moment you make a sarcastic remark, you invite people to stop, pause, and take a closer look—to see if you're serious. **It really should come across as a game.** There is a split second after you say something at odds with the situation at hand where someone might flick their eyes in your direction or pause to try to understand what you mean. This moment is solid gold—smile broadly, say something sassy, or play deadpan, and the other person will realize a game is afoot. Congratulations, you are officially bantering!

Take a look:

A: (walks in with a broken leg)
B: "Oh my God! Has something happened to your leg?!"
A: "Of course not. I just thought I'd look kinda cute wearing a cast."
B: "Got it. It does really bring out your eyes."
A: "Oh, do you think? Thanks, darling. You should see the bruise underneath; it's this really sexy shade of brownish yellow."

In this case, B gets the playful sarcasm and responds in kind. Instant banter!

Technique 4: Being Self-Referential

Wit and banter work, as you are probably starting to notice, because they **play with and subvert the ordinary conversational conventions.** One clever way of doing this is to quite plainly "break the fourth wall" of the conversation and draw attention to the fact of the conversation itself. This is less confusing than it sounds and happens frequently when people are flirting, platonically or otherwise!

A: "Well, here I am! So what are your other two wishes?"
B: (laughs) "Oh, wow, that was a terrible pick-up line."
A: "Wait, hang on, *a pick-up line*? Woah, woah, woah, I'm sorry, ma'am, but are you coming on to me? Awkward . . ."
B: (still laughing) "Okay, be honest, has that whole thing ever worked for you?"
A: "Well, I have a beautiful girl trying to chat me up, so I suppose it's working just fine!"

In this (admittedly cheesy to the max) exchange, the banter rests on the fact that both people are aware that banter is in fact going on. They are directly referencing the fact of pick-up lines and making the invisible visible. They are pointing to the conversation and deconstructing it.

You can do the same any time you consciously refer to the conversation itself and make that the source of the joke. When someone's giving a serious speech and says something like, "Well, I suppose this is the part where I share a heartwarming anecdote about my childhood . . ." that is ironic and self-referential. Add in a little self-deprecating humor or sarcasm and you have the makings of witty banter.

Banter Warnings

Banter can go wrong. Keep the following in mind to make sure you're not sticking your foot in it:

- Keep body language open, relaxed, and fun. Smile or do something deliberate to show you are joking, like wink or pull a silly face.
- Less is more. Keep things open-ended and don't keep trying the same tack if people are not responding to it.
- Don't plan things; be spontaneous. The best comebacks and one-liners often don't make a lot of sense, so don't worry about being logical or clever!
- Avoid "negging," which is insulting someone to put them on the defensive so that they are more receptive to your advances. It's weak and manipulative—and you can go way further without it.
- Teasing can be funny, but use a light touch. When in doubt, it's always best to tease yourself.
- Don't try bantering with strangers; the risk of offending them by accident is just too high.
- Avoid the obvious controversial topics. You'll have more luck with the everyday relatable topics.
- Never give an underhanded compliment ("Oh, I love how you don't care what people say about you!" or "Wow, your house is so lovely when it's clean"). If it takes too long for the other person to work out your true intention, they'll default to assuming you really do mean to insult them.

Try always to keep banter playful, light, and silly. The big focus is on building **rapport**, not on entertaining people or making sure they see you as clever or interesting. Banter should be like play—and that means the other person needs to be having fun, too. The end game is fun, connection, and relaxation—keep that in mind and banter will soon start to come more naturally for you.

PRINCIPLES OF SELF-DISCLOSURE

Picture this. You've met a new friend, and you're both very much still getting to know one another. One day you're both at a group gathering near a drinks table when they suddenly lean in closer, lower their voice to a whisper, and jokingly say, "Hey, can I tell you an embarrassing secret real quick?" while smiling and making eye contact.

Pause at this moment and ask yourself—how do you *feel*?

Does it suddenly seem like the rest of the world has gone quiet and it's just you and the other person? Does it feel like you've just been invited into a new, hidden room you didn't know about before? Or perhaps does it feel like you have just "graduated" in this person's eyes and have now been granted a new status as a slightly closer friend than you were just a minute ago?

This is the power of self-disclosure.

Now think about any people in your life who you like and who seem to like you, but with whom you somehow never feel like you're *progressing*. Maybe it feels like they're always a little at arm's length, and you're alienated or disconnected from them. Many friendships stall at this stage, especially friendships between men.

Why? Because the next level is one that can only be accessed by an increase in intimacy—and both sides are too afraid to take that next step. As a result, the two remain mere acquaintances, both secretly wishing there was more but not willing to risk going first!

If this sounds familiar, you might need a masterclass in the power of self-disclosure. If you've spent a lot of your life having difficulty with socializing, low self-esteem, or introversion, then much of your focus has probably been on minimizing the costs and risks of reaching out to people, on paying attention to yourself and how you come across, and on making sure that you're "saying all the right things" (see the previous chapter!). What you can miss on your mission to improve your social skills is the understanding that **vulnerability is essential for human connection.**

This is important—being a little exposed, being human, and being your unique and flawed self are not impediments to making friends; they are actually one of the ways we most firmly connect with one another. If you are determined to always be cool, calm, collected, and in total control, people may like and respect you . . . but it may still feel like there's something missing. The stakes are too low. A deeper connection never takes root.

Self-disclosure is when we intentionally share personal information about ourselves that other people wouldn't know unless we consciously chose to tell them. In other words, it's a choice, and depending on what we share, we invite more intimacy, more trust, and more authenticity. When you share something real about yourself, you also invite the other person to do the same, and that's how friendships develop and grow. Without the authenticity and bravery that comes with self-disclosure, you could stay trapped in Banter Land forever, like two comedians bouncing off one another but never quite *connecting*.

Self-disclosure has a few features. It can vary in:

Intensity

"I love cheese" is a self-disclosure on one end of the spectrum, whereas "I have a long-standing fear of being visible and seen for who I am because I'm afraid people will judge me" is right the way over on the other end. Frequency also matters—i.e., constantly "spilling your guts" versus sharing tiny tidbits only very rarely.

Effectiveness and Appropriateness

The extent to which sharing has actually created more intimacy and understanding, or how fitting the disclosure was to the conversation at hand. Is there a high reward associated with disclosing? Or is it the kind of thing that may be hit and miss?

Quality

Is what you're disclosing actually true? What kind of picture does it paint of the person you are? What does it say about the other person, your relationship with them, and what you want the relationship to be?

We've used the word "authenticity," but the truth is that self-disclosure is *transactional* and one of many social skills rather than a complete abandonment of the usual social norms. Transactional isn't a bad thing, though!

Think about a good friend you currently have, and try to remember what the process of getting to know them better was like. Chances are, you both took tiny and incremental steps to reveal more and more about yourselves. One day you dipped a toe in and confessed that you actually hated the class you both took. A little later they admitted that they were struggling too. A year on and you were sharing a little more private information about your relationships, your flaws, your hopes and dreams. They struggled with alcohol; you had an embarrassing dream to write a musical. Fast forward ten years and you've divulged the bigger secrets. Even when these disclosures have caused friction in the past, ultimately they led to a deepening of the sense of closeness.

The important thing is that, on the whole, disclosure has remained reciprocal and balanced. It is transactional because every time someone self-discloses, they are taking a risk. They are making a bet on that disclosure paying off, and hoping that you respond in kind and that the risk was worth the increased closeness. When you acknowledge and reciprocate, the "debt" is paid and you both now occupy a new, more intimate level of friendship. This is why so many companies do those cheesy "trust falls" with their employees during team-building workshops—they know that mutual risk creates trust. A real connection is one in which people have invested something of themselves, even if that's just something tiny at first.

You can probably see the problem: **If disclosure is absent or unbalanced, proper connections cannot form.**

If neither person ever discloses, or if disclosure is uneven, the transactional part of the process breaks down.

Self-disclosure is valuable *because* it is risky. That means the best strategy is not to bare your soul indiscriminately or get too deep and serious with someone you barely know. On the one hand, never sharing yourself can leave you isolated, but on the other, there's good reason why people can be hesitant to open up. Self-disclosure isn't always a good idea and should be avoided when:

- The topic is genuinely taboo, or it's inappropriate for that particular relationship. For example, sharing your sexual fantasies with your elderly mother-in-law.
- The disclosure is too much for the person, situation, or context involved. For example, you're at a celebratory party and you tell someone about your gruesome childhood abuse.

- While "true," the topic doesn't actually need to be shared, and doing so doesn't increase authenticity or let people know more about who you are. For example, confessing that you pick your nose (!).
- The disclosure can cause serious harm or destruction. This is the realm of secrets and dirty laundry. This is not the kind of thing you share to create trust, but rather the thing you share only once one hundred percent trust is *already* established. For example, disclosing an affair or confessing to a serious crime.
- The disclosure is not yours to share. For example, other people's secrets.
- Finally, there's no other way to say it, but the disclosure is just a major bummer. It fails to create trust and connection because it's so overwhelmingly burdensome and heavy, and others can't do much to help.

That said, when done correctly, self-disclosure will make people like you, trust you, and feel closer to you. Researchers have even found that **people like you more if they're the ones to disclose to you**, too (Greene, Derlega & Mathews, 2006). This is essentially what the process of making friends is: creating an upward spiral of mutual and deepening disclosure and trust. It's cathartic for you and you feel more aligned and authentic, and by hearing other people's disclosures, you enrich your understanding of other peoples' perspectives.

As with every other social skill we've covered, the art and mastery is in finding the balance. Too little and people lose interest, and everything feels shallow. Too much oversharing and you freak people out or cross boundaries. Just the right amount, though, and you find that sweet spot where friendship blossoms.

Four Easy Self-Disclosure Rules
Rule 1: Match your self-disclosure to theirs

Keep things symmetrical. Sure, someone has to break the ice and go first, but that's why you keep disclosures small when you're just getting to know someone: If they don't reciprocate, you haven't lost anything.

Rule 2: Gradually increase intensity

Not every relationship has to become "more." But if you do feel ready to move a friendship along to the next level, then dial things up gradually. Use disclosures like gear changes. There is an art to gauging exactly when to drop one in, but use your gut. If you feel like the conversation is stagnating and *both* of you are wanting it to move again, it could be time for a self-disclosure. You could tentatively offer a new opinion or share something about yourself they might be surprised by—just a small thing.

Then pause and note their reaction.

- If they ask questions and stay present, great, but don't push any further.
- If they pull back or end the conversation, that's your sign that they were comfortable where you were. No big deal.
- If *they* share something in return, consider this a positive sign—they want to progress too and are willing to reciprocate.

Whatever you choose, self-disclosures should feel seamless and fairly natural, rather than abrupt tone shifts. Never say something that you can't plausibly deny if it's very badly received!

Rule 3: Be positive

In all this talk of baring your soul and confessing secrets, you could be forgiven for thinking that self-disclosure is always slightly humiliating and gut-wrenching—not at all! Self-disclosure can also be about hopes and dreams that are close to your heart, or even positive thoughts and feelings about the other person. Tell people about the achievements you're proud of, or what you're looking forward to. Sharing your values and what's important to you can be inspirational and help foster connections that feel positive and healthy.

That said, you can also share "negative" things in a positive way. The trick is to remind yourself why you're sharing in the first place—to increase connection and trust. If you share an embarrassing secret about yourself but do so in a self-deprecating and humorous way, you ensure that the other person doesn't feel that the secret is a burden or something unpleasant they have to process.

Self-disclosure is not "dumping" heavy or difficult material in people's laps in the name of authenticity. We don't want to make them feel depressed or sorry for us. We're not complaining. Rather, we want to make them think "Oh, wow. This person is human, just like me. And they must really trust me to share that. I like that."

A good rule of thumb is to share only positive things at first and save the dark and difficult stuff for much later on—if you decide you need to share it at all. The bigger the disclosure, the better it is to err on the side of too late rather than too early; likewise, the more serious it is, the better it is to *prepare* to disclose rather than just blurt something out in the moment. A premature disclosure of this kind can make things very weird very fast.

Mini Self-Disclosures

The most effective kind of self-disclosure is the one that *only slightly* pushes the current state of affairs toward more intimacy. Look at where you are and then imagine just gently pushing on the current limit of how close you are to the other person. This is a mini-disclosure, and when done at the right time, it is more powerful than a gnarly heart-to-heart conducted when everyone's had a bit too much to drink! Here are some examples:

1. You've hung out with a new friend group a few times, but one day you say to them, "To be honest, I'm a little down and not really feeling it today, and I think I'll join you all on the next one!" You make this self-disclosure rather than coming up with an obvious excuse.
2. A colleague at work whom you've known a long time has asked you to look after their cat while they rush to visit their dying father in the hospital. You acknowledge their disclosure by making one of your own: "Oh, please don't worry about it. Last year when my mother died, I didn't know whether I was coming or going! I understand. Let me know what I can do to help."
3. You're on a date and order some food. The "getting to know you" phase is going well and there's a good vibe. You say, "I've been vegetarian for, like, twenty years now." You don't say more; you just wait to see their response—are they curious about your motivations? Do they share a little something about themselves? Or just yawn and start talking about something else?
4. You and your spouse are having a hard time. You sit them down and say, "Okay, look. I need to get this off my chest. I don't like the way you've been talking to me lately." You've been married for years, but this broaches a new, somewhat scary topic you've both been avoiding for a while.
5. You're on a moonlit beach, walking hand in hand with an amazing person you met six months ago. They've shared a bit more about their background, their past, their

hopes and dreams for the future. You say, "I don't really know how to say this . . . but I think I'm falling in love with you."

Each of the above disclosures varies in intensity and content. But each of them has a good chance of being effective because they only push the present situation a tiny bit further.

How to Respond to Someone Else's Disclosure
Now that you know the purpose self-disclosure serves, you can probably see how important it is to respond properly when someone offers you one. Usually, people do this in a bid to create more intimacy and closeness. It's an invitation. But don't feel that just because you've been given that invitation, you have to accept it.

If you do, make sure that at some point you then disclose something of equal emotional weight, or else ask questions to show that you are indeed willing to push the edge of your current intimacy a tiny bit further.

If you don't necessarily want to be closer to someone, respond to their disclosure with polite respect, but don't reciprocate. If you find yourself with a chronic oversharer, set any boundaries you think are necessary and keep conversations factual and distant. Chunking up or down questions can help create distance here! Recognize the risk that people take in sharing, however, and honor it, even if you don't want to return it.

Put it into practice: Now it's your turn. We've discussed storytelling, witty banter, and self-disclosure. The first thing to do for this exercise is to honestly ask which of these three is most out of your comfort zone. Then, set a small goal for yourself to practice precisely that skill. If you're nervous about storytelling, for example, challenge yourself to prepare a joke or interesting story, and then practice delivering it using the techniques mentioned here.

If self-disclosure is difficult for you, pick a person you'd like to create more intimacy with and ask how you can use self-disclosure to deepen your intimacy level just a tiny bit more. If you find yourself falling flat with witty banter, for example, try to insert more sarcasm or self-deprecation into your next, say, three conversations. How does it feel?

Summary:
- Though the real foundations of a good conversation are humility, curiosity, and open-mindedness, it's still worth learning how to tell engaging and entertaining stories. Storytelling is human, and anyone can be a good storyteller. But a story's value is in how it's perceived by the audience.
- The best stories have an attention-grabbing hook; they're short, precise, and have a relevant emotional core. In conversation, a story is meant to create connection and rapport, not showcase you as interesting. Prepare somewhat by building a story "library" beforehand, then use natural transition phrases such as "You know, that reminds me of . . ."to introduce the story. Remember that telling a story is still a kind of conversation.
- Witty banter is playful, clever, amusing conversation that speeds up rapport and builds closeness very rapidly. Anyone can learn to banter as long as they follow the rules: start small and build, banter WITH someone, not AT them, and a little goes a long way.
- Self-deprecating or self-referential humor helps you drop your ego and shows strength and maturity, putting people at ease. Be brief and very obviously exaggerate something

you're actually comfortable with. Be unexpected and use the element of surprise to grab attention and create spark and spontaneity. Flaunt conversational norms with playful sarcasm. The focus is always on building rapport, not on entertaining or impressing people.
- Vulnerability is essential for human connection, and appropriate self-disclosure creates trust, authenticity, and intimacy. Self-disclosure is intentionally sharing personal information that other people wouldn't know unless we chose to tell them. The most effective kind of self-disclosure is the one that *only slightly* pushes the current state of affairs toward more intimacy.
- Friendship-making is an upward spiral of mutual and incremental disclosures over time. Keep things symmetrical, gradual, positive, and small at first.

Chapter 4: When Ego Gets in the Way

THE NARCISSISM RATIO
By now, it should be clear that the art of socializing, being charismatic, and making friends is an *emotional* art, not a rational or intellectual one.

Charisma is nothing more than the quality that enables us to connect with and inspire others on an emotional level, without being coercive or threatening. That, in a nutshell, is what a friend is. To be charming, likeable, and trustworthy, you need to create a certain feeling in people. And that means that the focus is always on THEM, not US.

We can think of the narcissism ratio as the proportions of these two different points of focus. The higher the proportion of attention, consideration, and focus on the other person, the more charismatic and likeable we seem. The more we focus on *ourselves*, the more narcissistic we appear to others, and the less likely we are to form deep, trusting connections with them.

If in a conversation you refer to yourself ("I", "me," or "my") ten times as often as you refer to the other person ("you"), for example, then that's a pretty skewed ratio. But it's not as straightforward as that. There are many more subtle ways of dominating the conversation, steering things toward yourself, or being unresponsive to the other person that make you ultimately a conversational narcissist.

Who is the biggest threat to our own charm and charisma? That's easy: We are!

Are You a Conversational Narcissist?

Here are some of the signs.

You take more airtime.

Good conversations are not about you or the other person saying something interesting—rather they are about the connection between you both. However, if you're simply talking too much, there's a strong chance you're not leaving enough space for others. "Holding court" means you don't pay as much attention to other people's needs, perceptions, or expressions as much as you do your own. Naturally, you'll come across a little self-absorbed.

You always direct the topic.

Are you constantly the one who decides not only what the conversation topic is, but how that conversation unfolds? Another way to ask this question is, do you often find yourself annoyed that other people are slightly changing the conversation topic or direction, since it's not what you want to talk about? It may happen that you notice the other person do this, then simply carry on saying what you were saying before they spoke.

You interrupt.

First of all, interrupting is not *always* a major offense—sometimes people talk all at once simply because they're excited and want to emphasize and support what the person is saying (more on this later). But regularly interrupting is probably one of the most destructive conversational habits you can have. It's essentially sending the message "I'm more important than you; I deserve to speak more than you do." Interrupting is often felt by others to be extremely invalidating and undermining. It tells us that not only is a person not interested in what we have to say, but they are so uncurious about it that they are willing to cut us off.

You invalidate people.

If deep down you think that your perspective is the only one that really matters, you're going to hold other people's perspectives in contempt. You're going to think that they're unreasonable, uninformed, silly, unimportant, weird, secondary, stupid, bad, mistaken, or just plain wrong.

Validating someone is simply the act of acknowledging them and letting them know that they have value, and in their own way, they make sense. A conversational narcissist, however, sees themselves as the source of value, so if someone says something that doesn't directly refer back to them, they cannot acknowledge that person or see their value. They simply dismiss them. Without empathy, understanding, and insight, rapport crumbles . . . or fails to develop at all.

You brag and boast.

Naturally, a conversation should never be thought of as a platform to show how great you are. Most people know that they shouldn't go on too much about how amazing they are . . . but there are other, covert ways of bragging.

The notorious "humble brag" may be even worse than outright egotism ("Oh my gosh, I can never find clothes that fit both my tiny waist *and* my enormous bust. It's a real problem."). Other secret ways of blowing your own trumpet include name-dropping or constant one-upping (and that includes making sure you're always the one who has it the worst!).

You have an attitude of superiority.

A belief in your own superiority is the hardest thing to conceal. Any time you marginalize, judge, belittle, minimize, make fun of, or dismiss someone, it's obviously a bad sign. But many people convey a sense of their own superiority in other ways: They dish out unsolicited advice (often beginning with "As an XYZ . . ."), they lecture and preach to others whether they want it or not, and they attempt to qualify others or position themselves as the main arbiters of value in that exchange.

As an example, consider a man telling a woman out of the blue, "You don't need to wear so much makeup, by the way. In fact, as a man I can tell you that most men think a natural woman is more attractive." He thinks he is "helping" . . . but this comes from the belief that his own opinion on makeup is somehow absolute truth, and that anyone would be grateful to receive it as a kind of education!

Imagine two friends who are peers in all ways, but one of them consistently treats the other as though he is a younger brother, trying to correct him, instruct him, or tease his failures while adopting the position of someone wiser and more accomplished.

A related example is the person who thinks they know it all and considers it their sacred duty to enlighten and inform everyone around them. Pontificating at length as though one's personal opinions are actually profound philosophical edicts is not just annoying, it's boring. If someone senses that you think of yourself as genuinely more important than they are, you can kiss any rapport goodbye!

You manipulate.

It's hard to put your finger on exactly what manipulation is, but we all know it when we feel it. If you treat another human being like an object and merely as a means to an end, you are manipulating them. Again, this can be blatant, but it can also be incredibly subtle.

If you approach any conversation with the intention of positioning someone primarily in a way to serve your own ends, you're on shaky ground. This includes flattering someone so they give you what you want, being deceptive, trying to deliberately shift focus by blaming others or twisting facts, strategically playing the victim, throwing a tantrum to get what you want, intimidating people to get them to back off . . .

All of this is treating human connection as a mere tool and not as something with innate value in its own right. It's abusing other people and abusing your connection to them. A narcissist doesn't see people as they are but rather as extensions of themselves, who have value to the degree they can be exploited. Naturally, there are gray areas, but if you often find yourself thinking "What's in this for me?" then you might have a problem.

Okay, now time for the hard bit: ***All*** **of us are conversational narcissists . . . at least some of the time.**

If you are feeling insecure, nervous, or uncomfortable, you may start to turn inward and focus a little too much on yourself, forgetting the other person and the whole point of conversing with them in the first place (to connect with them!).

Even though all of the above signs look pretty serious, the fact is that most of us have a conversational narcissism ratio that's not as good as it could be. Sure, we're not comic book villains, but even little slips here and there may be seriously undermining your ability to be the charming, likeable person you could be. Why not do better?

The Power of the Support Response

You already have one powerful tool in your itinerary for centering the other person: questions. Let's look at another fantastic tool called the *support response*. First, consider the following conversation:

A: "So that's why we've both decided we're going to do a run every day. I think I've found my favorite type of exercise!"
B: "That's really cool. Running's great, but I think I prefer walking—easier on the knees!"
A: "Oh, totally. I get that. I think all the adrenaline makes you not really notice the little aches and pains. Yesterday was our record—three miles!"
B: "Running made me pretty tired. I ran for years, but I had to give it up. These days I do more strength stuff. You know, it's much better for you."
A: . . .

In this conversation, B is employing what is called a *shift response*—**when A says something, B responds in a way that brings the topic back around to themselves.** It shifts it back to B. In this short exchange, A makes two definite bids for emotional recognition from B, clearly wanting to talk about how exciting their new running hobby is and looking for a little validation that three miles is a pretty good run. But B doesn't respond, choosing instead to steer things back to themselves.

Notice how both of these shift responses act like a brake on the conversation. Can *you* think of anything for A to say to keep the conversation going? After a while, you can imagine A either losing interest or being polite and talking about B's topic for a while . . . then losing interest.

It's as though conversation is a game of tennis, and people hit the ball back and forth, sharing it equally. In this metaphor, the ball symbolizes the attention and focus of a conversation—i.e., who the conversation is temporarily about. A shift response is like never letting the other person get the ball. And if you do that, you're no longer really playing tennis!

A great way to improve your narcissism ratio is to use fewer shift responses and instead use a support response. Here's how that might look:

A: "So that's why we've both decided we're going to do a run every day. I think I've found my favorite type of exercise!"
B: "Well, congrats. I think I'm practically allergic to cardio, but hats off to those who love it. How long do you run for?"
A: "We've been keeping our runs to around two miles, but yesterday we broke our own record and did three!"
B: "Woah, look at you go! That's amazing."
A: "Aw, thanks. I'm pretty proud of myself."
B: "Are you going to be one of those crazy people who run a marathon every weekend?"
A: "Ha! Who knows, maybe. You going to join me?"
B: "Well, I'll do a marathon if you join me for a CrossFit class. Deal?"
A: "Oh my God, you do CrossFit?"

A support response is what it sounds like—it supports the other person as they share and express themselves. It doesn't work to pull attention from them, but sustains it and keeps it there. In this conversation, B asks questions but also supports A simply by asking questions and saying "That's amazing" and "Woah, look at you go!"

Notice something else interesting about the above exchange: By generously offering plenty of support responses, B does not lose out in the conversation in any way. In fact, the moment that A gets the validation they were looking for, *they, too, give a support response.* Now the conversational tennis begins. B can then take their turn and talk about themselves for a little while without having to fight for it.

This is an important point—support responses never mean that you take a back seat, are passive, or don't get to say your bit. **When used well, support responses lead to better, more fulfilling conversations for *everyone*.** Too many shift responses, however, tend to strangle conversations and leave both parties feeling like they're arguing over a scarce resource.

It's okay to talk about yourself, share an experience, or put your opinion forward. Just keep it balanced and offer plenty of support responses, too.

Short expressions that show you're listening and reflect emotional content:

"Wow!"
"Oh my God."
"Uh huh."

Supportive phrases and assertions:

"That's pretty interesting."
"You've clearly given this some thought."
"That makes sense."

Supportive questions:

"Then what happened?"
"So wait, how did you meet in the first place?"
"Would you say that's your favorite?"

You could try a kind of mixed response, too:

"Haha, that's hilarious (expression to show you're listening)! I would die from shock if that happened to me (*almost* a shift response). What did you do next (a supportive question)?"

By mixing things up this way, the conversation doesn't get too lopsided, the other person feels heard and supported, and you give them plenty of opportunity to ask you a question in turn.

ALBRECHT'S RULE OF THREE FOR CONVERSATIONS

If you consistently employ more support responses than you do shift responses, you will automatically avoid becoming a conversational narcissist. The great thing about support responses is how well you can combine them with the other techniques already discussed—for example, asking questions, using witty banter, self-disclosing, or maintaining curiosity. Let's look at one more way to ensure that you're getting the balance right: Albrecht's rule of three.

In *Psychology Today*, coach, lecturer, and author Dr. Karl Albrecht explains how **all conversations can be broken down into three fundamental components: declaratives, questions, and conditionals.** We're already familiar with questions, but what about the other two?

Declarations

This refers to any statement you make. **These are usually given as statements of fact—whether they are or are not.** "The sky is blue" is a declaration, but so is "This kind of weather is so annoying." Often, people will make declarative statements that are opinions wearing the disguise of fact. "It's not really possible to make a living as an artist these days."

The main characteristic about declarations, however, is the fact that they tend to invite a particular response from others in conversation. If someone simply states something, there isn't much room for other people's opinions, or for any give and take. The only real responses open to the listener is to do nothing, or else agree or disagree with what's been stated. As you can imagine, declaratives sometimes have the effect of shift responses, merely for the fact that they maintain focus on the speaker's perceptive and opinion.

Have you ever been in conversation with an annoying know-it-all? They were probably making too many declarations and not asking enough questions. Nobody wants to be lectured to when talking—they want the exchange to be a lively, dynamic give-and-take. People who rely too heavily on declarations in their communication end up being perceived as stubborn, self-focused, and a little boring. The conversation can become a soap box for their views rather than a shared, collaborative activity. At its worst, a conversation filled with too many declarations can inspire arguments!

Conditionals (or Qualifiers)

These can be thought of as modified, weaker forms of declarations. "This weather is annoying" is a plain declarative. "You know, in my opinion, this weather can be a little much at times" is very different. A conditional statement is softer and expresses itself while acknowledging that it is in fact an opinion and not the absolute truth.

Conditionals can begin with:

"If you ask me . . ."

"The way I see it . . ."

"I can't be sure, but I think . . ."

"XYZ is the case, wouldn't you agree?"

"Maybe XYZ is the case, I don't know."

"It seems like . . ."

"I'm happy to be proven wrong on this, but I do believe that . . ."

The trick here is that you are essentially conveying the same information you would with a declarative statement—but you are presenting it differently. It's more polite, more flexible, and more accommodating. It sends a strong signal to the other person that your priority in the conversation is not to "win" an argument or be right, but to maintain connection and rapport.

Questions

As we've seen, questions can come in all shapes and sizes. They can be open-ended or closed, they can chunk up or down, they can contain hidden assumptions and judgments, or they can be supportive and encouraging. The power of a question, though, comes from the fact that it respects the other person's role as co-creator and puts connection and interaction as the goal, with the factual content of conversation being less important.

Most people could drastically improve their conversational skills just by asking twice as many questions, but that said, you *can* have too much of a good thing. Ask too many questions in a row or ask too many of the same kind of question and you can obviously come across as a nosy interrogator—or even as though you are avoiding participating in the conversation yourself.

Albrecht's rule of three states that during a conversation, **you should avoid saying three consecutive declarative statements without including a question or qualifier.** Combined with the technique of support responses, we can see questions as supportive, declarations as an attempt to shift, and conditionals as a mix between the two.

By monitoring the balance of declaratives, questions, and conditionals in our speech, we can engage the other person more effectively. Albrecht suggests that after making a few declarative statements, we should redirect the conversation by asking a question, allowing the other person to contribute and take ownership.

Similarly, when responding to a question, balance out strong opinions with conditional or qualified responses. Note that the goal is not to completely center the other person at the expense of your own expression. It's also not necessary to censor yourself or pretend that you don't have strong opinions if you do. The goal is simply to *balance* both your needs and the other persons'.

- Too many declaratives: A tug-of-war conversation, a monologue, or an argument. Not enough curiosity or empathy.
- Too many questions: An interrogation or lopsided disclosure.
- Too many conditionals: Not a disaster, but can feel inauthentic or overly polite.
- Just the right balance between all three: magic!

Let's have a look at what a balanced conversation might sound like, and see if you can spot the declarations, the questions, and the conditionals. Note also where there may be a shift response or a support response.

A: "We were really nervous about getting a dog at first, but I'm so glad we listened to everyone's advice and got an older dog rather than a puppy."

B: "Yeah, I can totally see why people say you should do that. How old was your dog when you got him?"

A: "He was already ten years old!"

B: "Oh, wow."

A: "I know, he was a bit of an old man, to be honest. But it was great because we didn't have to do too much training. He was really mellow."

B: "Dogs can live for ages, though. He could go another ten years—I had a dog that lived to twenty-one."

A: "Really? That's crazy. I bet it was a small breed, huh?"

B: "Yup. A chihuahua. She was invincible!"

A: "Aw, cute. Did she go all gray in the muzzle?"

B: "She did. Blind, too, but we loved her. I really loved having a dog, but I don't know if I'd do it again. It's just too hard when they die, you know . . ."

A: "That is something I'm worried about. But I don't try to think about it too much. He's happy, so I guess that's what matters. Dogs can be tough. Do you have kids?"

Is this a balanced conversation? Let's investigate.

Speaker A managed to include:

- 3 declarations
- 2 support responses
- 3 questions (phrased conditionally, and always after a declarative)

Speaker B managed to include:

- 1 conditional response
- 1 question
- 1 support response
- 3 declarations

Verdict: The conversation is pretty balanced!

You might have noticed that when Speaker A was making their declarations, Speaker B supported them with questions, conditionals, and support responses, and then when Speaker B took their turn to make declarations, Speaker A reverted to asking more questions and offering support. You might have also noticed that both speakers gave somewhat mixed responses, which ensures an overall evenness:

A: "We were really nervous about getting a dog at first, but I'm so glad we listened to everyone's advice and got an older dog rather than a puppy." **(Declaration, almost a conditional).**

B: "Yeah, I can totally see why people say you should do that. How old was your dog when you got him?" **(Declaration/conditional, followed by a question—overall acts as a support response).**

A: "He was already ten years old!" **(Declaration).**

B: "Oh, wow." **(Support response).**

A: "I know, he was a bit of an old man, to be honest. But it was great because we didn't have to do too much training. He was really mellow." **(All declarations).**

B: "Dogs can live for ages, though. He could go another ten years—I had a dog that lived to twenty-one." **(All declarations—also a notable shift response).**

A: "Really? That's crazy. I bet it was a small breed, huh?" **(Support response, followed by a question. Speaker A acknowledges the shift response and supports it).**

B: "Yup. A chihuahua. She was invincible!" **(Declaration.)**

A: "Aw, cute. Did she go all gray in the muzzle?" **(Support response, followed by a question).**

B: "She did. Blind, too, but we loved her. I really loved having a dog, but I don't know if I'd do it again. It's just too hard when they die, you know . . ." **(All declarations, the last one quite strong, approaching a self-disclosure).**

A: "That is something I'm worried about. But I don't try to think about it too much. He's happy, so I guess that's what matters. Dogs can be tough. Do you have kids?" **(Declaration, a matching self-disclosure that acknowledges B's emotional content, and a question that both changes the topic but also potentially deepens it).**

The above conversation flows pretty well because both A and B are taking turns. When B says "Dogs can live for ages, though. He could go another ten years—I had a dog that lived to twenty-one," they are using this shift response to turn attention from A to themselves. This isn't a problem; having spoken a bit about themselves, A is happy for this to happen and immediately follows this shift in the conversation with both a support response and a thoughtful question: "Really? That's crazy. I bet it was a small breed, huh?"

Finally, you probably noticed the tiny self-disclosure near the end, which was introduced by B and sustained by A. If this conversation had been left to run for another twenty minutes, chances are that A and B would find themselves building more rapport and gradually creating more connection.

Now, reading the above breakdown, you might be wondering if it's really necessary to analyze conversations to this degree—rest assured, the answer is no! This is merely to illustrate Albrecht's rule of three and to show how supports and shifts feature in even a lighthearted and low-stakes conversation like this one. Take a look at an alternative path the very same conversation could have taken:

A: "We were really nervous about getting a dog at first, but I'm so glad we listened to everyone's advice and got an older dog rather than a puppy."

B: "Yeah, I can totally see why people say you should do that. How old was your dog when you got him?"

A: "He was already ten years old!"

B: "Oh, wow."

A: "I know, he was a bit of an old man, to be honest. But it was great because we didn't have to do too much training. He was really mellow."

B: "Dogs can live for ages, though. He could go another ten years—I had a dog that lived to twenty-one."

A: "Really? That's crazy. Well, like I said, our boy is ten . . . although he may actually be younger since he was a rescue and nobody is all that sure."

B: "Uh huh."

A: "They look at the teeth, you see. They make an estimate, but it's not always accurate. The thing is that if the dog wasn't really cared for in the past, their teeth can be in pretty bad condition. So they look older than they are."

B: "Makes sense."

A: "I mean, nobody knows. We decided when his birthday is and we just keep counting the years from that day! Hahaha! That's dog people for you."

B: "Oh, I get that. We used to do the same for our old chihuahua."

A: "Yeah? Toby's birthday was last month, actually, so we got him a little piece of steak. It was adorable . . ."

Let's take a magnifying glass to *this* conversation and see what happened.

Speaker A managed to include:

- A whopping 7 declaration statements, all in a row
- 2 mini support responses—that were immediately followed by declarations

Speaker B managed to include:

- 1 conditional
- 1 question
- 3 support statements
- 2 declarations

Verdict: This is not a balanced conversation, and it's likely quite tiresome for B. Fast forward it twenty minutes and either B will be bored to tears or the whole thing will have ended.

It all goes wrong at this exact moment:

A: "I know, he was a bit of an old man, to be honest. But it was great because we didn't have to do too much training. He was really mellow." **(This is a perfectly innocent declaration).**

B: "Dogs can live for ages, though. He could go another ten years—I had a dog that lived to twenty-one." **(Here, B is trying to shift the conversation to themselves. But note, however, that they are still maintaining and extending the overall topic).**

A: "Really? That's crazy. Well, like I said, our boy is ten . . . although he may actually be younger since he was a rescue and nobody is all that sure." **(A responds with some mild support, but immediately launches into another declaration. The effect is to briefly acknowledge B's bid to have the floor, but then refuse to give it).**

B: "Uh huh." **(What else could B say? The conversation goes downhill from here, and A then starts to lecture about dog dentistry and so on . . .).**

Admittedly, this is a very short and very simple conversation, but it does show just how quickly rapport can be lost if the balance of the three components is thrown off for too long. Again, there is nothing wrong with holding the limelight for a while, or sharing your opinion. The trouble comes in when you do not recognize that others wish to take a turn, or you actively steer the conversation away from them and back to yourself. Done once or twice, this can be forgiven, but if you do it consistently, you can expect that others will very quickly decide that you're a bad listener and that you have no intention of talking *with* them, only *to* them.

In almost every conversation, there will be a time when a speaker will make a shift response and signal that they want to speak, contribute something, or steer the conversation. Pay attention to it! If you ignore it, the conversation could lose momentum and start to feel disconnected. Of course, *you* might be the one giving a shift response and making a bid to talk about yourself . . . and realizing that the other person is not budging. We'll consider this situation in the next section.

INTERRUPTING—OR COOPERATIVELY OVERLAPPING?

There's not too much more to say about interrupting—it's bad and undermines rapport. But what about when interrupting isn't interrupting, but *cooperative overlapping*?

A professor of linguistics at Georgetown University, Deborah Tannen coined the term "cooperative overlapping" (CO) and explains how it's very different from interrupting. **CO is about talking along with the speaker, not to undermine or cut them off, but to validate what they're saying, give encouragement, and show that they're paying close attention.** She alternatively calls it "participatory listenership" and "enthusiastic listenership" and explains how different cultures have different expectations around this behavior.

Some people find, for example, that in certain countries or cities, interrupting is considered a normal and lively part of conversation, and it eases and encourages conversation rather than stops it. Cooperative overlapping is said to be common in Jewish New Yorkers, for example, who nevertheless find that others may see their communication style as too aggressive. Where they might feel that an overlapping, excitable conversation signals full engagement, others might see this as a sign that nobody is really listening to one another, and consider all interruptions to be a sign of rudeness.

The real problem only comes in when communication styles are not matched or aligned. When two different types try to talk, the interrupted speaker can get thrown out of whack and may stop speaking altogether or feel quite offended. This can create awkwardness all around. What to do?

According to Tannen, it's not an insurmountable problem once you're aware of what's going on. If you don't know someone well, try to get a sense early on what their style might be like. If they appear to be a cooperative overlapper and you're not, you can safely assume that you can carry on talking if they interject before you're finished. See it as a sign that they are listening and engaged with what you're saying (in effect, helping you say it), and take your time finishing and completing your point. When they're talking, try interjecting more often and see what response you get. It may feel a little strange at first, but you might find that more nonverbal engagement from you actually makes the conversation flow better.

If you yourself are the cooperative overlapper, be patient with people who might not be. If you chip in with a comment and they stop speaking, say something like, "Oh, I'm sorry, I wasn't interrupting you." If you find they are getting flustered, try to limit your responses to nonverbal ones while they're talking—for example, nodding your head, gestures, facial expressions, and eye contact.

Try to be alert of the different kinds of interrupting/overlapping:

Transitional Overlap

This is where someone jumps in and starts speaking close to the end (or what they think might be the end) of what the other person is saying.

A: "We've hired older folks; we've hired kids out of school. I can tell you we have a very diverse mix of employees. We'll hire anyone. What matters is your work ethic and whether you can get the job done—that's all that matters. I tell the interns that come through here, I tell them that it doesn't matter how much experience you have, but—"

B: "It's like some people think it's enough just to have the qualifications, just to be good on paper, when actually, you need to have a certain attitude as well, right?"

In this exchange, B is definitely interrupting, but in a way that doesn't really cut A off but adds fuel to what they're saying. If A was also a cooperative overlapper, they would interrupt B in just the same way!

Recognitional Overlap

Basically, "finishing a person's sentence."

A: "We've hired older folks; we've hired kids out of school. I can tell you we have a very diverse mix of employees. We'll hire anyone. What matters is your work ethic and whether you can get the job done—that's all that matters. I tell the interns that come through here, I tell them that it doesn't matter how much experience you have, but—"

B: "But it's about your mindset, exactly."

Progressional Overlap

This is when the first speaker is having difficulty expressing themselves and the second speaker interrupts to help cover over the gap and keep the conversation progressing.

A: "We've hired older folks; we've hired kids out of school. I can tell you we have a very diverse mix of employees. We'll hire anyone. What matters is your work ethic and whether you can get the job done—that's all that matters. I tell the interns that come through here, I tell them that it doesn't matter how much experience you have, but it's your . . . your . . . how do you say it? Not attitude, but, uh—"

B: "It's your mindset, your outlook. Like, your perspective on things."

A: "Yeah, exactly, your mindset. That's the thing that actually makes the difference, and blah, blah, blah . . ."

"Backchannel" Interrupting

In some cultures and in some contexts, people may like to frequently interject while a person is speaking precisely to support, encourage, and engage with what they're hearing. Strictly, they are interrupting, but the intention is the same as a support response. Japanese speakers, for example, may listen closely and repeatedly say "sō sō sō" throughout, which is a "phatic expression" (*Aizuchi*) that is a little like verbal cheerleading from the sidelines. African Americans may do something similar when they interject with expressions like "uh huh" or "yeah" or "I hear that" while someone is talking. Rather than either of these cultural practices being rude, they're actually a sign of active and respectful participation—or, if you like, a culturally unique way of listening.

Some people may be happy to overlap in some environments but not in others. It might feel fun to talk all at once when out on the town with friends, for example, but it can be overwhelming and confusing to do so when trying to solve a difficult problem as a group or in a professional context. Overlapping may also depend on other factors such as gender, class, culture, and context. It may be tolerated by some in big groups but not when in pairs, or it may be a behavior reserved for some occasions but not others.

Whatever the case, Tannen believes that **no style is better or worse than another**, only that it's worth recognizing the differences and keeping them in mind when you're trying to connect with someone a little different from yourself. Don't automatically assume that a person interrupting you doesn't care about what you're saying, or that the person who is listening quietly without interjecting isn't engaged with the story you're telling.

Mastering Turn-Taking

You've probably never thought about it before, but knowing exactly when it's your turn to speak in a conversation is actually a rather complex question and is resolved using many different conventions and norms. The way people organize themselves in conversations is a kind of meta-conversation—a social agreement that everyone speaking will follow the rough rules for engagement.

People and cultures of all kinds can agree that turn-taking should take place—it's just that they often disagree on the exact rules. How is airtime divided? How do you signal a change in turn? How long is each turn? If you find yourself repeatedly having difficulty in conversations, it may be that there's some friction or misunderstanding in turn-taking.

Imagine that every contribution to a conversation takes a particular structure: There's the introduction, the content or message itself, and the ending, where the speaker signals that their turn has ended and they're giving up the floor to someone else. There may also be other "rules," such as not leaving too much empty space between turns and not having more than one person have the floor at a time (with the exception of "enthusiastic listening").

So, what are these rules?

Well, that depends on who you are, where you are, and what you're doing. **A big part of learning to be charming, likeable, and a good communicator is to constantly be appraising the situation and adapting and adjusting yourself accordingly.**

Someone may signal that their turn is over and that you can begin your turn by:

- **Using eye contact.** They might talk for some time and then make eye contact with you when they're done (like serving the conversational tennis ball back to you!).
- **Pitch and tone of voice**. They may suddenly change these in a way that communicates that they're concluding their contribution.
- **Body language**. Different gestures can indicate that it is now your turn. The speaker can also signal that they're finished by sitting back in their seat, crossing their arms, or adopting some other "closing" movement.
- **Verbal cues.** A question is a very obvious one, but people can signal that they want you to jump in by mentioning your name directly, referring to you or your opinion, or saying something like "I imagine you and I differ on that, though," followed by a pause.
- **Slowing down or pausing.** Some people, especially those who favor an overlapping style, will sometimes literally stop in the middle of a sentence or slow right down. "And I was just like . . ." followed by a shrug indicates that the person probably doesn't intend to finish their thought! In some cultures, though, saying "You know?" or its equivalent is not necessarily an indication that the turn has ended, but could be more of an invitation for support responses (like "yeah" or "uh huh").

Linguists and anthropologists have studied turn-taking behavior for decades, and it's a rich and fascinating area. All you need to know as a budding good conversationalist and social butterfly is to be aware that these rules exist in the first place and that they may not always be the same from one situation to the next.

When you become aware of two people talking at once during a conversation, that's your cue to notice it and try to understand it.

Is someone (maybe you) interrupting?
Is it cooperative overlapping?
Do you and your conversational partner have different communication styles?
In a group, what is the general consensus for the "rules," and how can you match to that?

When They're the Conversational Narcissist

We'll end this book on a topic that's probably been lingering in your mind throughout: How do you deal with someone else who isn't a good listener, isn't charming, and is a conversational narcissist? How do you deal with endless shift responses or being interrupted? There's no point denying it. It takes two to tango, and if only one person in a conversation is listening actively, asking questions, and maintaining curiosity, that conversation is not going to go anywhere.

A word of warning: the more you improve your own conversational skills, the more you may notice how poor other people's are! **One big mistake you can make when encountering a conversational narcissist is to imagine that you can elevate things or rescue the conversation simply by being more attentive, understanding, and charming yourself.** More realistically, what tends to happen is that you don't rescue the conversational narcissist, but rather they suck you in, and soon you may find yourself competing with them and even resorting to your own tactics to wrestle the focus back from them and onto yourself—in other words, often the only possible way of talking with a narcissist is to become one yourself!

Instead, take a neutral and rational position: You cannot force self-absorbed people to pay attention to you. So, don't waste energy trying. If someone is incapable of genuinely seeing you, hearing you, or acknowledging you as a separate and valuable person, there is seldom anything you can or should do to change their mind. At best you can pay attention and see if there's anything you can learn from them (i.e., what not to do!) and then move swiftly on.

Using the "gray rock" technique is a way to protect yourself while maintaining your own standard of politeness. **Basically, being a gray rock means being unresponsive to manipulation.** It's a way of holding your own and making sure that you're not being ensnared by another person's attempts to dominate a conversation, mistreat you, or make you feel bad. Sometimes conversational narcissists create their own "reality distortion field" that can influence you—but only if you let it.

When you believe you may be in the presence of a conversational narcissist, consciously adopt the attitude of a gray rock: boring, dull, unresponsive. The reason is that narcissists do what they do because they want all attention to be on them. Make it clear that you're not really a viable source for this attention, and they'll lose interest.

While most of the time you would be interested in increasing intimacy and closeness, with such a person you want to do the opposite. Keep things shallow, neutral, and banal. Be as impersonal as possible. You are not violently pushing against them—you're just like a gray rock that doesn't do much of anything. You're bland. Remind yourself that your full, genuine, and empathetic attention is not a free-for-all but is something reserved for those people who can see it and appreciate it. For those who can't, your only obligation is to be polite, and that's for your benefit, not theirs.

Disengage if necessary. Never become defensive, sensitive, upset, or reactive. Don't give them any information (buttons to push or handles to grab you by!) but keep responses neutral and short. If you're feeling insulted or triggered, don't show it. Just manage the conversation as it is and disengage as soon as it's realistic to do so.

Manage your interactions with this person. Not everyone has the luxury of permanently avoiding a conversational narcissist. If you have to be around them, put "buffers" in place. You could ensure there's always an activity going on to distract you and give an excuse to escape. You could make sure you're never alone with them, or you could orchestrate meetings that have a natural but definite end. Keep it light and make sure you're not giving them an opportunity to insert themselves or dominate.

Don't be a doormat. In ordinary conversation, active listening, questions, and support responses tend to create more trust, liking, and understanding between people. Those who are secure in themselves will respond well and be happy to return the kindness and listen carefully to you when it's your turn to speak. Show this kindness to a conversational narcissist, however, and you're only inviting them to walk all over you. If you're in the presence of someone who cannot talk about anything other than themselves, give yourself permission not to ask them questions or give endless support responses! You will only leave the conversation feeling resentful and as though you've been taken advantage of.

Tighten up boundaries. The boundary that most needs defending is often the one around your time. Keep interactions with them as brief as possible. Don't share secrets or self-disclose, nor respond to their self-disclosures. Don't take any emotional "bait" but breezily move on from tricky topics. Be aloof but civil. Decide on the emotional frame that *you* want to hold, then stay there. If someone interrupts you, for example, don't sit there seething quietly while you let them talk, but at the same time don't get visibly upset and interrupt them in return. Calmly say "Oh oops, I wasn't finished speaking yet," then continue to speak. If it keeps happening, make your excuses and end the conversation.

With non-narcissistic people, it's wise to assume the best and keep trying to push past any awkwardness for the sake of that precious rapport and connection; with a conversational narcissist, however, the best strategy goes the other way. Cut your losses early on and leave—the world is full of interesting, attentive people who you can connect with instead.

Put it into practice: The final exercise is about boundaries. This book has been about creating connection, conversation, and friendships, but sometimes what's needed is to *reduce* the number of poor connections we have and draw a line against unhealthy conversation or friendships that have run their course. Try now to identify a current social habit in your life that you are ready to let go of, whether that's interrupting others or allowing others to interrupt you, talking about yourself too much, or not asserting yourself enough when others talk over you.

Perhaps, in a bid to improve your social life overall, you might like to think about a particular relationship that you'd like to minimize or detach from. Developing great social skills means you can improve any relationship and be calmer, more confident, and more likeable. At the same time, not every person can and should be your friend. Sometimes the best thing we can do is be honest about the people, behavior, and relationships that we're no longer happy with, and have the courage to move on from them so we can make more room for the kinds of connections we really want.

Summary:

- The biggest threat to connecting well with others is conversational narcissism—i.e., the tendency of centering ourselves, talking too much, steering the topic, interrupting, invalidating others, bragging, manipulating, or acting superior to others. Everyone has the potential to be narcissistic in conversation at times.
- A shift response is an attempt to bring the focus and attention of a conversation back to yourself. A support response maintains that focus and attention on the other person. A great way to reduce conversational narcissism is to use fewer shift responses and more support responses. When used well, support responses lead to better, more fulfilling conversations for *everyone*.
- Dr. Karl Albrecht says that all conversations can be broken down into three fundamental components: declaratives, questions, and conditionals. His rule of three is to never make three declarative statements in a row without a question or conditional statement.
- Declarations can be presented as statements of fact whether they are or aren't, and can shut down conversations or act as shift responses. Conditionals are modified, weaker forms of declarations that acknowledge their own subjectivity.
- "Cooperative overlapping" is different from interrupting. It's about talking along with the speaker, not to undermine or cut them off, but to validate what they're saying, give encouragement, and show that they're paying close attention. It can vary across cultures; neither way is right, but try to acknowledge and accommodate differences.
- Turn-taking rules can be complex and culture-bound, but a big part of learning to be charming, likeable, and a good communicator is to constantly be appraising the situation and adapting and adjusting yourself accordingly.
- When dealing with a conversational narcissist, don't try to rescue the conversation by being more attentive, understanding, and charming yourself, or you'll be taken advantage of. Instead use the gray rock technique and be aloof and unresponsive until they lose interest, and minimize contact as much as possible. Tighten up boundaries.

Summary Guide

CHAPTER 1: GETTING TO KNOW YOU . . .

- Dr. Jack Schafer's "friendship formula" is as follows: Friendship = Proximity + Frequency + Duration + Intensity. Friendship will develop according to the sum of all these four elements. That means that one element can be relatively weak if another compensates by being extra strong.
- Building friendships is about fostering increasing closeness—i.e., proximity. Greater frequency also means a stronger chance of friendship developing. The more frequently you engage with someone, the more they feel like part of your world. Friendship takes time to build, so greater duration of time spent together means greater chance of friendship. Finally, it matters how well you're able to satisfy another person's needs during any social interaction. The more you can, the better the chance of striking up a friendship.
- When making friends, deliberately find ways to increase proximity and the duration, frequency, and intensity of your interactions with people, in that order. Go slow!
- To create a reality distortion field, you will need to increase eye contact, be aware of your personal space, and stay present and open-minded in conversations. Charismatic, confident people are physically present, without being imposing or threatening, and their eye contact is natural. They do not let judgment, anxiety, or distraction undermine their presence in the moment. The key is to acknowledge people and make them feel important.
- The biggest impact you make on people does not come from what you *say*, but from how you *are*.
- Maintain reciprocal curiosity and the mindset that you can always learn something new from others. Be fully present, open-minded, and receptive rather than approaching with bias, judgment, or distraction. Instead of trying to convince others how fascinating you are, find what is fascinating about others. Conversations are co-creations!
- Genuinely connect to others by listening deeply, focusing on the person and not their story, and never making judgments or assumptions. Listen to understand, not to respond; listen primarily for emotion, not just fact. One way you can show that you're willing to really listen to people is self-disclosure.

CHAPTER 2: THE FRIENDSHIP MINDSET

- Give the gift of solid, respectful attention at all times. Listen generously, as though you are prepared to hear the value, the sense, and the meaning in everything you hear. Don't let your desire to seem like a good listener get in the way of actually being one. Let people know you are listening with small verbal and nonverbal gestures.

- Try not to let your own perspective impair your ability to understand somebody else's. Start from a position of ignorance and work your way up to real understanding, rather than making assumptions about what other people's experiences mean.
- To be a good listener, practice restating what you are told, paraphrase that content in your own words, summarize what you're hearing in a useful way (or else condense things by labeling the core emotion), then potentially reframe the story or gently suggest something new if this might help solve a problem or create an emotional resolution. Do this without assumptions, biases, or interpretations, but with a mind to truly understand the other person's point of view.
- Your response to someone's good news can vary, being passive or active, constructive or destructive. Aim for active, constructive responses that acknowledge and reflect the emotion and energy in a speaker's message.
- Give compliments—but keep them rare, sincere, specific, and appropriate.
- Avoid giving advice. Problem-solving, creativity, and conflict resolution are best achieved with a gentler frame shift and helping people discover what *they* themselves think, rather than telling them.
- Research suggests that talking about yourself makes you a little less likeable, while asking questions makes you a little more likeable. Open-ended and follow-up questions especially showed the greatest relationship to likability. People like those they believe are genuinely hearing them, seeing them, and reacting to them.
- Questions that chunk up or down allow you to vary the degree of detail at which you present or request information. Both approaches have their uses, but it's about balance, variety, and aligning with the other person. Become curious about where a current conversation is and whether it might need more chunking up or chunking down.

CHAPTER 3: TURNING ON THE CHARM

- Though the real foundations of a good conversation are humility, curiosity, and open-mindedness, it's still worth learning how to tell engaging and entertaining stories. Storytelling is human, and anyone can be a good storyteller. But a story's value is in how it's perceived by the audience.
- The best stories have an attention-grabbing hook; they're short, precise, and have a relevant emotional core. In conversation, a story is meant to create connection and rapport, not showcase you as interesting. Prepare somewhat by building a story "library" beforehand, then use natural transition phrases such as "You know, that reminds me of . . ."to introduce the story. Remember that telling a story is still a kind of conversation.
- Witty banter is playful, clever, amusing conversation that speeds up rapport and builds closeness very rapidly. Anyone can learn to banter as long as they follow the rules: start small and build, banter WITH someone, not AT them, and a little goes a long way.
- Self-deprecating or self-referential humor helps you drop your ego and shows strength and maturity, putting people at ease. Be brief and very obviously exaggerate something you're actually comfortable with. Be unexpected and use the element of surprise to grab attention and create spark and spontaneity. Flaunt conversational norms with playful sarcasm. The focus is always on building rapport, not on entertaining or impressing people.
- Vulnerability is essential for human connection, and appropriate self-disclosure creates trust, authenticity, and intimacy. Self-disclosure is intentionally sharing personal

information that other people wouldn't know unless we chose to tell them. The most effective kind of self-disclosure is the one that *only slightly* pushes the current state of affairs toward more intimacy.
- Friendship-making is an upward spiral of mutual and incremental disclosures over time. Keep things symmetrical, gradual, positive, and small at first.

CHAPTER 4: WHEN EGO GETS IN THE WAY

- The biggest threat to connecting well with others is conversational narcissism—i.e., the tendency of centering ourselves, talking too much, steering the topic, interrupting, invalidating others, bragging, manipulating, or acting superior to others. Everyone has the potential to be narcissistic in conversation at times.
- A shift response is an attempt to bring the focus and attention of a conversation back to yourself. A support response maintains that focus and attention on the other person. A great way to reduce conversational narcissism is to use fewer shift responses and more support responses. When used well, support responses lead to better, more fulfilling conversations for *everyone*.
- Dr. Karl Albrecht says that all conversations can be broken down into three fundamental components: declaratives, questions, and conditionals. His rule of three is to never make three declarative statements in a row without a question or conditional statement.
- Declarations can be presented as statements of fact whether they are or aren't, and can shut down conversations or act as shift responses. Conditionals are modified, weaker forms of declarations that acknowledge their own subjectivity.
- "Cooperative overlapping" is different from interrupting. It's about talking along with the speaker, not to undermine or cut them off, but to validate what they're saying, give encouragement, and show that they're paying close attention. It can vary across cultures; neither way is right, but try to acknowledge and accommodate differences.
- Turn-taking rules can be complex and culture-bound, but a big part of learning to be charming, likeable, and a good communicator is to constantly be appraising the situation and adapting and adjusting yourself accordingly.
- When dealing with a conversational narcissist, don't try to rescue the conversation by being more attentive, understanding, and charming yourself, or you'll be taken advantage of. Instead use the gray rock technique and be aloof and unresponsive until they lose interest, and minimize contact as much as possible. Tighten up boundaries.

BOOK 4: How to Speak Effectively:
Influence, Engage, & Charm

Chapter 1: Communication Fundamentals

The Ladder of Inference
In the chapter that follows, we're going to look closely at exactly what makes communication effective . . . and what makes it *mis*communication. We'll consider the importance of understanding the other person's frame of reference, how to frame your own position, what "chunking" is and how to use it, and how to adjust your mindset so you become a conscious, clean communicator.

But first, what is miscommunication? Have you ever been speaking with someone, feeling as though you are "reaching them," when all of a sudden, they say something that lets you know that you are both on completely different wavelengths? It can be a disorienting and frustrating experience, but miscommunication happens for a reason—and it can be avoided.

Poor communication arises as a result of a mismatch of perspectives, approach, or conversational skill.

Being an effective communicator means appreciating that the complicated process of communication doesn't happen by accident. **To avoid misunderstandings you need to consciously and actively take charge of the process**—and this is especially true when your message is subtle, nuanced, or very abstract.

If you examine any moment of miscommunication clearly, you'll see that understanding breaks down for a few reasons:

- One or both of you has failed to understand how the other is viewing things
- Faulty assumptions have been made, or someone has jumped to conclusions

In 1974, business professor Chris Argyris created a handy tool for better communication, which he called "the ladder of inference" (sometimes called "the ladder of inquiry"). The ladder is a metaphor for the way people think whenever they are given new information. It's about how new data and information is processed. What's useful about his metaphor is that it reminds us in a simple way that **different people tend to process information in different ways.** If we are unaware that this is happening, we can talk at cross-purposes—and miscommunication arises.

Before we look at the ladder, let's consider an example. Imagine a couple working together on a household budget. Jamie is looking back at the past six months and trying to find out where they overspent and why. Alex is looking ahead to the next six months and trying to figure out what kind of summer vacation they can afford.

They end up having an enormous argument, with Jamie thinking that Alex is not taking money concerns seriously, or taking responsibility for overspending, whereas Alex cannot see why Jamie is stuck on what is in the past and cannot be changed. They both find themselves saying "I'm just trying to get a handle on our financial situation!" and yet mysteriously they also both feel that the other one is getting in the way.

What's happened here?

According to Argyris, communication has broken down, and it's because Jamie and Alex are on different rungs of the ladder of inference. If you've ever experienced a communication breakdown of this kind, you'll know that it can be very subtle and hard to pinpoint. Often, we are only actually aware of our assumptions, expectations, and frames of reference *when they conflict with someone else's*!

But this is where the ladder comes in. It looks as follows. Imagine a ladder with each rung getting gradually smaller **from bottom to top**:

ACTIONS

BELIEFS

CONCLUSIONS

ASSUMPTIONS

MEANINGS

SELECTED DATA

OBSERVATIONS

Now imagine that this ladder is standing in a big puddle of water, which we'll call the POOL OF OBSERVATIONS. This pool contains all the possible observations we can make about the world—theoretically, there are infinite possibilities. The next rung up is OBSERVATIONS. These are all the observations that you select from the candidates of potential. We'll look at what causes you to select some observations and not others in just a moment.

The next rung is about the pieces of information you further select from these selected observations, SELECTED DATA—i.e., it's a subset. You're further narrowing down the data you are focusing on. The next rung is MEANING, which is the significance you attach to these selected observations. The next rung, ASSUMPTIONS, is what you do with this meaning. You extrapolate or make assumptions based on the meaning you've extracted from the observations.

On the next rung you come to CONCLUSIONS to make sense about what this all amounts to, and finally, these conclusions inform your BELIEFS about the world and your place in it. Consequently, every ACTION you take, the last rung, is informed by this long chain of inferences and meaning making. Furthermore, the ladder doesn't just go one way. Once you make meaning and take an action in accordance with those beliefs, then those beliefs actually tend to affect the data you are likely to select next time round on the SELECTED DATA rung.

Can you see where this is going? There are two potential problems:

1. Though everyone may begin in the same puddle of potential observations, each person ends up constructing *their own unique ladder* from those observations all the way up to the actions they take. If those ladders lead to completely different assumptions, meanings, beliefs, and ultimately actions, then conflict can arise.
2. Conflict can also occur, as we saw with Jamie and Alex, when two people are on different rungs and trying to talk with one another from different positions.

In our example, Jamie is on the SELECTED DATA and MEANING rungs, trying to understand what went wrong and piece it all together (and, honestly, assign blame . . .). Alex, however, is on the BELIEFS or ACTIONS rung, and is already looking for ways to move on from the fact that they overspent.

It may be, however, that even if Jamie and Alex were on the same rung, they may disagree on what meanings to ascribe to observations, and what beliefs and actions to take as a result. **However, good communication doesn't necessarily mean agreement—it means understanding.** Jamie and Alex can have a fruitful, productive conversation even though they ultimately disagree. At the same time, they can have an argument even when they both want the same thing and essentially agree!

How to Use the Ladder in Your Own Life

The ladder is an excellent way to identify, defuse, and resolve conflict. It's a way to shed light on misunderstandings and get everyone moving forward again. If you find yourself in a situation where you or others are "talking past one another," then this is your signal that communication is going to break down—or already has.

The first thing to do is check which rung each speaker is on. If the person you're talking to has an objection that comes from a rung lower than yours, it needs to be addressed first before moving on. Your discussion should focus on bringing you both up the ladder *together*. For example, if Alex identifies that Jamie is on a lower rung, then the objections made start to make more sense. Alex can now address them.

Jamie: "You're not listening. We spent five hundred dollars more last month on eating out than we said we would. That's a big deal!"

Alex: "Okay, it seems like you're really worried about how much we overspent. I agree with you, it's a lot. Why do you think it happened?" (Here, Alex is asking Jamie to move to the next rung, MEANING.)

Jamie: "Well, we were careless, that's all. We weren't paying attention."

Alex: "I agree. It crept up on us. Now I'm sure you'll agree with me, though, that there's nothing we can do about it now. And if we want to do better next time round, we need to start looking at the future." (Now, to the next rung—can you see the two ASSUMPTIONS made?)

Jamie: "Yes, okay. Let's do that."

Alex: "Unless we make some changes, we're going to be in big trouble (CONCLUSIONS). Now I know money's tight, but I still believe that going on vacations is very important, and I don't want to suddenly stop doing everything we enjoy (BELIEFS). So I think moving forward, I want to figure out some smart ways we can still do the things we love without spending too much money (ACTIONS)."

Jamie: "Yes, that makes a lot of sense. I want to do that too."

Now, there is no more disagreement in which Jamie keeps reiterating how bad they were to overspend, while Alex feels guilty for planning vacations. They're communicating again. Granted, in this example, we've kept things very simple and straightforward; in real life, each of these "rungs" may take a long time, perhaps even days. And though in our example Alex very neatly "leads" Jamie, in reality this process would be a lot more subtle, complex, and collaborative. There may well be disagreement or compromise. But ultimately communication is improved because people are reasoning together, rather than at cross-purposes.

The ladder can also be useful any time you are trying to get someone to understand your own actions, or proposed actions. Whenever you want to "bring someone around" to your point of view, don't start with the top of the ladder—bring them along with you and take each step of the ladder at a time so they can see how the inferences and assumptions of your argument gradually build on one another. It's true that someone understanding your thought process doesn't necessarily have to agree with you afterward. The good thing is that if you use the ladder technique, you will almost always avoid misunderstandings and miscommunication, and you will give yourself the best chance of actually being heard.

Another great thing about the ladder is that it shows you that the process of thinking contains many separate, *sequential* components—and skipping one can sometimes lead to sloppy thinking and, of course, miscommunication. It can be useful sometimes to use the ladder to slow down and examine your own thought processes.

Try working backward almost "forensically":

1. What beliefs have inspired your actions?
2. What conclusions do you have about a situation, yourself, others, or the world that informed those beliefs?
3. What assumptions are you making? (A great question is to ask whether you really have much evidence for them, and investigate what changes if you make different assumptions or none at all).
4. What meaning are you ascribing to your experiences?
5. What are you focusing on? What data are you selecting from your environment to act on—or else, what information have you discounted, ignored, or forgotten about?
6. Finally, can you look once more with fresh eyes at the observations around you? For a moment, can you do this without any interpretation?

Asking these questions can reveal interesting ways that our own thinking has gone astray, and if we can get a better understanding of that, we instantly become better communicators. After all, how can we expect clear and conscious communication with others when we ourselves are unclear on our motivations, expectations, and the meaning we ascribe to any situation?

The ladder can be used formally or informally, and for big complex chunks of data as well as more simple information. It is highly adjustable, but its strength is that it forces you to look at things you might have taken for granted. For example, you might use the framework in a meeting you are leading. If you understand the meeting as an exercise in getting everyone to "think together," then you can structure the meeting so that it moves deliberately from one rung to the other. This gives you time to iron out objections or confusions rather than rushing ahead to the higher rungs and risking a full-on conflict.

A few further key insights as you use the ladder in your own communication:

Nobody is "wrong." The ladder is not there to help you find out who is to blame! Also, the person who is higher on the ladder isn't necessarily faster, more intelligent, more correct, or more motivated. As we've seen, misunderstandings usually arise because of *mismatch*—that doesn't mean that there has to be a good guy and a bad guy. It just means something is not aligning.

Switch focus from content to process. Too many arguments are sustained because people are distracted by the content of what is being said—but usually the problem is the *way* it's being said, and the reasoning behind that. As you talk to someone, become tuned in to the way they are thinking—and the way you are thinking!

Keep your ego out of it. Disagreement and conflict have a way of activating our defenses and making us wrongly believe that we are the model of good reasoning, and everyone else is mistaken, stupid, crazy, wrong, bad, etc. But slow down and consider your reasoning, their reasoning, and the way the two are interacting. Remember that you are not just applying the ladder analysis to them, but to yourself as well. You might feel like you want to stand on the top of your own ladder and yell your opinion to all who will hear it, but this is just ego talking and will get you nowhere.

Ask questions. Finally, one way to become a better communicator is to actively engage them in the process of examining the underlying reasoning behind action and opinion. Ask with genuine curiosity. Why do they think XYZ? What facts do they know, and what do those facts mean to them? Why? How?

To conclude, most of us experience the objective world subjectively and selectively. We focus on specific facts only, interpret what those facts mean based on certain assumptions, come to conclusions based on these assumptions, allow these conclusions to shape our beliefs, and then let these beliefs guide our action . . . as well as determine what facts we focus on in the future. This process can be an opportunity to create a strong, effective, and healthy way of looking at the world, or it can become an unconscious echo chamber that ends up amplifying and replicating the same errors again and again.

Framing

If you're like most people, you listen to respond. You're reactive. You let conversations go whichever way they go.

But good communicators approach things a little differently. They are more likely to proactively set the frame for a conversation. **What is a "frame"? It's simply the way you position your line of thinking by your particular choice of words and expression.** It's the kind of thing that will appear to be everywhere once you know to look for it. It's how we develop our arguments, "lead" our listeners along paths of reasoning and inference, and deliberately use language for a special purpose we have chosen.

Consider the following speech made by Barack Obama at the 2004 Democratic National Convention:

> *"There's not a liberal America and a conservative America; there's the United States of America. There's not a Black America and white America and Latino America and Asian America; there's the United States of America ...*
>
> *We are one people, all of us pledging allegiance to the stars and stripes, all of us defending the United States of America. In the end, that's what this election is about. Do we participate in a politics of cynicism, or do we participate in a politics of hope?"*

Notice how he has structured his speech—notice the frame by which he is delivering his message. He did not simply stand up on the stage and announce: "It's important for us to remember who we are as Americans" or even "it's time there was an African American president, and I'll give you some reasons why." Rather, he took seventeen long minutes to lead the audience to this conclusion themselves. Note in the above that he asks a rhetorical question, to which the only answer can be "we participate in a politics of hope." Notice the rhythm and repetition in the way he lays out the artificial differences between different types of Americans, then leads to his conclusion: "we are one people."

Obama (and indeed anyone delivering a persuasive speech of this kind) succeeds not because he effectively shows people what he thinks, but because he constructs a compelling frame in which to communicate that message. His listeners, then, go a step further from understanding and are stirred up enough to be inspired by him and agree with what he says.

When the frame of a conversation changes, everything changes. Everything takes on a different meaning. Therefore, it's simply not something we can leave to chance. Obama, of course, would have had this speech carefully written by experts, and he may well have rehearsed it for hours. Obama was known as a powerful and persuasive speaker, and it's in big part due to his understanding of how to frame himself and his message.

George Lakoff is an author and professor of cognitive science and linguistics. In his book *Don't Think of an Elephant!*, he explains how talking to people's frames is a powerful way of having them really hear you, saying that we mistakenly think that,

> *"if we just tell people the facts, since people are basically rational beings, they'll all reach the right conclusions. But we know from cognitive science that people do not think like that. People think in frames ... to be accepted, the truth must fit people's frames. If the facts do not fit a frame, the frame stays and the facts bounce off.*
>
> *Why?*
>
> *Neuroscience tells us that each of the concepts we have—the long-term concepts that structure how we think—is instituted in the synapses of our brains. Concepts are not things that can be changed just by someone telling us a fact. We may be presented with facts, but for us to make sense of them, they have to fit what is already in the synapses of the brain. Otherwise, facts go in and then they go right back out. They are not heard, or they are not accepted as facts, or they mystify us: "Why would anyone have said that?" Then we label the fact as irrational, crazy, or stupid."*

So, **a frame is the way we work with pre-existing concepts to ensure that the message we're sharing has the highest chance of being received**. Interestingly, it's also why Lakoff recommends resisting the frame of someone you're pushing against by refusing to use their language. This is because it is language that builds the frame—and if someone is not working in your interests, then the frame they choose will not be the frame you want.

In Obama's case, framing is used to persuade. But frames can have other uses and are especially helpful in navigating difficult, uncomfortable, or emotionally charged conflicts. Maybe the other person just refuses to listen or believe you. Maybe you both keep saying the same things over and over, and it's escalating. What's the solution? According to Lakoff, you both need to find a way to *get into the same frame.*

As a good communicator, it's your job to find out what story you could tell that will resonate with the other person. Remember—it's not about facts. It's about all the many different ways to look at those facts, and what that means for two people who find themselves in a conversation about them. Here are a few things to keep in mind:

1. Make sure that, as far as possible, you begin every conversation with a good idea of where you want it to go. Be proactive.
2. What is your frame? Your source of truth? The framework you're embedded in? Really own this—it will help you find the metaphors and stories that will help you express your position.
3. Get the other person to see into this frame of yours by asking them questions. You want them to agree. Be careful and avoid using their story or their words.
4. Deliberately engineer the structure of your story so that it leads toward the kind of solutions you want. It's about focus.

Reading the above, you may think that setting a conversational frame may be a little manipulative. Isn't thinking in this way precisely the thing that leads to stubborn standoffs in conversations? Well, yes and no. **The truth is, we are all using frames all the time.** It's just a question of whether we're consciously aware of it, how those frames work, to what end, and in service of whom and what. Being a good communicator means understanding all this and proactively taking charge. This is more often than not a win-win scenario.

Let's look at an example. Imagine a potential client is interested but has concerns about the price you're charging. What you don't want to do in this case is bombard them with facts (you might call them "reasons") to change their mind. It won't work. What you need to do is consider the best frame for the case you want to make. And to do that, you need to understand the frame they're already in, the nature of their objections and fears, and what exactly it is you're asking them to do.

This might allow you to realize that the person is hesitant because they are unsure of the real value of what you're offering. They are very, very tired of being aggressively marketed to and just want something that works. So you say that they're right—it is expensive. There are people who don't buy because it's not in their budget, and that's okay. But you do have many satisfied clients who, having taken the leap, are now really glad they did—and you'd be happy to put them in touch. Otherwise, you totally respect their decision either way, and they know where to find you if they change their mind.

Can you feel the frame? Can you see how this response actually pulls the potential client into that frame with you? There is nothing in it for the person to push against—and a lot to agree with. As Dwight D. Eisenhower said, "Motivation is the art of getting people to do what you want them to do because they want to do it." In this example, you are using a frame that gives you the best chance of actually reaching this prospective client and getting them to behave in the way you want them to behave.

In the same way, a frame can change anything. It can turn a restriction and a limit into "safety" and "comfort." It can position a loss as a gain or a gain as a loss. It can appoint an adversary as a teacher, and a friend as a saboteur. The luxury fashion brand Hermes sells a handbag, the "Birkin." But not just anyone can buy the handbag; there are only a limited number available, and you have to be invited to spend the roughly fifty thousand dollars to have one. The company will only sell to those they consider worthy, and in fact don't even fully advertise their selection criteria, and do not display the bag in ordinary stores. Their tactics around this item are kept under a deliberate veil of mystery.

Hermes has completely inverted the conventional buyer-seller frame and created their own: In this frame, instead of the company marketing themselves so they are selected by the consumer, the consumer fights to be considered a potential buyer and feels privileged to cough up the fifty thousand dollars.

Every person you ever communicate with will have a lifetime of experiences behind them, and these have taught them in gradual increments to adopt certain beliefs and worldviews (hopefully not too many as bizarre as Hermes'). Many of these views will be unconscious. But that doesn't stop them from being strongly influenced by these beliefs, which seep through and infiltrate everything they do and say, as well as everything they're able to hear or agree with.

Think again about Obama's speech. There would have been many different people in the crowd that night, and a lot of them will have possessed viewpoints and frames that *didn't* match the one Obama was presenting. For example, many Democrats who are politically involved enough to attend conventions and rallies *do* tend to think that there is such a thing as a "liberal America and a conservative America, a Black America and white America"—after all, they were there to show support for the democrats, not the conservatives, and specifically for Obama himself precisely *because* he was a Black American, not because his race didn't matter.

This is the power of framing—it can so thoroughly change context, shift meanings, and create new understandings that it allows you to not only *have* a conversation but *steer* a conversation. This steering is so powerful that it can actually remake meaning entirely and cause people to completely change not just their opinions but the way they arrive at those opinions. Obama could have framed himself as a victim or as an angry avenger. He could have highlighted the frame of justice, or the frame of prosperity. He could, in essence, have chosen any frame in the world.

When someone uses their power to frame and influence in a good way, we call them leaders and are happy to be inspired by them. When their frames dominate and diminish us, we call them bullies and tyrants. Importantly—it's the same skill!

Reality is fixed . . . but the *meaning* of reality is dynamic and subject to change. It is not absolute but contextual, not passively received but actively constructed. This is where communication takes place, and where you have your greatest chance for making connections, being heard, and influencing others.

Chunking: Adjusting the Zoom Button

Take a look at this conversation:

A: Oh, wow, so you're a music teacher! How long have you been doing that?
B: Oh, about ten years now, at least.
A: Cool. And that whole time you taught the French horn?
B: Well, no. That's my main instrument, but I do oboe as well.
A: Huh. I've heard that the French horn is really difficult.
B: Yeah, it can be. A lot of my students end up quitting, sorry to say!
A: Oh, yeah? How long do they stay before they usually quit?
B: How long? Uh . . . I'm not sure. Everyone's different, I guess. I'd say the ones who leave do so pretty quickly. But that could be for all sorts of reasons. It's complicated, I think. But you know early on whether you love the instrument or not.
A: Oh, totally. So maybe, like, they'd quit after the first lesson?
B: Uh . . . no, not always. Sometimes a month? I don't know.
A: Do they ever tell you before they go or do they just disappear?

And on and on. What's your feeling about this conversation? Reading it again, can you spot the point at which is starts to kind of grind along? You can almost feel the moment where B starts to get bored. Why?

Before we consider the answer, let's look at another example:

A: Oh, wow, so you're a music teacher! How long have you been doing that?
B: Oh, about ten years now, at least.
A: Cool. That's a long time. Do you think you'll always teach?
B: Well, I do sometimes wonder. It's rewarding, but . . . people's attitudes to learning have changed so much over the years, you know?
A: I can imagine. People seem to just have less and less patience these days. What do you think's causing it?
B: Well, who knows. Take your pick, right? I mean, I have some very good students, so I can't complain.
A: Oh, I'm sure. Do you think that overall your students' motivations are changing over time?
B: Hm, could be. It's hard to say.
A: Do you think that you've had to adapt the way you teach them to accommodate for how different students are today compared with ten years ago? I often feel like we focus too much on technique in this country, and so little on the art side. Do you find that?

Now consider what you think of this conversation. It's completely different, but somehow something is still not quite working. The big problem with both conversations (other than A asking a barrage of questions and B being somewhat unresponsive) is a question of *chunking*.

In neuro-linguistic programming, the word "chunking" is used to describe the way in which we can group pieces of information. We can chunk "up" or "down:"

Chunking up means to ask questions or make comments in such a way as to combine information and make it more abstract and more general. It's the process of looking for things that are coming, or "zooming out" to see the overarching theme, pattern, or structure that simplifies all the smaller details you're looking at. So someone gives you a long list of all the pets they've had throughout their life, and you chunk up by saying, "So you're a real animal lover, huh?"

Chunking down goes the other way. It's when we ask questions or make comments that move the conversation from the general and abstract to the more specific. Someone says they love animals, and you ask them, "Do you have a pet?" In doing so, you're asking for a more *specific* instance of the general claim they've just made, i.e., zooming in.

Basically, chunking is a way to turn the dial on the level of detail occurring in a conversation. Let's return to our examples above. In the first example, Speaker A asks questions that lead to them zooming in on the idea of students quitting and exactly when they quit and why. It's as though each question drills deeper and deeper into this one chosen thread—perhaps to the boredom of Speaker B!

The second conversation has a different problem. Here, Speaker A keeps asking questions that open up the conversation to a more abstract level. But in time, these questions just seem to go nowhere. They are soon talking about students in general, and then all people and their total lack of patience, and then the entire system of music education in the whole country—there's a load of sweeping generalization and broad abstraction. Again Speaker B is not quite enjoying this flight into the abstract!

Chunking up questions/phrases/themes can look like:

- What does that mean?
- Let's look at the big picture . . .
- How does that connect to . . .?
- Why did all of that happen?
- What pattern is emerging?

Chunking down, on the other hand, could sound like:

- What happened next?
- Can you provide a specific detail? (For example, what was his name? How much did it cost?)
- Tell me more about . . .
- When did this happen, and in what order?

Which is better to use—chunking up or down? The answer is neither, because a good conversation contains a dynamic balance of both of them. We can zoom in and out to various levels of detail and abstraction according to our needs. (We'll explore this more in a later chapter when we look at "funnel questions.")

Start at a broad, general level and work your way down. This may correspond with more open-ended questions, but it doesn't necessarily have to:

1. Start with chunking up to define the "territory" of your conversation, state the parameters of the problem, or gently introduce a new conversation or topic.
2. Gradually chunk down, but **do not ask more than three chunking down questions in a row.** Find out things like specific goals, motivations, problems, interpretations, examples, etc.

3. Then zoom out again with another chunking up question. Again, try not to ask more than three of these in a row.

The point of zooming in and out is to avoid either extreme: Get too abstract and lofty and you risk creating a stiff, impersonal, and vague conversation about nothing and everything. On the other hand, linger too long on chunking down questions and you can get lost, stuck, or distracted by irrelevant details.

A good metaphor is to imagine that you and your conversation partner are mutually navigating your way up a winding mountain path, using a map. Sometimes, you'll both want to lean in and engage with the finer details of exactly where you are—the rocks and trees and so on. You'll focus on this turn or that turn, and the one foot in front of the other. But every once in a while, you have to consult the map and get a bigger picture of what you're doing. You need to look up and take in the horizon, or glance behind you to see how far you've advanced up the mountain and how much longer you have to go. You might even take a break and consider the whole reason for climbing the mountain in the first place! In any case, good mountaineers have both skills—they pay attention to the gravel beneath their boots, but also look up and around them and engage in the broader task.

The ideal conversation, then, would be a comfortable mix of the first and second of our examples above. For instance, instead of continuing to dwell on the students who quit, and exactly when they quit and why, Speaker A could take a metaphorical step back, allow the conversation to breathe a little, and take the opportunity to chunk up. Similarly, three or four chunking up questions into the second conversation is a good time to stop talking abstractly and probe for some specifics.

Conversational Extremist: The Nitpicker

In our examples, chunking up or down is something we can locate in a single question or comment. But it can often be more subtle than this. **"Nitpickers" are people who have a longstanding tendency to have conversations constantly take place on a concrete, literal, and detailed level.** The result can be a conversational style that is felt by others to be very dull, dragging, and uninspired. It's like the conversation gets "stuck in the weeds" and never really launches.

This is the person who, when you tell them you've met the love of your life, will be curious about what time in the morning you met them and what their name is and whether you spell that name with one L or two.

We tend to become conversational nitpickers ourselves for a few reasons. We may be anxious and trying to control the course of the conversation but inadvertently keep it muzzled to endless mundane details. We may be bored ourselves. The way out is simple: If you find that you or your listener is getting bored or distracted, sit back (sometimes literally!) and ask an open-ended, completely abstract question. Say something about an intangible concept. Introduce a metaphor, or even a controversial and nuanced opinion. This should kick the conversation back into gear.

Conversational Extremist: The Philosopher

The other extreme is the person who never, ever comes down from some towering abstract conversational heights and seems to always be looking down at humans and all the petty details of their lives ... a bit like a philosopher. These are the people who will constantly try to make isolate observations or single anecdotes mean something about a grander political, social, or philosophical narrative. You might want to rant a little about someone who was late, and they respond with a deep-and-meaningful deconstruction of the entire notion of lateness, of all mankind's tendencies to rebel against artificial segmentation of this imaginary construct called time, and to finish off, some complex psychoanalysis of the late person—not just this person in question, but all people who are late.

The conversational philosopher is someone who is always looking for theories, patterns, and overarching themes, but this can come across as pompous, cold, and irrelevant. The solution, here, is also obvious: Come back to earth with a question about *this* person's *specific* life in the here and now. This should immediately anchor and ground the conversation, with a side effect of making you seem more human, more approachable, and more relaxed.

Chunking up or down, then, is not just a cognitive exercise about how information is managed. It's also about the degree of openness or closedness in a conversation, the overall sense of flow, and the extent that either levity or seriousness is allowed to dominate.

Use chunking up questions when you want to summarize, contextualize, consolidate, or get some distance—theoretical or emotional. This is a focus on an overarching organization, on purpose and intention.

Use chunking down questions when you want to expand on some point, zoom in, confirm, or get to grips with the more "real" aspects of the conversation. This is a focus on how the overarching themes express themselves in specific ways, on unique experience, and on the details: who, where, when, how, what, and why.

Finally, **pay attention to chunking in conflict situations.** You may discover that at least part of the problem is that two people are talking with different chunking tendencies. For example, your boss may call you in with the intention of discussing an issue. Your boss keeps listing out all instances of this issue and expanding on the details of each. You get impatient because you are eager to understand what all of it means—what is the single insight or conclusion you are meant to come to? Your boss sees you wanting to boil everything down and find some common cause for each transgression, but assumes this means you are not accepting the fact that there are many offenses, not just one. You see your boss endlessly listing grievances but without synthesizing them into anything you can act on. And round and round you both talk, both unable to reach one another because you're operating at completely different levels of detail.

When communication has devolved to this extent, the way back to a shared frame of reference is to ask questions or make comments that *gradually* close the gap.

"What is that an example of?"
"Is there something that connects all these observations?"
"What one thing do you want me to take from this conversation?"

On the other hand, if you're having a conflict with someone who is being overly vague and abstract, try to help them zoom in by asking things like:

"Can you give me a specific example of what you're talking about?"

"When did this event happen? With whom? How?"
"Can you pinpoint the exact moment it all went wrong?"

Think Before You Speak

"I just call it like I see it."
"I'm being honest."
"That's not what I *meant* to say."
"I'm just being me."
"I don't do small talk."

Have you ever said any of the above? One major impediment to health, effective communication is a set of subtle but very damaging beliefs about what is actually required of us as humans when we speak to others. **Some of these beliefs come from the idea that as long as we are authentic, sincere, and share our emotions, that's enough; in other words, our intentions matter, and how we articulate ourselves is less important.**

Nothing could be further from the truth! Good communicators know that you cannot just, well, blurt out whatever enters your mind. You need to be deliberate. You need to consciously *filter* what you say. You need to speak with purpose and discipline. If you've ever said something you later regretted or really "put your foot in it," then this is a sign that you could use more deliberation in the way you communicate!

The first thing is to subtly challenge the idea that communication is solely about expressing yourself, your position, or your emotions. It is not really relevant whether you have a strong feeling about something, whether you feel like you're right (or even if you *are* right!), or whether you are overcome by this or that impulse in the moment. Since communication is a social activity, it involves others, and that automatically means that a portion of all communication is *simply not about you*. People who understand and work with this insight are ultimately better at communication than those who keep on stubbornly insisting "it's not my fault that they misunderstood me!"

Being a conscious and careful communicator means you avoid causing offense or misunderstanding, you boost your credibility and maturity in other peoples' eyes, and you generally keep yourself out of trouble! Speaking without thinking, however, often occurs because we're impatient, we're conversational narcissists (more on this later in the book), we are not good at listening, or simply we're excited and get carried away with sharing what we want to share.

Not everything you think and feel needs to be shared. Not everything that pops into your head needs to be expressed. To decide what qualifies an idea to be shared, ask yourself the following questions:

1. Do I have good motives?

Is what you're going to say helpful or useful to yourself or anyone else? Be honest about what your motives are. Many people butt in during conversations to share some tidbit of information that is completely irrelevant, simply because it satisfies their own ego to say something and impress others. Be real and assess whether what you're saying moves things forward and contributes to the shared goal of the conversation (i.e., not some hidden agenda of your own).

Some people will say something along the lines of "if you can't say something nice, don't say anything at all." But sometimes, you *will* have to express something that's not "nice," especially if you are defending a boundary or addressing conflict. Still, your motives should be to share any grievance or disagreement with the intention of clarifying and resolving it, rather than to blame and shame. This is why motive matters. You may be able to fool the other person that you are saying something out of concern or genuine misunderstanding, but at least be honest with yourself and check whether you're speaking for some other, less noble reason.

2. Is it true?

Opinions, perspectives, and desires are one thing. But ask if, beyond this, you are actually saying something you know to be a falsehood. This may seem an obvious point to labor, but often we insert little falsehoods into what we say without being conscious of it. We exaggerate, we minimize, we omit important information, or we present our best guess as more certain than it really is. Again, it ties into motive. Are we genuinely and honestly sharing what we know, or are we trying to come across as an expert?

In the realm of our own perceptions and experiences, of course, nothing is really "true" or "false"—it is our unique experience. But be careful that you never act as though something being true *for you* automatically makes it true for another person. Here, being truthful means owning and acknowledging your own perspective, while not overstepping and behaving as though that perspective were truth.

3. Am I breaking confidences?

It goes without saying: never share something you've been asked to keep private. Gossip is awful and degrades the speaker, the listener, and the person being talked about in equal measure, but you can still break confidences even without technically being in gossip territory. Ask yourself this question: If the person you're talking about was present, would they be okay with hearing what you're saying about them?

4. Is it considerate?

No, you don't always have to be *kind*. Some situations in life call for communication even when we don't like or approve of the person in front of us, or where "kindness" isn't really appropriate. But you do have to be civil, polite, and considerate. You do have to show the other person a degree of non-negotiable respect. Sometimes, what you want to say may be true, it may be necessary, and you may be well within your rights to say it—but that still doesn't entitle you to be rude about it. In this case, remember that etiquette and manners are not something you do merely for the other person's sake, but something you do to communicate a degree of respect for yourself.

An option is to use the THINK acronym—which stands for True, Helpful, Inspiring, Necessary, or Kind. As we've seen, you don't need to have all of these, but if what you want to say ticks only one or two boxes, you're probably better off keeping silent or rewording your message.

All of this can only be achieved when you do something essential: **stop and think. Get into the habit of pausing before you talk, or even just *mentally* pausing**. Even a few seconds of forethought can be enough (deep down, we usually know whether something is a good idea or not even without going through the above questions—we just need to slow down enough to realize that we know!). If you're not really sure, then err on the side of staying silent. It's always possible to speak up later; it's never possible to un-say what's already been said.

Understanding "Clean Communication"

Imagine that a woman says to her husband, "Can you please take out the trash?"
Now imagine that she instead says, "Can you please take out the trash for a change?"

You can probably see which one is "clean" communication, and which one is a little *dirty*. Saying "for a change" adds a hostile blaming element that is not part of the main message, but forms a secondary piece of communication. This charge may be added in consciously or unconsciously. On the other hand, clean, smooth communication conveys a message without adding in any kind of "negative charge."

Any time your communication is serving a double role of delivering extra shame, anger, ridicule, guilt-tripping, manipulation, lies, and so on, it's no longer clean. Imagine the husband hears the second phrase from above and responds, "Take it out yourself." The wife may then (rightly) see this as an attack and respond, "Why are you so mean to me? All I did was ask you nicely to take the trash out!" As you can imagine, a fight ensues, in part because the wife's initial communication was *unconsciously* unclean. That didn't stop her husband from responding to what she was really communicating!

Whether consciously unclean (arguably a bit easier to deal with) or unconsciously unclean, this type of communication is a kind of *anti*-communication. It creates misunderstandings, hurt feelings, and barriers. Have you ever had a conversation with someone who on the surface seemed to be saying and doing all the right things, but you still somehow felt bad afterward? Maybe you had a weird physical sensation in your gut, or you felt like something was amiss. It might have felt like you were being lied to, manipulated, or subtly insulted . . . chances are, you were the recipient of some unclean communication.

Let's take a look at another example. The wife says to the husband, "Can you please take the trash out?" The husband hears this and, in his mind, interprets it to mean something like, "You're a lazy good-for-nothing and I have to talk to you like a child!" He responds in the same way, "Take it out yourself!" As you can see, the misunderstanding is now on the part of the listener/receiver. Here, the husband is overly sensitive, and has allowed his own issues to distort the message he's receiving. Again, the communication is unclean.

Whether snags happen on side A or side B, and whether they are done consciously or unconsciously, they can degrade communication. Even worse, little snares and hiccups can compound over time, creating animus and a feeling of negativity that is hard to shift once it's underway. This "toxic residue" can lead to more intense conflict in time or even a big blow out, so it's best to keep on top of communication as it happens, practicing, if you will, a kind of routine "communication hygiene." This cleans up little misunderstandings and conflicts before they become big ones.

You'll know that there is some residue in your communication with someone when one or both of you feels:

A little wary, nervous, or uncomfortable
Any combativeness and defensiveness
Lies, deception, or lowered trust
General upset or high emotional intensity

Now, the "dirt" in communication can be accidental, or it can be deliberate. If it's accidental, the idea is to stop, take a step back, and address it. Many innocent mistakes turn not-so-innocent if not addressed in this way. "Hey, I just wanted to talk to you about something. You asked me earlier to take the trash out, and it felt like you were kind of implying that I don't pull my weight or something. I don't know if I've got that wrong; is that what you were trying to say?" Importantly, in addressing something, you need to work hard not to introduce more unclean language!

If, however, the unclean communication is intended, then the approach is to go in to conflict resolution. "Well, actually, if we're going to be honest about it, I have been feeling like I'm doing too much of the housework lately." The thing is, communication can be clean even during conflict. So long as messages are being shared *without* introducing extra negativity, then the conversation is clean and likely to be productive.

First make a promise to yourself that you will use clean language as often as you can. Make a commitment that you will be straightforward, honest, and respectful, and will never resort to underhandedness, passive aggression, or innuendo. This takes a degree of conscious maturity as well as discipline.

According to clean communication experts Matthew McKay, Patrick Fanning, and Kim Paleg, the ideal communication attitude is "**taking responsibility for the effect of what you say**." It also means owning the consequences of your speech, even, and maybe especially if, you're not quite conscious of what you're doing. Do your best to create a conversational space where you can work honestly and respectfully through any conflicts or disagreements. Leave out harmful speech, accusations, "barbed" language, and insinuations that might hurt and attack another person—and do it no matter how upset or wronged you feel. Follow the "ten commandments of clean language" to keep you on the straight and narrow and spare yourself and others a load of unnecessary drama:

1. **Don't use judgment words and loaded terms** ("pigsty" or "lazy").
2. **Don't use "global" labels**, i.e., make sweeping generalizations or use absolute statements ("you haven't taken out the trash in two weeks" rather than "you're an untidy person," which takes a swipe at the person's *entire being*, not just their behavior).
3. **Don't send "you" messages** of blame and accusation ("I'm stressed" is better than "you're stressing me").
4. **Stay away from old history**—stick to the issue at hand and let bygones go.
5. **Avoid negative comparisons** ("You're a slob just like my ex was").
6. **Never threaten, even subtly** ("If you can't be bothered to do the trash, it makes me wonder why I bother to do any of *my* chores"). Control and manipulation only create escalating defensiveness.
7. **Describe your feelings** rather than use them as a weapon or a "point" you've scored ("You've really gone and riled me up this morning! Why do you always insist on hurting me like this?").
8. **Keep your body language open, relaxed, and receptive**. Call off a difficult conversation until you're calmer, if necessary.

9. **Use whole messages.** Incomplete messages are more likely to be taken out of context. A whole message contains observations, thoughts, feelings, and needs/wants. For example, "I see the trash is piling up (observation), and I realize you haven't taken it out for a long time (thoughts). When I see that I have to do it, even though it's your chore, I feel overwhelmed and annoyed. I'd really like for you to keep up your end of the housework as we agreed (wants/needs)."

10. **Be clear.** If you have a question, ask. If you want something, request it. Avoid using passive language, innuendo, or hints ("Is there some special reason you've decided to let us all live in filth, or . . .?"). Be direct and clear.

Summary:

- Poor communication arises as a result of a mismatch of perspectives, approach, or conversational skill. People process information differently, but to avoid misunderstandings, communicate consciously and use the "ladder of inference." It shows the unique way that people use their experiences to make meaning: observations > selected data > meanings > assumptions > conclusions > beliefs > actions.
- Conflict can occur when people are on different rungs. To improve communication, see where people are and how their ladder of inference is working for them, then speak to that, in sequence, and without blame or shame.
- Good communicators deliberately create their own frames during conversations and position their line of thinking by using specially chosen words, expressions, and images. Change frames and you change meaning.
- Deliberately engineer your conversational frame and invite the other person in using pre-existing concepts they're familiar with to improve the chances they'll be receptive. Remember that reality is fixed, but the *meaning* of reality is dynamic and subject to change.
- Chunking is about the way we group information. Chunking up is grouping specific instances into a larger overall abstract pattern or theory, while chunking down makes inferences from the general to the specific. Keeping the level of detail varied and appropriate creates a better flowing conversation than one that relies too heavily on chunking up or chunking down.
- It is a mistake to think that authenticity, expression, and sincerity are enough—*how* we articulate ourselves matters. Consciously filter what you say: Is it true, kind, and helpful?
- Take responsibility for what you say and practice clean communication—i.e., without hidden negative meanings.

Chapter 2: Mastering Style and Tone

Eliminate Crutch Words and Empty Language

So, um, you probably already, like, know what crutch words are and, well, how they can undermine your communication and stuff, you know. Right? If that makes sense?

It's not uncommon to feel a little flustered when speaking. It's not uncommon to feel distracted, unprepared, or unfocused. After all, the communication we're talking about is everyday communication—not carefully crafted speeches and presentations. Natural speech is often a little disjointed, loose, and open-ended. Crutch words or "filler words" can act like necessary padding or pauses to help us catch our breath, collect our thoughts, and process the next thing we want to say.

The trouble is when this kind of fluff language takes over and starts detracting from the overall message. **A crutch word helps prop you up, but it can make you harder to understand, hurt your credibility, and distract from what you're saying.** So much of what we say is socially and culturally coded, and filler words can come with an enormous set of assumptions, insinuations, and prejudices.

Words like *um, ah, well, you know, like, so, right, okay*, and *hm* can be like little speed bumps that interrupt the flow of your message. It's easy to see why—if you're talking to someone who is showing you that every third or fourth word they use essentially has no meaning, are you likely to pay more or less attention to what they say? The irony is that in using crutch words to fill an awkward silence, we end up diluting our message and making it *less* likely that people pay attention to all those other, non-crutch words.

More than this, using crutch words can actively annoy people and signal a subtle lack of conversational awareness and etiquette. Consider that when you open your mouth, you are "taking the floor," even if it's in a very casual and free-form setting. You are holding the mic, so to speak. If people get the sense that you are hogging this position without really saying anything, they are likely to get annoyed or bored, and they may be tempted to interrupt or just ignore you.

Get Comfortable with Pausing

To get rid of an overreliance on crutch words, you need to learn to do one thing: embrace silence. Usually, filler words and fluff are there to deal with a mild sense of anxiety, to fill the void, and to keep up feeling of flow when you're not quite sure what you're saying next. But if you actively embrace those (natural) pauses in speech, you empower yourself to be a more proactive, conscious, and confident speaker. You are not afraid of awkward silences—you are actively using them as one of the many tools you have in your conversational itinerary.

If you have a bad crutch word habit, don't worry—this can actually be used to your advantage. By replacing every crutch word with a thoughtful, assured pause, you communicate a few powerful things to your audience:

You are confident, either in yourself or in what you have to say. You do not feel that you need to quickly say your piece or rush through what you're saying for fear that you'll be interrupted or ignored. In treating your own message with this kind of attention and respect, you convey to others a belief in its value, and they can't help but do the same.

You show consideration for your audience. If someone is blundering and blathering on with very little thought for how clear their message is or how it may be coming across, they signal a disregard for the other person. All of us need to carefully consider how we present ourselves, and too many filler words can make for a boring and confusing listening experience for an audience. However, if other people get the sense that you are being deliberate about how you speak, you create a frame of mutual respect and consideration, which automatically elevates whatever conversation you're having.

It helps you stay calm. A pause is a moment in which you can gather yourself—and it's also a moment for the audience to process and digest what you're sharing. It's the difference between gobbling down a meal without thinking versus savoring each bite and pausing after each mouthful. The breath is connected to our state of anxiety—and if we're talking *constantly*, we're usually not breathing, and this fuels anxiety. Just stop, take a breath, and let the conversation expand a little and relax.

Finally, a pause can actually help you make your point. It's a mistake to think that silence is empty space or some kind of lost opportunity where you could have been speaking instead. A pause has power. Pausing at the right moment can alert your audience to the fact that you're about to say something important. It can help you build suspense and then release it. When you pause after something important, it can show the audience that you want them to really think about what you've just said. It gives you time to lean on other, non-verbal elements of your communication—such as your eye contact or body language. This can be more effective that just talking and talking.

Here is a two-step exercise you can try to break the crutch word habit and come across with more confidence and clarity.

Step 1: Pay attention. Actually listen to how you currently speak. This requires awareness in the moment, but it's even better if you can somehow record yourself during a conversation so you can play it back and see just how often you're relying on crutch words. You may be surprised! Try to notice not only when you're resorting to filler and fluff, but also to how this is impacting the conversation, how people's energy and attention levels are changing, how the conversation is flowing, and how anxious or confident you feel. Recording may be difficult, but you can also gain some insight by filming yourself telling a story. The idea is to get a good snapshot of the role this kind of language is presently playing in your life.

Step 2: The next bit is difficult but becomes easier with practice. Just keep quiet! Force yourself to say nothing instead of using a crutch word. You don't have to speak in a smooth, uninterrupted flow—just stay quiet if you're not sure what to say. Try to teach yourself that a pause is not a problem. Sure, if you just go silent for longer than five or six seconds, your listeners may start to wonder, but you may discover you seldom need that long to gather your thoughts, and that people are rather tolerant and will wait.

Then, repeat step 1 and notice how different it feels to pause instead of um and ah. Notice how you feel and how other people respond to you. You may also find that pausing in this way has other related benefits: You speak more slowly, more deliberately, and with more assuredness. You find yourself taking yourself more seriously!

The Dangers of "Hedging Language"

Imagine someone said the following to you:

"I was just wondering, I don't know, maybe we could potentially slow down a little with this new launch, just until we have more clarity on the funding situation. I don't mean to offend or anything, don't get me wrong, and I suppose this could just be, like, my issue, but I just feel that we could possibly pause here and, uh, reassess. Do you know what I mean? Haha, sorry if all that doesn't make any sense!"

Do you get the feeling that this person is calm, confident, and self-assured? Do you get the feeling that they are knowledgeable, competent experts? Are you inspired to listen to them and come along to their point of view?

Probably not. "Hedging" or "softening" language is a way to reduce what we're saying, to make it smaller, more polite, and less certain. It absolutely has a place whenever tact, diplomacy, and etiquette are required. In fact, it plays a vital role in communication of all kinds. However, like filler words and crutches, it can do more harm than good.

Imagine the same message conveyed as follows:

"I think we're moving a little fast on this. I would prefer personally to slow down until we have more clarity on the funding situation, although I do appreciate this may not be the majority view. What's your take on it? Is it essential that we launch this week?"

The message is the same, but the frame has positioned the speaker in an entirely different light.

Watch out for the following:

Maybe, could be, might, possibly, potentially, etc. Using these words is often an attempt to convey the uncertainty of the information, but it only makes *you* look uncertain.
Instead, say: *What you mean. Be direct and assertive without being rude.*

Does that make sense? Sorry I'm not making sense. Don't deliberately invite people to devalue what you say. Usually, people say this not when they're afraid of being misunderstood, but when they want to signal submission and compliance.
Instead, say: *Nothing. Say what you mean, and if the other person misunderstands, they can ask for clarification.*

Do you know what I mean? Right? Don't you agree? This can come across as excessively seeking approval or validation . . . and consequently communicating that you don't feel sure in what you're saying. This can put people on the spot or make you seem needy or unreliable.
Instead say: *"What's your opinion on this?"*

I feel, I suppose, it's just me, I wonder, I'm worried, etc. Using "I feel" when you really mean "I think" or even "I believe" weakens your position. Using lots of emotive, self-effacing, or self-referencing language can create a frame that makes you look reactive and passive.
Instead say: *"I think,"* or simply state your perceptions without personalizing or psychologizing them.

Hedging language, as you've probably noticed, tends to happen more with women. Whether women are naturally more effusive and submissive in conversations, or social norms have conditioned women to diminish themselves when speaking up, is a moot point. Whatever the truth, sadly there *are* some asymmetries in the way people perceive male and female speakers. A woman, for example, may be perceived as bossy and domineering when behaving in ways that are considered merely assertive for men, yet if she uses hedging language, she will not really be taken seriously. In the same way, a man may be encouraged to present himself as more certain and in control than he really feels, causing misunderstandings. Yet if he uses softer, more hedging language, again he will be perceived as *less* trustworthy and competent, even when this really signals a more nuanced and sophisticated understanding of his own message.

All of this is to say that something like hedging or crutch words are not *absolute* phenomena, but rather something that interacts with culture, gender, and so on. Furthermore, you may consciously choose to use hedging if you actually want to come across as non-threatening (for example, in diffusing conflict or in a tricky negotiation).

When speaking (especially in a professional context), it's almost always better to be

- concise
- calm
- clear

This **does not** mean rude or curt.

Upspeak and the Mystery of Tone

A related linguistic phenomenon is what is called upspeak (also called uptalk, "valley girl speak," or high rising terminal—HRT). Even if you've never heard the name of this phenomenon, you already know what it is, and you've heard plenty of it whether you know it or not!

Upspeak is when the last word of a declarative sentence (i.e., a statement) is said with a rising pitch, the same way a question does.

In 1993, journalist James Gorman wrote an article for *The New York Times* where he put a name to this phenomenon. It's not just a linguistic phenomenon but a complex stereotype that focused on upper-middle class young women who lived in the Southern California valleys. This way of speaking became wildly popular and emulated by many, but it also came to be vilified culturally and denigrated as a highly aggravating way to express yourself.

Since Gorman's article in the '90s, communication experts have given the standard advice to completely avoid this kind of inflection in your own speech, unless you want to bore, annoy, or alienate your listeners. Phrasing statements and questions can understandably make you seem unsure, lacking in confidence, and perhaps even unintelligent.

Many theorists have criticized this criticism itself, suggesting that picking on this perfectly arbitrary vocal variant says more about the critic's hidden sexism or reaction to the lifestyle or culture that they assume it represents.

Dr. Kami Anderson is an interculturalist and linguist and claims that,

> "Uptalk is a lilt that is commonly used to soften communication. It's a way that people use paralanguage, or the sound of their voice and intonations, to appear more friendly, personable, and approachable ... We begin to perceive the ways in which we show empathy or compassion with our voices as a weakness, when in actuality it is a demonstration of our ability to consider the perception of others in the workplace. Socialization has indeed made the practice of uptalk more noticeable in women because it is perceived as a gendered communication trait, but ... that perception is an extension of the workplace practices."

What Anderson is saying, in other words, is that there isn't anything inherently bad about upspeak, except for the fact that it is not considered masculine. But this may be misguided. Studies (Lakoff, 1973, 1975) have found, for example, that people chairing meetings tended to use upspeak three to seven times more often that their subordinates. The conclusion is that upspeak actually has a role in asserting leadership and tends to be used by higher-status individuals. Rather than creating a frame of imposing demands, upspeak establishes an intention of collaboration and ease, which may be just as important in the workplace.

So, should you avoid upspeak or embrace it confidently? Well, as with anything to do with language and communication, the answer is: it depends.

If you are a woman, refusing to apologize for your normal speech patterns is likely to give you a valuable sense of assertiveness and confidence. This also applies to your regional accent and any vocal markers of class or social status—if a certain linguistic idiosyncrasy is yours, then "own" it.

Excellent communicators do not all speak identically, and they are not afraid to be distinctive in the way they speak. However, they do all share the ability to be **conscious** of what they are saying, how they are saying it, and the effect they are having on others. Women do not need to speak like men do in order to be taken seriously. However, if a woman becomes aware that she is coming across as uncertain, unconfident, or nervous, then she can consciously take steps to remedy this. *The key, then, is not whether you use upspeak, but whether your total expression is one of confidence and poise.*

Upspeak, like any vocal style, is likely to become grating if overused. Record yourself and try to spot instances of rising pitch. Experiment with taking those same words and giving them a neutral or even downward inflection at the end. Notice the effect it has on you, your message, and your listener. A little upspeak here and there is probably a good thing and contributes to articulate, varied, and lively tone, but too much can be a bad thing.

The Five Types of Communication Tone

Why exactly is it that upspeak can be such a problem? One reason is that it creates an inappropriate communication tone. **A communication tone is a little like a vocal frame.** It's about how you use words and phrases to establish the kind of communication that can happen. A company will tend to use a more formal tone with shareholders and investors, but adopt a friendlier, more persuasive tone in marketing to its customers. Naturally, the tone we use—our register or the way we "pitch" our message—has a lot to do with the reason we're communicating in the first place. Upspeak, then, can be a problem if it conveys a tone of informality and casualness in a situation that calls for more formality and restraint.

Tone of voice expresses your message, your intention, your feelings … but it also affects how people see that message, and the intentions and feelings they ascribe to you. **In essence, there are always two streams of information every time we communicate: what we are saying and all the extra data that comes from how we say it.**

Type 1: Informative

This is the communication tone that is neutral, objective, and calmly rational. It's the way your doctor speaks to you, or the language of an encyclopedia or service professional. The actual data itself is front and center, not the person sharing that data, or the context, or the relationship between speaker and listener.

Type 2: Humorous

In other words, comedy and fun. Well-paced levity can ease tensions, make you stand out from the crowd, or get your point across quickly. In the wrong place, humor can be disrespectful, unprofessional, or just weird.

Type 3: Respectful

This is a step or two beyond just informative—it's deliberately polite and considerate, seeking to be pleasant, inoffensive, and accommodating. This is almost exclusively the tone of communication between strangers or people in shared public places, where etiquette and social norms stave off the most common misunderstandings or awkwardness.

Type 4: Formal

The kind of tone you find in academic and professional settings. Formal speech uses longer words, longer sentences, and no slang or colloquialisms. Its emphasis is on correctness and a certain portrayal of high standards.

Type 5: Informal

The opposite: a more conversational tone. The voice you use outside of professional situations, either with friends or family.

Miscommunication can occur when we are using a tone that doesn't suit the context or the message, or we are communicating with someone who is using a different tone from ours. For example, you are using an informal and overly familiar tone with an employee you're in the process of disciplining, you are using a humorous tone in a difficult situation with people you don't know well, or you are using a respectful and informative tone when someone has raised a personal grievance with you. **The problem is not the tone but the mismatch between the tone and the intention.**

Effective communication depends on many different factors—what you're saying, your empathy levels, the platform or medium, and so on—but tone may be the most important. A Grammarly and Harris online poll found that fifty-three percent of knowledge workers felt that the tone of a message was more important than the content. That means that clarity and factual accuracy are only a part of a good message—the way those facts are framed is also important. Furthermore, "intent is not the same as impact"—in other words, simply feeling a certain way means little unless you are able to actually convey that to your listeners.

How can you be more conscious of tone in professional settings?

It can be a difficult balance to strike. Here are a few tips to navigate what can be tricky waters:

Strike a balance between friendly and business-like
Only you will know about your unique workplace culture and context, but try to imagine social niceties and friendliness acting as a kind of buffer or lubricant. For example, you might make a comment about the weather or ask how a person is, but *for the purpose of* easing into business and quickly warming up before talking more formally. The friendliness is there to assist but is not the main focus. So, that means that a ten-minute conversation about details of your personal life, or an impassioned rant about the weather, is inappropriate.

Be confident but not arrogant
One way to do this is to focus on the content—be clear, calm, and assured in what you're saying, but don't let this turn into *personal* confidence or, even worse, egotism. The surest way to hold your own without conveying a sense of superiority or haughtiness is to show no hesitance in sharing your own opinion or position, but be graceful enough to ask their opinion, request help, or admit that you're wrong, unsure, or don't know.

Aim to be concise but never curt
You can almost always get your message across with fewer words than you think! You're communicating for a reason. What is it? Make sure that you are clear on the crux of your message so that when you deliver it to your audience, you can do so with minimal distraction or irrelevancy. In other words, get to the point! However, the ordinary conventions of politeness will go a long way in stopping you from coming across as rude or too blunt. Ask questions, say please and thank you, and always add a little buffer before and after what you say, rather than just blurting things out.

Instead of being emotional, be compelling
We've seen that hedging language, upspeak, and using too many crutch words can make you appear weak or overly emotional. You are never required to pretend you don't have feelings or emotions, but a professional and self-regulated person takes on the responsibility of being selective with how they express this emotion. It doesn't matter if you're "right" to feel how you feel—people seldom continue to listen to someone who is overcome with anger, fear, or upset. Instead, make your case with compelling arguments, give your evidence, and be as persuasive as you can. If you're worked up, you may need to take a step back and cool off before deciding what to say and how.

Be genuine but also stay flexible
You need to "be yourself" (in all contexts, not just professional ones), but that doesn't mean that you should relentlessly center your own perspective at the expense of the people you're talking to. You might be a genuinely straight-talking, no-nonsense kind of person, but if the person you're talking to is more nuanced, sensitive, and delicate, then respect that and dial down your tone. You can still be who you are, but be considerate of how the message, the context, and other people may require you to adjust and adapt.

Overall, professionalism is about awareness—it's about knowing that what you say has impact, and deliberately taking steps to speak in a way that gets you what you want while respecting the context and the people you're talking to. Returning to the question of upspeak, then: you may well be perceived as frivolous, uneducated, or annoying if you use upspeak in a professional capacity because it simply does not fit the context. But by the same token, someone who is using an overly stiff and formal communication tone in a casual setting is making the same mistake and showing that they lack situational awareness.

The answer to "What's the best tone to use?" is always "the tone that best matches the context and which will most likely be received by my listeners."

How to Use Signposts
What is the function of road signs when you're driving? They're there to let you know what's coming up, to alert you to exactly where you are, the direction you're going in, and where you're likely to end up if you carry on your route.

Conversational "road signs" serve a similar function. They are verbal and non-verbal markers that tell your listeners what kind of "journey" they're going on, where they are, and where you are taking them. The concept of signposting is most seen in public speaking, where the speaker is expected to move the audience through a sequence of clearly marked key points arranged in a logical argument with clear transitions from one idea to the next. This helps the audience "connect the dots" and see your argument as a whole.

It's easy to forget just how important it is to do this. When you are on your own, the things you already know occupy your mind in a diffuse, all-at-once state. You have already formed your opinions, made your connections, and arrived at your conclusions. It's easy to forget that when you open your mouth to speak to others, *they haven't done all this*. This is why signposting is so important. You need to structure your thoughts and ideas as an organized narrative, with one step leading to the other.

Signposting is commonly thought of as a way to keep your listeners engaged and listening to what you say. But it's more than this. Signposts help your audience come along with you on a cognitive journey so that they can truly *understand*, arriving at your conclusion as a matter of process rather than simply having you tell them some disconnected bits of information. Signposting helps guide listeners through a unique perspective. It helps facilitate their mental processing and categorization of the information you're sharing—and do so in a way that helps make your case.

If you're driving along a road that suddenly ends, splits without warning, or takes you to a surprise destination, you'll feel disoriented or even totally lost. The same thing happens when you signpost incorrectly—and your audience will not want to continue listening to you. In the same way, a long car journey where there are no signs at all and no indication of how far you've gone or what's coming next can lead you to feel bored and irritable. That's why some speakers fail to hold anyone's attention—they've failed to use any signposts.

Now, signposting is not just for people making corporate presentations or keynote speeches. It's for anyone who wants to hold people's attention for longer than two minutes, or tell a good story. The skills are the same. Take a look at the nine most common types of signposts and how to use them.

Transitioning to a New Point

Though you are presenting the audience with a thread of reason that runs all through your argument, you are not just jumping from one idea to the next. You need to signal when you are moving on to a new distinct idea or point, even if it is related to the previous one (and frankly, it should be).

- "Moving on to my second point..."
- "Another separate but related issue is..."
- "Now that I've told you about... I want to switch and talk about..."

Bear in mind that signposts can be verbal but also nonverbal. You can signal a change in idea by switching to a new slide on a presentation; or, in a more casual context, literally listing out points on your fingers; or altering your expression or body language to show that you're changing tack.

Providing More Details on One Point

Help the audience visualize the hierarchy that your ideas fall into so they can easily see which ideas are offered as main themes and which are given as secondary examples, evidence, or counterpoints of those main themes.

- "I now want to say a bit more about..."
- "If we zoom in on..."
- "Taking a closer look at this point here..."

As you can see, many verbal cues are in fact verbal in nature (zoom in, take a look, etc.) and help your audience to visualize.

Linking Similar Points Together

You might need to add a related point to the one you've made already. Make sure you signal that you are giving another point that is distinct, but still related to the previous one, to make sure that people don't think you're broaching an entirely new idea or even offering a counterargument. Don't just make a point—let people know its relationship to the point before it, and to the argument in general.

- "In the same way..."
- "To explain this, we need to understand a second idea..."
- "What that implies is..."

Introducing the Opposite View

It can be extremely disorienting to hear a person go on at length about something that seems to be the opposite of the point they're making. This happens when they don't use a deliberate signpost that signals "I'm about to tell you something different from the main point I'm making." It might seem obvious to you as the speaker, but remember that your listener hasn't arrived there yet, and you have to show them both sides, making it clear that they are, in fact, in opposition.

- "Nevertheless…"
- "On the other hand…"
- "Critics of this line of reasoning tend to say that…"

Changing Topic

It's frustrating when there is no verbal or non-verbal gap in a person's stream of speech, but they have completely switched topic without telling you. If you do this, you risk leaving your audience behind completely and wasting your breath!

"Now, let's consider something completely different…"
"I'd like to pause here and take a look at something else for a moment…"

Changing Topic—But Just for a Moment

When you are reading written words, you can usually see when the author has placed some extra information in brackets. But when you are speaking, you might "open a bracket" and leave your audience hanging and wondering when you will close it again. You need to use signposts to show your listeners that you have taken a temporary detour to express some other loosely connected point, but that you will return again shortly. It's great if you can clearly show what the detour is, why you're making it, how it relates, and how soon you're coming back to the main "road."

- "As a quick side note…"
- "Let me deviate for a minute…"
- "Now, to get back to our original argument…"

Returning to Earlier Points

Repetition can be deathly boring if done out of carelessness or lack of skill, but extremely powerful if done consciously and on purpose. Return only to those points that are genuinely most important—a common technique is to conclude by reiterating the claim you made at the beginning.

- "Because of how important it is, I'll say it again…"
- "To recap…"
- "I'd like to return, then, to what I said earlier…"

Returning to Previous Examples

The same can be done with more specific examples, points of evidence, or little details. The effect can be to draw your listener in and encourage agreement, especially if you incorporate a rhetorical question or question tag:

- "Remember when I mentioned . . . ?"
- "Let's go back to the start of the story, shall we?"
- "You'll remember Frank, who you've already met at the start of the story . . ."

Summarizing

Naturally, at the end of speaking, you want to pull everything you've said together and present it nicely with a bow on top. The flow of a presentation is usually to present your point, elaborate on it and support it, then summarize it to close. Having a decisive conclusion is a courtesy to the listener, but it also helps you emphasize and reiterate and close in a controlled, deliberate way—the same way you put a period at the end of a sentence.

- "So to wrap up . . ."
- "To summarize all that . . ."
- "To close this off . . ."

Now, while all of this seems pretty clear on paper, there is a knack to doing it well in real life! In a way, a formal presentation in a professional context is easier since we have time to prepare and plan. In more natural, casual conversations, all the same rules apply, but we often have to think on our feet.

Before we end this chapter (isn't *that* a nice signpost?), let's consider one bad habit that will totally destroy other people's willingness to listen to you. Have you ever been socializing and felt yourself trapped in a "conversation" with someone who simply would not stop talking? It's as though once they opened their mouths, they could not physically close it again. You felt bored, irritated, and desperate to run away. Why? Poor signposting.

To make sure that *you're* not being this person (and yes, you could be, considering how seldom anyone actually tells someone else "you're boring me to tears"), pay attention to the structure of what you're saying. Even if you only speak for fifteen seconds, what you say needs to have a main point, it needs to be introduced, supported, or expanded on in some way, then concluded. If you don't, you risk trapping you both in a never-ending story.

Avoid:

"Going off on a tangent"—Does the piece of information *directly* relate to your main point? Leave it out. If you insist on saying it, wait your turn to speak next and launch a different, separate thread.

Repeating the same material—Say what you need to, say it once with a little expansion, then drop it. Your listeners heard you!

Starting the story too early—If you want to tell someone about an interesting person you met, don't start the story a month before when you were reading a book that reminded you to go to an event that you went to and met someone, who then in turn introduced you to the second person . . . Just start at the point you met them.

Carrying the story on for too long—Have a clear idea of where the "punchline" is. Once you've made your point, don't then get tempted to start up a fresh idea or expand some auxiliary point. It will feel like you're overstaying your welcome, so to speak.

Delving into pointless detail and rebuttal—If you dwell too long on some minor detail of the story, it's as though the car has stalled on the journey. Your listeners will simply register you as having gotten distracted from telling your own story, and they'll stop paying attention. Similarly, don't get too carried away entertaining every little possible variant or argument against what you're saying—you don't have all day!

If you've ever been accused of "talking too much," rest assured that you *can* become a better storyteller. It's about quality, not quantity. The irony is that it's usually when we feel that people aren't listening that we tend to do worse with signposting and structuring our speech. But the truth is that if you are clear and organized and have enough consideration to deliver your message in a digestible form for your audience, they will often return this consideration by listening to you for a lot longer than you'd think.

Summary:

- A few crutch words like *um*, *ah*, *well*, *you know*, *like*, *so*, *right*, and *okay* are natural, but too many can undermine your credibility and make it more difficult to understand you. Instead, become aware of the habit and consciously replace crutch words and empty language with confident silence. Being calm and thoughtful shows consideration for your audience and gets your point across more effectively.
- Likewise try to avoid hedging or softening language and instead be clear, concise, and confident in your expression.
- Your communication tone is like a vocal frame you set, so pay attention to whether you are being informative, humorous, respectful, formal, or informal. No tone is wrong, but a mismatch between tone and intention, or tone and context, can be a problem.
- Be especially conscious of upspeak (making statements with the intonation that belongs to questions), and ask whether it may be damaging your credibility or interfering with your message.
- With tone, strike a balance between friendly and business-like, confident and arrogant, concise and curt, emotional and merely compelling, and so on. Professionalism is about awareness and deliberately taking steps to speak in a way that gets you what you want while respecting the context and your audience.
- Especially with public speaking, use signposts—which are verbal and non-verbal markers that tell your listeners what kind of "journey" they're going on, where they are, and where you are taking them. Use a signpost every time you want to transition, give further detail, link points, change topics, offer a counterpoint, or summarize.

Chapter 3: Painting with Words

The Art of Vivid Language: Use Imagery and Rhythm

Whether you're speaking to one person or an entire audience, if you want your listeners to really absorb what you say to them, paint them a picture ... that is, help them paint their own *mental* picture of what you're saying. Verbal expression is a fundamentally human characteristic, but long before we evolved even this, we processed our world in pictures via five senses deeply embedded in the real, physical world. That means that if we can talk in such a way as to address and engage this pre-verbal world of imagery and sensation, we allow ourselves to connect with other people on a deeper level.

This is what vivid language does, and visual imagery and rhythm (sight and sound) are two powerful components. Those who are naturally talented speakers find themselves drawing on these extra-verbal skills without consciously realizing it. But once you're aware of how to do so deliberately, you might find that a whole world of expression opens up to you, and you instantly become a more compelling, relatable, and vibrant speaker.

How to Paint the Picture

All words are representations of ideas, but, as they say, a picture paints a thousand words. **Images are richer and work more quickly and more effectively on listeners.** Using imagery can actually bypass language in a way, and transmit information that feels closer to lived experience, and not just something that someone is telling you about. To get a hang of using imagery in conversation, you need to master the use of three tools:

1. Concreteness
2. Simile
3. Metaphor

Concreteness is about being embedded in the world, about being real. You can define a technical term a million different ways, but the moment you give someone an example of what you're talking about, they will instantly understand it on a deeper, more tangible level. Many highly skilled orators (like politicians or motivational speakers) will make abstract theories and concepts instantly relatable by boiling them down into real terms—instead of talking about the economy, they talk about people sitting around a kitchen table doing the family budget. They talk about specific people, specific places, and real events. In the same way that emotional responses are processed more quickly in the brain than rational ones, things we can touch, see, smell, etc. are processed more easily and more quickly than symbols and abstractions.

Simile is one way that we can tether an abstraction to something else—usually something less abstract. It's a comparison that usually uses *like* or *as*. For example:

"It was like a kick in the teeth."
"As easy as pie."
"They descended on the buffet like a plague of locusts."

Metaphor is another way to tether abstract to concrete and make illuminating comparisons. An oft-repeated metaphor that many of us will remember from school is the classic "the mitochondria is the powerhouse of the cell." Metaphors directly state that something *is* something else in order to compare two different but related ideas or objects. The mitochondria metaphor works because none of us have actually seen mitochondria, and the way in which they generate energy is rather complex and vague.

However, if a teacher tells you it's like a powerhouse, you very quickly and clearly understand the message: This is a part of the cell that generates energy. The concrete has been tethered to the abstract, of which you now have a better grasp. For proof of how impactful metaphors can be, ask yourself how much of the mitochondria's technical functioning you can remember from school—not much right? But if you're told once that it is a powerhouse, you're likely to remember that little detail for the rest of your life.

Concrete similes and metaphors add power and depth to what you're saying. Depending on how extreme the comparison is (i.e., how unalike the two things are in real life), you can inject enormous color into what you're saying, giving ideas a positive or negative spin (think about the effect of calling cigarettes "coffin nails"), evoking a particular emotion, or even adding a dose of humor.

Consider the funny story tells of how Keats and Shakespeare were arguing in heaven over who was the best wordsmith. They agreed to spontaneously compose some poetry/prose to describe the next person who walked over the hill. When a man with severe rickets emerged, Keats looked at the very bent legs and hesitated before saying,

"See over the hill there strode

A man whose legs are very bowed."

This was well and good, but then it was Shakespeare's turn, who said,

"Alas what manner of man is this,
who carries his balls in parenthesis?"

And Keats had to admit that Shakespeare was, after all, the superior wordsmith!

Other ways to add color and depth to your language:
- Use imaginative adjectives. Forget about "nice" or "beautiful" and try to use more specific, unique words—they will stick in the listener's memory, and even if they don't understand the word, you may still come across as intelligent and erudite.

- Use the power of detail. This is not unlike zooming in and zooming out again with chunking. You could speak for forty minutes about how you struggled for money in your youth and how it made you the resilient, light-hearted person you are today. Or you could just say, "Growing up we were so poor, we went to KFC to lick other people's fingers."
- Be a little unexpected. When people hear cliches, they stop thinking. Instead be fresh in the way you describe things and don't be afraid to say something that will make people sit up and say, "Wait, what?"

Rhythm and How to Go with the Flow

Most people think of music as soon as they hear the word "rhythm." There's good reason for this—**language is musical by nature, and so much of the meaning it conveys comes down to its rate, its articulation, its flow, and the way it moves through time**. Rhythm is the way that sounds or words repeatedly change in a regular fashion. When someone strikes a drum in a periodic way, we "tune into" this beat, allowing ourselves to sync up with it, predicting the next beat and thus feeling as though we are somehow aligned. It's the same when people speak: If someone is delivering their message with a repeated, consistent rhythm, it provides a kind of aural scaffolding onto which we can sync, our comprehension is deeper, and we are more engrossed.

For example, if they speak quickly and with rapid-fire sentences, we might feel alert, even a little anxious and hurried. If they repeat certain phrases over and over, and every point they make is delivered using the same sentence structure, we start to be almost lulled into that rhythm ourselves, coming through sheer repetition into line with the message being shared. Take a look at a few ways you can consciously control the rhythm of your speech to achieve certain effects.

Parallelism

That is to say, *grammatically* parallel, i.e., the structure of the sentences are repeated or equivalent in some way. This is typically done when you are listing out things—even just two things. Using parallelism can make your message feel more coherent and convincing, and you may seem a lot more conscious and in control as a result.

Consider both these sentences:

Give me liberty or give me death.
Give me liberty or death.

The difference may seem small, but there is one, isn't there? Though they say precisely the same thing, the first one seems more solid somehow. Consider also:

Better to rule in hell than to serve in heaven.
Better to be a ruler in hell than to serve in heaven.

Again, the meaning is essentially the same, but in the first sentence, both clauses take the same form—rule in heaven is compared to serve in hell. The structure is mirrored, and so the expression feels more fluid. The second mixes two forms and the effect is lost. If, however, it were changed to "better to be a ruler in hell than to be a slave in heaven" it would be parallel and sound better. Finally, consider the form of individual words themselves:

I love skiing, painting, and my dog.
I love skiing, painting, and walking my dog.

Can you see how in the first sentence, the expression feels disjoined because one thing in the list (dog) is not like the other two? Even if only unconsciously, a listener may perceive this lack of coherence and organization and ascribe it to your overall message. Use parallelism when you can—even if it's only in small ways—and your speech will feel more whole, more connected, and stronger.

Repetition

Closely related to this is repetition, which you might end up doing when using parallelism (for example, consider the repetition of "give me" in the example above). There is a definite tendency for the human mind to assume that the things it is exposed to repeatedly must somehow be truer (psychologists call this the illusory truth effect). That's why if you want to convince or persuade your audience, or even just drill a point home so they can really grasp it, then you'll need to repeat your message more than once.

Repetition is a little like putting text in bold underline—it tells people what is important, and it helps you structure your ideas by summarizing and synthesizing main ideas. In many ways, it's also a way to incorporate parallelism, resulting in a message that not only "sounds right" but is more easily understood. Think about Winston Churchill's famous "we shall fight them on the beaches" speech:

> We shall go on to the end. We shall fight in France, we shall fight on the seas and oceans, we shall fight with growing confidence and growing strength in the air, we shall defend our island, whatever the cost may be. We shall fight on the beaches, we shall fight on the landing grounds, we shall fight in the fields and in the streets, we shall fight in the hills; we shall never surrender.

This section came at the very end of a long and impassioned speech filled with so much other rousing imagery, that by the time the crowds heard this section, the almost literal drumbeat repetition of *we shall fight, we shall fight, we shall fight* left them in awed silence. Conservative member of parliament Chips Channon later said that "he was eloquent and oratorical and used magnificent English; several Labour members cried." Churchill's speech is regarded as a masterpiece of oration, precisely because it was able to stir the emotions so far beyond the purview of ordinary language that it was more like poetry or music.

Alliteration and Assonance

Alliteration is really a form of repetition, but what is repeated is single sounds and letters, in this case consonants. Alliteration works best when the repeated sounds actually connect in some meaningful way with the message itself. For example, "the girl read a book by a babbling brook" repeats the "b" sound and, consequently, emphasizes the bubbling sound of the water, painting a subtle picture. In Shakespeare's "fair is foul and foul is fair: hover through the fog and filthy air," the repetition of the "f" sound almost seems to become the filthy fog itself.

In your own speech, you don't need to get too carried away or it will feel forced. Just be aware always that the literal sound of the words you choose is also part of the message. If you really want to emphasize your negative opinion of a character, you might say so much more by calling him "slimy and sleezy" than if you had just called him "a shady guy."

Assonance, on the other hand, repeats vowel sounds and letters within words, rather than at the beginning. Some examples are "free as a breeze" (can you almost hear someone saying *wheee*?) and "no pain, no gain." When using either alliteration or assonance, remember that a little goes a long way. Don't overdo it or the effect may feel a little trite!

How to Be a Masterful Storyteller

Have you ever tried to tell a joke and sadly watched as it fell flat? Or maybe someone else was trying to tell you such a joke, and somehow bungled the delivery.

Think carefully about exactly *why* the joke failed. One obvious reason is that the punchline was mangled or the logic and flow of the story was disrupted somehow. But a far more likely reason was that the joke failed to evoke the right emotions.

A joke is just a very short story that is meant to evoke a small set of reactions (humor, shock), but it tells us a lot about the way **human beings react not just to "information" but to narrative. They do this not solely by having a cognitive grasp on what they're told, but on making an emotional connection to it.** Those who understand this process end up being the proverbial good storytellers, and it's a very rarified art, indeed.

Even if you aren't literally telling a joke or delivering a classic story to an audience, you will at some point need to incorporate storytelling in your communication. Perhaps you have to give a work presentation, convince someone of your viewpoint, flirt and get someone to like you, summon up some compassion for yourself when you've done something wrong, inspire someone to act, make a complicated argument for something, or simply tell people about what you did on the weekend without boring them to tears!

As you can imagine, good storytelling is not just about words, but also how we use our voice, body language, gestures, facial expressions, and even visual aids. Let's look at how.

Tip 1: Use stories to support what you're saying

Consider a story a tool. Give your audience an example of what you're talking about, or show them a story that quickly captures or demonstrates the point you're making. You don't need to explain *why* you have told the story, however: People will intuitively grasp it and make their own conclusions (and become more engaged in the process).

For example, if you wanted to create a feeling of rapport and make yourself seem relatable and real, you might share a touching story from your childhood that would resonate with anyone. If you wanted to quickly explain the rather complex view you have on commitment to one's dreams, you could quickly tell a little story about the difference between a chicken and a pig when it comes to bacon and eggs (punchline: "the chicken is involved, but the pig is really *committed*!"). Another way to use stories is to have them introduce a certain point. Perhaps you want to answer a question about what you do for work by explaining how one day, you started to wonder if there was a better way to chop an avocado …

The best stories are those that quickly make their point and directly speak to our emotional experiences or our five senses. Use metaphor, simile, and vivid language to make complex topics seem more accessible. Finally, ensure your audience can draw links between the story and the current situation, by saying something like, "And that goes to show . . ." or "after that day everything changed," and so on.

Tip 2: Set the scene, present the tale

All of us instinctively know what a good story is—we knew it even when we were children! To tell a compelling story, you'll need to do the same. Give some background context by telling your audience when and where the story took place. Bear in mind this is just to briefly sketch the stage the story unfolds on, so to speak—don't get distracted on these details or worry too much about accuracy. If the weather, for example, doesn't really feature in the story, don't bother mentioning it at length.

Another tip is to deliver your story with a slight increase in volume than you ordinarily would be used to. People will register this and pay closer attention—we can't help it! Once you have their attention, however, keep it by being careful with your pace. Don't go too fast (i.e., because you're nervous and worried about holding their interest) or too slow (people will resent it and stop paying attention). Instead, imagine that you're delivering interesting nuggets of information at a uniform pace. You can pause and slow down a little on purpose to heighten anticipation, but only do so if you will then release that tension by revealing a big payoff at the end.

Keep your speech varied and dynamic. Modulate your voice between high and low pitch, high and low volume, and varying sentence lengths and structures. You can even use rhetorical questions to draw people in and encourage them along the main beats of the story. This is the meaning of being articulate—being able to speak with ease and flexibility the same way a gymnast moves with ease and flexibility through their routine. Depending on the situation, you might find it useful to almost play the parts of different roles in the story—subtly change your voice, accent, facial expression, or way of speaking when delivering the lines of a speaker in the story.

Tip 3: Keep it short

Brevity is the sole of wit. A short, pithy story has the greatest chance of impacting your listener and staying with them long afterward. A short story is easier to digest and simpler to understand. This is not to say that you can't have success telling longer stories (after all, people love things like TED talks) but that you will need to work harder to maintain people's attention. Consistently imagine yourself in the other person's shoes. They will always be listening *for a reason*; they'll be primed and on the lookout to spot the lesson, the punchline, or the big idea. If you make them wait for it, or bury it somewhere underneath loads of irrelevant detail, they may give up listening and decide the payoff is not worth it.

Tip 4: Make it mean something

Human beings love stories, but not because they are merely entertaining. It's the way people have transmitted meaning and value for all of human history. Stories are told to make points, to convince, to pass down wisdom, to warn, to teach, to make the complicated easier to understand . . . and yes, occasionally to entertain.

It's a good idea to try to embed your story in some larger framework of meaning. What did you learn from the anecdote you just shared? What did this event teach you? How did life change because of this story? What does it all mean? In a persuasive presentation, you can indulge a lot in suggesting an interpretation for your listeners; in more casual contexts it's usually better to hint at the "moral of the story" rather than lecture too much. In traditional cultures, storytellers are lauded not when they have good yarns to tell, but when they are best able to "prescribe" the right story for the right listener, as though it were medicine. Know your audience and the kind of narrative they are likely to respond to, and you will speak to them on deeper level.

Tip 5: Start with a bang

A "hook" is what it sounds like—something to grab ahold of your audience. The sooner you have a hook to catch them, the better. It's almost always a good idea to start with your main point, or at least strongly hint at it. Consider the opening lines of Jane Austen's *Pride and Prejudice*: "It is a truth universally acknowledged, that a single man in possession of a good fortune, must be in want of a wife." This is not only a great hook, it's also a single-sentence summary of the entire novel's central theme. Then there's George Orwell's *1984*, which opens with *"It was a bright cold day in April, and the clocks were striking thirteen."* Immediately the audience is given a question to mull over—what kind of world is this?

Of course, these are novels with authors who have had time to think about these first lines. When telling a story on the spur of the moment, you can still be impactful, however, simply by remembering that you need to start with something that will immediately catch attention. One clever way of doing this is to actively downplay something that is quite absurd: "Oh? I didn't tell you about the time a crocodile ate my lunchbox? Well, the first thing you need to understand was that I never liked that lunchbox anyway . . ."

To do this effectively, you need to understand the story in full for yourself before you open your mouth. There's nothing worse than someone who starts telling you a story and halfway through it's clear that they don't know where they're going with it (or worse, when to stop!). Every story needs to be a concise, self-contained entity that has a beginning, middle and end. Even if it's not a joke, it needs a "punchline." Knowing the main point will help you identify key "beats" or story points along the way and stay on track. But remember: these beats are not a list of dry, objective facts. They are a carefully curated string of *emotional experiences*. You describe the day (it was hot, your legs were sticking to the car seat) and how excited you were (you show this excitement in your facial expression, voice, and posture). The girl of your dreams waltzed up to you and smiled, and it was like an angel had spoken (simile) . . . These are all emotional nuggets rather than data points!

Some final hints and tricks:

A story can be interesting and true, but if it's not **relevant** to the listener or to you or your message, don't tell it. In ordinary conversation, unless encouraged to do so, never tell a story that is longer than about a minute (this, by the way, is quite a long time).

If a particular detail is not intrinsic to the logic of the story, leave it out entirely. ("It was Thursday and that was when he usually had his spin class, but that day the class was canceled because the instructor had broken her toe last weekend at the carnival. You know, the one they're hosting to raise funds for that church thing we saw in the paper. Anyway, that's why he was free on *that* Thursday even though he ordinarily wouldn't have been, so he bumped into my friend . . ." It's easier to just say "One day, he bumped into her.")

When rehearsing for a presentation, record or film yourself first and do practice runs—many people are surprised to see that they need to stand up taller, speak more slowly, and breathe more deeply! Finally, gauge reactions as you go and adjust your story in real time. If you realize that the other person is not familiar with the TV show/book/idea you're talking about, then stop talking about it!

Summary:

- If you want your listeners to really absorb what you say to them, paint them a mental picture. Do this by using vivid and concrete imagery, similes (using *like* or *as*), and metaphors to connect abstract ideas with more real-world ones. Use adjectives and interesting details and be a little unexpected.
- Language is musical by nature, and much of the meaning it conveys comes down to its rate, its articulation, its flow, and the way it moves through time. Pay attention to the rhythm and flow of your speech.
- In parallelism, we repeat certain structures to create an effect. Repetition drives our point home and makes it seem more true, as do alliteration (repetition of initial consonant sounds) and assonance (repetition of internal or vowel sounds).
- Human beings react not just to "information" but to narrative; to be a good storyteller, you need to go beyond sharing information and facts, and help your listeners form an emotional connection to what you're saying. Good stories enlist the use of our voice, body language, gestures, facial expressions, and even visual aids.
- Make sure that your story illustrates supports or connects to your larger point or circumstance. Set the scene but don't dawdle on unnecessary detail. Start with a bang and keep things at a moderate pace, being concise. Be relevant and interesting, and if you can, practice your story ahead of time!

Chapter 4: Communication's Most Underrated Skill

Asking the Right Questions

Communication is certainly about what you say and how you say it. But that's only fifty percent of the conversation, right? In this chapter, we'll take a closer look at the important but sadly overlooked skills of listening, asking questions, and allowing the other person to shine during conversations. Becoming a better communicator is not the same as becoming a better public speaker. Knowing how to carefully present your ideas is only one half of the story—your listener is the other half, and unless they are on board, you will only ever be engaging in a monologue, not a dialogue.

One of the easiest and most natural ways to connect with the other person is to just ask questions. So many poor communicators could instantly improve by doing this alone.

But asking the *right* questions is also important. What's more, you need to pay special attention to how you ask them and when. Mastering the questioning process means you gather more and better-quality information, you build stronger connections with others, you inspire trust and liking, you learn, and you may even find yourself being helpful in someone else's learning process. In short, good questions allow you to access the best that communication can be.

Have you ever been in a conversation where it felt you were being interrogated? Think back to a memory like this, or just imagine what that kind of scene would look like. Now, what are the kind of questions that an interrogator asks?

Did you do it?
Where were you the night of the eleventh?
You knew the victim, right?

All of the above are closed questions—meaning they have only one short possible answer. Yes or no, or some other tiny, single-word snippet of information. A closed question is like a little dart that demands only one specific kind of information from the other person. It's closed because, in effect, it closes the whole world of potential answers down, usually just to one or two options. Consequently, it closes the conversation itself down. Once you answer a closed question, there's very little else for you to do.

If you use only closed questions in conversation, you risk coming across as an interrogator, because others will feel that you are deliberately and forcefully closing off avenues in this way. The other person will rightly feel that they are sitting there at your mercy, being probed. It's not fun, and it usually peters out pretty quickly.

That said, closed questions have their uses, too:

- You can use them to confirm your understanding of what you've been told ("So you were a history major, then, right?")
- You can use them to make conclusions or summaries of what's been discussed so far ("So we've all agreed to never go to McDonalds for lunch again, right?")
- You can also use them as part of frame setting, i.e., to set the tone and scope of a more formal or structured conversation ("Were you satisfied with your service at McDonald's today?")

Imagine closed questions like periods in a sentence—you only need a few, but when used correctly, they help structure your sentences and give you a pause now and then. Use too many and everything will feel too rapid fire and staccato.

In what situations can we use open-ended questions? That question itself is a good example of one! We are opening the range of possible answers, and in so doing, opening up the conversation. We are inviting the other person into the mix and allowing them to have a turn at directing the conversation's course. Open-ended questions show curiosity and interest in the other person, without allowing assumptions and prejudices to pre-select what we already think the answers will be.

Open-ended questions allow you to:

- Develop and extend a conversation, expanding on a point or deepening your grasp of it ("So what exactly made you so interested in the medieval period in the first place?")
- Flesh out an idea or concept and find out more details about it ("What other specific budgeting issues do we want to discuss in the meeting on Friday?")
- Probe for opinions and unique perspectives ("From your point of view, what do you think went wrong with this program?")

As you can probably see, good conversational flow contains *both* open and closed questions.

How to Use Funnel Questions

Funnel questions are what they sound like: questions that guide information in increasing detail down a narrowing path. Like a funnel, the process begins wide and broad with open questions, and steadily narrows to a point with closed questions. Each question leads on from the last, but is a little more narrowed in scope, becoming progressively more closed and detailed.

Using such a technique, you ease the other person into answering more direct and specific questions, while balancing this with invitations to supply additional information as they go. Because it strikes a balance between probing/interrogating and genuine conversation, this technique is most often used in occupational settings—for example, job interviews.

Imagine that an interviewer attempts first to put the interviewee at ease by asking very general open-ended questions—how they are, whether they found the journey to the office okay, etc. This soothes any tension. Slowly and gradually, the interviewer leads, in increments, to more and more targeted questions:

So how are you finding this amazing Californian sunshine?
I hope the big move is going well—what's the new neighborhood like?
Great. So, if I recall correctly, your previous job was in our branch in Minnesota. Can you give me a rundown of your time there?
I'm interested in hearing more about your work with fundraising around that time.
Can you tell me more about the team members?
Can I ask how much you were able to raise?

You can see the funnel at work if you attempt to answer these questions—you'll see that the answers will get progressively shorter but more specific as they go, responding with something like "Eight hundred thousand dollars" at the end. Importantly, this is an easier and gentler way to ask such questions; consider how uncomfortable it would have been to ask the final question first. The interviewee might have felt put on the spot or interrogated, whereas with some "warm-up" questions that naturally lead from one to the other, this question is not likely to feel like an imposition.

Here's a summary of how to ask funnel questions:

1. Begin with open-ended questions

Think of these not even as questions but as invitations to share information—as the other person wishes to share it.

2. Ask for additional explanation

Ask for clarification based on the answer to the above question. These are questions that help you understand the motivations, reasoning, and cause/effect relationships behind certain situations, as well the person's perspective on it all. You're not merely being polite and making small talk—you use the answers you're given to inform your next questions.

3. Ask for more details according to what you're told

Narrow the funnel one step at a time. You might ask for examples, justifications, explanations, or more specific instances or pieces of evidence or support. Take another step closer to the specific information you're looking for. This may require just one question or it can take many, depending on the topic.

4. Finally, reverse the funnel

This final step is optional, but you can also start working the funnel in reverse again, using the very detailed answer you got to inspire another funnel that begins with broad questions again. For example, after you're told that the fundraising team generated eight hundred thousand dollars, you can immediately sit back in your chair and say, "Okay, that's impressive. How did you do that?" The conversation continues with you getting the information you want, but without badgering or leading the other person.

Funnel questions are not only for formal or professional situations, however. They can be used any time you are trying to extract some information from someone, but in a way that is easy, comfortable, and personable. A psychiatrist, for example, might need to find out whether a patient had suicidal thoughts, but this is a difficult question to ask, and so it's best to lead into it with a long series of funnel questions. The psychiatrist doesn't rush through the conversation, and genuinely listens to answers (i.e., doesn't give the impression that they are "hunting" down just one desired response). Gently, the psychiatrist keeps zoning in on those aspects of the patient's answer that will most likely lead to ideas around depression and suicide. Near the end of the funnel, the psychiatrist begins to use words like "specifically" and "exactly" to continue narrowing down. But with the psychiatrist's inviting, encouraging language and a genuine desire to listen, the patient never feels manipulated or hurried along, and the psychiatrist gets the information they want.

In your own conversations, whoever you're speaking to and whatever information you're trying to get, keep the image of a funnel in mind. Never make sharp jumps from very general to very specific—and always lead gently from one into the other.

How You Structure a Question Matters

It goes without saying that the question you ask determines the answer you get. But when you really grasp what this means, you understand just how much of a difference question structure can make. Ask a poor question and you get a poor answer!

Take a look at these different question types/forms and notice how their structure influences the kind of answer you might get:

Probing questions

That is, questions that get right to the core of the matter. These are typically closed questions and are more direct, targeted, and focused, often using "narrowing language" such as *exactly* or *specifically*, or else uses question words that inspire a single answer—when, where, who.

"Exactly how much will it cost if we want to send the whole office the course?"
"When is the latest I can get back to you on this?"
"What evidence do we currently have that the diagnosis made at the time was correct?"

(Notice in this last instance that the question is probing without necessarily being closed).

Leading questions

As though you are taking the other person by the hand and pulling them along with you on your train of thought—which isn't always as bad as it sounds! There are a few ways to do this.

- **By making an assumption**—"How much will you be willing to invest in your wellbeing today?" (Assumption: you are in fact going to invest!). "What did I do wrong here?" (Assumption: I have actually done something wrong). Note that this is one way that a frame is created—the frame is built up on "shared" assumptions.
- **By deliberately asking for agreement, compliance, or support**—"It's expensive, don't you think?" or "I think we both want the same thing here, right?" Even if the other person doesn't feel compelled to verbally respond, you are still leading them, and the focus is still on them coming along with you.
- **By making your desired answer the easiest one**—Let's say you want someone to say yes. You could say, "Shall we have a break?" and be far more likely to receive that yes

than if you asked, "Shall we pause here or continue on?" The latter question is psychologically felt as offering two fifty-fifty options, whereas with the former, the easier response seems just to agree/nod/say yes. In the same vein, asking, "It's noon—what do you want to do now?" is the question least likely to have the other person spontaneously agree to a break like you want them to.

- **By presenting two "options"**—the key here, of course, is that you're happy with either option! Technically and logically, they *can* say "neither," but they may instead default to choosing one of the two you have presented.

Rhetorical Questions

As we all know, rhetorical questions aren't actually questions at all, but statements that are made in such a way as to encourage and elicit agreement. For example, "Isn't this new layout so much easier to work with?" Strictly speaking, this isn't a question form, but rather something you are dressing up as a question in order to frame it as something you are seeking their agreement on, rather than just *telling* them. If you just say, "The new layout is better," you are potentially inviting disagreement or simply stating a personal opinion, and the other person's perspective is irrelevant. If you make it a rhetorical question, however, you are signaling that you are *not* simply telling someone, but acknowledging the value of them being in agreement with you—it's halfway between arguing that you're right and politely asking for their agreement!

To conclude, here are a few tips for using questions in a proactive, conscious way:

- Whatever you do, don't forget to ask questions entirely—even poorly formatted questions are better than none at all!
- Want to create a feeling of rapport or develop a conversation? Use open-ended questions.
- Want to get particular information out of a person? Use probing questions or closed questions—so long as they are at the end of a funnel!
- Want to persuade someone, close a deal, or make a sale? Use leading and rhetorical questions.
- In conversations of all kinds, make sure you are mixing things up—don't have three questions of all one type right after one another, for example.

How to Be a Truly Effective Listener
Many people *think* they are good listeners. Few of them are right!

Being an effective listener is about so much more than comprehending what you're told, or simply behaving in a way to make it appear that you are paying attention. In an attempt to be better communicators, many of us will begin with our side of things and try to improve the way we speak; the truth is that you can drastically improve all your relationships by starting on the other side and becoming an excellent listener first.

Good listening is actually a collection of different skills: It's about hearing, understanding, interpreting, and responding, and it's something that we do *with* someone as the conversation unfolds in time. A good mindset shift is to realize that listening well is primarily about the other person—you know you have truly listened if your listening has created an outcome that the other person intended and wanted.

The HURIER Method

Judi Brownell from Cornell University created the acronym HURIER to help people remember the key skills behind masterful listening: Hearing, Understanding, Remembering, Interpreting, Evaluating, and Responding. Here are the components of Brownell's model:

H: Hearing

Here, "hearing" means any and all processes that result in you acquiring new information through your senses, and can include things like sight and touch as well as sound. Good listeners can synthesize information on all these channels; it's what makes us say "I hear you" when we are in fact responding to emotions implied in facial expressions, gestures, and posture. Even when it does come to auditory sensation, there is a lot to listen for beyond the basic facts of the message. You can hear the tone, pace, pitch, volume, and articulation of the voice. You can hear the accent, the rate and depth of breath, and the little clues that hint at certain emotions.

To really hear someone, make sure that it's the only thing you're doing. Don't multitask or daydream about what you'll say once they stop talking. Don't get distracted by devices or passersby. Just sit in the person's presence and be receptive to what they're sharing, without needing to hurry or rush them through to a conclusion. If you really can't give them your full attention, there's nothing wrong with postponing the conversation until a time when you can.

Example: You're catching up with an old-school friend you haven't seen in ten years. You sit somewhere quiet and give him your absolute full attention, noticing the subtly different accent he now has, the slight tiredness in his voice, and the fact that he's speaking quite slowly. He is telling you a story about a new promotion at work, and you notice his voice speeds up and gets a little formal as he does so.

U: Understanding

Naturally, you want to comprehend the *meaning* of what you're told once you carefully receive and absorb it. Making sense of what you're told is a process that starts with them and ends with you as you put together the pieces of information they've shared.

Once a message leaves its sender and floats across the void in order to reach the listener, there are countless ways for things to be lost or distorted. One of the worst things you can do as a listener is to assume you have heard and understood when you haven't. Consider how a certain word or phrase may mean slightly different things to them than they do to you because of cultural or generational differences. Consider how differently they may use certain imagery, cultural references, or even what they consider to be courteous and good-mannered.

Luckily, this is precisely what communication is for—to close these gaps and dissolve these potential misunderstandings. Check in with the other person to see whether the version of their message you've received is something they recognize. If you're not clear on something, ask for clarification. Paraphrase what you've been told, saying, "Have I got that right?" Take your time and ask questions rather than assume you know certain details, and importantly, don't interrupt people as they speak—you might miss out on crucial information.

Example: He's summarizing the last ten years of his work for his company, and you're missing some of the details since you're not familiar with his industry. You ask him at one point, "So you say you're a consultant now but actually you're still technically employed by them, right?" You're not only trying to understand what this word "consultant" means to him linguistically but also emotionally.

R: Remembering

It is a mistake to think of listening as "passive." As you listen, you are holding all the details of what you're told and actively assembling them as you go, collaboratively creating the meaning with the other person. To do this, you need to be able to recall what you've been told earlier. That may mean details from five minutes ago, or it can mean something you were told last year. Not only does effective listening require you to remember details, it requires that you put these details together.

If you think, "But my memory is terrible," then don't worry—most problems with remembering during conversations are actually not about memory but about *attention*. You usually "forget" something not because your memory is bad, but because you weren't properly attending to the stimulus in the first place. To improve your memory, simply slow down, pay close attention, and actively link everything you're told with everything you've already been told right there in the moment. You can then use this to inspire further questions or requests for clarification.

Example: He starts talking about his family, and you think: Hang on, he's telling me now about his sister . . . but which sister was that? So you say, "That's so interesting! I remember you mentioned your sister when we spoke on the phone last week. Is this the same sister?" He says, "Oh, no, this is my younger sister." You make a mental note that he has (at least!) two sisters. This little interlude will fill in any of your own memory gaps **and** *make it appear that you are an attentive, careful listener.*

I: Interpreting

The first three letters explain how you receive information and consciously connect it with other information, and in so doing deepen your comprehension of what it all means. From that point, naturally, you can't help but interpret the message. It's as though we zoom out a little and look at everything around the message—the context, the speaker (their biases, goals, expectations, etc.), the additional nonverbal information being shared, any hidden subtext, and so on. These things can add depth and richness to a message, or they can even change a message completely into something else.

Note *everything* you can observe about what the person in front of you is communicating:

- Their nonverbal cues such as body language, voice characteristics, expression, and so on
- The underlying emotional meaning behind their words
- The context of the conversation and why it is happening
- How the other person may be responding to you
- The speaker's personality, biases, blind spots, and style of expression
- Cultural, generational, gender, or even socioeconomic factors

Example: You notice an overwhelming emotion of stress and exhaustion in your old school friend, and how his new professional demands and commitments seem to have changed the way he speaks. You note how all of this comes together with a somewhat shy but intense personality, and you observe his style of dress—very somber and businesslike but quite expensive clothing.

E: Evaluating

Once you've gathered all of this data together, the next step is obviously to decide what to do with it. Crucially, this comes at the end, not the beginning, so you can make sure you're in possession of the *entire* message before coming to any conclusions. Now, evaluating does **not** mean you decide whether you believe the person, whether you like them or what they're saying, or whether you agree. This is not a question of judgment but rather appraisal. Here we need to be on guard against our own assumptions and prejudices. Too many of us are too quick to jump into this stage before we've given the other person the chance to express their full message, or ourselves the chance to properly and thoughtfully digest it. Keep reminding yourself that there is no rush, and you don't even have to come to an evaluation if you don't yet feel you're ready.

Example: You start to conclude that your friend's work and occupational status has become a big part of his identity. Though he is very casually telling you about his life, and idly complaining about being overworked, you wonder if part of him relishes the label of "workaholic" and if in some subtle way he is showing off. This, however, is a temporary theory, and you don't jump to conclusions just yet. What's more, you acknowledge that much of this interpretation may come from your own values around work and money, your history with this friend in school, and the fact that you used to be a little competitive back then . . .

Keep an open mind. Listen to what they're saying, not what you might think they're saying or what you wish they were saying. This is the stage where a little neutral judgment and objectivity can go a long way. You don't have to be emotionless, just be clear about what it emotion and what is logic. Recognize your ideas as separate from theirs, and identify any influence from biases, beliefs and values—whether theirs or your own. Finally, make a clear distinction between the speaker and the message they're sharing. Listening means hearing the message—not jumping to conclusions that fit in line with our assumptions about who the person is or should be.

R: Responding

The very last step is to respond. Yet, how many of us jump in to respond before the other person has even finished speaking? We skip right over the understanding, the remembering, the interpreting, and so on, and leap in to share our message. The usual result is something that resembles less a conversation and more a competition.

Importantly, you are responding—i.e., what you say is in direct reaction to what they have said. It is an answer, something that connects to their contribution and expands it, continues it, even contradicts it sometimes, but still speaks to it in some way. Have you ever talked to someone who patiently waited for you to stop, then proceeded to talk about something completely different? Chances are you not only felt they weren't listening, you probably felt invalidated or a little insulted, too. Good dialogues are co-created—they are not simply two people monologuing beside one another.

If during the course of the other person's speaking, you watch as your chance to share a particular idea has come and gone, do not try to force the conversation to backtrack so you can make your point. Let it go and engage with the conversation where it stands. When you "rewind" conversations this way, you are essentially telling the other person that all of their contribution beyond that point was unnecessary and unwanted—don't be surprised if they quickly lose interest after that!

Your response should *demonstrate* that you have gone through the HURIER acronym and have not only understood but processed what you've been told. Reflect on their message and show them what that idea looks like in your world after you've passed it over your own perspective and values. In a way, it's this final step that proves to the other person how thorough your listening has been. This is because you actively prove that you have taken on board what they've said and engaged with it.

Example: You mull over the whole encounter and everything your friend has said, and as a result of all that processing, you say, "Well, you've clearly got a lot on your plate right now! I have to admit that these days I'm a little allergic to overtime myself and haven't done the daily grind for a long time. I think I just want to live a little more slowly, you know? Do you think you'll cut back at some point? Or are you enjoying the hustle and bustle?" This is a thoughtful response that shows that you've heard, understood, and processed what you've been told, and you also share some of your own perspective. It isn't judgmental, but curious and collaborative.

You may choose to respond in a million different ways, depending on the message and what your goals are. You may ask questions, show empathy, do a chunking up/concluding statement to signal the end of the talk, or dive in deeper to show that you're interested in continuing. Be aware that expounding on your opinion is seldom something that others appreciate or ask for.

Social media platforms like YouTube encourage a kind of illusory conversation that is really just an isolated person talking into a screen, with no chance for the listener to respond or steer the conversation. Consequently, people today lack certain listening skills and may mistakenly think that a good conversation is one in which each person gets an opportunity to opine and make a little speech. They may unwittingly focus on how to accurately express themselves and forget to make space for the other person's expression. Using the HURIER acronym, however, reminds you of the relative importance of different components of a conversation. It is almost always a good idea to *start* with a thorough and attentive processing of the other person's message, and only *then* launch in with your own.

If you routinely fail to do any of this, you may find yourself earning a reputation as a conversational narcissist, which is what we'll explore in the next section.

Don't Be a Conversational Narcissist!

The term was first coined by sociologist Charles Derber in his 1979 book, *The Pursuit of Attention*, but sadly, conversational narcissists have existed for a long, long time. **A conversational narcissist is someone who has, basically, failed to understand the social, collaborative, and joint nature of conversation, and who uses the medium instead to *gain attention for themselves*.** Instead of using the chance to engage with another to learn and connect, such a person uses conversation as a way to bolster their own ego, to demand attention and recognition—in other words, they see others as audience members!

Now, don't just assume that this horrible affliction just happens to other people. As part of his research, Derber listened in on more than 1500 talks and had to sadly conclude that *most* were conversational narcissists, despite being well-intentioned. Being self-absorbed and trying to make everything about you, it seems, is actually pretty common. But it also means that you are missing out on opportunities to have more genuine, more informative, more satisfying conversations with people (not to mention coming across as a bore!).

Conversational narcissism can be understood as a kind of default that we all fall into when we fail to make efforts to truly listen. Sadly, conversational narcissism tends to reproduce itself—a big trigger for behaving this way is often the sense that we are not being listened to, because the other person is too busy with themselves to pay us attention. Yet, the more we try to make the conversation about *us*, the more the other person feels the same way and responds by trying to edge their way into the limelight. Ultimately connection is lost and the conversation becomes a battleground or dissolves entirely.

The first step is to fully own your part of the conversational contract. You cannot do anything about other people's behavior, but you can go a long way to model genuine listening and create a frame of respect and collaboration rather than self-absorption.

Reframe the Way You Understand the Purpose of Conversation

Why do people talk at all? Is it to prove how great they are, to show off, to elicit praise and flattery? Is it to show how much you know or have someone agree with you and confirm your views? While most of us want to say *no*, be on guard for when you might be speaking within this frame. Constantly remind yourself that the overarching purpose of any communication is to connect. A good conversation is not something you fight over with the other person to win, and it's not something you begrudgingly share with them, anxiously waiting for your turn so you can snatch attention back from them. Rather, it's like a dance you do together, something you *co-create*. If you find that your conversation partner is seeming to get in the way somehow, this is a sign you're doing something wrong! It should never be a competition.

Don't Jump Ahead

We have all had the experience of quietly thinking to ourselves what we plan to say the moment the person in front of us shuts up. Our eyes may even glaze over as we stop listening to them and instead think about the fantastic argument we're going to make once they're done with whatever it is they're blabbing on about . . .

It's a bad habit! As much as you can, try to stay present with what the person is saying. Don't rush ahead to try to imagine what they are going to say next, and likewise don't start thinking of your own response. Remember the HURIER model and tell yourself that you can respond after you've really listened, understood, and processed the message. Another good idea: remind yourself that you actually don't have to respond at all. It is not a requirement for you to weigh in or for you to hurry to get your equal share of airtime. Confident, secure speakers don't need to dominate the conversation, because they prioritize the flow and are enjoying the dialogue—who exactly is speaking is not so relevant.

Avoid Advice

As a general rule, never give unsolicited advice—and be careful even if it is solicited. Ask yourself, when was the last time you desperately wanted to hear what someone else thought you should do? It's not often, right? But you probably do find yourself wanting to be heard, respected, and empathized with on a fairly regular basis. Commit to offering the same thing to others.

The truth is that most people give advice because they like the way it makes them feel: wise and powerful. Most people dislike receiving unsolicited advice precisely because they can sense this unconscious motivation. Rather than getting enamored with your own vision of what the other person should do or what their situation means, become curious about how *they* see it, what *they* value, and what *they* are trying to accomplish. If you catch yourself wanting to say, "Well, I think you should . . ." try asking a question instead.

Stop Centering Yourself

When you are being a conversational narcissist, it is as though you are moving through the conversation with a certain thought hovering in your awareness: "What has this got to do with me? What can I get out of this? How can I make sure this road is leading back to me somehow?"

So they may say something about scuba diving, and you immediately think, "What has scuba diving got to do with me? I know—I did a scuba diving course when I was a teenager, and I have a pretty funny anecdote about a stingray. When they're done talking, I'm going to share my anecdote."

Or maybe they say that they've gained five pounds over Christmas and are feeling a little bad about themselves, and you immediately think, "Well, that's sad and all but what can I get out of it? I'm pretty good at stuff like this. I know all about nutrition and fitness. As soon as they stop talking, I'm going to share my brilliant diet advice and then they'll think I'm clever."

Granted, few people literally think in such selfish terms, but the effect of continually centering yourself is the same regardless. Instead of talking about the other person, or about the topic in general, you are constantly making the focus of the conversation *yourself*. This is tricky because everyone wants to talk about themselves to some degree . . . but do it too much and people will tire of you and find you difficult to connect with. Imagine your attention and focus is a beam of light. Constantly shine it away from you and onto the topic or the other person. The frame is not "what about me?" but "this idea is interesting, what's this?" or "hey, tell me more about you."

Watch Out for Passive Conversational Narcissism, too

Our description so far has been quite over the top, but you can dominate conversations in subtler, more passive ways. If someone keeps sharing something with you, but you fail to ask follow-up questions, it's like you're being a tossed a ball that you repeatedly let fall to the ground. The "game" never goes anywhere. Sometimes people signal their lack of interest in someone else by simply not giving any supportive responses, not asking any questions, or even not acknowledging that they've heard the message. This can be a conscious or unconscious way of controlling the conversation, since eventually the other person will just stop talking . . . and then you can jump in and have the limelight again!

What If *They're* the Conversational Narcissist?

Sadly, chances are they will be, at least some of the time. You might be wondering if it's worth going to the effort of asking questions, listening empathically, and de-centering yourself if the other person will only grab the opportunity to hog the conversation. This can be tricky to deal with. Always start by giving others the benefit of the doubt and ask them about themselves before sharing details about you. If they simply never ask, well, you can politely disengage and make sure you're not wasting more time than you strictly have to.

You never have to suffer in silence while being talked at, and you shouldn't feel bad for wanting to disengage from a boring, one-sided "conversation." Try as much as you're willing to gently steer them onto something else, but if they're not budging, cut your losses and bail! Sometimes people are having a selfish day, and sometimes they're just plain old selfish. Be polite but end it. Whatever you do, don't get embroiled in a fight for attention—you can never convince a conversational narcissist to care about you, and you can certainly never beat them at their own game.

Summary:

- One of the easiest ways to connect with another person is to just ask questions. The right questions help you gather more and better-quality information, build stronger connections with others, inspire trust and liking, learn, and help other people learn, too.
- Closed questions (those that have very short or one-word answers) can be used to confirm your understanding, make conclusions or summaries, or set the tone and scope of a more formal or structured conversation. However, they can kill a conversation and make it feel interrogatory.
- Open questions (any possible answer) allow you to probe for depth and can keep a conversation lively and open-ended. Use both in the "funnel question" technique, which probes for information down a narrowing path of increasing detail, starting broad and progressively becoming more specific. Start with open questions, then drill down for more detail as you go, eventually reversing the funnel if necessary.
- Good listening is a collection of different skills: hearing, understanding, interpreting, and responding. The HURIER method asks us to Hear, Understand, Remember, Interpret, Evaluate, and Respond, in that order. Remember that listening is active and includes both verbal and nonverbal material.
- Avoid being a conversational narcissist, who is someone who uses conversation to gain attention for themselves, rather than connect with others, share, or learn. Reframe the way you understand the purpose of conversation and understand that it's not about you or your ego. Avoid giving advice, interrupting (or thinking about what you want to say), or centering yourself in the dialogue. Similarly, don't be afraid to disengage when you encounter a conversational narcissist.

Chapter 5: When It All Goes Wrong . . .

Effective Conflict Resolution

Conflict exists whether we like it or not. **It's inevitable that disagreements will arise whenever and wherever people have to deal with one another due to their inherent diversity of opinion, taste, and experience.** In certain cases, conflict can even be thought of as desirable, since it ultimately strengthens bonds, forces people to communicate better, and helps them collaborate in realistic ways. In this chapter, we'll look at ways to manage conversations that have gone bad, or navigate those that may prove challenging.

In an article published in the *Journal of Managerial Sciences* in 2009, Professor Abdul Ghaffar of Qurtuba University argued that conflict is necessary because it draws our attention to the most relevant issues, encourages participation, helps people recognize and benefit from their differences, and raises awareness of problems. It can help both parties clarify their desires, blind spots, and boundaries.

The Different Types of Conflict

Most of us just want to avoid conflict, but this prevents us from learning more about it and becoming better at handling it when it inevitably arises. Not all conflict is the same—take a look at some variants:

Affective Conflict
"Affective" here indicates that the conflict is heavily tinged with emotion. Think interpersonal clashes that are filled with high levels of rage, fear, sadness, guilt, and so on.

Substantive Conflict
This is when people (often a group) disagree about the task at hand or the goal they are jointly working toward, i.e., disagreement over what constitutes a fact or "reality." In professional settings, it can thoroughly undermine an organization's effectiveness.

Conflict of Interest
This occurs when there is tension in how limited resources are allocated between two or more parties. Usually, each party agrees on the fundamentals of the situation, but they are in essence competing for the same resources and are therefore at odds.

Retributive Conflict
As the name suggests, this describes a conflict where one or both parties is engaged in punishing the other for some perceived crime—usually an instance of that party trying to punish them!

Conflict in Values
This is not a disagreement about facts (i.e., what is) but about principles, values, and beliefs (i.e., what could or ought to be).

Goal Conflict
This occurs when people cannot agree on a shared goal.

Displaced Conflict
This is a kind of secondary conflict; both parties may shift their hostilities onto a third, unrelated party, or focus on irrelevant issues and fight about those instead of the *real* problem.

Of course, people are endlessly creative in the ways they clash with one another, so any particular conflict can be a unique blend of a few of the above or change over time from one to another. Understanding the type of conflict you're dealing with is a great first step in resolving it. As we've already seen, getting an insight into the unmet emotional needs behind conflict (that is, relatedness, certainty, autonomy, fairness, and so on) can give us a way forward in addressing those needs and relieving conflict.

The Thomas Kilmann Model

Kenneth Thomas and Ralph Kilmann are the two researchers behind this method of conflict resolution. According to the model, people come into conflict simply because they have different ideas, values, motivations, or wants. The main way around this difference is to use plenty of both assertiveness and empathy. Broadly, however, the model outlines five conflict-resolution strategies: **competing, avoiding, accommodating, collaborating, and compromising.**

Each strategy is a quite different approach to navigating conflict. None is *right*—each has their own pros and cons, and the one that will work best is the one that most accommodates the unique facts of the circumstances. Empathy and assertiveness are present in all five models, but in varying degrees. You can imagine a matrix with empathy on one axis, and assertiveness on the other. Let's take a closer look.

1. **Competing**

On the matrix, this strategy is high assertiveness, low empathy.

This is the tactic of working out disagreements using aggression or competition, which can be thought of as low-key aggression. Whatever the degree, it's about working *against* the other person, not *with* them. The strategy is great when you genuinely are in a position of control or authority, and also when you don't necessarily have the time, money, or energy to solve the problem or be overly empathetic. This tactic can actually work (if "work" means bring some kind of resolution to the conflict), but obviously, it won't win you any friends and your competition may alienate people to the extent that they no longer want to "play" with you.

2. **Avoiding**

Characterized by low assertiveness and low empathy.

This position is basically attempting not to engage at all. You don't defend your own position or make your point, but you're also not making any special attempts to listen to the other person's concerns. Naturally, there's a time and place for this approach. If you know for certain that you have very little power in the situation, and that the other person is unlikely to budge or listen, then it makes sense to just walk away. The approach becomes a bad choice if the conflict is actually your responsibility or even your fault, and a response to it is expected. Not responding can come across as disrespectful or weak and may actually increase negative feelings and create a bigger conflict down the road.

3. **Accommodating**

The approach using low assertiveness but high empathy.

This is the peacekeeper's tactic. Such a person will try hard to work things out, make concessions, and find some harmony. They'll tend to go along with satisfying others' needs just to keep the peace and err on the side of not expressing their own needs. This way of doing things is a good strategy to take when you don't have much power and are highly invested in a harmonious outcome. If there is a genuine but tricky conflict in a relationship that is very valuable to you, being accommodating can work—so long as it doesn't go too far and you become a doormat.

4. **Collaboration**

Uses high assertiveness and high empathy.

The approach of working together on a problem. Here, you balance your own needs and desires with the other person's, and you value both equally. A typical technique is to try to find some common ground or a shared goal and work from there. This approach is a great one if both sides can genuinely say that they want to come to an agreement. The approach will waste time and muddy the waters, however, if one or both parties is not really interested in finding a way forward—collaboration takes *both* sides working together, not just one. If there is low trust or reason to believe that there cannot be a reasonable shared goal, this approach is not ideal.

5. **Compromising**

This last strategy can be seen as the middling approach, somewhere right in the middle of both assertiveness and empathy. Compromising means embracing difference and disagreement without letting it jeopardize the relationship. It's a balancing act and a way to get people who disagree to nevertheless get along. Typically, the solution is for each party to move ahead with a plan that suits them in some ways but not all. Certain rules can be put in place to protect you, but you are also required to be flexible enough to abide by the rules of others, even if you don't particularly like them. It's an approach that can really work since both parties will by definition leave with something they want.

VOMP

You might like to combine the above model with another framework introduced by Crosby Kerr Minno Consulting called VOMP. **It's a simple acronym that can help you pause, regulate your own emotional response, and plan to respond in a conscious, measured way.**

Here's what the VOMP acronym means:

Ventilation

In other words, let people "air" their side of the conflict. So much trouble and misunderstanding can be avoided if people speak up and speak honestly. Keeping secrets, mulling silently over resentments, or even outright lying about how you feel will only prolong the negative feelings. But this ventilation process is not the same as solving the problem, nor is it a chance to escalate negativity by throwing blame or accusation. It's not necessary to decide if you agree or not, or counter with objections or corrections—just listen. Simply share your side of the situation and give the other person a fair opportunity to share theirs.

Ownership

There are seldom any conflicts between adults where there is a bad guy and a good guy, with the bad guy shouldering one hundred percent of the blame. Try to take responsibility for your portion of the conflict and "own" your part of it. This takes humility initially, but if you can acknowledge it plainly and move on, you may find it's actually a relief to stop being defensive. What's more, it can invite the other person to "put down their weapons" and frankly take responsibility for their portion of the conflict, too.

It's important, however, that you don't take on *more* than your fair share. Granted, it's not always possible to neatly portion out blame, and you might be arguing precisely because you can't decide who's more to blame. But in this case, say something like, "I acknowledge my part in the problem" in a more general sense, and move on. Never knowingly take on more of the blame in an attempt to gain an upper hand—it's dishonest and usually backfires.

Moccasins

This refers to the old advice to "walk a mile in the other person's moccasins. Both sides need to actively try to understand the conflict from the other one's perspective. Again, this is not the same as acquiescence or agreement. It just means that you make efforts to notice what the other person is going through and how they see things (including your behavior).

Plan

Finally, you need a way forward. Conflicts need to *end* at some point. Once you have both shared your views, listened, taken ownership, and so on, it's time to collaboratively decide on how you'll move on. What will be different? How will you avoid the same problem in the future? What rules or new expectations are there? Any new goals, reassurances, or commitments? Whatever they are, they need to directly address what each person has shared in a realistic and practical way.

Now, while the above may seem great on a theoretical level, you can probably already tell that it may be difficult to apply in real-life situations, especially when tempers are flaring. One of the best things you can do when you notice that a conflict is occurring is to *get a little distance.* Pause and make space. This will allow you to downregulate those strong emotions—which as we've seen get in the way of more rational thought processes—and help you slow down and look carefully at what is happening. The conflict will still be there, but you will have a strategy for moving forward.

So, a general strategy for all conflicts is:

1. **Pause and step away** (if possible). Use the distance to become conscious of both sides' unmet needs, their concerns, and their goals. Process your feelings and take a moment to cool off.
2. **Decide on a strategy** using the Thomas Kilmann model. Think carefully about the degree of both empathy and assertiveness you'll need to best resolve the conflict. Don't forget to think about the other person's approach, not just yours.
3. **Consciously attempt a conflict-resolving conversation**, as we've explored in earlier chapters on "crucial conversations." Plan a time and place, conduct yourself with civility and compassion, and do your best to come to a mutually satisfying resolution.

Uh Oh—We Talked and There's Still Conflict

Let's be honest. You can do everything "right" and still find yourself facing an unpleasant situation. Sometimes, the best thing you can do is to compassionately detach and try to move on as soon as possible. Not every situation has a comfortable resolution for every party, and not every problem has a solution. Sometimes, hurt feelings remain hurt, and relationships or connections are damaged or terminated.

Nevertheless, even though you may find yourself in a stalemate and unable to compromise much further, try to at least come to some sort of inner resolution with yourself. Ask honestly what you can learn for next time. You will get over the dispute a lot faster if you know deep down that you have allowed the negative experience to make you a better communicator going forward.

How to Master High-Stakes Discussions and Stabilize Intense Emotions

So far, we've looked at ways to take control of your conversational frame, to convince and persuade, to ask useful questions, and to use tact and deliberation as you conduct yourself in dialogue. All of this, however, becomes far more difficult if we find ourselves in the middle of a distressing conflict situation. Chances are, you've been there before: Emotions are running high, things feel a little volatile and unpleasant, and you may even notice that you're acting impulsively . . . sometimes to your later regret.

Conflict is human, and being destabilized now and then does not mean you are a poor communicator. Nevertheless, it is possible to learn skills that will help you navigate these tricky situations *as they are happening*—which is the time when you most need to communicate well!

Let's talk about **crucial conversations**. These kinds of talks combine three key features:

1. High stakes (i.e., there is a lot to lose on both sides)
2. Opposing viewpoints
3. Strong emotions

Notice that in the list above, we have not mentioned the topic of conversation—people can and do get into conflict over "minor" or "unimportant" topics. The truth is that the topic is usually secondary. What's primary is what is currently at risk, how both parties are differing in the way they are approaching that risk, and the (let's face it, interfering) effect of strong emotions like fear and anger.

Let's all own up to it now: Most of us are simply not very good at crucial conversations. If something is important to us and we sense threat, strong emotions result... and that usually sees calm rationality and control fly out the window. If the other person does the same, you have a spiral that carries you both down into conflict. Have you ever considered that every single act of *physical* aggression started out as a verbal disagreement, maybe even just a silly misunderstanding? In other words, the spiral can take you far, far away from where you want to be.

Returning to our metaphor of the ladder of inference, it's clear how different beliefs, experiences, emotions, and perspectives create our "pool of meaning" and potentially lead to us clashing with someone who has done the same thing, only with a very different set of raw ingredients. Many would argue that it's easy to be a good communicator when the stakes are low—everyone agrees and the feeling either way is pretty neutral. But you will really put your communication mastery to the test by seeing how well you can navigate, defuse, and resolve conflict as it unfolds in the moment.

Whether your crucial conversation is to give negative feedback, to break up with someone, to apologize for a wrongdoing, to ask an embarrassing question, to set a difficult boundary, to clear up a confusing misunderstanding, to find a compromise between two opposing needs and rights, to smooth over hurt feelings, to restore trust, to solve a shared problem, or to cut off contact entirely, know that everyone finds these kinds of conversations difficult. Also know that in a very tricky conversation, there is seldom a way through that is completely easy and painless. So, keep that in mind as you read about the ways you can ease a conflict. No matter what happens or how badly things have already deteriorated, you can still do your best to move forward with respect, dignity, and a spirit of cooperation.

How to Navigate a Crucial Conversation

First and foremost, be as clear as possible from the outset exactly what the problem is. What is the issue, concern, or conflict? It seems too obvious, but before you get engrossed talking to the other person, clarify in your own mind what you see as having gone wrong. Is it one event or a pattern? Try to locate the issue and be as concise as you can.

This will help you **understand the purpose for the conversation**. The purpose should be, naturally, to address the problem you've identified. If you simply bring a grievance or a boatload of unhappy feelings to place at the other person's feet, it will only be felt like an attack or a confrontation. Know *why* you are having this difficult discussion, i.e., what you hope to actually achieve when it's done. If we're honest with ourselves, we may be tempted to start a conversation for the unconscious reason of hurting the other person somehow.

Once you are clear on all this, you can plan ahead and **choose a time and place to have the discussion.** Don't spring it on the other person or just launch into it without enough time to prepare mentally (granted, this is not always possible, but if you can, try to slow things down so you are in control and not merely reacting). Make sure you have a moment where you won't be distracted or interrupted, and avoid times where you know you or the other person will be tense or busy with something else.

Try to make the environment as supportive as possible. It might be a push to remain "positive," but you can do a lot to keep things calm, safe, private, and comfortable. It's far easier to deal with any difficult feelings or ideas when you feel like you're in a supportive "shelter" in which dialogue can unfold.

Once the groundwork is laid, the next part is probably one of the most difficult things any of us will be called to do in life: **be genuinely compassionate**. You will naturally feel some inner resistance to the other person—that always happens if the stakes are high—but the good news is that you don't have to agree with the other person or fake your feelings or allow them to mistreat you. You only have to maintain an empathetic awareness of the fact that they are also finding the situation difficult, just like you. That's all.

So, that's how you lay the emotional groundwork and approach the conversational space with an intention to listen, to cooperate, to resolve. Never underestimate the power of holding this attitude—you might not say or do anything differently, but your stance will be perceived. The next thing to do is lay the theoretical groundwork, and this means to **carefully separate evidence from interpretation, fact from opinion**. Usually, this is exactly where the conflict itself lies—each of you believes you are in possession of a fact, when really you are both arguing over different interpretations of that same fact.

Carefully teasing out what is true and what is merely a perception of or response to the truth can often make up the bulk of a difficult conversation. On the other hand, you might discover that you are both actually operating from a slightly different set of equally true facts—uncovering the assumptions on both sides can do a lot to lessen the size of the dispute, lowering those strong emotions.

As you talk, try to remember to "**question the question**." What this means is to dig a little deeper than the face value challenges, concerns, questions, or issues that are raised. This will help you move past knee-jerk reactions and overly emotional defensiveness and see to the real causes beneath. Ask yourself (or them!) what someone is *really* communicating when they say what they say. But don't stop there—examine your own statements and questions in the same way and see if you can use "clean communication" to say what you really think, feel, and want.

Finally, the key to managing difficult conversations is to **take responsibility for managing your emotions**. Yes, you probably want the other person to do it as well, but you cannot do this for them! Stay calm and in control, and the best you can hope for is that it inspires the same of the other person. You are not required to lie, to be fake or overly stiff, or to assign yourself the role of "emotions policeman"—simply acknowledge and express your emotions but without letting them dominate or steer the conversation.

Regulating Your Own Emotions

You might like to reframe "controlling" your emotions as "self-regulation." Being in control of yourself emotionally doesn't mean you suppress, repress, or judge your own authentic emotional experience. Rather, it means that you never, ever allow this perfectly understandably human reaction to *get on top of you*. In a difficult conversation, you *will* feel strong emotions. But your skill as a communicator is about you feeling these emotions and doing the right thing anyway.

In his book *Emotional Intelligence*, Daniel Goleman claims that emotional responses occur far, far quicker than rational ones. The part of our brain that controls our emotions, called the amygdala, is activated long before we start using the prefrontal cortex, which controls our analytical thinking. This is a survival mechanism that evolved to let us react quickly to danger. The downside, though, is that it means we're predisposed to first act with blind emotion, and with our rational, conscious minds trailing far behind. If we know that when we're in the heat of the moment, we can't think as well, then the way to think better is obvious: put a damper on our emotions.

Dr. David Rock created the SCARF model in 2008 to help his patients better understand emotional reactivity and how to manage it during difficult conversations. Rock claimed that we need to start with an understanding of where strong emotions come from in the first place. He believed that people always act so to gain access to rewards while avoiding threats. They do this in accordance with five potential human needs:

1. Our need for **Status** relative to other people and to feel important
2. Our need for **Certainty** and knowing the future is predictable and in our control
3. Our need for **Autonomy** and the ability to feel like we determine our lives
4. Our need for **Relatedness** to others and to feel like we belong socially
5. Our need for **Fairness** and justice

If one or more of these needs are not being met, a person might start to react emotionally, since it feels like a threat. In high-stakes conversations, then, **one of our main goals should be to lower this sense of emotional threat so that we can start to access our slower and more rational thinking process—and find our way out of the problem**.

Sounds reasonable, but how do you actually do that? The steps outlined above (setting practical and emotional groundwork, engaging your compassion, planning a time and place, etc.) are all going to help, but so will some of the following principles:

- Before you do anything, just observe. Note your own emotional responses that you're bringing to the table and try to put a label on them.
- Next, try to observe the thought process, interpretations, and personal narratives that are set in motion by these emotions. Take an inventory of your opinions, your assumptions, your understanding of the purpose of the conversation, your interpretation of a shared event, and what you see as the ideal outcome.
- Think about what your thoughts and feelings are telling you about the need that is currently going unmet. Are you feeling that your autonomy is threatened? Are you scared about losing relatedness or feeling angry about an attack on your sense of fair play?
- Use your understanding of all these things to start to put a frame around the discussion. These are not just space and time limits, but personal boundaries. For example, you might decide that you want to have a mediator present or make it clear upfront what you are and are not willing to accept during the course of the conversation.

If you find that your emotions are getting the better of you, stop, take a deep breath, and consciously remind yourself of why that emotion is there. Try to address it and then refocus on what you've identified as your goal. Keep your eyes on a potential solution and don't be distracted by emotion. If you notice strong emotions in the other person, you can do something similar. Try to ask compassionate questions to get to the root of what they're feeling and why, and try to find a solution in which both of you have your needs addressed.

It will feel so much easier to get a handle on strong feelings if both of you know a potential way forward and have a clear plan for what can be practically done about the problem.

Assertive Communication

John asks Lana if she wants to hang out. Lana isn't interested in the least, but she's also afraid of coming across as rude, so she agrees. The two go on a date, and just as it's about to end, John pushes to meet again; Lana feels the whole thing is getting pretty awkward by that point, but instead of saying she's not interested, she makes an excuse . . . and a plan for date two.

Fast forward a month and John and Lana are having an outright conflict. Lana is mad that she's been pestered by John, and John thinks it's awful that he's been strung along. What part of their communication was wrong? Well, all of it—the moment Lana failed to communicate her position assertively, she avoided temporary discomfort and replaced it with a much bigger problem later on. In an attempt to not hurt John's feelings, she ironically ends up *really* hurting them.

Most of us feel a little uncomfortable "asserting" ourselves now and then. The thing to remember is that **communicating your needs, limits, and perspective with firmness and clarity actually saves you from a lot of future discomfort and awkwardness.** In fact, it can help you avoid a world of conflict and misunderstanding.

With good reason, most of us have been socialized to acquiesce, to cooperate and find harmony in social situations (some of us have been socialized to do this quite a lot!). We may unconsciously hold the belief that to be polite, we have to say yes . . . which means that saying no means we're being impolite. But is that really true? Sometimes saying no is the kindest and most courteous way forward, and saying yes is the quickest route to negative feelings, misunderstanding, and even disagreement.

None of us have infinite resources and infinite time, and this means at some point, we all have to choose what we want to focus on and what we will have to pass up on. Furthermore, we will often encounter other people who have made different choices about their priorities and values than we have. This means that we have to say no to certain ideas, events, projects, commitments . . . but also to people.

Good communicators know that this isn't a problem and not something you have to apologize for. In fact, gracefully asserting your own limits and boundaries is a way to help you more smoothly navigate social relationships, remove stress and drama, and command respect from others. It is never a zero-sum game where your needs and wants are pitted against someone else's—communicating assertively still leaves plenty of room for *everyone's* needs to be met, without resentment, passive aggression, guilt, or shame.

It may seem counterintuitive, but having firm boundaries that are well communicated can actually bring you closer to others. The first step is to drop the assumption that assertiveness means being forceful, rude, dominating, or unkind. It means truly understanding that asserting yourself does not diminish anyone else.

If Lana had kindly but firmly said, "You're great, John, but to be honest I'm not interested," it may have been awkward for a short moment, but ultimately, there would have been more clarity, more respect, and more understanding between them.

What Makes Assertive Communicators Different

If you're someone who can recognize Lana and John's story in your own life, you may have trouble asserting yourself. You may be an intelligent, self-aware, and well-spoken conversationalist who is good at listening and uses plenty of "clean" communication. Yet if you are routinely failing to speak up for yourself, and saying yes when you mean no, chances are you're going to have more than your fair share of conflict.

Assertive communicators are **not** loud, pushy, or arrogant. They never bully others, and they also don't make hints or threats or use other passive-aggressive approaches. To really understand an assertive communicator, you need to see that their approach is one of *balance*: what is being balanced is their needs, rights, and limits, and their respect for everyone else's needs, rights, and limits. They are essentially saying: *I value and respect you. And I also value and respect myself.*

The *and* is important. An unassertive communicator will value and respect other people but not themselves, and an aggressive communicator will value only themselves and nobody else. The effective, assertive communicator understands that the magic happens somewhere in the middle.

Ten Essential Assertive Communication Habits

1. **They make direct, clear, friendly eye contact.** They are present in the moment and aware of themselves and others. There is an honesty and sincerity in their company.
2. They hold their bodies in ways that are neither too rigid and stiff, nor weak and overly yielding. They **stand tall but relaxed**. They don't slouch or cower, but neither do they have any force or tension in their gesture or posture.
3. **They use a tone of voice that is steady, calm, and in control.** It is one hundred percent unnecessary to raise your voice to assert yourself. In fact, violent or overly emotional language most often signals a loss of control and lack of security in one's own position.
4. They have facial expressions that are **open and receptive**.
5. **They pay attention to when and where** they assert themselves by raising issues at the right time and place so they are most likely to be well received.
6. **They never, ever resort to blame or accusation**. Especially never threaten (for example, "If you don't do this for me, I'm leaving you"). When we try to manipulate people this way, we are essentially only communicating our powerlessness. Asserting ourselves is about knowing who *we* are and what *we* want. We are stating our limits on our behavior, not making demands on someone else's behavior. If someone cannot respect a boundary, then we follow through; we do not use our boundaries and assertions to control others.
7. They have **crystal-clear expression**. There is no room for wishy-washiness here. Say "I'm afraid I can't do that for you" rather than "Hmm, this is a little difficult. I'm not sure . . ."
8. They use **positive language**. Having limits is not the end of the world, and saying no to something doesn't make you wrong or bad. That means it's perfectly possible to say no while keeping things friendly and polite. Assertive communicators also know how to frame their statements in terms of what is being gained rather than what is being lost. For example, "Could you put your socks in the laundry hamper? Then we'll have a nice

clean room" instead of "Could you stop leaving your socks everywhere and making the place look like a pigsty?"
9. **They avoid criticism**. Again, for example, phrases such as "I know I'm being silly about this, but could you please not say that word?" and "Do you not have manners?" are just plain criticisms rather than assertions (and yes, one can be critical of oneself!).
10. **Finally, they gracefully accept when they are told no**. One of the best ways you can communicate to others that you take personal boundaries seriously is to respect other people's—no ifs, ands, or buts.

Well, so much for the habits of assertive communication, but that still leaves us with the question of exactly *how* to say no, to set down limits, to turn people down, or to raise grievances. Let's take a look at five different types of assertion—each one best suited for a particular social situation. Bear in mind that each will be most effective when the above ten habits are firmly in place.

Type 1: Basic Assertion

This is essentially a clear, neutral statement of our goals, ideas, emotions, limits, requirements, or feelings. It is something we are saying about ourselves. It is not the same as "truth," but it is the same as "our truth," and we state it plainly and confidently. For this reason, it's important for this type of assertion to use "I" statements.

"I can't eat dairy, as I'm intolerant."

"I feel a little disappointed that the plans have been canceled."

"I think this is a bad idea."

"I need to leave at five if I want to make my appointment."

Basic assertions are best used in those low-stakes, everyday situations where you need to make others aware of your needs, limits, and perspectives. They help us make the tiny course corrections to daily life that mean we avoid bigger misunderstandings later. Just remember to keep things short and sweet and don't make your claim as though you are inviting opinions or asking for permission. If you can't eat dairy, just say so with as much clarity and simplicity as you would say "the sky is blue." If you launch into a five-minute speech about why you can't and how you're sorry for being inconvenient, you're going too far.

Type 2: Empathic Assertion

Sometimes, though, what you are asserting will impact another person—sometimes quite negatively. The fact that someone will be unhappy with us setting a boundary doesn't automatically mean we aren't entitled to that boundary or that we are doing something wrong. But what it does mean is that we are obliged to consider and acknowledge their feelings. This is where empathy comes in handy. Crucially, empathy doesn't mean we capitulate to unreasonable demands or apologize for having limits. It means we have limits *while still having empathy for the fact that others might not like it.*

Use this type of assertion when you know that the other person might not like what you're saying. Begin with your acknowledgment of their thoughts, feelings, and opinions; genuinely and kindly show empathy for their position, then reiterate your own with the same level of kindness. Here, you need to pay more attention to finding *balance*. Making a firm assertion should not mean you're rude, and simultaneously being kind should not mean you have to soften your assertion.

"I appreciate that it's not convenient for you, but I simply won't be available that day."
"I know this hasn't been easy for you, either, but that's my decision."

Type 3: Consequence Assertion

Let's ramp this up a little. The consequence assertion is for those times in life when you need to communicate an if/then quality to your assertions. You need to let other people know that there are consequences to their behaviors and exactly what those repercussions will be. This can be an extremely tricky thing to navigate since the wrong tone or choice of words can make it seem like you are trying to forcefully control or modify someone else's behavior, manipulate them, or make ultimatums.

It's worth thinking carefully through your message for some time before speaking up. Sort it out in your own mind first and be honest about whether you may in fact be trying to strong-arm the other person or use guilt, shame, or obligation to control them. You need to understand for yourself how *you* will behave in certain conditions—not try to set the other person's behavior for them. Often, tactics like this can backfire because the other person calls your bluff, quickly revealing that you are not in fact prepared to follow through with the consequences, and that your assertion was nothing more than a plot for control.

Before you make a consequence assertion, ask whether there are other options before escalating this way. Only resort to this kind of assertion when you feel boundaries have already been violated or ignored, and when you realistically feel that you can and will follow through with consequences. When you make the assertion, keep all the ten points from above in mind; the firmness of your assertion comes from your own conviction, *not* from how blunt you are or how loud you speak.

"If you keep speaking to me like that, I'm going to have to insist we go our separate ways."
"Unless you can produce the documents we've requested, I will need to raise an issue with the ombudsman."

Type 4: Discrepancy Assertion

Of course, people do make mistakes, and nobody is perfect. Sometimes, people step over the line or break a clearly stated boundary by accident or just because they're not paying attention. If you've already made an agreement with someone and they then fail to follow up on their side of the deal, then you may need to make a discrepancy assertion. This is when you draw the other person's attention to the difference between what was promised and what was delivered. In a way, agreements, contracts, and deals are simply boundaries that both parties set. If you're in a professional or more formal context, you will need to know how to politely but firmly draw attention to moments when agreements have been dishonored.

The best way to do this is to frame it initially as a misunderstanding, and position the request for correction as something that you are *jointly* embarking on:

"The requested documents appear to not have been submitted yet. If they already have, please ignore this message and accept our apologies. If not, please be reminded that the due date has now passed, which is in violation of the contract."

This frames the issue neutrally, without making threats or placing blame, but rather shining a light on a discrepancy and subtly pointing out the natural, obvious consequences. Should such an assertion *still* be ignored, then the clear next step is to follow through with those consequences.

Type 5: Negative Feelings Assertion

If you have a personal situation in which you have a strong grievance you want to share with the other person, then you need to know how to assert how you feel. You want to call attention to the negative feelings you're experiencing as a result of their behavior. This can be done in a calm, controlled, and, yes, even respectful way. You will feel better for articulating your pain, and you will also give the other person plenty of opportunity to rectify things.

Importantly, this is the kind of assertion best made in private, in interpersonal relationships, and is usually inappropriate for professional contexts. Include a few key components: an objective description of their behavior, the objective impact of that behavior on you, your feelings as a result, and a clear statement for how you wish them to behave in the future:

"You were half an hour late this morning. As a result, I missed my appointment and won't get another one for two weeks. I'm absolutely livid. I need you to promise me that this won't happen again, and that you'll set alarms for yourself like we talked about."

Bonus: The Broken Record Technique

In an ideal world, you'd state your boundary and people would instantly hear you and respect your limits. In the real world, there are some people who can't help but test this boundary and push and push to see how much you really mean it (for example, every two-year-old in the world!). Such boundary-pushers will try all sorts of tactics to get you to budge. The broken record technique, however, makes you impervious to these tactics, because you don't react—you simply restate your assertion over and over and over again, like a broken record.

If you budge even a little, the nagging might continue, so be sure to be boringly consistent and make the same assertion again till the other person gets tired of trying to push you. Though you can paraphrase the language, do not change the message in the least, or add or take away anything. Be like a smooth, grey rock that simply cannot be negotiated with.

"Can you look after Buster?"
"I'm allergic to cats. I can't, I'm sorry."
"But he'll be in the other room most of the time."
"I can't, I'm sorry. As I said, I'm allergic."
"But you won't even be spending that much time with him."
"Yeah, I know, but I can't. I'm allergic to cats."
"Wow, you are so mean, you know that?"
"Okay, fine, but I can't do it, as I said, because I'm allergic. Sorry."

Give and Take: The Art of Feedback

Effective communicators are just as good at giving feedback as they are at receiving it.

Let's take a look at each skill in turn. First, how do you *give* good feedback?

As with so many of the other communication skills we've explored, good feedback is done consciously and deliberately. Be mindful of your language and keep in mind the ultimate purpose of communication. In this case, the goal of giving feedback is not to shame, control others, or make yourself look smart. Rather, it's about communicating something that will ultimately be useful to the other person—and possibly to you as well. That means that your goal is to avoid as much as possible anything that will interfere with the other person hearing something genuinely useful.

The Best Way to Give Feedback

Whatever situation you find yourself in, try to make sure your feedback follows these criteria:

1. It is about actions, choices, words, and behaviors, and not about people

2. It contextualizes that behavior by clearly describing the effect it has on you

3. It is specific

4. It is timely (i.e., delivered as close to the behavior as possible while staying appropriate)

If you are unhappy with an employee's behavior, but you tell them while they are in the breakroom with their colleagues, "You're irresponsible and have ruined things with this client," then you have not given them feedback, but more or less insulted them. Notice that every one of the above four rules is broken. A better approach would be to call them aside in a specifically planned meeting and say, "Breaching the client's privacy by sharing their personal information is not only illegal, it reflects really badly on me and means I have a lot of work to do now." This is specific, delivered at an appropriate time and place, and targets what the employee has actually done, rather than who they are as a person ("irresponsible"). This passes the test of being "useful" because it shows the employee exactly what they have done wrong and why it has inconvenienced you, whereas the only response to the previous feedback is to feel bad!

Of course, not all feedback is this "negative." Sometimes you will want to let someone know when they've done something right, and all the same principles apply. Sure, sometimes you just want to compliment someone, but if you intend to give feedback, be specific and make sure it's something the other person can actually use or act on. For example, "You're such an amazing employee" may feel nice, but "I really appreciate how you take initiative—it makes my life so much easier!" is more actionable and useful.

The Situation-Behavior-Impact (SBI) model is a framework that can help you ensure you tick all the boxes when providing feedback. SBI makes it more likely that other people will hear your feedback and take it onboard, rather than resist it, ignore it, or take offense. Here's how it recommends you structure your feedback:

S is for Situation: First describe the situation. Yes, you guessed it—you should aim to be as neutral and objective as possible. Be straightforward and describe things how an uninvolved third party might describe them. For now, just state the facts.

B is for Behavior: Now you move on to describing the behavior of the other person. Again this is just description—you are not interpreting, passing judgment, or saying what you think either way. Also avoid trying to mindread and guess why they have behaved as they have, or what they want or value. You want to cultivate an open, curious, and respectful frame here.

I is for Impact: As before, state your own resulting thoughts, feelings, or behaviors. As far as possible, try to focus on information that is quantifiable or can be measured. Be too vague and you'll get lost. Instead, focus on external, observable behavior and describe it in terms of how you've experienced it. Importantly, don't make blanket statements about what their behavior *is* more generally. Stick to how it affects you.

If you follow the above outline, you will likely avoid a few pitfalls: you won't get distracted by irrelevant behavior or either of your personalities or values because you'll focus only on specific actions. You won't cause offense or resistance because you are not attacking the person but making observations about their behavior, and in such a way that they can't help but see the same thing. Finally, you avoid overstepping and making claims about their behavior more generally because you only focus on the zone of control you're in charge of: how their behavior affects you. In our previous example, if you had told your employee that their being irresponsible was something that everyone thought, and that they always behaved this way, and that they were probably irresponsible in their personal lives, too, you'd naturally be overstepping!

Instead, keep your focus narrow, stick to one issue at a time, and be specific with it. Try to avoid observations about their judgment, choices, values, personality, and so on, and focus on what they have concretely done. Rather than frame someone's performance on a presentation as them being nervous, focus on how they spoke too quickly or stared at the floor a little too much. And instead of saying something like, "People can't hear you in the back," say "I had trouble hearing everything you said."

Other ways to help feedback go down smoothly:

- Ask questions. Be curious about their perspective on the issue and show that you have respect for it.
- If possible, give the person a way forward: Make a plan for the next move. How can progress be measured? Let them know.
- Don't draw things out—receiving feedback can be uncomfortable, so get to the point fast.

The Best Way to Receive Feedback

First things first: receiving feedback (of any kind) is never a problem. Even if it feels really bad in the moment or catches you by surprise, and even if it seems dangerously closer to being an insult and doesn't follow any of the rules discussed in the last section. Being an effective communicator means you have enough faith in yourself that you do not fear other people's opinions, whatever they may be. That said, there will probably be times in life where feedback throws you. Here's how to handle it with grace and turn it to your advantage.

Feedback can vary according to two dimensions: It can be expected or unexpected, and it can be positive or negative. That gives us four possible combinations.

If feedback is expected and positive

Hooray for you!
This one's easy—celebrate your achievement and be proud of yourself. If you like, make a note of what worked and commit to continuing to do it.

If feedback is expected and negative

For example, you've been called in for a performance review after a disastrous year. It hurts to hear, but you know there's truth in it; the way forward is to take action. Set objectives and goals for yourself and get moving—don't allow yourself to wallow in self-pity or be tempted to passively blame others. One of the best ways to empower yourself in the face of shortcomings is to find out exactly what you can do to learn. Any temporary embarrassment you feel will fade away; in fact, you can take a less-than-ideal situation and impress others with your ability to turn it around.

If feedback is unexpected and positive

In other words, a pleasant surprise. Bear in mind that feedback isn't always necessarily correct—and that applies to praise and compliments, too. Think about how valid the feedback is and ask what you can do to apply it to your life if it is valid. What did you do that worked? Repeat this behavior or see if you can make it a habit. If someone has complimented a skill or attribute, see if you're doing everything you can to support and develop that trait in yourself.

If feedback is unexpected and negative

We saved the worst for last. Hearing from out of the blue that you've done a bad job can be difficult, and it will always be so, no matter how high your self-esteem! The first thing to remember is not to react immediately, if possible. Remember that strong negative emotions can dampen your slower, more rational mind from stepping in, so try to just absorb and process what you've heard before reacting.

Next, seek to validate what you've been told. Sometimes feedback is completely groundless; sometimes it's right on the money—chances are, your bad feedback falls somewhere in the middle. Be honest with yourself. Look at the impact you might have had on other people, and think about things you might have previously overlooked. Keep in mind that everyone will have different expectations, values, and beliefs. Keep in mind also that even if someone has delivered their feedback poorly, it doesn't mean there isn't potential value in what they're saying.

Once you've processed things in this way, again orient yourself toward action.

What can you practically change given this insight?
What can your next step be?
What new goals does this inspire?
What are you currently doing that isn't working?

Whatever you do, try to remember that **feedback is about actions, not people**. That means that even though it's human to respond emotionally to feedback, you can cut yourself some slack and resist judging yourself, your personality, etc. If it helps, reframe things so that there are always three parties: you, the other person, and the issue at hand. Whether you are giving or receiving feedback, try to imagine that you're always on the same side as the other person, and it's you versus the issue, rather than you versus them.

Summary:

- Conflict is inevitable whenever people differ, but it can be managed with grace and tact. Try to understand the type of conflict: affective, substantive, conflict of interest, retributive, conflict in values, goal conflict, or displaced conflict from somewhere else.
- According to the Thomas Kilmann model, people come into conflict simply because they have different ideas, values, motivations, or wants. There are five conflict-resolution strategies according to degree of empathy and assertiveness: competing, avoiding, accommodating, collaborating, and compromising. Each has pros and cons and is best used in specific circumstances. Compromising (medium assertiveness and medium empathy) is usually a good bet all around.
- VOMP is an acronym that can help you pause, regulate your own emotional response, and plan to respond consciously during conflict. It stands for ventilation (speak your peace), ownership (own your part in the conflict), moccasins (have empathy), and plan.
- Crucial conversations are characterized by high stakes, opposing viewpoints, and strong emotions. Be clear and understand the conversation's purpose, then pick the right time and place. Show compassion, take responsibility, and separate fact from fiction.
- Regulate your own emotions by being aware of the underlying needs they express: status, certainty, autonomy, relatedness, and fairness.
- Be assertive and communicate your needs, limits, and perspective with clarity and kindness. Be clear, calm, firm, open, in control, and respectful. Decide on the type of assertion that best fits your needs: basic, empathic, consequence, discrepancy, or negative feelings assertion.
- When it comes to giving or receiving feedback, remember that it is about behaviors and actions and not about people. Be kind, but also don't take things too personally.

Summary Guide

CHAPTER 1: COMMUNICATION FUNDAMENTALS

- Poor communication arises as a result of a mismatch of perspectives, approach, or conversational skill. People process information differently, but to avoid misunderstandings, communicate consciously and use the "ladder of inference." It shows the unique way that people use their experiences to make meaning: observations > selected data > meanings > assumptions > conclusions > beliefs > actions.
- Conflict can occur when people are on different rungs. To improve communication, see where people are and how their ladder of inference is working for them, then speak to that, in sequence, and without blame or shame.
- Good communicators deliberately create their own frames during conversations and position their line of thinking by using specially chosen words, expressions, and images. Change frames and you change meaning.
- Deliberately engineer your conversational frame and invite the other person in using pre-existing concepts they're familiar with to improve the chances they'll be receptive. Remember that reality is fixed, but the *meaning* of reality is dynamic and subject to change.
- Chunking is about the way we group information. Chunking up is grouping specific instances into a larger overall abstract pattern or theory, while chunking down makes inferences from the general to the specific. Keeping the level of detail varied and appropriate creates a better flowing conversation than one that relies too heavily on chunking up or chunking down.
- It is a mistake to think that authenticity, expression, and sincerity are enough—*how* we articulate ourselves matters. Consciously filter what you say: Is it true, kind, and helpful?
- Take responsibility for what you say and practice clean communication—i.e., without hidden negative meanings.

CHAPTER 2: MASTERING STYLE AND TONE

- A few crutch words like *um*, *ah*, *well*, *you know*, *like*, *so*, *right*, and *okay* are natural, but too many can undermine your credibility and make it more difficult to understand you. Instead, become aware of the habit and consciously replace crutch words and empty language with confident silence. Being calm and thoughtful shows consideration for your audience and gets your point across more effectively.
- Likewise try to avoid hedging or softening language and instead be clear, concise, and confident in your expression.
- Your communication tone is like a vocal frame you set, so pay attention to whether you are being informative, humorous, respectful, formal, or informal. No tone is wrong, but a mismatch between tone and intention, or tone and context, can be a problem.

- Be especially conscious of upspeak (making statements with the intonation that belongs to questions), and ask whether it may be damaging your credibility or interfering with your message.
- With tone, strike a balance between friendly and business-like, confident and arrogant, concise and curt, emotional and merely compelling, and so on. Professionalism is about awareness and deliberately taking steps to speak in a way that gets you what you want while respecting the context and your audience.
- Especially with public speaking, use signposts—which are verbal and non-verbal markers that tell your listeners what kind of "journey" they're going on, where they are, and where you are taking them. Use a signpost every time you want to transition, give further detail, link points, change topics, offer a counterpoint, or summarize.

CHAPTER 3: PAINTING WITH WORDS

- If you want your listeners to really absorb what you say to them, paint them a mental picture. Do this by using vivid and concrete imagery, similes (using *like* or *as*), and metaphors to connect abstract ideas with more real-world ones. Use adjectives and interesting details and be a little unexpected.
- Language is musical by nature, and much of the meaning it conveys comes down to its rate, its articulation, its flow, and the way it moves through time. Pay attention to the rhythm and flow of your speech.
- In parallelism, we repeat certain structures to create an effect. Repetition drives our point home and makes it seem more true, as do alliteration (repetition of initial consonant sounds) and assonance (repetition of internal or vowel sounds).
- Human beings react not just to "information" but to narrative; to be a good storyteller, you need to go beyond sharing information and facts, and help your listeners form an emotional connection to what you're saying. Good stories enlist the use of our voice, body language, gestures, facial expressions, and even visual aids.
- Make sure that your story illustrates supports or connects to your larger point or circumstance. Set the scene but don't dawdle on unnecessary detail. Start with a bang and keep things at a moderate pace, being concise. Be relevant and interesting, and if you can, practice your story ahead of time!

CHAPTER 4: COMMUNICATION'S MOST UNDERRATED SKILL

- One of the easiest ways to connect with another person is to just ask questions. The right questions help you gather more and better-quality information, build stronger connections with others, inspire trust and liking, learn, and help other people learn, too.
- Closed questions (those that have very short or one-word answers) can be used to confirm your understanding, make conclusions or summaries, or set the tone and scope of a more formal or structured conversation. However, they can kill a conversation and make it feel interrogatory.

- Open questions (any possible answer) allow you to probe for depth and can keep a conversation lively and open-ended. Use both in the "funnel question" technique, which probes for information down a narrowing path of increasing detail, starting broad and progressively becoming more specific. Start with open questions, then drill down for more detail as you go, eventually reversing the funnel if necessary.
- Good listening is a collection of different skills: hearing, understanding, interpreting, and responding. The HURIER method asks us to Hear, Understand, Remember, Interpret, Evaluate, and Respond, in that order. Remember that listening is active and includes both verbal and nonverbal material.
- Avoid being a conversational narcissist, who is someone who uses conversation to gain attention for themselves, rather than connect with others, share, or learn. Reframe the way you understand the purpose of conversation and understand that it's not about you or your ego. Avoid giving advice, interrupting (or thinking about what you want to say), or centering yourself in the dialogue. Similarly, don't be afraid to disengage when you encounter a conversational narcissist.

CHAPTER 5: WHEN IT ALL GOES WRONG . . .

- Conflict is inevitable whenever people differ, but it can be managed with grace and tact. Try to understand the type of conflict: affective, substantive, conflict of interest, retributive, conflict in values, goal conflict, or displaced conflict from somewhere else.
- According to the Thomas Kilmann model, people come into conflict simply because they have different ideas, values, motivations, or wants. There are five conflict-resolution strategies according to degree of empathy and assertiveness: competing, avoiding, accommodating, collaborating, and compromising. Each has pros and cons and is best used in specific circumstances. Compromising (medium assertiveness and medium empathy) is usually a good bet all around.
- VOMP is an acronym that can help you pause, regulate your own emotional response, and plan to respond consciously during conflict. It stands for ventilation (speak your peace), ownership (own your part in the conflict), moccasins (have empathy), and plan.
- Crucial conversations are characterized by high stakes, opposing viewpoints, and strong emotions. Be clear and understand the conversation's purpose, then pick the right time and place. Show compassion, take responsibility, and separate fact from fiction.
- Regulate your own emotions by being aware of the underlying needs they express: status, certainty, autonomy, relatedness, and fairness.
- Be assertive and communicate your needs, limits, and perspective with clarity and kindness. Be clear, calm, firm, open, in control, and respectful. Decide on the type of assertion that best fits your needs: basic, empathic, consequence, discrepancy, or negative feelings assertion.
- When it comes to giving or receiving feedback, remember that it is about behaviors and actions and not about people. Be kind, but also don't take things too personally.

www.ingramcontent.com/pod-product-compliance
Lightning Source LLC
Chambersburg PA
CBHW080322080526
44585CB00021B/2440